ACCLAIM FOR JOHN TAYLOR'S

The Count and the
Confession

"Narrative nonfiction at its best. . . . You will be hooked on this tale of lust, love, greed, and murder."
—*The Roanoke Times*

"Mr. Taylor . . . has a gift for vivid descriptions, telling details and polished prose."   —*The Wall Street Journal*

"Combine your favorite Gothic tale with the popular board game Clue and you'll come close to realizing what a fascinating story John Taylor spins."   —*The Orlando Sentinel*

"A classic whodunit, a tale of 'did she or didn't she?'. . . . This though, is nonfiction."   —*The Washington Post*

"Taylor manages to navigate an extremely complicated case with humor and color to spare."   —*New York Daily News*

"A gripping story of a suspicious death and the mysteries that surround it even a trial, a conviction, and a decade later. . . . Taylor gives enough information to allow each reader to form his one-person jury."
—*Richmond Times-Dispatch*

"In Taylor's richly detailed account, this strange but true case makes for one mesmerizing whodunit."   —*Pages*

JOHN TAYLOR

The Count and the

Confession

John Taylor, a journalist for more than two decades, has been a contributing editor at *New York* magazine and a senior writer for *Esquire*. He is the author of *Falling*, which *Entertainment Weekly* ranked as one of the five best nonfiction books of 1999, *Circus of Ambition*, and *Storming the Magic Kingdom*, a *New York Times* Notable Book of the Year. He lives in East Moriches, New York.

The Count and the
Confession

The Count
and the
Confession

A TRUE MYSTERY

John Taylor

VINTAGE BOOKS

A DIVISION OF RANDOM HOUSE, INC.

NEW YORK

FIRST VINTAGE BOOKS EDITION, JUNE 2003

The Library of Congress has cataloged the
Random House edition as follows:
Taylor, John.
The count and the confession : a true mystery/ John Taylor.
p. cm.
1. Monroe, Beverly.   2. De la Burde, Roger Zygmunt.
3. Murder—Virginia.   4. Trials (Murder)—Virginia.   I. Title.
HV6533.V8 T39   2002
364.15'23'09755612—dc21   2001048481

Vintage ISBN: 0-375-72583-0

Author photograph © Jeannette Walls
Book design by J. K. Lambert

www.vintagebooks.com

Printed in the United States of America
10   9   8   7   6   5   4   3   2   1

FOR JEANNETTE

Contents

The Count and the

Confession

CHAPTER I

The Last Door
on the Left

What do you take to prison? Beverly Monroe had no idea. But her attorney had given her a list of some basic items she was supposed to bring—white underwear, rubber-soled shoes—and during the weekend before she was scheduled to surrender, in addition to setting aside money to pay her estimated taxes and signing papers giving her daughter Katie power of attorney, she packed. Each of her three children wanted her to have something personal of theirs to take with her. Her younger daughter, Shannon, gave her a blue thermal Patagonia she'd gotten for Christmas. Katie had Beverly take her plaid flannel L. L. Bean pajamas. Gavin, her oldest child and only son, bought her a necklace, which she wasn't sure she would be allowed to keep.

Beverly also packed some of their old socks and a yellow tennis sweater that had been Shannon's in the seventh grade. She added writing paper, her German dictionary, her French phrase book, and a few of her favorite books, including Peter Mayle's *A Year in Provence* and a volume of poetry by Herman Hesse. Since she wasn't supposed to bring a suitcase, they put everything in a small cardboard box.

On November 9, 1992, exactly one week after she had been convicted of murdering Roger de la Burde, her children drove her up to the Powhatan County sheriff's office. The day was dry but cold. They took Beverly's dark blue Mercury Sable, following the Midlothian Turnpike west out of Richmond's suburbs and up to Route 13, a looping, narrow-shouldered road that ran through rolling fields past the Mennonite church and the local farm bureau office before reaching the village.

Greg Neal, the Powhatan investigator who had first interviewed Beverly back when everyone thought Roger's death was a suicide, waited for her in the sheriff's office. Neal seemed unwilling to look Beverly in the eye, she thought. He turned her over to one of the uniformed deputies, Tommy Broughton. Carrying her small cardboard box, she followed Broughton and a female secretary out into the parking lot and climbed into the back of an unmarked Chevrolet Caprice. A rack on the dashboard held a shotgun.

Broughton headed up to Maidens Road, which wound north through stubbled cornfields and stands of pine. Beverly's children followed close behind in her Mercury. Every minute or so, Beverly looked back and waved to them through the rear window. Throughout the trip, the secretary kept up a stream of polite conversation about the accomplishments of their respective children, as if they were at a church social.

They reached the slender bridge that crossed the James River. Beverly looked out at the dark green water. It was low at this time of the year, the muddy banks below the tree line exposed. Roger's estate, Windsor Farm, was three miles downriver, invisible beyond a bend.

Just outside Goochland, a small town on the north bank of the James, Brougton turned onto River Road West. Beverly saw the store where Roger had bought the fiberglass canoe he had used only once. Broughton pulled into the Virginia Correctional Center for Women, a cluster of old brick buildings with slate roofs and white casement windows set among magnolia and pecan trees. It was surprisingly pastoral. There was neither a wall nor a fence. Black Angus grazed in a pasture across the road. They passed a guard booth and stopped at an administration building. Beverly looked back at her children. The guard had halted them at the booth. They waved. She waved back and then followed Deputy Broughton inside.

———

The prison's intake room was noisy and chaotic. Guards in navy blue uniforms were bantering with other guards behind a counter as they passed heavy keys back and forth and signed clipboards. One of the women on the jury that had convicted Beverly worked somewhere back there. Beverly put her box on the floor. The guards ignored her and Deputy Broughton. After a few minutes, a door opened and a heavyset African-American woman, wearing a white jumpsuit with gold buttons, beckoned Beverly into her office.

The woman brusquely introduced herself as Ms. Wendy Hobbs, the warden. There was also a big man wearing mirrored sunglasses in the office. He sat watching Beverly in silence. The warden didn't introduce him. Instead, she launched into what seemed to be a prepared speech. Don't think that you're going to be treated any differently, she told Beverly, just because your case has had all this publicity and you've had a privileged existence. Here, you're nobody special. Here, you're not different. No one is going to cater to you. You're a prisoner and you'll be treated the same as all the other prisoners. Don't expect anything else.

Beverly just stood there and listened. She knew Warden Hobbs was making a point of cutting her down to size, and she said nothing. There wasn't any response she could think to make.

When the speech was over, Warden Hobbs dismissed her. Two guards escorted her across the grounds and down a tree-lined slope to a low brick building. A barred door opened and then closed behind them with a horrible electric buzzing noise. The building smelled powerfully of Lysol. In a waiting room, two other guards looked through her belongings and put them in a plastic bag, which they kept.

They told her to strip, then searched her body, gave her a towel to wrap around herself, and led her down a hall to a laundry room. A shower stall with a mildewed plastic curtain was wedged between the industrial-size washers and dryers. There were roaches on the floor and walls. One of the guards squirted a glob of anti-lice soap into her hand and instructed her to wash herself with it.

Beverly Monroe was the sort of woman invariably described as petite—a word she hated. She seemed fragile, with her delicate bones and thin skin and startling hazel eyes, but she was actually strong and athletic. She skied and played tennis. She enjoyed hard labor—breaking soil with a mattock—and liked to think of herself as a woman who was up to almost any physical challenge.

But the water in the shower was so cold that it shocked her. With only the one thin towel, she couldn't dry her hair. The guards gave her Katie's flannel L. L. Bean pajamas to wear, then led her past another barred door, which opened and shut with the same horrible electric buzz, and down a quiet corridor. It had a low ceiling and brick walls painted white. On both sides of the corridor were doors with horizontal slots. Beverly saw the eyes of the people behind the doors watching her as she passed.

The guards stopped at the last door on the left, gestured for Beverly to enter, and locked the door behind her. She found herself in a small rectangular room. It had a metal clothes locker, a bunk bed with a plastic mattress and plastic pillow but no sheet or pillowcase, and, in a doorless nook, a toilet flushed by pulling a chain that hung from the tank suspended above it. There was one dim overhead bulb and a single begrimed casement window. The window was partially open, and the chilly November air poured through the gap. Beverly tried to close it, but the crank was broken.

Beverly sat down on the bunk bed. Time passed. She had no way of measuring how much—twenty minutes? forty? After a while, she got up and paced off the room's measurements. It was two and a half feet from the bunk to the metal locker and twelve feet from the door to the window. She began to feel that the walls were closing in on her, literally moving inward. She thought she would have to hold them apart with her hands.

———

After dark, someone passed a bologna sandwich in a plastic bag through the food slot in the center of the door. Beverly had no appetite and didn't even open the bag. She never ate bologna anyway. She lay down on the lower mattress and stared up at the crisscrossed wires holding the mattress above her.

She thought of Warden Hobbs's lecture. She didn't consider herself privileged. In her own mind, she was an independent, hardworking divorced woman, a mother of three children—grown but still struggling to find their way in life—who rarely spent money on herself, preferring instead to double her mortgage payment on the odd occasion when she could afford it. But she realized that to others she certainly seemed privileged. She had had a good job at Philip Morris. Roger, with whom she'd been involved for twelve years, collected art and claimed he was a Polish count. Back in February, they had attended a masked ball at the Virginia Museum of Fine Arts. A photograph of Roger dancing with the museum director had appeared in the newspaper. Five days later, he had been found shot to death by a single bullet from his own revolver. Now she was serving the first day of a twenty-two-year sentence for murdering him.

Beverly knew nothing about criminal justice or the Virginia penal system. She had no idea when she would see her children again or when she would be set free or what prison would be like. The fact that her life had fallen apart so swiftly and so absolutely at times had terrified her—and at times enraged her—but mostly it filled her with disbelief.

Unable to sleep, she lay on the plastic-covered mattress, shivering in Katie's pajamas as the November wind whistled through the open casement window.

CHAPTER II

A Farm on the River

1

Early in the evening of February 29, 1992, Roger Zygmunt de la Burde was alone in his bedroom at Windsor Farm, dressing for a ball. The property was on Huguenot Trail, bordering the James River west of Richmond, Virginia. It dated back to the seventeenth century. Charles Carter Lee, the oldest full brother of Robert E. Lee, had acquired it in 1853 and it earned a footnote in Civil War history when, after surrendering to Ulysses Grant at Appomattox, Lee and his officers returned to Richmond along Huguenot Trail, spending the last night before they finally disbanded in the farm's fields.

Burde had lived at Windsor for twenty-five years, first with his wife, Brigitte, and their two daughters and then, after the girls left for college and he and Brigitte divorced, by himself. Windsor was a working horse farm, with 220 acres of pasture and woodland. The dozen or so horses grazing on his fields belonged to other people, who stabled them at Windsor. Burde had little interest in animals, crops, or gardening. He was by profession a chemist and had, until retiring four years earlier, worked in the research department of Philip Morris, where he had been the co-author of some seventeen patents. But most of Burde's money had come from real estate speculation. Over the years, he had acquired row houses in Richmond's Fan District, tracts of rural woodland, even a small island in the James River. At the moment, he and various partners owned some thirty properties.

Burde took his tuxedo out of the closet. The ensemble had a wing-collared shirt and a rakish green-and-black-plaid jacket with black silk lapels. The jacket, when he tried it on, felt tight. Burde led an active life. He was an accomplished skier and an aggressive tennis player, who liked to rush the net after serving and was often called for foot faults. But he had a weakness for fatty food—meat and cheese and desserts—and in the last couple of years he had gained twenty-five pounds. Most of it had gone straight to his gut. He felt himself aging.

Burde was sixty. He had an olive complexion, an infectious smile, and penetrating dark eyes. Women considered him handsome, and this encouraged his vanity. The sagging skin beneath his jaw dismayed him, as did his receding hairline; he'd had a hair transplant that had not come out as well as he'd have liked. In fact, it looked terrible. And he worried about his health. He suffered from insomnia and heart pains and high blood pressure. Recently, he had discovered blood in his semen—and that, he could tell you, was a sight to tighten the sphincter.

Burde was originally from Kraków, Poland, where he grew up during the Nazi occupation and came of age under postwar Communist rule, which he found even more oppressive. His father, a lawyer, had managed a small factory, and his family, considered part of the reactionary bourgeoisie, was forced to surrender its house to a workers' collective.

After receiving a Ph.D. in chemistry from Kraków University, Burde determined to flee his Soviet-bloc country. During a trip to East Berlin, he slipped into West Germany, then made his way to the United States, living in Buffalo and Chicago before settling in Richmond when Philip Morris offered him a job in the 1960s.

Burde claimed he was a count. He was descended, he told people, from a French aristocrat who had settled in Kraków after the Napoleonic Wars. His letterhead said ROGER Z. CTE. DE LA BURDE.

Burde's neighbors and colleagues never knew how seriously to take these claims. They considered the man himself an extraordinary oddity. He could be witty and engaging, an enjoyable raconteur of wickedly funny stories told in thickly accented English, but he also had what to people in the

Virginia piedmont seemed to be strange European eccentricities. He bowed. He wore ascots and smoking jackets. He collected abstract and African art. He routinely propositioned women he scarcely knew.

They also considered him unscrupulous. After the local fire department put out a fire in a cottage at Windsor that contained part of his art collection, the blaze started up again the following night, and that time Burde tried to fight it alone with nothing more than a garden hose. His insurer, Lloyd's of London, refused to honor the policy, citing the suspicious circumstances; Burde sued and the case was settled out of court. That was only one of the many lawsuits he had been involved in. Moreover, he had been tried and acquitted of extortion—for threatening a business partner's girlfriend—and tried and convicted of trespassing and malicious destruction of property—for cutting down a neighbor's trees.

But to his friends, Burde's roguishness was part of his charm. He thought of himself as a man who brought a little dash to whatever he did. He liked to cook and he would throw ingredients together ad hoc—whatever was in the refrigerator—and present his guests with dishes he named Chicken Windsor or Shrimp de la Burde. He believed in the idea of style. He had a white suit he put on if he felt the situation could accommodate whimsical flair and a long black leather overcoat that he draped across his shoulders like a cape.

He was given to sudden enthusiasms—in the last few years he had taught himself to speak French and to play the piano—and devoted to high culture. His taste in music ran from Telemann to Bill Evans; in books, from Goethe to Lawrence Durrell. But his foremost enthusiasm was for African art. He had, as F. D. Cossett, an art critic for the Richmond *Times-Dispatch,* once noted, "one of the best collections of African sculpture in the country."

Burde had begun assembling it on an extended trip to Nigeria in 1968, and owned more than four hundred objects: fetish dolls, spears and headdresses, vases and bowls and chairs and brass works, Benin hip masks, Ogboni ceremonial staffs, Ere Ibeji twin-cult figures, and wooden Yoruba statues. On more than one occasion, Powhatan County deputies, dispatched to the house after something had triggered the burglar alarm, were startled, when they pointed their flashlights into the dark windows, by some bulging-eyed monster that turned out to be a mask.

Despite its size and the unquestionable value of some of the pieces, a taint had become attached to Burde's art collection after he lied about its provenance. To avoid acknowledging that he had violated Nigeria's antiquities law by exporting valuable historical artifacts, he claimed that his father, Rudolph, had collected the pieces during trips to West Africa in 1912 and 1916. Confronted by an associate curator of African art at the Metropolitan Museum of Art, he sheepishly admitted that he may have embellished the facts. But that was fifteen years ago, and Burde had worked since then to restore the collection's reputation. For two years he had been putting together a book about it, complete with photographs of the important pieces and essays by five academics.

Aside from the book, which was still unfinished, Burde's life lately was full of vexations. After leaving Philip Morris, he had sued the company for a share in the profits from one of his patents, and, instead of settling as he hoped it would, the company had countersued. Burde also had money problems. Most of his wealth was tied up in illiquid real estate, and in the past year he had grown so short of cash that he had concocted a scheme to sell forged art created by a local stonemason, who changed his mind and backed out before the project could get off the ground.

That was just as well, Burde later decided, because he subsequently learned that a man named Wojtek Drewnowska had reported him to the FBI for trafficking in fraudulent art.

Drewnowska had good reason to feel hostile toward Roger. Burde had been having an affair with the man's wife, Krystyna, who now represented Burde's most pressing worry: Two months ago, in December, after leaving her husband and their two teenage children, she had become pregnant by Burde. Recently, she had drafted an agreement spelling out terms of his support for her and the child and was pressing him to sign it. Krystyna also wanted him to leave Beverly Monroe, who had been his primary companion for the past twelve years, so that Krystyna could move in with him at Windsor to see if they were suited for marriage.

Beverly knew about his affair with Krystyna but did not know that Krystyna was pregnant. If Beverly found out, the long relationship Burde had enjoyed with her would quite possibly be destroyed. Upheaval now seemed not just inevitable but imminent.

Burde's entanglement with the two women had become terribly complicated. This evening he would be leaving the pregnant Krystyna alone on her birthday in order to accompany Beverly and her family to the ball at the Virginia Museum of Fine Arts. Burde did not feel particularly guilty about this. He was used to doing as he pleased, without much regard for the feelings of others.

From his bedroom window Burde had a view of the James River, high with the early runoff from the Blue Ridge Mountains. The view was through a gap in the trees on the neighboring property. When the Armentrout sisters had refused him permission to create that gap by cutting down the trees, he had hired someone to do the job anyway. The man had leveled a couple of acres' worth of trees—mostly sycamores, some two hundred years old and so big that you couldn't get your arms around them—and left them toppled in the river in violation of water-conservation board restrictions. Burde had paid the fines and settled the suit the Armentrout sisters brought against him, and now he had the view he wanted.

It was dark by the time Burde finished putting on his tuxedo. He switched on the outdoor floodlights, set the alarm and locked the front door, and crossed the gravel driveway to his sienna-brown Jaguar sedan. Overhead, stars glimmered in a clear but moonless night sky.

———

Roger and Beverly, Katie and her boyfriend, Alan Block, and Gavin and his date, Michelle, arrived at the museum just as the ball was getting under way. It was a masked ball, celebrating Mardi Gras, and some people wore full costumes. One woman was covered in peacock feathers; another had on an Indian headdress. A third wore a Muslim veil that trailed to the floor.

Beverly had bought everyone in her group a handheld mask. Laughing, made slightly giddy by the infectious silliness of the party, they raised the masks to their faces and joined the throng climbing the stairs from the main lobby, passing the string quartet and moving through the Cochrane Court, with its Roman floor mosaic and the Italian table donated by John Branch, then through the European Gallery and down a narrow dark corridor hung with Picassos and Braques before finally entering the Marble Hall. The huge chamber, its walls and floor and columns paneled in glistening pink marble, was crowded with revelers. There were King Tut masks, green monkey masks, catcher's masks, sequined black masks, and masks made of paraffin and glitter that simulated melting ice. The conversational roar bounced off the soaring walls. Some people were dancing in front of a swing band, while still others gazed down on the spectacle from the catwalks overhead.

Burde liked to talk about "the people who matter."

"The people who matter play golf, they don't watch football in bars," he would tell his daughter Corinna. "The people who matter ski—they don't go to movies at the multiplexes." He wanted not just to count them as his friends but to be regarded as one of them. On this night, the people who, in Burde's mind, mattered in Richmond—bankers and lawyers in their thirties, the party being geared to the younger set, but also older people like James Dyke, the state secretary for education, and Ambassador Walter Rice and his wife—were at the ball. And so was he.

Burde had social aspirations for Corinna and was disappointed that she hadn't come. The kind of privileged young men Burde wanted his daughter to marry were here. Beverly had called Corinna to try to persuade her to join them, but she had refused. Relations between Burde and his two daughters were tense. Colette, the oldest, had moved to New Orleans, but Corinna was still in Richmond and Burde was constantly critical of her—of the jeans she liked to wear, of the boy named Buster she had dated, of the modest condo she'd bought, and the wooden cable spool she used as a coffee table. Over Thanksgiving dinner at Beverly's house this past fall, with Beverly's children and friends present, he'd started yelling, literally yelling, at Corinna about her lack of ambition, as he saw it, calling her a "loser," and she'd had enough.

That disappointment notwithstanding, Burde was in his element at the museum. He always loved a party. He bowed to women and kissed their hands. He drank white wine from the cash bar. He told off-color jokes and passed along real estate tips to men. "Now is the time to invest," he'd been saying that week, "because blood is running in the streets." He had never been enthusiastic about Katie's boyfriend, Alan, who, while a bright young lawyer, came from a modest background, but that night, he suddenly embraced Alan, kissed him on the cheek, and said, "I'm so glad Katie has you." A short while later, when a conga line began snaking through the Marble Hall, he joined it.

Roger often gave parties at Windsor, and he made conspicuous charitable donations. He had arranged for exhibits from his collection at the University of Richmond and Virginia Commonwealth University, and he had tried to befriend prominent philanthropists like Sydney Lewis, a discount-chain retailer who had underwritten the construction of the Marble Hall and filled it with his own modernist collection. But because of his legal battle with Philip Morris, his sharp-edged business style, his dubious background, and his aggressive social climbing, many of "the people who mattered" in Richmond had always looked askance at Roger. This past fall, despite a vigorous campaign by Charlie Valentine, a friend from one of Richmond's oldest families, Burde was denied membership in the bastion of the city's establishment, the Country Club of Virginia. And a few months earlier, curators at the Virginia Museum, whom Burde had been trying to persuade to sponsor an exhibit of his African art to coincide with the publication of his book, had turned him down; the collection was still too controversial.

Since then, a woman named Katharine Lee had been appointed the museum's new director, and Burde hoped to charm her into reversing the decision. As the ball reached its climax and the raucous swing band launched into a tune by Count Basie, he asked Katharine Lee to dance. Roger was a good dancer. He liked to throw in little moves he'd picked up in Africa, shimmies and shakes that Beverly and her family found hilarious. He and Katharine Lee began to jitterbug. A photographer for the Richmond *News Leader* saw them and sensed the night's shot. His exploding flash caught Roger, in his wing-collared shirt and plaid dinner jacket, swinging Katharine Lee across the floor by the hand. His face had a look of rapturous concentration.

It was the last photograph taken of him while he was alive.

2

On Wednesday, March 4, Beverly Monroe arrived home from work at around six o'clock. The last four days had been emotionally harrowing. On Sunday, after the ball, she had been at Windsor helping Roger with his book when she found a copy of the support agreement Krystyna Drewnowska had drafted. Roger broke down. In the long conversation that followed, he acknowledged that Krystyna was pregnant. He had been talking for years about finding a surrogate mother to bear him a male heir, but Beverly was unsure if Krystyna was merely a casual mistress who had agreed to serve as a surrogate mother, as Roger insisted, or a true lover.

After they talked for hours, Beverly left in the early evening, to avoid encountering Roger's attorney, who was coming in from out of town to discuss Roger's lawsuit against Philip Morris. Beverly herself worked at Philip

Morris, as a coordinator in the patent department. Some people at the company regarded her with suspicion for continuing to see a man who had filed a lawsuit against it, so she made a point of drawing a very distinct boundary between her job and her relationship with Roger. She didn't want to be seen anywhere near his attorney.

The next morning, she drove back out to Windsor before going to work, to give Roger some old photographs of the two of them that he'd mentioned the day before. His attorney's car was still in the driveway, so she left the pictures on the front steps without going into the house. Roger called later. He asked her to take the afternoon off and spend it at Windsor. Beverly agreed. It was a brisk, sunny day. They sat on redwood chairs on the front lawn and tried to talk calmly about the big question that hung over them.

That evening, Roger dropped by Beverly's house, thirteen miles from Windsor, on Old Gun Road in Chesterfield County. He brought a bouquet of flowers and asked her to come to Windsor on Wednesday for dinner. It would be like old times, he said, but they weren't to talk about anything serious.

The following night, Tuesday, Roger again appeared without warning at Beverly's house. She was playing the piano when he arrived. She rose and offered him some food or wine.

"No," he said. "Just play."

He pulled a chair up to the piano and sat listening with his hands folded in his lap. When, after half an hour, Beverly stopped playing, Roger asked her to continue. Finally, she said she needed to eat something. Roger brought her a piece of cheese and they sat on the red couch in the room Beverly called her library. Roger said his heart hurt and asked Beverly to press her hand against it. She did, for twenty minutes, until he said he felt better. Hoping to break Roger's unsettlingly quiet mood, Beverly put on a tape of Saint-Saëns's adagio "The Swan." When it was over, Roger asked her to play it again, then a third time. At nine-thirty he said he was tired and left.

Roger called Beverly several times at the office the next day. He wanted her to come out to Windsor as soon as possible and to bring her flute. Beverly wasn't able to leave the office until after five. She got caught in traffic and reached Old Gun Road at six o'clock. She called Katie, who was living in Charlottesville, to discuss their plans for the weekend, found her flute, and climbed back into her blue Mercury for the twenty-minute drive out to Windsor.

There was still some light in the sky. Following Huguenot Trail, known officially as Route 711, Beverly left the suburban landscape of Chesterfield County south of Richmond—a place of strip malls, brightly lit self-service gas stations, vinyl-sided tract houses, and intersecting eight-lane highways with interminable stoplights and crawling traffic—and headed west into the pastoral quiet of Powhatan County.

The road was narrow and relatively ungraded and it twisted and dipped as it followed the contours of the hills. Huge rolls of baled hay lay unraveling in the wet pastures. The weather that winter had been mild and dry, but heavy rainfalls late in February had fed the dormant woodlands. The loblolly pines had a green bristling quality, and the tiny blooming flowers of the red maples created a rust-colored mist around their black branches.

Houses, sometimes clustered together but most often isolated, stood between the stretches of uncleared forest. The smaller houses, with rusting tin roofs and wide porches, had been built close to the road. The large estates, some dating to the eighteenth century, were set farther back, at the end of long, straight drives that receded behind immaculately cropped lawns. Beverly passed the hand-lettered signs at their gates: KESWICK PLANTATION, EASTVIEW, GRAYFIELD, NORWOOD, HILLWOOD.

Thirteen miles out of Chesterfield County, Huguenot Trail dropped into a hollow, crossed a tiny spring-fed rivulet known as Fine Creek, then began a long ascent up a shoulder of land that pushed out toward the river. To the right, a bluff of shaggy pasture, enclosed with post-and-rail fencing, blocked the view. Beverly slowed near the crest of the ridge. On the left side of the road stood a sturdy iron historic marker with black-on-gray lettering:

LEE'S LAST CAMP

Here Robert E. Lee, riding from
Appomattox to Richmond to join
his family, pitched his tent for the
last time on April 14, 1865. He
stopped here to visit his brother,
Charles Carter Lee, who lived
nearby at Windsor. Not wishing to incom-

mode his brother, Lee camped by
the roadside, and the next day
ended his journey at Richmond.

On the opposite side of the road, where a gravel drive lined by shade trees cut up through the pasture, a small sign read:

WINDSOR FARM
STABLES

Beverly turned in at the drive and followed the gravel lane up over the crest of the ridge. The sun had fallen behind the tree line to the west. Below, on the far side of the long pasture, was the white brick house, its lit windows glowing in the dusk.

3

Shortly after eight o'clock on Thursday morning, March 5, Joe Hairfield left his house on Huguenot Trail to make the two-mile drive to Windsor. He was going to discuss his working relationship with Roger de la Burde. Hairfield was an energetic, straightforward, and uncomplicated man. He had gotten to know Burde two years earlier, after federal marshals had arrested a man who was renting Windsor's fields to pasture his cattle and charged him with dealing marijuana wholesale. Once the marshals seized the dealer's livestock, the pastures at Windsor had gone uncut. Thistle and johnsongrass began to overtake them.

Originally, Roger had hired Joe's teenage son to help around the farm during the summer, for five dollars an hour, but soon enough—being that the job was a little more than a fifteen-year-old boy could handle—Roger hired the father to help the son out for an additional six dollars an hour. They mowed the pastures and repaired the fences. The barns and stables also needed repair, but that was beyond the scope of a summer job, so in September Roger told Joe that if he would restore the outbuildings, the two of them could go into business boarding horses and share the profits. Joe undertook the job and in the process became Roger's farm manager. He oversaw the teenagers Roger was always bringing in to do the manual labor, deciding whom to hire and whom to fire, what work needed to be done in what order, and what equipment needed to be repaired. He was in charge of receipts and the payroll, and at the end of each week he would come to Roger for the money that was needed.

Windsor, an expensive proposition, cost $15,000 to maintain in a good year, and Roger invariably complained about expenses. "Joe, you're breaking me," he would say. "You're absolutely *breaking* me."

While it was true that Roger complained about everything, nothing, it seemed to Joe, pained the man like parting with money. When one of the tenants in the rental cottage had to move out before his lease was up, Roger infuriated the fellow by keeping his security deposit, even though the fellow had given advance notice. And Roger never had signed the contract Joe had drafted spelling out the partnership arrangements for the boarding business. He kept putting it off. Joe hoped to settle the matter this morning. It would put their relationship on a more professional footing.

Just as Joe was turning into Windsor's driveway, he encountered Beverly Monroe's blue Mercury about to pull out onto Huguenot Trail. Joe knew Beverly fairly well. She was at Windsor most weekends. She liked working outdoors—doing actual labor, not just gardening—but she was also demure and proper. Her voice, with its refined Carolina cadences, was so quiet you sometimes had trouble hearing what she said.

Joe and Beverly both rolled their windows down and talked from car to car over their idling engines. Beverly explained that she was concerned about Roger. She had been over to see him the night before, she said. His usual practice was to call her when she got home to make sure she had arrived safely. Last night the call never came. So she had called him, only to receive a busy signal. She had tried several more times that night, and again this morning, but the line was still busy. Now she was afraid that something might have happened to him. He had recently been complaining about chest pains. He could have had a heart attack. She'd just been at the house, but the door was locked and no one had answered the bell.

Joe suggested they go back and try again. Beverly followed him down the driveway. They stopped beside the pair of massive yews in the circular turnaround. Everything was still. The morning air felt damp and chilly, and the grass was wet with dew. The first swordlike leaves were pushing up through the earth in the two big iris beds that flanked the house.

Joe left Beverly and went down to the barn to try to raise Roger by using the phone there. The line was busy. When he returned to the house, Beverly was just standing by her car, in her khaki trench coat, doing nothing. It seemed peculiar. Joe asked her if she had tried the doorbell again. She said she hadn't.

"Try it," Joe told her, adding that he would return to the barn and call Roger's secretary, Barbara Samuels, who had a key to the house.

This time when Joe returned from the barn, Beverly was sitting on the front steps.

"Did you try the doorbell?" he asked.

"Yes."

Beverly seemed perplexed but not particularly agitated. Joe told her to keep trying the bell while he circled the house to look in the windows. He made his way around to the back, where the land dropped down through a grove of hickory, ash, and willow trees to the river. The first few rooms Joe peered into were empty, but then he worked himself in between the two old boxwoods, the ones they were always pulling bagworms out of, that stood in front of the library windows. Craning to peer up over the air conditioner, he saw Roger lying on one of the couches. It looked like he was asleep.

Joe went around to the side of the house, jimmied open the lock on the sliding glass door that led into the library, and pushed aside the heavy gold curtains. It was a strange room, and utterly silent now. A row of crocodile masks hung along one wall. On the bookshelves were roughly carved wooden figures with teeth and bones attached to them by rotting hemp cord. In the center of the room, a pair of boxy contemporary couches, upholstered in a nubby beige fabric, faced each other on a silver Oriental carpet. A coffee table stood between them.

Roger was lying on his side on the couch nearest the sliding door, facing into the backrest. Joe circled the couch. Roger had on dark sweatpants and a navy sweatshirt with a dark horizontal stripe around the chest. He had taken his shoes off, and his feet, in white socks with slightly dirty soles, were tucked together as if he had been napping. His bifocals rested on the coffee table, next to a copy of *Time* magazine opened to an article about the painter Toulouse-Lautrec and some of the material from the book he was preparing on his African art collection.

As Joe approached Roger, he saw a bullet hole in his forehead. He could tell right away that Roger was dead. The upholstery in front of Roger's head was spattered with dried blood. Blood had streaked across Roger's face and pooled below his right eye, which was swollen shut, the eyelid purplish. The blood had matted his hair and soaked into the striped, tasseled cushion on which his head rested. Joe recognized Roger's revolver, a .38 Special with a double-action hammer, on the couch next to him.

Even though Joe had no doubt Roger was dead, he instinctively lifted Roger's hand to take his pulse. The hand was cold and heavy, pale on top and liverish underneath. Rigor mortis had set in.

There was no note that Joe could see, but it seemed clear to him that Roger had killed himself. He started back out the sliding glass doors just as Beverly appeared on the patio.

"Don't go in," Joe said. "Roger committed suicide."

Beverly rushed past him into the room. Sobbing, she knelt by the couch and leaned her head on Roger's shoulder. Hairfield went into the foyer. He saw that the telephone had been taken off the hook. He replaced the receiver, then called the Powhatan County sheriff's office.

—

Greg Neal, a deputy in the Powhatan County sheriff's office, was at home on the morning of March 5 when the dispatcher called to tell him that Roger de la Burde had committed suicide. It was Neal's day off, but he was one of only two investigators in the department. The other, Captain Vernon Poe, was scheduled to appear in court that day, so the task of investigating the death, and writing the report on it, fell to Neal.

He dropped by the office first, to collect the cameras and equipment, then, in the department's unmarked 1988 Ford Thunderbird, he drove over to Windsor. Neal knew Dr. Burde, as he thought of him. He had served papers on one of the tenants in Burde's rental property a couple of years earlier. As he had been leaving, Burde had stopped him and demanded to know what he was doing. It was a brief conversation, no more than thirty seconds, but Burde was a forceful man and he made an impression on Neal.

When Neal reached the house, two police cars were parked out front. Deputy Morris and Deputy Lane, uniformed patrolmen from the sheriff's department, had arrived a few minutes earlier. Deputy Morris briefly explained the situation: apparent suicide; body discovered by the deceased's longtime girlfriend. Then he showed Neal the library.

Neal had been with the Powhatan County sheriff's office for almost eleven years. Originally from West Virginia, he had lived in Powhatan County since he was thirteen, attended Powhatan High School, and put in four years as an auto mechanic, first at Condrey's Texaco then at Adams Pontiac, before making the switch to law enforcement. After graduating from the police academy, he worked the road for seven years as a patrol deputy, handling burglaries and assaults. When he started doing investigations, they mostly involved uncomplicated rural crimes that tended to be either spontaneously conceived, badly planned, or stupidly executed—and therefore pretty easy to solve. The death of Roger de la Burde, Neal would admit later, was the most unusual case he'd ever handled.

But it didn't seem that way that morning. As Neal first surveyed the scene, he had no reason to doubt what he'd been told: that Burde had committed suicide. Even so, one thing that struck him right away were the black marks on the fourth and fifth fingers of Burde's right hand. They looked like gunpowder stains, but they were more extensive than any such stains he'd ever seen before. And it was not primer residue, which is usually invisible. It was obviously powder. The stains puzzled Neal. He thought maybe Burde had wrapped his hand around the cylinder of the gun when he pulled the trigger.

There were a few other things about the scene that struck Neal as well. There was an ashtray with two cork-colored Marlboro cigarette butts on the coffee table. And there was a great deal of partially burned paper in the fireplace. As Neal set about taking photographs of the scene, he made a point to include pictures of these curious details. He also slipped paper bags over Burde's hands, to keep them uncontaminated until the coroner had a chance to swab them. The swabs would be sent to the state forensic laboratory, which would conduct a gunshot residue test to determine if Burde had actually been holding the gun.

The sheriff's department had no hard-and-fast rules about how a suicide, as opposed to a homicide, should be investigated. That was left up to the case agent's judgment. And so, operating on the assumption that Burde's death was a suicide, Neal did not do many things he later wished he had done. He did not have the troopers secure the house, or even the library, with yellow crime-scene tape. He took the gun into evidence, but not the pillows or the sofa. He did not collect the cigarette butts or the burned material in the fireplace. Nor did he search the house for signs of forced entry.

He did walk through the rooms. He examined the contents of Burde's wallet, which he found in the bedroom. He looked into the dead man's office and saw a computer, but he didn't turn it on. He flipped through the papers on the desk but left the drawers unopened. Since everyone assumed it was a suicide, Neal saw no need to scrutinize the place too closely.

Burde's body lay on the couch until Lester Brown, the local medical examiner, arrived at around eleven-thirty. He too treated the death as a suicide, staying for only thirty minutes and neglecting to record the temperature of the corpse. Shortly thereafter, a hearse from the Rose-Bennett Funeral Home brought the body to the morgue at the Office of the Chief Medical Examiner, on Fourteenth Street in Richmond, where it was placed in cold storage to await the autopsy.

4

Barbara Samuels, Burde's part-time secretary, reached Windsor around nine o'clock and began calling the members of Roger's family. Joe Hairfield also called Beverly's secretary at Philip Morris, Darlene Shannonhouse. Dee, as she was known, arrived by ten. She found Beverly sitting in the kitchen, crying endlessly. Her speech was almost incoherent and she kept repeating herself. Unable to get much of an accounting from Beverly, Dee went off to find Joe Hairfield, hoping he would explain what had happened.

"We came in and we saw Roger lying on the couch," Joe said.

"What did you do?" Dee asked.

"I took the gun out of Roger's hand," Joe said.

"Haven't you ever watched *Perry Mason* or *Matlock*?" she asked. "That's the last thing you do. You leave those things intact." Her own outburst embarrassed her. She was usually a polite person. "What were you thinking?" she asked.

"I don't know," Joe said.

He seemed clearly chagrined.

———

Beverly's son, Gavin, shared the house with her on Old Gun Road. He was her oldest child, a tall, mild-mannered young man who had done poorly in high school, joined the army, made a few false starts after his discharge, and finally returned to live with his mother and enroll at Virginia Commonwealth University. He'd risen early that morning to take a biology exam and had then gone to the Fitness and Wellness Center on Midlothian Turnpike, where he worked as a trainer. His mother, the manager told him when he arrived, had called but hadn't left a message. That was a puzzler; she never called him at work. When he couldn't raise her at the office, he drove home, a quarter-mile away, to check the answering machine. There was a message. "Gav, call the farm." His mom's voice sounded like it was cracking.

Gavin called Windsor and spoke to Dee Shannonhouse.

"You need to come out here," she said.

"Why?" he asked. "What's happened?"

Dee wouldn't say.

Gavin drove quickly out to the farm. Dee's mysteriousness made him nervous. He wondered why his mother had been unable to talk to him. Had Roger hurt her or something? He never had before, but that was all Gavin could think of.

When Gavin saw the squad cars clustered in front of the house, his heart froze. Dee Shannonhouse was in the living room. "Something's happened to Roger," she said.

"He didn't kill himself, did he?" Gavin asked. That was Gavin's first thought. Because the guy absolutely hated his life.

———

Katie Monroe, Beverly's second child and older daughter, had graduated from George Mason University Law School two years earlier and was working as a clerk for Judge Bernard Barrow of the Virginia Court of Appeals. While the appellate judges heard cases in four venues around the state, Judge Barrow lived in Charlottesville and maintained his office there, and Katie had moved to the town for the year of her clerkship. When she returned from lunch that day, a message from Gavin awaited her. "Family emergency. Call immediately."

Katie was slight like her mother and had Beverly's alert hazel eyes. Her mind was quick and analytical; she thought of herself as resolutely right-brained and a member of a diminishing species, the Virginia progressive. After learning of Roger's death, her first concern was for her mother. Beverly's father had killed himself twenty-two years earlier. What, Katie wondered, would another suicide by a loved one do to her mother? She took the back roads to Windsor, through Fluvanna and Goochland Counties, veering around tractors and semis hauling log-laden flatbeds.

When she pulled up at the house, Krystyna Drewnowska was sitting out front on the steps by herself, crying.

"What are you doing here?" Katie asked, and then, without waiting for a response, entered the house.

The question sounded rude, she knew, but she had met Krystyna only once before, during a party Roger and Beverly had given the previous November at Windsor. Krystyna had made several clumsy attempts to usurp, or so it seemed, Beverly's role as hostess by bringing plates to guests; then, before leaving, she had gotten into a heated argument with Roger in Polish. Katie had the impression that Krystyna was another one of the unhappy, grasping women who tried to worm themselves into Roger's life.

After comforting her mother, Katie returned to the kitchen and asked Roger's daughter Corinna why Krystyna Drewnowska was at the house.

"She's pregnant," Corinna said.

That's perfect, Katie thought. Roger, in her view, had been a terrible father. Because he'd alienated his daughters, he'd decided he had to have another child—he'd been talking for two years about conceiving a "male heir"—but once one was on the way, he committed suicide, leaving the child and the mother to fend for themselves.

Krystyna came back inside. She was a striking woman, Katie felt, not a natural beauty, but striking. She wore her thick blond hair cropped at her jawline, spoke in heavily accented English, and dressed sleekly. That afternoon she had tied a bright yellow scarf around her neck.

But it was clear to everyone that Krystyna had no real allies among those who had gathered at the house. Beverly said little to her. When Roger's exwife, Brigitte, passed her in the hallway by the back porch, she made some sharp comment in German. A little while later, Katie noticed, Krystyna was gone.

———

Shortly before two o'clock, Deputy Neal, who had been at Windsor all day, asked Beverly to follow him into Roger's bedroom, down the hall from the library, and give him her version of what had happened the night before. Neal was a round-shouldered, soft-spoken man with a close-cropped brown beard that hid the beginning of a double chin. He sat down on the bed and took out a notepad. He didn't ask many questions. He didn't have to. Beverly Monroe turned out to be one of those people who, once they got started talking, wouldn't stop.

She had arrived at Windsor sometime after six o'clock, Beverly told the deputy. She and Roger had intended to talk over some "difficulties" but decided to delay the discussion until the coming Friday. Instead, they played the piano together, then Roger told Beverly to lie down on the couch and read a *Time* magazine article on Toulouse-Lautrec while he fixed a dinner of shrimp and rice. It was, Beverly said, a peaceful, pleasant evening. Roger kept telling her how nice it was to have her there, kept repeating that word—*nice*. After dinner, Roger decided to work on his book. Beverly brought out the research and Roger began to leaf through it but soon quit. His earlier cheerful mood dissipated. He began to act as if something was eating him.

A number of things had been worrying Roger in the last couple of years, Beverly told the deputy. The upkeep of the farm was one: No one in his family was interested in helping him maintain it. His two daughters were a disappointment. Not too long ago, Beverly said, Roger had asked her why God punished him with children like this. Also, the ongoing lawsuit with Philip Morris was getting him down. And he had health problems. He complained about his chest and heart, and he was afraid of prostate cancer.

Furthermore, Beverly confessed, Roger had been unfaithful to her in recent years. While she had come to accept these infidelities, Roger knew that she knew, and this distressed him. But the crucial issue in Roger's life, Beverly told Neal, was that for the past year and a half he had been obsessed with having another child. He had talked about finding a surrogate mother. Even though Beverly was fifty-four, they had discussed the possibility of her bearing the child. Beverly admitted that she had been willing to entertain the idea and had gone so far as to ask her daughter Katie if she would supply an egg.

That idea hadn't panned out. Instead, Roger had begun an affair with Krystyna Drewnowska. Krystyna had left her husband, Beverly said, had tricked Roger into making her pregnant, and had been trying to get him to marry her. When he refused, she drew up a child-support agreement and demanded that he sign it.

Once the child he had thought he wanted was actually on the way, Beverly explained, Roger felt trapped. He saw no way out of the situation. While his whole life was one large tissue of lies, Beverly said, he had always remained in control of things. But with Krystyna determined to bear this child against Roger's wishes, and to hold him financially responsible, he felt he had lost control.

Roger had been tired the night before, Beverly told Neal. He had become melancholy. When they had played the piano, he had insisted she play one particular piece, Wayne Shorter's "Lady Day," over and over. After dinner, he had taken a nap and when he woke he had told her he loved her and said how sorry he was for making such a mess of their lives. He also said that although he had demanded Krystyna get an abortion, it was now too late for her to undergo the procedure and he hoped they could all work it out. Beverly said she assured him they could. She urged him to call Krystyna right then and resolve the matter. "No," she recalled him saying. "I'll call her later so I can explain it to her in Polish."

Around nine-thirty, Beverly said, she collected her things and prepared to leave. Roger walked her to the door, where he put his hands on her face and kissed her. "Please don't leave me," she recalled him saying. He told her he loved her, then said, "Good night, *engelchen.*"

Roger usually called her when she got home, Beverly continued, to make sure that she'd arrived safely and to wish her good night. But that evening he didn't call, so she called him. Each time she tried, however, the line was busy. It was still busy in the morning, so she drove out to Windsor. Unable to get Roger to answer the door, she was leaving to go to work when she encountered Joe Hairfield, and he broke into the house and found the body.

Neal put his notepad away and thanked Beverly. She seemed to him to be likable and truthful, and to be genuinely grieving. He told her he'd talk to her again at a later date and drove back to the sheriff's office. He had begun by then to wonder about the nature of Burde's death. He was thinking it could be a suicide, but he was beginning to see some problems. Those stains on Burde's fingers still puzzled him.

———

Since the police were not treating the house as a crime scene, no one who was there that day felt they needed to, either. Quite a few people had gathered at Windsor by mid-afternoon, and ever since the hearse had carried off the body, many of them wandered in and out of the library, unable to resist the temptation to stare at the couch on which Roger had died.

The couch upset Corinna. She asked Gavin to get rid of it. He and Joe Hairfield and the husband of Roger's occasional bookkeeper, Hazel Bunch, trooped into the library and on the count of three hoisted it up. Gavin was startled to see a pool of blood on the carpet beneath the couch. It was creepy. Gavin figured it must have trickled out of Roger's body overnight and then seeped down through the pillows. Struggling with his end of the couch, Gavin accidentally stepped in the blood and tracked a bit of it across the floor.

They carried the couch outside and heaved it up onto the back of a pickup. They went back in and rolled up the bloody rug and brought that out as well, then drove down to the barn and left the couch and the rug there, on the hay-strewn floor.

———

Beverly's youngest child, Shannon, was studying art at the College of William & Mary in Williamsburg. Late that afternoon, when she returned to the little room she rented near the campus, there was a message on her answering machine from Gavin saying that Roger had passed away the previous night. There was nothing in the message about how or why.

Shannon's first thought was that Roger had had a heart attack. She had in a way expected it. He had been complaining for a year about heart pains, and his diet was terrible. He'd eat sausage and hard cheese for breakfast, and late at night she'd often catch him in front of the fridge with a spoon in one hand and a half-gallon of Pet ice cream in the other. A heart attack was something she thought she could deal with.

But at the same time she flashed on the dream she had had just the night before. It had been so vivid that recalling it gave her goose bumps. It began as a typical running dream. She was running after someone, a man, she didn't know who, and she caught up with him and put a hand on his shoulder and turned him around and it was Roger. He was crying. A mist surrounded them. She put her hands on both sides of his face, which was odd, because when she was a kid living with her mom after her mom left her dad, she'd never wanted Roger to kiss or hug her. To her, Roger had been this gross old Polish guy.

In the dream, however, she reached out to Roger. He was crying and saying good-bye, and at that moment what felt like a thunderclap woke her up. It was four o'clock in the morning, but the dream had so disturbed her that she sat up in bed and wrote down a description of it in her journal.

Instead of trying to call Gavin or her mother, Shannon immediately got into her car, a little beige Plymouth Champ, and made the one-hour drive from Williamsburg to Windsor. On the way, she thought about the dream. It seemed totally flaky, but at the same time it was an undeniable premonition. It was almost dark when Shannon reached the farm. By that time denial had set in. It must be a mistake, she told herself. Roger couldn't really have died. He must be in the hospital.

There were a few cars parked out front, but none of them belonged to Katie or Gavin or her mother. The front door was open. Shannon walked in, through the dining room and into the kitchen, where she came across Corinna and Joe Hairfield and Barbara Samuels. Corinna was holding her hand in the shape of a pistol, index finger extended, turning it upside down and pointing it toward her forehead. Shannon realized from what Corinna was saying that Roger had killed himself with a pistol. Her legs buckled, she lost her senses for a moment, then, just to get away, blindly turned and fled down the hallway.

5

Shortly after dawn the following day, William Jefferson, who was completing his fellowship in forensic pathology at the Office of the Chief Medical Examiner in Richmond, arrived for work at the state's Consolidated Laboratory Building on Fourteenth Street. The morgue was in the basement, near the bay where the hearses and ambulances dropped off the bodies. They were kept overnight on rolling stretchers in a large cold-storage room, called the cooler, that was connected to the morgue by a massive steel door.

Richmond had one of the highest per capita murder rates in the country at the time. Jefferson never knew how many corpses would be waiting when he arrived for work. On any given morning there would be from one to twelve bodies, and sometimes as many as five or six of them would be riddled with bullets. The fellowship had provided Jefferson with a lot of opportunity to concentrate on homicide autopsies.

The morgue was large and cool, with overhead fluorescent lighting, walls of sheet metal, and cinder blocks painted white. It was dominated by three autopsy tables that were perforated to allow fluids to drain down to the brown tile floor. Dr. Marcella Fierro, the deputy chief medical examiner and a woman who had acquired a degree of local fame as the model for the sleuth-pathologist Kay Scarpetta in Patricia Cornwell's mystery novels, assigned Jefferson to conduct the autopsy of Roger de la Burde.

The body, still dressed in sweatpants and sweatshirt, the hands bagged, was wheeled from the cooler and placed on a table. There were several other doctors and assistants at work in the lab that morning. As Jefferson proceeded with the autopsy, Fierro occasionally looked over his shoulder and made comments, but she was also working on several other cases in the room.

Jefferson and the assistants, George Coy and Robert Smith, stripped the body, which was cool to the touch, and examined it. Rigor mortis was passing, but the jaw and arms were still stiff. They measured the body—68.5 inches from head to toe—and weighed it: 209 lbs. Speaking to a scribe, who stood beside him marking up a body diagram on a clipboard, Jefferson noted an appendectomy scar, the stigmata of scalp scars from a hair transplant, and "a charcoal gray staining" on the fourth and fifth fingers of the right hand. He avoided making any assumptions about what had caused the stains. All he could do was describe what they looked like.

Jefferson and the assistants photographed the body and wounds, took X rays, and washed the body down. Jefferson measured the bullet hole in the forehead. It was a quarter of an inch in diameter. He cleaned the wound. The ring of soot burn and powder that surrounded it was $15/16$ of an inch in diameter. It looked to Jefferson like a typical contact wound. There were copious amounts of muzzle residue and lead deposits just under the skin. And there were star-shaped tears in the skin of the type that occurred when a gun muzzle was pressed against flesh. Under those circumstances, the gunshot discharged pressurized gases beneath the skin, and as they expanded, the gases tore the skin. Jefferson recovered two small lead fragments in the skin near the entrance wound. They had been shaved off the bullet when it entered the skull.

Jefferson made a Y incision in the trunk, cutting from each of the two shoulders inward and down to the xiphoid, at the lower end of the sternum, then down to the pelvis. He folded back the skin, and examined the major organs. The victim, he observed, had a mild constriction in the left coronary artery. Both his lungs were congested. He had an uncircumcised penis and a markedly enlarged prostate gland. Everything else seemed within the normal limits. The stomach contained partially digested shrimp, tomatoes, and a leafy green vegetable that looked to Jefferson like spinach. The state of the contents suggested Burde had died two to three hours after eating.

One of the assistants sawed off the top half of the skull and removed the brain. Using what the pathologists called a brain knife, for serial slicing, Jefferson cut into the tissue to trace the bullet path. The bullet had entered the right frontal lobe, passing backward and leftward and downward. Along the path, it fractured the bone around the eye, causing those tissues to bleed, severed the brain stem, and did damage to the cerebellum. Under those circumstances, Jefferson knew, death would have been instantaneous.

Jefferson found a single large-caliber bullet in the posterior fossa, at the back of the brain, where it had come to rest. He lifted it out with his fingers.

When the autopsy was complete, Jefferson released the body back to the cold-storage locker, where the funeral home would pick it up. Since the fatal gunshot wound was said to be self-inflicted and since the deceased had been shot in the head and not through the clothing, there was no need to keep the clothes. Jefferson had them sent back to the funeral home along with the body. The bullet fragments, gunshot residue kit, and the bags from the hands were forwarded to the evidence room of the Office of the Chief Medical Examiner pending a final disposition of the case. Then Jefferson sat down to dictate a provisional report.

During the autopsy, the pathologist had seen nothing that contradicted the story that the deceased had committed suicide. Making a determination of the manner of death, however, was beyond the scope of his responsibilities in this case. In his report, under the heading for cause of death, he stated, "Gunshot wound to head and brain."

When he was finished with the report, he forwarded it to Marcella Fierro, who read it over, approved it, and initialed it.

———

That same morning, an article appeared in the Richmond *Times-Dispatch* with the headline, ART COLLECTOR FOUND DEAD IN POWHATAN. The article reported that the authorities were investigating whether or not Roger de la Burde had committed suicide and quoted Captain Vernon Poe of the Powhatan sheriff's office as saying, "It's really too early to tell." An article in the Richmond *News Leader* gave even greater prominence to the official uncertainty, declaring in its lead sentence, "Police have not determined whether the shooting death of Roger de la Burde, a Powhatan art collector, is a homicide or a suicide."

Poe's desk was right next to Greg Neal's in the sheriff's office, a series of windowless rooms underneath the county courthouse in the small village of Powhatan. Neal had shown Poe the Polaroids he'd taken of the death scene and of Burde's body. It seemed to Poe that the bullet's entry hole, just above the deceased's right eyebrow on the side of the forehead, was in an unusual spot. Most suicides who chose to end their lives with guns, he told Neal, shot themselves in the mouth or the temple.

As Neal was thinking this over, he got several calls from people who knew Burde. One man said he had been friends with Roger since they were both young college students in Poland. It was the funniest thing, the way this guy talked, like Bela Lugosi in a vampire movie. Mr. Neal, he said, I just *vant* to let you know, Roger de la Burde, you *vould* see him as *veirdo*, but *zat*'s his lifestyle. If Dr. de la Burde had committed suicide, he *vould* have wrote you a book, my son, not a note, a *book*, and before he finished it he *vould* have changed his mind.

Neal also received a call from Krystyna Drewnowska. He had talked to her briefly the day before at Windsor and she had said she didn't think Burde would have committed suicide. Now she had heard Beverly's story about leaving Windsor at nine-thirty and calling Roger from her house only to hear a busy signal. The story didn't make sense, Krystyna said. If Beverly Monroe had left Roger that night, she explained, and had called at ten, at eleven, and at twelve and gotten a busy signal, she would have been back on Roger's doorstep by one A.M.

The calls kept coming in. Neal was amazed. A woman who said she had a "mature adult relationship" with Burde called to insist he would not have killed himself. A little later, Neal received a call from a Don Beville, who identified himself as Burde's friend and publisher. Beville said Burde had called him around ten o'clock the night before the body was found. The conversation had been short, but what Roger had said was so unusual and he had sounded so strange that Beville had written down the words. It was "a new day," Roger had declared, adding that he was going to "make some changes" in his life and that "the weight of the world" was off his shoulders. Roger didn't seem depressed, Beville went on. In fact they had made tentative plans to get together for lunch the following day. Roger had said he would bring a friend.

———

Carl Baker, the superintendent of the Virginia state police, had also begun to wonder if Burde's death was a suicide. The previous year Wojtek Drewnowska, Krystyna's ex-husband, had come to the state police to complain that Burde had seduced his wife, and in doing so had involved her in certain illegal activities, some sort of art fraud. Wojtek had demanded that the police launch an investigation into those activities. Nothing much had come of this—the charges had been pretty hard to substantiate, and given the circumstances, Wojtek may simply have been trying to create trouble for the man who had stolen his wife. But now that Burde had turned up dead, Baker thought the Powhatan County officials should be made aware of this background. Baker told Dave Riley, one of the senior agents in the Bureau of Criminal Investigations, to contact the local Powhatan investigator, fill him in, and offer the assistance of the state police.

Greg Neal welcomed Riley's call. He said he had felt rushed during the investigation at the scene. He'd had to serve as his own crime-scene tech person, which meant collecting all the physical evidence—dusting for prints, taking measurements and photographs—as well as talking to the witnesses.

Riley was sympathetic. When investigating a case, he never served as his own crime-scene tech person—that spread you too thin.

As a result of being overworked, Neal said, he had not been as thorough as he might have been. And he did have some concerns about the case. All in all, Neal told Riley, he'd like to have a second look at the scene.

6

On Saturday morning, Corinna called Beverly. Since her father's death had been announced in the papers, she said, she and her mother were worried about security at Windsor. Also, Roger had left some instructions, written a few years ago, stipulating to the IRS that in the event of his death he had already given specific possessions to certain people. Corinna wanted to know if the Monroes would help her and her mother move these things out. Gavin and one of his fraternity brothers, Dave Fleenor, rented a truck, and drove out to Windsor with Beverly, Katie, and Shannon.

It rained off and on all day. Brigitte took charge of the operation. She had crocodile heads and abstract paintings taken down from the walls and stored in boxes. She had Persian rugs rolled up and wrapped in plastic. It was hard work. They all still felt confused and grief-stricken by Roger's unexplained death, and they reacted in different ways. Shannon retreated into herself, depressed, because someone they loved had taken his life and no one knew why. Beverly kept seeing mementos that distracted her with memories of Roger. Katie sat down on a couch in the middle of the day and cried. Gavin tried to joke. Corinna got angry. "Why did my dad have all this junk?" she cried out in frustration.

By nightfall Windsor looked as if it had been stripped. On Brigitte's instructions, Gavin and Dave Fleenor had transported some of the stuff to a storage bin. They also took things to Corinna's apartment and to Brigitte's. Past dinnertime, they were still carrying boxes and rugs up into Brigitte's apartment. On the last run, when it was getting time to relax and crack a brew, Brigitte started asking them to move her furniture around and lay down some of Roger's rugs. Gavin and Dave looked at each other. What was going on? Were they supposed to redecorate her frigging apartment?

Then Gavin shrugged. Brigitte was a grieving widow. He and Dave Fleenor stayed at Brigitte's, carrying couches back and forth and spreading out rugs, until late at night.

———

That night, a security guard at the Philip Morris plant in south Richmond received a call from a woman asking to speak to a plant supervisor.

"In reference to what?" the guard asked.

"It's very personal," the woman said. She sounded middle-aged and had a whispery Deep South accent.

The guard asked her to be more specific.

"It's about Roger Burde."

"It's about an employee?"

"Ex-employee," the woman said. "He was a scientist," she added. "He was suing Philip Morris."

When the guard asked her to call back during office hours, she said she needed to speak to someone immediately.

"Why can't this wait until Monday?" he asked.

"Because there's a lot of problems out here now."

"With the product or what?"

"Sir, I am not at liberty to tell you that."

The guard put his supervisor, Bobby Williams, on the line. Yes, Williams said, he was familiar with Roger de la Burde, a former employee in research and development. Yes, he knew the gentleman was deceased. No, he did not know the gentleman was engaged in a lawsuit against Philip Morris.

"Well," the woman said, "I'm trying to tell you that these people out here that are suing for him—"

"Suing *for* him?"

"Yes."

"Okay."

"They're taking it upon themselves that—they're trying to say that Philip Morris killed this person and they're spreading it around everywhere. I mean *everywhere*."

"Okay."

"Now does that give you *any* idea of what I'm talking about?" The woman said she needed to speak to one of the Philip Morris lawyers that night. "They're spreading the word that Philip Morris killed this person. And they in turn are going to turn around and sue Philip Morris for a zillion, billion dollars, you know? And it's stupid."

The supervisor said all he could do was recommend that she call Hunton & Williams, Philip Morris's primary law firm in Richmond, on Monday.

"You're not taking this very seriously, are you?" the woman asked.

"Yes, ma'am," Bobby Williams assured her.

———

The next day, Brigitte called Beverly again. Windsor, she said, now looked too bare. Would the Monroes help return some of the things they'd all removed the day before? Katie and Shannon rolled their eyes when they heard this. But the family drove back out to the farm and pitched in rehanging paintings.

Afterward, Corinna stopped by Beverly's house to talk to Katie. She had seen the article about her father's death, with its reference to a possible homicide investigation, in the *Times-Dispatch*. It seemed unnecessary, she said, since her father had clearly killed himself. She didn't want her family to be dragged through a homicide investigation. Do we have some say in that? she asked. Is there any way to prevent it?

Katie, whose job as a clerk for an appellate judge had given her a good introduction to criminal law, realized that Corinna thought a homicide might be a crime like assault or rape, in which it was necessary for the victim to press charges in order for an investigation to proceed. She explained that in a homicide, since the victim was not there to decide whether or not to press charges, the state stepped in, much as it would with a minor or anyone else unable to give informed consent, and assumed the responsibility for bringing charges.

"You can call and tell them how you view it," Katie said, "but you have no control over their decisions."

———

A wake was held for Burde that evening, at the Joseph W. Bliley Funeral Home on Staples Mill Road. Roger would have hated it, Shannon decided. The funeral home was in the middle of nowhere, across the street from a Grease Monkey lube shop. There was heavy organ music, and Styrofoam crosses and gaudy flower arrangements were all crammed into a dark little room. It was so tacky and plastic, Shannon thought, perfect middle-class suburban-strip-mall America. She stayed real quiet, standing close to her mom the whole time, holding her hand and squeezing it tight, because she was concerned about her.

Roger's body lay in an open casket in a room next to the chapel. Charlie Valentine, who had tried to get Roger into the Country Club of Virginia, came up and placed an old golf club in the casket. The club had belonged to his father. The gesture seemed to say: You bet there's golf in heaven. Beverly and her children went to the room and stood in the doorway for a minute, but then Beverly decided not to approach the casket. That just wasn't Roger, she felt. He wasn't there at all.

———

There was a gathering at Windsor that night. Roger's sister, Monique, and her husband, Alan Huber, a dentist in La Jolla, California, and their son, Sig, were there, as were the Monroes, a Polish friend of Burde's named Kot Unrug, and Sheldon Gosline, a young graduate student in Egyptology at the University of Chicago, who had gotten to know Burde while he was a curatorial intern at the Virginia Museum. Talk turned to the question of a suicide note. Nobody, they realized, had systematically searched the house for one. The guests spread out through the rooms to look.

They didn't find a note. What they came across, in Roger's bedroom, were mass cards, photographs of the venerated Black Madonna of Czestochowa, and a letter to Burde from a Polish nun chastising him for his irreligious life. Burde, while raised a Catholic, had never been devout, and this unexpected cache, these references to unexpiated sin and divine judgment, suggested to the guests that he may have been going through some sort of religious crisis in his finals days or hours. Monique, a flamboyant woman given to bright clothes and dramatic gestures, found a Ouija board, and some of the guests used it to try to summon Roger's spirit. Suddenly

Monique thought she saw something and ran to the window. What was it, Gavin wondered, a bloody apparition? This is too much, he thought. This is weird, weird, weird.

Sheldon Gosline was staying with the Monroes. He didn't know them well and had expected to sleep at Windsor, but Beverly, who'd extended the invitation, had seemed distressed, so he thought he would go and give comfort where comfort was most needed.

Back at Old Gun Road, he and Katie and Shannon sat up discussing Burde's character and what might have happened to him. Sheldon had all sorts of theories. He pointed out that Roger had died on Ash Wednesday. He thought that was symbolic. It was a penitential day, he said, a time when Catholics were concerned with self-examination and death.

Sheldon was also a student of African culture. After leaving the Virginia Museum, he had lived with Roger for a couple of months to help him with his book. He told Katie and Shannon that Roger was heavily influenced by Nigerian religion. Eshu, the Nigerian god of chaos, was a particular force in Roger's life, he said. Eshu was two-sided; he had a face that was at once both black and white, and he confused people by showing one man the black face while simultaneously showing a second man the white face. Roger also had two faces, Sheldon said, and he sowed similar confusion by showing people only one or the other of them.

Shannon was fascinated. Sheldon had pieced together all these graduate school–type theories like the squares of a quilt. They stayed up talking until two A.M.

The next morning Shannon's eyes felt like slits.

7

On Monday, Greg Neal drove up to First Division state police headquarters, on Brook Road in Henrico County, north of Richmond, where Dave Riley worked in a small, low-ceilinged office with two other investigators. Three metal desks and a row of metal filing cabinets took up all the space. Riley had the desk near the window, with a view of the parking lot.

Neal knew a lot of the state police guys, but he had never heard of Riley and at first he didn't like him. Riley seemed to think Neal was a rube who didn't know what he was doing and had muffed the death-scene investigation. Riley didn't actually come out and say as much—this was just Neal's impression. He was admittedly sensitive on the matter.

The 35mm photographs Neal had taken of the death scene were still at the processor. But he had brought Polaroids of Burde's right hand, with the dark smudges on the fourth and fifth fingers, and of Burde's body lying sideways on the couch.

Riley, who did think the death-scene investigation had been mishandled, studied the photographs. The smudges on Burde's fingers resembled gunpowder residue, he thought. But he could not understand from looking at them how they occurred as a result of a suicide. In fact, at first, he was in the dark as to how they could have occurred as a result of *anything*. The pattern of the stains was truly bewildering. Burde was right-handed, but if the stains on that hand were from gunpowder, the two investigators reasoned, Burde could not have used it to pull the trigger, since the gunpowder was discharged mainly through the muzzle and the cylinder. His right hand would have to have been close to the source of the discharge, which meant he would have had to have used his left hand to pull the trigger.

Neal explained his concern about the position of the body. Riley agreed that it was unusual. Typically in a suicide, Riley thought, the person would sit in a comfortable chair or lean against a comfortable tree or lie in bed propped up by a couple of pillows. In those final moments of life, comfort was key. And the person was usually deliberate about positioning the gun. He would aim for a direct shot in the side of his head or would stick the barrel in his mouth and point straight up. The suicide's goal was to kill himself instantly. He wanted at all costs to avoid botching the job and winding up maimed but alive. That Roger de la Burde would lie on his side and shoot himself in a complicated manner that involved somehow holding the gun with his left hand just did not make a lot of sense.

Riley had been assigned to as many as sixty homicide cases—he'd never sat down and counted them. Some, like the one where an inmate decapitated, or nearly decapitated, another inmate in the old Richmond penitentiary, were pretty straightforward. Some, like the case in the Northern Neck, where a Peeping Tom had murdered a young woman after watching her and her husband make love in their trailer, were more complicated. And then there were others, like the Parkway murders along I-64, that remained unsolved mysteries. Of those sixty-odd cases, Riley had been the lead agent, the one with his name on the case and exclusive control over the investigation, on fifteen to twenty. It was, he felt, an impressive record, and it gave him confidence in his instincts and judgment.

Riley had a gut feeling that this case would prove to be a homicide. It was, at that point, just a hunch, but as hunches went, it was powerful. In Riley's mind it approached near certainty.

————

Roger de la Burde's funeral was held that same morning. An organist played some Bach pieces that Beverly had suggested. There were not many mourners, and they had spread out in isolated clusters in the chapel's pews. Brigitte, Corinna, and Burde's older daughter, Colette, who had come up from New Orleans, sat in stoic silence. Roger's sister and her husband were there with their son, Sig, who sat next to Krystyna Drewnowska. Burde had an illegitimate German daughter named Sylvia, who had flown in over the weekend, and she sat with her German fiancé. Beverly and her children occupied a pew down in front.

The priest, who hadn't known Roger, had asked Katie Monroe to gather reminiscences, and his remarks sounded canned and secondhand. The service, Beverly felt, wasn't very nice at all. It just wasn't.

Afterward, the funeral procession made its way through a light rain toward Hollywood Cemetery on a bluff of the James. The cemetery, which dated from 1849, contained the graves of American presidents James Monroe and John Tyler, figures from the Confederacy such as Jefferson Davis and Jeb Stuart, and members of old Virginia families like the Randolphs and the Branches.

Roger, Katie Monroe thought, was finally joining the Richmond aristocracy.

The hearse, trailed by a line of cars with their headlights on, passed through the wrought-iron gates and followed a winding narrow road through steep hills covered with ash, cedar, beech, and elm trees and crowded with weathered tombstones, mossy crypts, marble angels, obelisks, and crumbling headless cherubs.

Corinna had wanted all of her father's vehicles—the Jaguar, the little Mercedes, the Citation, and the Dodge van—in the procession. She had asked Gavin to drive the Jaguar, Roger's favorite car, and to serve as one of the pallbearers, and Gavin had been happy to do both. He had talked to Corinna a lot over the weekend. She was definitely stunned by what had happened, but she hadn't had a very loving relationship with her father and

Gavin hadn't seen her shed a single tear. Didn't mean she wasn't grieving, though.

The procession halted on a northern slope near an ivy bed, on the far side of a knoll that held Fitzhugh Lee's grave. The rain had died away by the time the final words were spoken over the casket. As the mourners dispersed through the soggy grass, Krystyna walked up to the grave alone and laid a single flower on it.

Afterward, Corinna de la Burde telephoned Greg Neal. For the better part of a year, Beverly had been telling Corinna that she was worried about Roger, who seemed increasingly despondent and forgetful. Corinna had dismissed these concerns at the time. She didn't see her father that often— her job as a sales representative with 3M meant she was on the road several days a week, and she had little inclination to spend her weekends at Windsor—but when she did see him, he seemed like his usual self. Now she began to think she should have taken Beverly's warning more seriously.

Corinna told Neal that he would probably hear a lot of people who knew her father saying it was impossible that Roger killed himself. But her father was, in her opinion, a very intense man. He experienced radical mood swings. His motor was racing all the time. He jumped from project to project. He constantly changed his mind. Anyone who knew her father as well as she did would suspect that he had a chemical imbalance of some kind. The fact was, he'd been unhappy recently. And there was a history of suicide in his family. His mother had once tried to kill herself.

The only thing that bothered her, Corinna told Neal, was that her father had not left a note. Her father had always been obsessed with what would happen to his property and investments and art collection in the event of his death, with who would receive what and under what circumstances. In addition to his will, which he was always revising, he'd written detailed instructions spelling out what his children, mistresses, relatives, and friends should do if he died. Which made it very surprising, Corinna said, that if her father had killed himself, he hadn't left an extensive note.

8

Dave Riley was a true Civil War buff. He haunted souvenir shops and battlegrounds and went to re-enactments. He knew that Robert E. Lee—

whom he considered second only to God—had stopped at Windsor on the way back from Appomattox. So the farm interested Riley for historical reasons. And now that he was considering Burde's death as a possible homicide, he wanted to get a feel for the place. Studying the layout, taking a visual impression, was something he did on every case.

Riley also wanted to talk to someone neutral who knew as much about Burde as possible, and he could think of no better person than Barbara Samuels. Secretaries, in Riley's experience, knew all the secrets. So he called Samuels and arranged to meet her at the farm the day after the funeral.

Neal went with him. Neal had now come around to liking Riley. The state police investigator was a little full of himself, but that was hardly a crime. Riley clearly had more training and experience than Neal did. And Riley seemed to have realized that while Neal may have made a mistake or two investigating the death scene, he wasn't completely ignorant. Grounds existed for a working partnership.

Corinna was at Windsor with Barbara Samuels when the two officers arrived. The first thing Riley did was walk through the ground floor, to eyeball it. People had been coming and going, so there was no intact crime scene. Riley and Neal dug through the ashes in the library fireplace, but there was nothing in there except some glossy magazines that had been partially burned. These didn't seem to Riley to be evidence of much. Anybody could buy a glossy magazine at a newsstand.

The officers sat down to talk to the two women. Riley played it close to the vest. If the case was a homicide, he didn't yet know who the possible suspects were, and he didn't want to reveal his thinking to any suspect who might be hoping the police would just write the death off as a suicide.

If Burde had been found dead in a car in downtown Richmond, Riley thought, a whole range of people could be suspected of killing him. But if Burde had been shot with his own gun while napping on his own couch in his own house, the murderer had to be someone who had access to the house, who knew both that Burde had a gun and where he kept it, and who was on intimate enough terms with him to get into the library and right up next to the couch while he was asleep. Those conditions considerably reduced the universe of potential suspects. In fact, Riley believed, you were talking about a handful of people.

The daughter Corinna, obviously, was one. So was the secretary, for that matter, but Riley had to start somewhere and the secretary was more likely to be neutral than anyone else.

Riley talked to Barbara Samuels alone in the kitchen. She was a short, stout woman who looked to be in her early forties and wore her hair in tight black curls. She had been working as Roger's secretary two to three days a week for the past two and a half years. She typed letters, took dictation at the computer—a little of everything.

Burde didn't seem suicidal, Samuels told Riley. He was looking forward to finishing his African art book. He had a ski trip planned, with Beverly Monroe, only a week and a half away. And he had recently said something that Samuels found revealing in light of his supposedly having killed himself. When a teenage boy had committed suicide in Powhatan a short while back, Roger had told her that the youngster's death was a tragedy. "There's no reason ever to give up," she remembered him saying. "There's always hope."

At the end of the conversation, Samuels told Riley she wanted to share with him some details of Burde's life, but not while Corinna was in the house.

———

When Riley returned to Windsor two days later to see Barbara Samuels alone, there was something he felt he had to get on the table right away. He asked her if she had been having an affair with Burde.

No, she said very matter-of-factly. Roger had tried, she had refused him, and he had given up. He didn't hold it against her. The overture hadn't worked, so he had moved on to something else. And she hadn't held it against him, because she knew that was just the way he was: He tried with every woman.

There had been some sexual activity between Roger and Hazel Bunch, the local bookkeeper who came in from time to time, and possibly with some of his other help. But the two main women in his life, Samuels said, were Beverly Monroe and Krystyna Drewnowska. Roger felt torn between them but had been thinking of leaving Beverly for Krystyna.

Riley wondered if Samuels was in some way biased against Beverly. He did not have the feeling that she was. Samuels clearly liked Burde and felt loyal to him. But she also seemed to have started out liking Beverly, and she didn't seem to have any special love for Krystyna. If anything, she didn't seem particularly crazy about either of the women at this point. In Riley's mind, she passed the neutrality test.

Riley was one week into a case that had yet to be declared a homicide, but after talking to Barbara Samuels he believed he had his primary suspect. Beverly Monroe had had the opportunity to kill Burde, since she was at his house the night he died and was apparently the last person to see him alive. She had had the means, since she knew about his gun. And now, if the information provided by Samuels was true and Burde had been planning to leave her for Krystyna, it was clear she had had motive.

Of course, Krystyna was also a possible suspect. She too had motive, if it was true, as Beverly had claimed, that Burde was going to end his relationship with her. But if Krystyna had killed Burde and was hoping to pass it off as a suicide, she would hardly have called Greg Neal and insisted that the case be investigated as a murder. That, in Riley's view, spoke for her innocence.

Krystyna's husband, Wojtek, was also a possible suspect. Since Roger had more or less stolen the man's wife, Wojtek clearly had motive. But Riley didn't think Wojtek would have had the sort of easy access to the house that the killer apparently enjoyed.

Riley felt he had to follow the evidence, and in his mind at this point it was flowing in the direction of only one person: Beverly Monroe.

———

After the funeral, Beverly had been inclined to go straight back to work, but then everybody, including her boss, Jim Schardt, the head of the Philip Morris patent office, had told her, no, she should take the week off, so she did. Shannon had never seen her mom in such a state. She couldn't sleep. She had no appetite. She was given to uncontrollable fits of crying. Her face was swollen and raw; her eyes were puffy and red. She was thin and kind of ashen-colored and unkempt, not her usual groomed self. She was really traumatized.

On Friday, Corinna came over to Beverly's house with a copy of Roger's will and an accompanying letter he had written for his beneficiaries. It was evening and Beverly had just finished dinner, some turkey soup that Donna, Jim Schardt's wife, had brought over. It was the first thing she had been able to eat in days.

Beverly had never seen the will. But Roger had told her that while he was leaving Windsor to Corinna, he was giving her the right of lifetime tenancy there, with no restrictions. She knew he had done this because she was the only one who cared enough about the place to put in the effort and labor to maintain it. Far from being a gift, the lifetime tenancy was a sort of burden, an obligation she would carry out for Roger's sake.

Sitting at the kitchen table, she read the letter, which was addressed to her, to Roger's ex-wife, to his two legitimate daughters and his one illegitimate daughter, and to his Polish friend. It contained, like most things Roger wrote, misspellings and grammatical lapses.

Dear Brigitte, Colette, Corinna, Beverly, Sylvia, and Kot!

I am addressing this letter to you as the most important people in my life and those whose life are inextricably involved in my purpose of existence. . . .

It is my duty to explain a few words that the purpose of my will is to reward those who were especially instrumental to the development of the welfare of our Family. Regrettably, they were often not the direct members of my family, who often took for granted that what was produced through decades of hard work and tremendous personal sacrifices.

In my last thoughts I want to remember Beverly Monroe, who at a tremendous personal sacrifice built our family's security, and recognition, who gave me relentless support, who stood by me in moments of weakness and never abandoned her vision and her highest personal principals. Beverly's contributions to our family were often made at the expense of her personal welfare. I love you, I respect you, and I am grateful to you Beverly. I am appointing you hereby as one of the Executors of the Estate and hope you will fulfill this obligation with vision.

My daughter Corinna de la Burde, who I love with every breath of my life and whom I have learned to respect over the last few years, I appoint as the second Executor of my Estate. Corinna, you are a real de la Burde who will preserve the dignity of the name and will always be guided by fairness, loyalty, and common sense. Today it is up to you to carry the torch of the family forward. . . .

My friend Konstanty Unrug, you have been an inspiration and a guide on many cross roads of my life. . . . I am appointing you as third and alternate Executor. . . . I don't believe that Inner Blindness in our family is eternal. . . . I still hope for Colette and Sylvia and I want you to be their guide.

Colette, I love you very much. . . . Since you are a Countess, it is your duty to yourself to act as a countess in your daily life. Until now you have chosen only to detract from your beauty, from your intelligence, and from your own accomplishments. And that for no obvious purpose! . . . I pray to God that one day you will realize how close you are to becoming a real caring Person and a Winner in life. To do so, God must open your eyes so that you can learn to:

—Care deeply for other people and especially for your family members.

—Use your energy towards higher goals instead of low class pursuits.

—Associate with people from who you can learn and after who you can model yourself rather than with those you can dominate and subjugate to mood swings.

—Dress up, lose weight, look up and better yourself. . . .

Nothing will give me greater pleasure than to live a bit longer, observe your transformation and have a chance to rewrite my will, so that you can be a much greater beneficiary than you are now. . . .

Brigitte, I cared for you deeply all my life. I protected you, and wanted to share with you but your lack of interests, lack of ambition and goals, your passive and negative attitude was unbearable. There was no competence, no caring, and no desire to help or share. Ever! As unbelievable as it is, you would do virtually nothing, for yourself or others when it required your sacrifice or even a slight discomfort. For that reason, no discretionary judgment should be left to you with the disposition of the assets which I am leaving through you to the children. . . . Any discretionary judgment left to you will lead to a blunder or will be relegated to lawyers, bankers, or financial planners, who will do their job in a typical "institutional manner," without real regard for family welfare. . . .

Sylvia, I am learning about you and I want to give you the benefit of the doubt. Let me see that you can care for others in addition to yourself and [your son] Benjamin. Let me see that you are willing to make personal sacrifices so that you may accomplish. . . .

> I greet you and love you!
> Until we meet again.
> Roger de la Burde.
> 6/28/89

Despite its overwrought, self-important, hectoring tone—typical Roger, she thought—the letter consoled Beverly. It indicated that Roger had valued her above all others in his life. That was something she could grab and hold on to, she felt, something real.

———

Krystyna Drewnowska, who had a Ph.D. in biochemistry, supported herself by working in the hematology department of the Medical College of Virginia for $36,000 a year. Within days of Burde's death, she asked her obstetrician to arrange a paternity test to establish Burde as the father of her unborn child. She also consulted an attorney, John Moore, about any claim the child may have on the estate. Moore told her about the "pretermitted heir" statute, which stipulated that if the deceased named any children in his will and then had additional children after the will was signed, the latter were entitled to a portion of the estate equivalent to the portions received by the named children.

Krystyna also gave her attorney a letter Beverly had written Roger in 1990, a year after he began his affair with Krystyna. Krystyna had found the letter on a nightstand in Burde's bedroom at Windsor. She had read it and, thinking it might be useful one day, made a copy of it.

A few days later, Krystyna left the country. She would remain abroad for the next eight weeks.

———

John Moore passed Beverly's letter along to Greg Neal, who read it with considerable interest. Five pages long, angry and bitter in tone, with words underlined and placed in quotation marks for irony and emphasis, the letter had been prompted by an article on prenuptial agreements in *Time* magazine that Roger had sent Beverly. It reviewed their relationship, the various discussions they had had about marriage, and the obstacles Beverly felt Roger had created to avoid it. She complained about the restrictions he had always placed on their relationship; about his postponing a final divorce even though he and Brigitte were legally separated; about him seeing other women (Roger had been involved with a woman named Donna at the time he began his affair with Beverly); about his earlier insistence that she keep her own marriage together; and about the pressure he had put on her, once she did get divorced, to marry an older man, a "geezer," they called him, for the money.

Dear Roger,

I am returning the article for you to recycle. I had already seen it and read it, objectively, I think. The manner in which you sent it was rather impersonal, but still seems to require an answer, expected or not.

You've always made your priorities very clear, in one way or another, and by one condition after another on me, or on us, and have found many reasons, ever since I have known you, to avoid any genuine commitment. There have been a whole string of conditions or restrictions or barriers imposed, and I hate to drag these out again in full view; but if you will look back, you may possibly see what all this represents to me. And if you will really consider where we have come from and where we are now, you will see that none of these attitudes or actions that created the "conditions" reflects or supports any intent to be "only with me" or to plan any future with me.

Not that awful beginning pitch line, with the conditions carefully drafted into a formal presentation of what it took to be with you; not the follow-up "condition" that I would "just have to lump it" while you continued to hang onto Donna and keep her involved; not the one after that, which warned me to keep my marriage intact, "or else;" nor the opposing conditions & demands imposed at the same time to make that utterly impossible; nor when the marriage and family did blow apart, the "condition" that it was strictly my problem and "really had nothing to do with" you, as you backed away on more than one occasion; nor the further "condition" that was then attached to my family and to me as we became viewed as inferior and a mess and an imposition; nor the "conditions" and threats for more time and energy and more work "for us," when things were going the very worst for me.

Certainly not, when you realized that I was going to handle the divorce and the rest of it—and would be free—and came up with the great "geezer" way out. Not only would it not effect your life and your "base," which was so "good & strong & loyal" and superior, but "my security" would be somebody else's problem. But even that condition came with more conditions, all running counter to be workable, and putting pressure on me to perform some unrealistic coup, to con some 60 or 65 year old wealthy man out of his money, some stranger who would not want <u>anything</u> from me, not even a prenuptial agreement (which, by the way, you thought had no real effect). And as your reward for this wonderful solution to your "future with me," you demanded a new Mercedes Benz convertible. Sounds funny now, but it wasn't. That was the only consequence that you ever really envisioned.

Other conditions grew out of everything around me: My job, every facet of my life with you, family, friends. Some I could handle okay. Others I managed to get around, like "Geezer." And there was always the "ultimate" threat and condition that I should have to put up with and accept your "weaknesses" so that you could be unfaithful and disloyal but still pretend that it didn't really affect anyone else. I refused this one, and still do, because it was destructive and unworkable, just like "Geezer."

I did still love you through all those awful times, but only determination, really stubbornness, and a knowledge of what you <u>could</u> be, kept me going. However, if there had ever been any doubt about your intentions, it was completely erased as I watched you after Brigitte left—and I saw all the new set of conditions and barriers develop. Now they were based on the rationale of getting her back and preserving the family "structure" <u>so</u> that you could provide so much better for my "security"!

Never once did you think about life or a future with me, nor how those months and years of backtracking would affect "us." True, you did set another seemingly noble condition—"that you wouldn't stop seeing me"— but that was foolish, and I tried to get you to see it as another impossible impasse you were setting up. . . .

Now, in your mind, you've never done or thought anything other than to want and plan to be with me "all along." In reality, <u>not one</u> plan or move has ever been based on that "wish," and most have been completely counter to any such possibility.

<u>And now,</u> you are pushing two more new, major, long-term conditions and obstacles into place, and <u>neither</u> have <u>anything</u> to do with loving me or trusting to "protect" me, or us.

Wedging the relationship, whatever it is or was, with Krystyna in between us was already enough to "do me in." I had to start turning away and being realistic. And if anything remains alive over the past few months, your wanting to have a <u>baby with someone else</u> was overkill. So, your insistence on a take-it-or-leave-it prenuptial agreement is somewhat superfluous.

If you had ever actually asked and planned for me to marry you, which you haven't, the words have only come up occasionally in unfocused and meaningless statements or jokes or as a backdrop for these conditions that had begun to take precedence in your mind, but if you had asked, I would have enough difficulty with a decision just because of the unpredictable nature of your impatience and temper.

I also see no future based on your <u>unwillingness,</u> not <u>inability,</u> to be faithful and maintain respect and trust in a marriage.

True, those issues are my "conditions," but they are also ones which benefit and sustain us both and are vital to love and to marriage. You certainly do not need another situation of sourness & resentment in the home. If the hurt and absolute caring and kindness are not there, why bother to set up that kind of situation? It wouldn't last, agreement or not. And I don't want that, for you or for me.

So, save your legal protections and arguments for the next time. You had <u>better</u> have one in place before anybody moves in with you. Strange that such an obvious and valid need never occurred to you. . . .

All of this discussion—and please pardon the rambling—is not to try and back you down or to "win". A change of heart now or later would not change the reasons for insisting on it, or your perception of me that has been the basis for those reasons.

I see no other way around or through this impasse, nor the other recent "obsession." You've closed me out, just like always, but more finally this time, and I have to go on with some kind of future. You seem to think that I have a decision to come up with, but you have already made it.

We will both live with the consequences, and I hope you have considered those more fully than you did the other conditions.

Yes it hurts, hurts my feelings, insults my sense of justice and honor and integrity, but I have lots of practice and experience putting rejections from you into perspective, and behind me. This time, it will be harder, because it means giving up on you, and giving up goes against my nature, but it has to be done.

Guess that's it. I will continue to care, for that's also my nature, and to be a "friend to the family" & to you, for what it's worth.

Neal showed the letter, which was undated, to Riley. It seemed to contradict the description Beverly had given Neal of her supposedly harmonious relationship with Burde. Instead, it confirmed the scenario they'd been given by Barbara Samuels: that Burde had been easing out Beverly in favor of his younger, pregnant mistress and that Beverly was angry at both Burde and Krystyna. What they seemed to have on their hands, Neal thought, was a classic scorned-woman situation.

9

In the third week of the investigation, Riley decided it was time to hold what he called a skull session with the commonwealth's forensics people. The meeting took place in the conference room in the chief medical examiner's office, upstairs from the morgue. It was a windowless room, with one large conference table. Plastic body models stood on shelves, and portraits of distinguished past pathologists hung on the walls. Riley and Neal, the deputy chief medical examiner Marcella Fierro, and the pathologist Dr. William Jefferson all attended, as did Ann Jones, a firearms expert in the forensic science division, and Larry McCann, a psychological profiler for the state police, who was helping Riley develop an interview plan for Beverly Monroe.

Neal brought along the prints, now back from the processor, of the 35mm photographs he had taken at the death scene. He handed them around. One of the pictures showed Burde's face in profile; he was lying on the sofa with his eyes closed, his two slightly cupped hands in front of him. The sooty black marks were clearly visible on the insides of the fourth and fifth fingers of his right hand. These marks had not been tested to determine the nature of this substance, but everyone at the meeting, studying the pictures, assumed it was some sort of gunpowder residue.

If Burde had killed himself, Riley told the others, he could not have used his right hand. Had he used it, his fingers would have been gripping the butt of the gun, and there would be no way to account for the sooty stains on the fourth and fifth fingers, which Riley felt had to have been caused by gunpowder discharged from the front of the gun. Would a right-handed man kill himself with his left hand? It seemed if not inconceivable at least unlikely. Ann Jones agreed. She said she didn't think suicide fit the circumstances of the case.

Burde's Smith & Wesson .38 was identical to the one state police undercover officers used, which meant that there were plenty of them in surplus. Riley had drawn one. Taking it out now and showing it around the conference table, he announced that he had a theory of how Burde died. He then climbed up on the table and lay on his side, in the position in which the dead man had been found.

Burde, Riley said, had woken up when the gun was pressed to his head by the killer. He demonstrated with the Smith & Wesson. At that final instant, he explained, Burde had thrust his hand out in a protective gesture and wrapped his fingers around the cylinder just as the gun was fired. The soot stains on his fourth and fifth fingers came from cylinder flash, gunpowder discharged through the front of the revolver's cylinder.

"That's not cylinder flash," Ann Jones said. "That's muzzle flash."

Jones, who thought Riley too opinionated for someone who was not a forensics expert, told him she believed his conclusions were inconsistent with the evidence. Riley asked her how muzzle flash, which would have come from the front of the gun barrel, could have darkened the deceased's fingers. Ann Jones demonstrated by clasping her right hand to her forehead, palm against skin, and inserting the barrel of the gun between the fourth and fifth fingers. Burde, she said, was not extending his hand, palm outward, toward the gun. If that had been the case, the gunpowder residue would have been more diffuse. His hand was instead palm inward, cupping his head.

The same close-up photograph that showed Burde's charcoal-stained fingers also showed a slightly curved imprint, noticeably darker than the surrounding skin, on the palm of the right hand. Marcella Fierro said she had seen many cases in which objects that people were holding at the time of death, or objects that had been placed in their hands at the time of death, left such imprints. As the body cooled and the blood settled, the weight of the object pressed down on the flesh and molded it into a pattern identical to the contours of the object.

The imprint on Burde's hand, Fierro pointed out, resembled a gun butt. She believed that the butt of the Smith & Wesson had probably lain overnight in his hand before Joe Hairfield removed it.

If the death was suicide but Burde hadn't shot himself with his right hand, Fierro asked, how then had the revolver ended up in that hand? The only conceivable way would have been for Burde to have shot himself with his left hand, thrown the gun up in the air, and caught it with his right hand. But that would have been impossible, Fierro explained, since the bullet severed the brain stem, rendering the man instantly immobile.

The forensics, the people at the conference table agreed, seemed to rule out suicide. What made more sense—what was in fact the only scenario that made any forensic sense to them—was that someone had killed Burde while he was sleeping. The murderer had slipped the gun between the fingers of Burde's right hand as it cradled his resting head, fired once, then placed the gun in that hand to make the wound appear self-inflicted.

At the end of the meeting, Riley asked Ann Jones if she could devise a test that would confirm this theory. Jones said she thought she could.

"Go to it," Riley told her.

CHAPTER III

The Magic Writings

1

Beverly Monroe had returned to work the week after the funeral. Her job required her to conduct state-of-the-art patent searches for research and development, to abstract the patents the scientists generated, to coordinate foreign patent applications, and to track the patents claimed by competitors in the thick *Official Gazette* published every week by the U.S. Patent Office. Staying abreast of all the paperwork took organization and diligence. Beverly had only been gone a week and a half, but the patent abstracts were backing up, and she had to lay the groundwork for the semi-annual meeting between top New York executives and the research team leaders, where it was decided which foreign patent applications the company should make.

Going back to work was more difficult than Beverly had imagined. She wasn't herself, and more than that, the whole world seemed different. It had an eerie, unfamiliar quality.

Dee Shannonhouse, her secretary, was struck by the change in Beverly's personality. Beverly seemed to find it difficult to talk. She would break down at every other sentence. She seemed so uncertain that she asked Dee to double-check her work. And her mind would drift. Dee would look up from her desk and see Beverly staring blankly at the wall, as if she didn't know what she was doing.

And a lot of times Beverly didn't. She would forget where she was. Her daily commute—from Old Gun Road to Robious Road to the Midlothian Turnpike and down around to the Philip Morris plant in south Richmond—had become confusing. Sometimes she forgot altogether that she was driving. She found herself talking to Roger. "Why'd you do this thing?" she'd ask him. "Why did you do this?" Roger seemed to be with her in the car, but he said nothing. She felt walled in by his silence. He was as still and unforthcoming as he had been that day she found him dead on the library couch—a memory so powerful that at times it threatened to obliterate all her other memories of him.

These were the thoughts that would go through her head. And then there she would be at Philip Morris with no memory of the trip. Once, she drove right past the gate.

What added to her confusion was that her thoughts of Roger were intermingled with memories and feelings, buried for years, about the suicide of her father. Dallas Duncan, known as D.C., was raised on a dairy farm in a cove outside Marion, North Carolina, a small town near the Catawba River. When he was twenty-two and working in the Marion post office, he married seventeen-year-old Anne McCall, the daughter of a Marion businessman who owned a hosiery mill and a funeral parlor. Six years later, Dallas took a part-time job as a rural mail carrier in Leeds, South Carolina, a tiny hamlet 110 miles south of Marion, bought the retiring mail carrier's house, and moved his young family across the border.

Leeds was an isolated village in a region of sandy soil, fir trees, scrub pine, and cornfields. Two miles down a dirt track from the paved road that ran between the towns of Chester and Carlisle, it consisted of one store, the small post office, and a brick schoolhouse, where Beverly and her three brothers accounted for four of the seven students. Their house had come with two hundred acres of wooded land, and the family worked together clearing and then cultivating it. They grew corn and cotton and red clover, raised cows, and planted tomatoes and beans in the vegetable garden and zinnias and verbena in the flower beds.

As a child, Beverly found life in Leeds idyllic. She went barefoot in the summer. She gathered blackberries, swam in the creek that ran alongside the house, and hiked an old logging trail to fish in the Broad River. She took piano and dance lessons. She worked, too, helping her father sort mail and driving the route with him. He sent her and her brothers out in the pastures to cut the johnsongrass and pull the bitterweeds and wild onions that, if eaten, would spoil the cows' milk. The corn had to be hoed twice before harvest, and she spent days in the seemingly endless rows with nothing but a hoe and a jar of water, which she placed under the wild plum tree that provided the only shade in the fields. But she came to love fieldwork, even cotton picking, when the entire family and the black laborers they hired competed to fill the first bale.

Dallas, who preferred freedom to prosperity, worked only half a day. In the afternoons he taught Beverly and her brothers to box and hunt, to play baseball and basketball. He organized footraces and card games. He was a tirelessly physical man, tall and broad-shouldered, quick enough to catch a black snake by its tail and then break its neck by cracking it like a whip. He dug a pond and stocked it with catfish and bream. He built a horseshoe pit and then a clay tennis court in the backyard. He also had an independent wife, who worked full-time for the railroad, first in the relay station at Leeds—where she took the telegraph messages sent down by the central headquarters and hung them on a pole suspended next to the track so the engineer could reach out and snatch them as the train flew past—and later as the first female stationmaster in Carlisle.

But what most distinguished Dallas in that part of the South Carolina piedmont was his interest in books. He had amassed a considerable library, filling two full walls of the living room. He had books on agriculture, and on history and politics. He had Dale Carnegie's exhortations to self-improvement and the novels of Thomas Wolfe. He bought volumes of poetry and paid Beverly and her brothers twenty-five cents each time they memorized poems like "The Raven" or "In Flanders Fields."

The school in Leeds stopped at the seventh grade. Beverly attended high school in Chester, thirteen miles to the north, and then Limestone College, up near Spartanburg. After graduating with a major in chemistry, she had a choice between a job in the research department at the Millikin mill in Spartanburg and a teaching grant in the chemistry department at the University of Florida. Dallas urged her to go to Gainesville. "Don't settle down here," he said. "Seek wider horizons." It was the first indication she'd ever had that her father might in some way be disappointed with his own life.

In the fall of her second year at the University of Florida, she met Stuart Monroe, a Ph.D. candidate in the chemistry department, and within a year they were married. They moved to Wilmington, Delaware, when Stu found work with the Hercules Corporation, and then to Ashland, Virginia, after he was offered a job as a chemistry professor at Randolph-Macon College.

The village of Leeds changed beyond recognition during those years. When a chemical company set out to acquire property near the Broad River, Dallas hoped it would buy his land. Instead, the company purchased a nearby parcel and built an immense chemical plant, a gleaming facility with metal tubes, piping, storage tanks—like something from outer space, Beverly thought when she went back. Dallas Duncan sold his cattle and stopped farming. Within a year, the johnsongrass, bitterweeds, and poison ivy had taken over. Scrub pines sprang up. Weeds subsumed the clay tennis court. Dallas still had his vegetable garden and his flowers and he still had the daily mail route, but Beverly's mother, Anne, had come down with a thyroid disorder and retired from the railroad. One Sunday morning, a fire that started in the furnace burned the house beyond recovery. Dallas sold his land to a paper company, receiving much less than the $75 an acre he thought it was worth, and he and Anne rented a small house in Carlisle.

Dallas planted an iris bed, built a sandpit for his grandchildren, and speculated in the stock market. But the visible signs of his aging, his graying hair and slackening skin and mottled hands, angered him. He would lose his temper because he was unable to lift a heavy log that would have posed little challenge when he was young. He became withdrawn and moody, given to long silences and sudden enraged outbursts.

Dallas had always been a prolific letter writer. He wrote almost weekly to Beverly in Gainesville, Wilmington, and Ashland. Now his letters, once so literate and vivid, became difficult to comprehend. One consisted of little more than columns of numbers. He was deteriorating mentally. Anne, worried, had taken all the guns out of the house, but Dallas managed to borrow a rifle from a neighbor, and on a sunny early-summer morning in 1970, a year after a sell-off in the stock market had hurt his investments, he told his wife he was going to check the mailbox. Anne heard a shot and ran outside. Dallas had killed himself in the woods across the street.

When Beverly heard the news, she left immediately for South Carolina. Throughout the long drive down, she kept telling herself that what her brother had told her on the telephone couldn't be true. Her father had been too strong to commit suicide. But when she walked through the front door of the house in Carlisle and saw her three brothers and all these other people gathered around and heard her mother crying hysterically in her bedroom, she knew it was true. Her father, the man who had always epitomized masculine vitality, who had cleared two hundred acres of South Carolina scrub pine and could break the neck of a black snake with one snap of his wrist, had killed himself.

When Beverly returned to Ashland, there was a letter waiting for her from her father. He had written it shortly before he died. Beverly opened the envelope. It contained several sheets of indecipherable scribbles. She couldn't read them; she couldn't even bring herself to look at the pages once she saw how incomprehensible they were. She folded them back in the envelope and filed them away in the box where she kept all his other letters.

In the years that followed, Beverly never really talked to her mother about what had happened and why. In her own mind Beverly decided that her father had been growing weak, that he knew it, and that he had determined he didn't want the rest of his family to watch him disintegrate. Dwelling on something like this—something you could never understand or change—only caused pain, so she had stopped thinking about it until Roger's death brought it all back.

———

Toward the end of the week she returned to work, Beverly received a call from Greg Neal. She hadn't heard from him, or anyone in the sheriff's office, since the day Roger's body was discovered.

The investigation was almost complete, Neal said. They just needed to tie up a few loose ends concerning the suicide. There was another officer who wanted to talk to her and go through the background again, to get the paperwork in order. They could all meet at Windsor.

"Would that be okay?" Neal asked.

"Sure," Beverly said.

2

Beverly made the twenty-minute drive out to Windsor at around nine o'clock on the morning of March 26. The weather was misty and damp, just like it had been on the day, exactly three weeks earlier, when she and Joe Hairfield found Roger's body. On the drive over, she kept having flashes, seeing Roger as he'd been that day, lying on the couch in his dark sweatshirt and sweatpants, his feet in those white socks tucked neatly together as if he were napping. By the time she reached the farm, she was already in tears.

Several cars were parked in the driveway by the yews. Beverly tried to pull herself together. Barbara Samuels met her at the door. Greg Neal was there with another man, whom he introduced as Special Agent David Riley. Riley was bulky, with a reddish-brown mustache and aviator-style glasses. His large front teeth and slight overbite gave him a deceptively boyish appearance. Beverly told Mr. Riley she was pleased to meet him.

"Call me Dave," Riley said.

Beverly agreed to do this.

"And can I call you Beverly?" Riley asked.

"Certainly."

And from that time on, it was Beverly and Dave.

———

Like Beverly Monroe, Dave Riley had a father who had killed himself. It might have been suicide, it might have been an accident. His father had run the waterworks in what was then Princess Anne County, down near Norfolk. He was a fun-loving and popular but hot-tempered man who always carried a gun. Every few months, he and Riley's mother would get into a fight and she'd go home to her family and he'd come after her and threaten to shoot himself unless she returned. "Come home, honey!" he shouted on one of these occasions. They were standing in front of her parents' house. When Riley's mother said no, he climbed into his truck and put his gun to his head, as he'd done before. She turned her back and the gun went off. Riley was two. He grew up thinking his father had died a natural death.

His mother remarried, to a sergeant in the Virginia Beach police department. While his stepfather could be generous and funny, he was even more hot-tempered than his father, and sometimes violent toward his family. Like many policemen of his day, Riley's stepfather took advantage of his authority in small ways, fishing while on duty and flashing his badge instead of paying at the local drive-in. So although Riley grew up around cops, hunted and fished with them, and watched them work, he didn't particularly want to be one. Riley wanted to be an illustrator for *Field & Stream*.

He spent three semesters at Old Dominion University in the late sixties before a little matter of the army caught him up. While he was in training to fly helicopters, an irregular cardiogram led to his discharge. After a brief foray into commercial art—arranging mannequins and decorating windows at Sears; it was fun but didn't pay enough—he ended up as a state-police road trooper in Richmond. Between the traffic accidents and the drunk-driving arrests, he did some investigative work, mainly in narcotics, and performed well enough that in 1980 he was promoted to special agent at First Division headquarters in Henrico County. He liked the job so much that he'd never taken a promotion exam since.

———

Riley had no intention of letting Beverly Monroe know he considered Burde's death a homicide, much less that he considered her the likely murderer. Summoning her in for an official interrogation and advising her of her Miranda rights would instantly create an adversarial relationship. She would clam up and insist on a lawyer. But if he could lull her into a false sense of security, if he could allow her to believe she had successfully gulled the police into thinking Burde had killed himself, she might say or do something that would betray her. She might even agree to take a polygraph test.

Riley had been planning his encounter with Beverly for more than a week. He had talked to Larry McCann, the police department's psychological profiler, about how best to approach Beverly. He had drawn up a list of inconsistencies he could use to confront her: that other witnesses contradicted her claim that Burde was suicidal; that her own claim that she thought the barn door was locked and didn't know it was never locked hardly jibed with the fact that she'd been visiting Windsor for thirteen years; that other witnesses contradicted her claim that she never had a key to the house. He had also made notes of questions to ask Beverly.

Didn't you have a key? Everyone said you had a key.

Did you ever handle the gun?

Beverly, after several calls & no answer, weren't you concerned he still wasn't answering till after midnight, yet you went to bed w/out reaching him or going back over to check on him, especially since you said he was having chest pains.

And he had jotted down ideas for ruses he could use to trick her, to test her responses.

Tell her we found a print in a crevice of the gun that definitely was not Burde's. See how she reacts.

Weren't you still there when Burde made the call to the publisher, Beville, about the appointment the next day? Insinuate Beville understood she was there.

Have you ever expressed to Burde that you were through with him? Tired of his excuses for not marrying you? Your frustration w/ him over his lies and other women? Told him you had the ability to blackmail him?—if no, show her the letter.

Tell her I <u>know</u> she had already found the body, but was afraid, due to the circumstances, to be the one to find him—she feels guilty about it. Or, that she was actually in the house <u>when</u> he killed himself and is afraid to say so. Tell her, these two above situations are the only explanations to explain her strange statements and actions when his body was found the next day.

Weren't you asleep on the couch when he killed himself?

You <u>were</u> there when he did it because he was on the wrong couch! That everyone sees him use [the other couch]. You had to be there!

Going into the meeting, Riley had wanted to have enough information about Beverly to be able to establish a rapport, so he had called Barbara Samuels. She filled him in on Beverly's background. Beverly was cultured, Riley learned. She was interested in art, classical music, history. Riley had once been interested in art himself. He'd have that going for him. Plus, he too was interested in history, another point of common ground. To put himself in the frame of mind where he could carry on an intelligent conversation with her, he also listened to some classical music. He could never remember the titles to classical pieces, but even so, the music helped him understand who Beverly was.

As the final step in preparing for the interview, Riley had gotten out his old navy blue suit. It would give him that patina of culture.

———

Despite Riley's casual manner at the farm that morning, he was observing Beverly carefully. It had been his idea that they meet at Windsor. He wanted to see how she would react at the scene of the crime, if in fact it was a crime. But Beverly walked in, Riley thought, like she owned the place, so he didn't get anything out of that.

After the introductions, he led Beverly into the kitchen at the rear of the house. The two of them sat down at the round Formica-topped table. Barbara Samuels had not turned the heat on and the house was cold.

Riley began by explaining that he'd been brought in to make an official determination about the cause of Burde's death. He himself, he said, thought it was probably a suicide. However, Jack Lewis, the commonwealth attorney for Powhatan County, was a little cynical. Lewis had a few lingering doubts that needed to be put to rest before the case could be officially closed, and he had sent Riley out for additional information.

Riley told Beverly that he was investigating the death from a psychological perspective. He was trying to determine Burde's state of mind in the final days of his life. He wanted to know what she could tell him, he said, because she was perhaps closer to Roger than anyone.

"You have a history together," Riley said. "I know there was a lot going on in your lives. Can you tell me what led up to this?"

Beverly struck Riley as intelligent, articulate, attractive, and sophisticated. She was also, Riley thought, extremely cooperative, almost surprisingly so. Riley had brought a suicide-assessment form with him. He asked her a couple of questions from it to get the ball rolling, so to speak, but once she started talking, he found that he didn't even need the thing. She required no prompting. All he had to do was sit there and nod and take it all down.

———

Beverly talked for nearly two hours. From time to time, she broke down in tears, but for the most part she retained her composure. In the last year, she told Riley, Roger had become depressed, confused, and so forgetful that she had taken to writing down what he said so she could later prove to him he'd actually said it. But, in retrospect, it seemed he'd always had psychological problems. He tried to dominate every aspect of the lives of those around him. He sought out people he felt he could manipulate. He could be cruel to loved ones.

"Would it be accurate," Riley wondered, "to say that Roger had a Jekyll-and-Hyde personality?"

Beverly agreed that it would. She said Roger had asked her to marry him several times, once literally getting down on bended knee, but she had refused, because she didn't believe he would be faithful. The Sunday three days before he died, when Beverly had found the agreement Krystyna Drewnowska had drafted, he had again suggested that he and Beverly marry and together raise the child Krystyna was carrying. Beverly had said she'd need to think about it.

Beverly then described how she and Roger spent his last evening, how he had fixed a shrimp dinner, then become melancholy when the subject of Krystyna came up. He had talked to Krystyna, he said, and she had rejected his idea that she give the child over to him and Beverly to raise. Beverly tried to encourage him, but he became disconsolate and finally rolled over into a fetal position on the couch, his back to her. That was his state of mind in his final hours.

Listening to Beverly, Riley maintained an air of studied neutrality. He had not wanted to give the slightest sign of disbelief, to do anything that might make her less than relaxed or cause her to rethink her willingness to cooperate. And now that she had finished her story, which he was prone to consider an utter fabrication—from what he understood, Burde wasn't about to marry Beverly or anybody else—the time had come to broach the true reason for the meeting.

Would she be willing to submit to a polygraph examination? he asked. Keeping his voice friendly, he told her that since she was the last one to see Burde alive and had been present when his body was discovered, this was a natural step for the investigators to take. They had other people who could also technically be considered suspects, he said, and they would probably ask them to take polygraphs as well. But for obvious reasons, it made sense for Beverly to go first. It would establish a precedent for the others.

Riley tried to suggest that the test was a mere formality, a minor nuisance that could be taken care of quickly, and, in fact, the sooner the better. "It would be convenient," he said, "if we could finish this up today."

When Beverly said she was afraid the state of her nerves might somehow adversely affect the test, Riley shrugged off this concern and she agreed to take it. He gave her the directions to First Division headquarters and told her to appear at one o'clock. The less time that passed between her agreeing to the test and actually taking it, Riley thought, the less opportunity she would have to reconsider.

———

Beverly had eaten nothing all day. After Riley left, Barbara Samuels fixed her a cup of instant coffee. Beverly, unaware that Barbara had been providing Riley with information about her, sat talking with Roger's secretary for a few minutes, but she worried about being late for the one o'clock appointment and she soon left.

It was raining hard by then, and Beverly had to hold the steering wheel with both hands and lean forward to peer through the windshield. Despite Riley's detailed directions, she got lost a couple of times. She still was not thinking clearly. But each time, she turned around and kept going. She reached the police station right at one o'clock.

3

Riley was waiting for Beverly in his office on the second floor. But he wasn't holding his breath. In fact, he didn't consider the odds greater than fifty-fifty that Beverly would appear. He expected her to consult with her daughter Katie, who, Riley had learned, was a lawyer, or with another attorney. Come one o'clock, Beverly, or more likely somebody representing her, would call and say that on advice of counsel, she had decided not to take the test. That would be the course of action any attorney would urge. And if Riley himself were Beverly's attorney, that would have been his advice as well.

In Riley's experience, a polygraph was only accurate about two thirds—or maybe three quarters—of the time. He'd known people who failed polygraphs who were later proved to be innocent, and he'd known certifiably guilty people who passed polygraphs. In fact, a certain type of criminal—the sociopath—loved to take a polygraph, because the truth had no meaning to him. Even so, a polygraph was a useful tool in building a case. The results definitely moved things in a certain direction.

———

First Division headquarters was in a brick-and-cement building with brown-tinted windows on an undeveloped stretch of Brook Road, just off I-295 in Henrico County. Beverly parked her Mercury in the lot out front—near a flatbed trailer bearing a silver barrel emblazoned with the words STATE POLICE BOMB SQUAD—and hurried through the rain to the lobby. Beverly had never been in a police station before, but the atmosphere was unexpected. It was more like a motel lobby, with a brick floor, cushioned chairs, and a pleasant receptionist behind a wooden desk.

Riley appeared, thanked her for coming, and escorted her to an elevator. Upstairs, there were corridors with offices, all very plain and very quiet, nothing like the bustling police stations, crowded with desks and ringing phones and officers wearing shoulder holsters, that you'd expect from watching television. But the long, anonymous corridors were disorienting. As she followed the investigator down a hallway, she realized she wasn't even sure what floor she was on.

Riley led her into a small room and introduced her to the polygraph examiner, Wyatt Omohundro, a huge, balding man, a giant, with a ponderous, looming presence. Omohundro had Beverly sit down at the side of the room's lone desk. The room was bare as well as small. On one wall was a large mirror. Naïve as she felt herself to be in this situation, Beverly knew that the mirror had to be one of those one-way observation windows. She decided it was best to ignore it.

Omohundro, who had a slow, rumbling voice and a heavy Southern accent, explained the process and told her that he himself would be the one to inform her of the results. "Basically," he said, "when I get through, I grade the charts, I reach a determination, I will look you right in the eye and tell you the determination."

He read her, as required by law, the standards of practice, which stipulated that she give her written permission to be administered the test and that she had the right to end the examination at any time. He then passed Beverly the form.

"Is it standard for someone to do this without a lawyer?" Beverly asked. "My daughter's a lawyer. She's concerned with everything I do."

"Sure, I can understand," Omohundro said. It wasn't his job to urge her to talk to an attorney. His objective was to secure her permission and then administer the test with no one else present. He and Riley had already decided that if she insisted on calling a lawyer, they would simply abandon the polygraph. He indicated the standards-of-practice form. "Just sign your name right there."

Beverly signed. Omohundro then passed her a permission form. "When you sign your name, you're simply telling me that you're here of your own free will," he said. "If you read this and sign this form, you still have the right to walk away at any time you want to."

Beverly still wanted Omohundro's advice on legal representation. "If a person does this, would it be wrong to have a lawyer?" she asked. "Should I get a lawyer?"

In a casual voice, Omohundro said, "Well, some do and some don't."

Beverly asked how reliable polygraphs actually were.

"In situations where there is a clear specific issue," Omohundro said, "the polygraph is extremely accurate." The reason it had a bad name, he explained, was that private examiners, without the proper training, sat on pasteboard boxes in the back rooms of convenience stores running dozens of job applicants at a time and charging a hundred dollars a person.

He then handed Beverly another form.

VIRGINIA STATE POLICE

ADVICE OF RIGHTS

- Before we ask you any questions, you must understand your rights.
- You have the right to remain silent.
- Anything you say can be used against you in court.
- You have the right to talk to a lawyer for advice before we ask you any questions and have a lawyer with you during questioning, if you wish.
- If you decide to answer questions now without a lawyer present, you still have the right to stop answering at any time.
- You also have the right to stop answering at any time until you talk to a lawyer.

WAIVER OF RIGHTS

- I have read this statement of my rights. I understand what my rights are. I am willing to make a statement and answer questions. I do not want a lawyer at this time. I understand and know what I am doing. No promises or threats have been made to me. No pressure or coercion of any kind has been used against me.

"It all sounds so serious," Beverly said.

"Well, this is a very serious matter," Omohundro told her. He then read the form aloud.

"My one question," Beverly said, "is whether I should or shouldn't have my daughter here."

Omohundro ignored the question. "Okay," he said. "Do you understand your rights as I've explained them to you?"

"Yes," Beverly said.

"With your rights in mind, do you waive your rights?"

"Yes."

Beverly then signed the form. Omohundro signed as a witness. For the next hour, Beverly and Omohundro talked about her relationship with Roger, about the child Krystyna Drewnowska was expecting, and about the events on the evening of March 4 that Beverly had already described to Neal and to Riley. She spoke quietly, but her manner was serious and polite. She struck Omohundro as refined and intelligent. He had been a polygraph examiner for more than fifteen years and had run, he figured, thousands of suspects. She was not the usual polygraph subject.

"Now, listen," he said when she had finished. "I've got some very heavy questions I've got to ask you. This boils down to the very reason as to why you're here so we can put this thing away forever and ever and ever."

He turned to the questions he had formulated for the polygraph.

"Do you know who shot Roger?"

"I think he killed himself."

"You think it was Roger that killed himself. Okay. Did you yourself shoot Roger?"

"Oh no." Beverly's voice was practically inaudible.

"You did not."

She raised her voice slightly. "Oh no."

"Listen to what I'm saying. At the very moment Roger was shot, were you there?"

"No," Beverly whispered.

"You did not see this happen. Before Roger was shot, did you know he was going to be shot?"

"No. Let me tell you something—"

"I'm trying to help you by not letting you go into too much detail," Omohundro said. "At the same time, I don't want to cut you off."

He asked a few more questions and then drew the pre-test interview to a close. "I want you to just sit and relax," he said. "The bad part is over now. I'm going to go in and make a few notes and write a few questions down, and when I come back, we can get this over with."

After he returned with his list of written questions, Omohundro hooked up the polygraph attachments. He told Beverly to sit very still, look straight ahead, and remain silent. He was going to cut the instrument on, he said, and he would have to balance the machine's readings on her present condition. If she talked, laughed, moved, or coughed, he would be unable to balance her in.

Once he had balanced his readings, Omohundro took out the pack of notes that he had previously formulated from what was known as the SKY (Suspicious Knowledge and You) test. He began to read the questions, marking a plus or minus on the chart paper to indicate whether she answered in the affirmative or the negative.

"Were you present when Roger died?" he asked.

"No," Beverly said.

"Did you yourself fire the shot that caused the death of Roger?"

"No."

———

Riley was in the tiny observation room, watching through the one-way mirror. The room was dark, the only light filtering in through the mirror, and it was crowded. All three stools by the window were taken. The rest of the people were packed in behind. Greg Neal was there, and some of the other investigators, and also a couple of the secretaries, who knew about the case from having typed up the investigators' reports. A crowded observation room was typical on an interesting case. Riley kept going in and out of the room. Watching this kind of stuff made him antsy. It was nerve-racking.

———

Omohundro conducted two separate tests and ran each one twice to ensure accuracy. At the end of each test, he pulled the rolls of paper from the machine and, leaving Beverly hooked up to the monitors, took them to an office across the hall, where he graded them. Riley joined him. Riley liked to think of the scrawled readings on the charts as the magic writings. He studied them. On the hot questions, he saw, Beverly's answers indicated a classic deceptive. They were *way* over there.

Riley now knew that there was a strong possibility not only that Burde's death was a murder but that Beverly had killed him. His initial hunch about the case, it seemed to him, was verified. He told Omohundro that this may be their last chance to talk to Beverly. He didn't think that she would put up with much in the way of confrontation at this point. If they pressed her too hard, if their talks with her veered into an interrogation, she might simply get up and walk out. Go through the routine, Riley told Omohundro. Inform her of the facts, but don't lean on her.

Omohundro returned to the interrogation room. It was almost three o'clock. Beverly had been in the room for close to two hours without a break. She was pale and red-eyed, but she sat patiently at the side of the desk, awaiting the results. Looking her straight in the eye, as he had promised her he would, Omohundro informed her that her answers indicated deception on the relevant issues.

"You're kidding," Beverly said.

"No, I am not kidding," Omohundro told her. "You are not telling the truth."

———

Riley had returned to the observation room to watch Beverly's reaction to the results of the test. She didn't appear to him to give anything away. This was a pivotal moment in the unfolding investigation, one for which Riley had been planning for over a week.

Riley had attended a number of special training courses during his career, and taken the famous John Reid course on interrogation.

John Reid, who worked at the Chicago police crime lab in the 1940s, had helped develop the polygraph machine and co-wrote *Criminal Interrogations and Confessions*. Reid's technique was to present suspects with scenarios or "themes," as he called them, that would appear either to explain the suspect's suspicious behavior or to lessen his culpability. The suspect would think the theme offered him a way out of his predicament. But what the theme really offered was an opportunity for the interrogator to link the suspect to the crime. If, for example, an interrogator could get a suspect to admit that he was at the scene of a crime but only as a bystander, the suspect might seize on this as an opportunity to explain away his presence; meanwhile, the interrogator was placing the suspect at the scene. In trials prosecutors liked to show that a criminal had the opportunity, means, and motive to commit the given crime, and if investigators could elicit an admission that a suspect was at the scene, it took care of the opportunity factor. John Reid also taught that a suspect, in accepting an investigator's theme, usually had to change his story. That put him at a tactical disadvantage and allowed the interrogator, and later the prosecutor, to question his credibility. Finally, Reid taught, once the suspect had accepted a theme, the interrogator could point out its inherent contradictions, thereby paving the way for a full confession.

For days, Riley had been thinking about the theme he could present to Beverly if she failed the polygraph. The theme would have to enable her to explain why she had failed the test but at the same time remain consistent with her basic story. Riley had no intention of accusing her of murder. Beverly, he felt, was too intelligent and cunning to confess to the killing, which had signs of premeditation. To accuse her of murder, to become adversarial, would terminate her cooperation immediately. John Reid, who had encouraged the Chicago police department to abandon the old third-degree style of interrogation, had taught that the interrogator should present himself to the suspect as a sympathetic person trying to work with the suspect to reconcile his story with the polygraph results. The theme was the instrument of such a reconciliation.

It had already occurred to Riley that he could suggest to Beverly that Burde had committed suicide and that she had been present. He could then give her two possible explanations, a tactic Reid called "presenting the alternative question": either she had lied because she didn't want people to know she'd been present and been unable to stop Roger from killing himself or she didn't remember it because she had blocked it out. The beauty of this theme was that it explained both why Beverly would say she was innocent and why the polygraph would indicate deception. It placed her at the scene but seemed to get her off the hook. If the forensic tests later proved that Roger's death was a homicide, Beverly's acknowledgment that she had been present when Roger killed himself was the equivalent of a murder confession. In fact, if the forensics indicated homicide, Beverly's confession would be tantamount to an admission that she had gone so far as to kill Roger and then stage a suicide. That constituted first-degree murder.

———

After Omohundro confronted Beverly with the results of the polygraph, he asked, "Isn't it true that you killed Roger?"

"No," Beverly said.

"Well," Omohundro said, "Agent Riley would like to talk to you."

For Riley, watching from the observation room and refining his theme in his head, this was the cue to enter.

As Omohundro left the interrogation room, he encountered Riley outside. Later he would recall he had then told Riley he had switched off the tape recorder but that Riley could turn it back on—without letting the suspect see—by flipping the switch located on the inside of one of the desk legs.

But after Riley entered the room and sat down, he did not turn on the tape recorder. Instead, he pulled his chair close to Beverly, to create intimacy. He was so close that his knees were touching her knees and she could feel his breath on her face. He took one of her hands in his own and began by telling her that if, as she said, she didn't kill Roger, there had to be some reason why she had failed the polygraph.

Let's try to work out what it is, he said. He didn't believe she was telling him everything, he continued. Her story simply didn't add up. Why, for example, was she so concerned about Roger when she woke up on the morning of March 5? Why had she gone down to the barn when she couldn't get into the house? Why was her behavior so strange to Joe Hairfield?

And there were other inconsistencies in her story, Riley said. She had told him and Neal that after dinner on the night of March 4, she and Roger had watched a program on PBS about Charles de Gaulle. But the show, Riley said, had not been broadcast that night; it had aired on an earlier night. Furthermore, he continued, someone had reported to the police that she'd said that when she left Windsor that night, Roger had been asleep on the sofa. It had also come to the attention of the police, Riley said, that she had called the medical examiner's office and asked the time of Roger's death.

Beverly said she had no explanation for these inconsistencies. She remembered the program on de Gaulle quite clearly but had no recollection of calling the medical examiner's office. It was all quite baffling, just as baffling as the fact that she had failed the polygraph test.

Riley proposed an explanation: She had been present when Roger killed himself but didn't want anyone to know.

Beverly resisted this idea. I just can't explain why I failed the test, she said.

But Riley kept pushing it. People quite often wouldn't admit to such things, he said. There were lots of reasons. Maybe they found it too painful. Maybe they felt responsible. Maybe they were afraid they would be blamed for what had happened.

Riley had pulled his chair even closer to Beverly and locked her in eye contact. He believed that working a theme required complete immersion in the role and the moment, as well as the ability to improvise. You learned to bob and weave and commiserate. You had to be prepared to let the theme take you in unexpected directions. And you had to be persistent. You had to repeat the theme again and again. You had to overcome every objection the suspect made to the theme. You had to make it clear to the suspect that he was not going to be able, by simply persisting in his deception, to make you give up.

Perhaps, Riley said, you're afraid you'll be accused either of shooting Roger or of driving him to do it.

Beverly shook her head. When she didn't seem willing to admit she was present when Roger had killed himself, Riley moved on to his second possible explanation.

Maybe, he said, you were so traumatized by Roger's suicide that you blocked it out. Sometimes, he went on, when people are involved in traumatic incidents, the shock is so bad that they can't recall the actual event. If they remember it at all, it's more like a dream. That's a natural fact, he added. That's documented.

Beverly seemed more responsive to this idea. To drive it home, Riley added that when he was a boy, his father had committed suicide in front of him. He had blocked it from his memory, he said, and only knew what people told him about it.

That was a lie. Riley had not been present when his father killed himself, and the event had taken place when he was much too young to remember anything about it. But Riley had no compunction about lying to Beverly. Misleading suspects, who were trying to mislead him, was part of his job. John Reid, who encouraged the practice, called such fabrications "transitional themes," since they offered the suspect a "crutch" that made it easier to admit guilt.

At that point, the way Riley saw it, he was acting with Beverly and doing a darn good job. She was acting with him, and she *thought* she was doing a darn good job. Each was trying to out-act the other. And Riley now felt he had won the contest—he'd be the one taking home the Oscar—because

Beverly seemed to go for the idea that if he'd blocked out the memory of a loved one's suicide, she might have done the same. So Riley said, Now, what do you remember? Is there anything you can remember?

With Riley leading the way, prodding, making suggestions about details, insisting again and again that this was the only possible explanation for the failed polygraph, and with Beverly at first reluctantly consenting to his proposals and then, in a tentative, halting voice, offering possibilities of her own, they together constructed a series of events from the night of Roger's death that Riley convinced Beverly she had blocked from memory.

What must have happened, they agreed, was that she and Roger had been lying opposite each other on the two couches in the library at Windsor. She had fallen asleep and was awoken by a loud crash. Looking over, she saw Roger and the gun and fled from the house in shock. When she returned to her own home, she could not remember the evening, but she knew something was terribly wrong, which was why she kept trying to call Roger that night, why she slept badly, and why she returned to Windsor early the following morning.

After working out the scenario with Beverly in a conversation that lasted an hour and a half and was witnessed by the people in the observation room, Riley turned the tape recorder back on—he would later insist that he had only then realized he had forgotten to do so at the start of the interview—and tried to get Beverly to reiterate on the record the scenario the two of them had just worked out.

"Beverly," he said. "When you got up to go out, did you see a note?"

"No."

"Did you see a note on the table?"

"No."

"All you saw was the gun."

"That's right."

"You saw the gun and you remembered the noise."

"I have this vision of him lying like that—"

"You have this vision. You remember him lying on the couch. You remember seeing the gun and then you remember that you went home. You had this unconscious feeling that something was wrong. You couldn't remember what."

Beverly murmured in a confused manner.

Riley returned to the image of Roger lying on the couch. "You remember seeing him there," he said, "and all night long, all you wanted to do was go to him and be with him and see that he was found, and it just ate at you all night long."

Beverly again gave a confused murmur.

"It's eating at you right now," Riley said. "Beverly, you're going to sleep better. You'll sleep better if you remember this. You'll sleep better."

"I'll try."

"Tell me again," Riley said. "Just look through me right now. Look through me right now and tell me again. You hear the noise. You're asleep or you're in a sleepy state. You're on your couch. You remember jumping and somehow you remember standing there and seeing the gun. . . . You remember standing over him and seeing the gun at some point and you remember leaving the house and making the phone calls. And you remember leaving him asleep on the couch."

"That's the vision I had," Beverly said. Her voice sounded uncertain.

"You know now he didn't walk you to the door," Riley said. "That's what he always did before."

"Yeah."

"But you know now that's not true. You know he didn't really walk you to the door, because you left him asleep on the couch."

"I have this vision of him from some other time—" Beverly began.

Riley cut her off. "Yeah, but you left him asleep on the couch," he said. "And you remember looking down and seeing the gun. And you just could not face it. You could not face telling people, calling and saying, 'I was there when this thing happened.' It was just too much for you to deal with at that moment. And it was just overwhelming."

"That's a hard thing to admit," Beverly said.

"It's hard to admit, sure. But it's not hard to understand." Riley returned to his theme. "You knew all night he was there and you didn't sleep a wink."

"No," Beverly told him. "I know I didn't sleep a wink."

"You didn't sleep all night long."

"At the time I couldn't understand why—"

Riley cut her off again. "You'd have these flashes," he said. "You'd see that gun in his hand. You'd have these flashes all night long seeing that gun in his hand."

"I don't remember," Beverly said. Uncertainty again seemed to overtake her.

"Don't let this thing go away from you," Riley warned her. "Don't rationalize it away. Don't do that."

"I won't. I won't."

Riley reminded her that there must be some reason she had failed the polygraph.

"I get shivers, " Beverly confessed, "and I don't know exactly where it comes from."

"It comes from that night," Riley said. He again brought up the image of Roger lying on the couch. "Your conscious mind wants to tell you he walked you to the door, but you know that can't be right, so your unconscious mind says out loud, 'I left him asleep on the couch.'

"And that's what you did!" he added vehemently. "You left him asleep on the couch. And then you walked out, and you got in the car, and the whole thing, you said to yourself, you rationalized as a dream. And you drive down the driveway and you go to the gas station," he continued, replaying the entire sequence. "You start thinking, If I call him, maybe he'll answer the phone."

Beverly struggled to visualize the events Riley was encouraging her to recall. Suddenly, one clear, if irrelevant, memory did appear to her. "I bought water," she said.

Riley wanted her to focus on his scenario. "You called him," he said. "And you knew he wouldn't answer the phone, but you kept hoping that he would. And then all night long you didn't sleep, because you knew where he was. And you couldn't stand the thought. You thought, What a horrible person I am, because I have left him without somebody to take care of him. And it ate at you all night long. That's the worst thing that's bothering you," Riley suggested. "Isn't it? Tell me the truth."

"I think so." Beverly's voice had become almost inaudible.

"You feel guilty that you left him on that couch all night long, and you feel like people won't forgive you for that," Riley said, then tried to reassure her. "What did it delay? What did it hurt?" He took a breath and tried a bit of humor. "It put me to a lot of trouble, I'll tell you that."

Beverly didn't grasp the humor. "I'm sorry," she said, genuinely apologetic.

"That's okay," Riley told her. "They pay me for that. They pay me to get to the truth. My job is to find the truth. Okay? So don't worry about that."

"But I have to tell you this," Beverly said. "If you hadn't said I was with him, I would have never—"

Riley interrupted her, saying, "But you do remember now, don't you? Tell me yes. Tell me you remember."

"I remember some of it."

Riley reiterated the scenario. And then he brought up a new point, a contradiction that had to be resolved for his theory of the case to make sense. Beverly had said she left Roger's house at nine-twenty the night he died. However, Roger's publisher, Don Beville, had said Roger had called him at around ten, which meant either that Roger was alive after Beverly left or that Beverly had not in fact left at nine-twenty. If she had killed Roger, she must have been at the house when that final phone call was made.

"I know you didn't leave as early as you told me you left," Riley said. "You said you left at nine-twenty. You left later than that. Not a lot later, but maybe an hour or so later."

"But how can you know that?" Beverly asked.

"I do. I know that. Because Roger made a phone call. And he probably made the phone call while you were asleep."

"To Don Beville," Beverly said.

"You were asleep," Riley repeated. "I know that you were. I could picture this, because I've seen this situation a thousand times with me and my wife. She's asleep on the couch. She's got the TV on, maybe the music's on, maybe she's been reading, maybe the dog's in her lap, whatever it is, and she's sound asleep. She does it every night. And I go make calls, I work, I do all kinds of things . . . and come back at some point and . . . wake her up and it's time to go to bed."

Beverly said she didn't hear the phone call.

"You wouldn't have heard it," Riley told her. "Because you were asleep."

Riley repeated the scenario once again, focusing on the idea that while Beverly had suppressed the traumatic memory, her unconscious had been plagued by guilt over abandoning Roger's body. "All night long this thing that was eating at you: 'I left Roger there, the family is not going to understand.' " Riley was still holding Beverly's hand, his eyes boring into hers. "You couldn't leave him there. You couldn't count on when somebody would find him. You didn't want him left there for a day or two days, you know that."

This idea did not register with Beverly. "I don't remember saying anything or thinking like that."

"You might not want to accept it consciously, but you know from talking to me what happened, don't you? Give me that much."

"Okay."

"You do know that, don't you?" Riley asked. "Tell me yes."

"Yes, I guess so." Beverly paused. "I wish I could see it somehow."

"You can see it, you can see it," Riley said. "You still have a hard time describing it, but you see it."

If Beverly described these memories, regardless of how uncertain they now seemed to her, to someone outside First Division headquarters, that would serve as a second, independent confession. And the prosecution could call as a witness the person to whom Beverly confessed. "When you get through putting it together, when you feel comfortable with it, call Corinna," Riley suggested. "Don't block this out of your mind again, because this will ruin you," he warned. "If you can't deal with it, you'll put it out of your mind again and it will torment you forever."

Riley felt by then he had gotten as much as he was going to get. "You want to go home now?" he asked.

"Yeah, I really must," Beverly said. The questioning had gone on for almost eight hours, interrupted only by that late-morning cup of coffee with Barbara Samuels at Windsor and the confusing drive to headquarters.

"I'll walk you outside," Riley said. "Let's use the stairs."

———

Beverly was by then so exhausted that when she got up to leave, the blood left her head. She felt as if she were going to pitch forward. Riley had to help her into her raincoat and hold her up by the arm as they walked down a flight of stairs to the lobby and then out to the sidewalk. They stood under the metal awning that protected the front door. It was raining heavily by then. The falling water rattled on the awning.

Riley had talked incessantly all the way from the interrogation room. He was trying to make the point that everyone experiences guilt when their loved ones die. Outside, he began to tell Beverly how his first wife had had a stroke from an aneurysm when she was thirty-three and suffered brain death and he had had to decide to take her off life support. "I had to pull the plug," he said.

It was kind of like saying he too had had to end the life of someone he loved.

Riley handed her his card. "Call me tomorrow, Beverly," he said. "Let me know how you are."

He seemed genuinely concerned.

Beverly turned the Mercury around in the parking lot and headed out into the rain. It was too late to go to the office, she decided. She drove south on I-95 toward the river. The rain hammered the windshield. Her eyes were full of tears, and she had a hard time seeing. The rush-hour traffic was particularly heavy. Just short of the turnoff to her house, she found herself stuck in a bottleneck at Robious Road. Although she'd had nothing to eat all day, she was too exhausted to prepare anything once she got home. And anyway, she had no appetite. She lay on the living room couch and stared out through the windows at the dark, rain-swept sky.

4

Beverly Monroe had played guard on her high school basketball team, and during her senior year, when the team made it to the state championship, she was described as "most athletic" in the Chester High School yearbook. She was also Miss Senior Class, an honor student, and a member of the student council. Her chemistry teacher, Miss Chick, encouraged her to become a scientist. She was one of only three or four female graduate students enrolled in the University of Florida's chemistry department.

But a girl growing up in the South in the 1940s and 1950s learned—no matter how talented and accomplished she was, no matter how bright and competitive—to place a premium on manners, to cultivate a sweet disposition, to be gracious and deferential. Beverly Monroe had always had a hard time saying, "No, I don't want to do that." It was considered rude. And so time and again at crucial moments in her life, out of a simple desire to be accommodating, she'd ended up doing what other people wanted her to do.

During high school and college she dated Carol Fields, a tight end on the Chester High football team. Beverly's father discouraged her from marrying Carol. Carol is a wonderful guy, Dallas would say, but he's too unsettled, too easily distracted; he wouldn't make a good match. At the start of her second year in the master's program at the University of Florida, Dr. Butler, her professor in organic chemistry, invited the entire chemistry department to a weekend party at his lake house outside Gainesville. There, during a day of waterskiing and badminton, she met Stuart Monroe, who was working toward his Ph.D. Stuart was tall, lean, personable, and a good dancer. He and Beverly started dating regularly.

While Beverly liked Stuart, she had no particular sense of intimacy when she was with him, no feeling she was with someone who genuinely understood her. But dating Stu had its advantages. The male students in the chemistry department, and the single professors, pestered her constantly for dates. She did not enjoy dating for the sake of dating, but as long as she was not involved with anyone, hopeful men asked her out, and how many times can you say you've got other plans? Dating Stu solved the dilemma posed by the illusion of availability she had projected.

That fall, she met another graduate student, Richard Thayer, from Kentucky. Stupid as it sounded, she knew the first minute she laid eyes on him that he was the one. Richard and Beverly were thrown together frequently during the year, in classes and study sessions, on weekend road rallies. But a professor they shared, Dr. Jones, told Richard that Beverly was involved with Stuart Monroe, so Richard never made an overture. When one of Stu's fraternity brothers got married on St. Simons Island, below Savannah, Beverly and Stu attended. It was an expensive society wedding, with chests of iced champagne and a white-jacketed orchestra, and in the middle of it, Stu asked Beverly to marry him. Beverly, flustered, tried to evade the proposal lightheartedly, but a few weeks later she received a congratulatory letter from Stu's mother, as if the marriage had already been decided. When Beverly tried to talk to Stu, he let her understand, without saying so explicitly, that his mother would be crushed if the plans, as they were now being called, fell through. Beverly, afraid of upsetting or offending Stu and his family, turned to Dr. Jones. It was a Sunday. They were in the lab. Dr. Jones was writing formulas on the chalkboard. He told her Stu would make a good husband. She asked about Richard Thayer. Dr. Jones said that Richard had a girl in Kentucky he intended to marry. Dallas Duncan agreed with Dr. Jones. "Stu's a great catch," Dallas said. "He's earning a Ph.D., he'll get good job offers, your combined salaries will be excellent, and besides, you like the same music."

Some things about Stu bothered Beverly. He had attended the Virginia Military Institute and was fastidious and wedded to routine. He could also be inflexible. When Beverly's old boyfriend Carol Fields called her after hearing the news, he heard the doubt in her voice and tried to discourage her from going ahead, but she could find no good reason why she shouldn't marry Stu. She was finishing her master's degree. She knew she wasn't a gifted scientist. Lab work bored her. She had no real desire to pursue a career in chemistry. She did not, she realized then, have any particular goals at all. And she was twenty-four years old. In 1961, women her age got married if the opportunity presented itself.

After the wedding, Stu and Beverly rented a small house near the campus while they finished up their respective degrees. Stu was doing polymer research; Beverly was studying carbon ions. Although they were both full-time students, Stu expected Beverly to do the housework and prepare the meals. He was, she learned, obsessively meticulous. He numbered his record albums and played them in order. He had a similar method for organizing and rotating his ties. But what was most important, and what seemed to Beverly glaringly obvious, was the fact that there was no genuine emotional connection between the two of them. A few months into the marriage, she realized it had been a mistake.

When Stu completed his academic work, he took a job doing research on polyolefins with the Hercules Corporation in Wilmington, Delaware. Beverly remained behind in Gainesville to finish her thesis and take her oral exams. Richard Thayer returned to campus, unmarried, and the two of them began to spend time together. When Richard let Beverly know that he had feelings for her, she decided to end her marriage. She called Stu in Wilmington and told him that it wasn't his fault; they had both made a mistake, but they needed to acknowledge it now, before it was too late.

Stu, mortified by the idea that his new wife might suddenly leave him, called Beverly's parents, who drove down to Gainesville, arriving the week before her oral exams. They tried to appear reasonable, but they were scandalized and devastated. They urged Beverly to reconsider, or at least to take her time, to do nothing rash. Beverly did not learn this until years later, but Dallas also spoke privately with Richard Thayer and asked him, man to man, to do the honorable thing, stand aside, and give the young couple a chance to make their marriage work. Richard agreed and abruptly disappeared. When Beverly called his apartment, no one answered. She thought he had decided to cut off a relationship that was becoming complicated. To her parents' relief, the crisis subsided, and after passing her orals, Beverly moved up to Wilmington.

———

Like Stu, Beverly got a job at Hercules—in the patent library downtown, not at the research center out by the golf course. The company generated two or three patents a week. Each one had to be abstracted, filed, and docketed. Beverly liked the work. It allowed her to use her education in chemistry without having to spend time in a lab. She was earning $8,000 a year and Stu, $14,000; together, as Beverly's father had predicted, it amounted to a considerable income. They bought a new split-level and Beverly learned to play golf. When Gavin was born in 1963, she switched to working part-time.

Stu saw his marriage to Beverly in terms of roles: his was to pursue his career and provide most of the income; hers was to raise the children, keep house, and prepare the meals he expected to be served at six, twelve, and six. They rarely talked about anything except the logistics of their lives, bills and car repairs, dinner menus and tee times and choir practice at the Presbyterian church they had joined. Beverly felt like they didn't know each other at all. While they rarely argued, much less fought, neither felt affection for the other.

When Gavin was six months old, Beverly decided for the second time that she was going to leave Stu. But then Stu discovered a large melanoma on his back. Diagnosed with skin cancer at the age of twenty-nine, he underwent difficult surgery and was sent to the Mayo Clinic, where the doctors told him he couldn't consider himself clear of the disease until he had been in remission for five years. Beverly decided it would be dishonorable to leave him then. Marriage entailed duty, and it was her duty to stick by her ailing husband.

During his recuperation, Stu realized that he could not bear the idea of returning to Hercules. He detested the corporate regimen, which to him was exemplified by the ringing bell at the lab that signaled the start and finish of every day. It reduced science to shift work. When Stu took a job teaching chemistry at Randolph-Macon College in Virginia, where he had studied as an undergraduate, the Monroes moved a second time, to Ashland, a small town fifteen miles north of Richmond.

———

Katie was born just before Stu and Beverly left Delaware. Six years later, after a surprise pregnancy in 1971, Beverly gave birth to her youngest child, Shannon. In Ashland, the family lived in a brick Colonial house on Maple Street and took an active part in all the social rituals of small-town-college life. They attended musical performances and plays at Blackwell Auditorium. They rooted for Randolph Macon's basketball and football and baseball teams. Both Stu and Beverly sang in the choir at the Duncan Memorial Methodist church. Stu taught his children to ride bikes, coached Gavin's Little League teams, and bought a lot on Lake Caroline, where the family retreated on weekends to picnic and fish from the aluminum johnboat Beverly's father had given them.

But Stu took long sabbatical journeys during the summer, to lecture at other schools or to do research, leaving Beverly with the responsibility of looking after the children for two or three months at a time. And even when he was at home, he felt at times as emotionally unavailable to his children as he was to his wife. After work, he liked to sit in the living room undisturbed while he drank a gin and tonic and read the newspaper. As a young girl, Katie would sit across from him in silence, wanting to jump into his lap but feeling that the raised newspaper represented a barrier her father had erected to ensure that she didn't encroach on his private emotional terrain. And while she rarely heard her parents argue, she also saw that they never hugged or kissed each other the way the parents of her good friend Gwen Andrews did.

During those years, Beverly's sense of civic responsibility became acute. She had given up chemistry and patents but she worked at the college library part-time and joined an environmental group and the Ashland Planning Commission. During Christmas, she had her children deliver baskets of food to the poor elderly couples who lived in the old wooden apartment houses down by the railroad tracks. One winter they helped people affix plastic insulation to their windows. After a hurricane ravaged the Virginia tidewater, she asked each of her children to donate an item of their favorite clothing—it had to be favorite, not cast-off—to the families who had lost their homes. Driving through town, she would notice a trash-strewn street and the following Saturday she would announce to her children, "We're going to pick up litter along Ashcake Road. I was down there the other day and it's a mess." And that's what they would spend the day doing.

In the mid-1970s, a young theology professor at the college developed a romantic attraction to Beverly. He was also married; in fact, he and his wife and Beverly and Stu played tennis and went dancing together. While he and Beverly did not have a physical affair, Beverly maintained, their involvement proceeded beyond flirtation into a decided emotional intimacy. They exchanged affectionate letters. She signed hers Sunshine; he signed his Columbus. When Stu found some of the love letters, he felt betrayed and insisted on a separation. They divided the house. Beverly and their two daughters shared the upstairs while Stu and Gavin lived on the first floor. The arrangement was impractical, however and after a couple of months they abandoned it.

But Beverly grew increasingly restless. By the late seventies, with Katie and Gavin in high school and Shannon beginning elementary school, her duties as a mother took up less of her time. She read Simone de Beauvoir's *The Second Sex* and began to feel she had sacrificed her own identity for the sake of her husband's. She and Stu now rarely talked at all, but from time to time he would utter vague remarks that led her to think he was set on another separation, a permanent one. She decided she needed to be financially independent and in 1979 applied for a job as a patent coordinator at Philip Morris. The company hired her that October.

———

The Philip Morris plant, its tall tower emblazoned with the Marlboro, Kool, and Benson & Hedges logos, sat flush against I-95, next to the James River in south Richmond, in an industrial neighborhood of docks, warehouses, and train tracks. The smell of roasting tobacco hung in the air. The plant had a huge manufacturing center as well as the research-and-development facility, where as many as six hundred scientists studied every aspect of cigarette production: flavor chemistry, vapor chemistry, filter chemistry, tobacco chemistry. They analyzed paper perforation, which controlled a cigarette's burn-rate, and ignition propensity, a euphemism for the tendency of cigarettes to start fires. They experimented on exotic projects such as the smokeless cigarette, a battery-operated device that would heat tobacco to create smoke and its attendant flavors without actually causing combustion. They examined the texture of the tobacco leaf, to determine ways to prevent the minute crumbling that occurred when the shredded leaves were rolled into cigarettes.

The tobacco industry generated fewer patents than other industries, since much of the information it produced—techniques for enhancing flavor or controlling the levels of nicotine—was secret and remained proprietary. Nonetheless, Philip Morris required a substantial patent operation. Beverly, together with three attorneys and two secretaries, all of whom worked out of a small suite of offices connected to the research center by catwalks, monitored the flow of Philip Morris's patents and conducted state-of-the-art patent searches for its scientists.

Two months after joining the company, Beverly attended the annual

Christmas party in the cafeteria. She still felt like an outsider and was standing by herself against the wall wondering whom to talk to when a man in a dark suit walked over, bowed slightly, and introduced himself, in a thick Central European accent, as Roger de la Burde. He had receding black hair combed off his forehead, black brows partially hidden by large glasses, and dark eyes that regarded her with a directness and curiosity that seemed out of place in the congenial Southern atmosphere.

In the weeks that followed, Roger began dropping by the patent office at lunchtime. He would sit in front of Beverly's desk, his hands folded, his face serious, talking intently about art and music and books. Beverly felt at times that he was putting on an act, but she was also drawn to him. He was stimulating and provocative. He challenged her. He had genuine passions, and he conveyed, as her father had done, the sense that life truly was an extraordinary gift, one squandered by so many people who failed to learn, to absorb culture, to embrace new enthusiasms.

Beverly's knowledge of real estate and zoning—acquired both from her father and from her work on the Ashland Planning Commission—impressed Roger. They began taking small trips during lunch, to look at property or to the Marsh Gallery at the University of Richmond to see an exhibit. Sometimes they stopped for a picnic lunch on a hillside slope overlooking industrial east Richmond. Roger would bring a book, by John Updike or Theodore Dreiser, or a copy of *National Geographic* with an article on something like the Ottoman empire, and read to her as they ate.

Beverly soon heard all the office gossip about Roger. He was not considered a company man, one of the lifers who got to the plant early and sat in the cafeteria smoking and talking about the price of Philip Morris stock. He was a talented intuitive scientist, but he hated committees and writing reports. He left others to work out the details of his ideas, and some of his subordinates had accused him of stealing their research. He often arrived at the office late, either because he had been up the night before or because he'd risen early and gone out to view real estate. Sometimes during lunch, he crept under his desk and took a nap. Philip Morris, he'd made it clear, was not his life.

Like most of the women at Philip Morris, Beverly also heard about Roger's affairs. He was at the time involved with a former legal secretary, a divorced woman with three children, whom Roger had persuaded to leave her job and become a real estate agent. Before that, there had been an English teacher who played the guitar. Roger himself was candid with Beverly about these affairs, and she was, somewhat to her surprise, uncritical of them. He had what he called a "European attitude" toward marriage and adultery. Marriage, he explained on more than one occasion, involved creating a family to produce heirs and to forge alliances for the sake of social and financial advancement. It needn't have anything to do with romance. Indeed, romance was often better left out of it.

———

Beverly's new job, together with the time it took her to commute from Ashland to the plant, required long hours. She usually left the house by seven and returned at seven. This new schedule disrupted Stu's routine. His wife, after absorbing some fashionable feminist ideology, was disappearing in the morning, leaving him to get the three children off to school and to clear and wash the breakfast dishes. One day, coming down to find a dirty kitchen and Beverly gone, he became so enraged that he began smashing the plates.

Later that summer, Stu decided to purchase a new house, without first informing Beverly. She was startled by the decision, but she didn't object. The house Stu bought, six miles out of Ashland, on Horseshoe Road in rural Hanover County, was a modern place, next to the South Anna River and behind the Hanover Country Club. Beverly actually liked it. She had more room to herself there. Roger, who was always looking for ways to promote his art collection, encouraged her to start writing about art. That fall, she published an article about a small show at the Virginia Museum in an art journal in Washington, D.C.

She wrote two more articles by the end of the year, staying up until two or three in the morning to finish them. Seeing the pieces published gave her a new sense of her capabilities. Gardening and sewing began to seem pedestrian by contrast. And raising her children, she felt, had been largely an exercise in unappreciated devotion. She could, she realized, be someone other than the dutiful self-sacrificing wife she'd been for the last eighteen years.

Stuart became jealous of Beverly's relationship with Roger. On New Year's Eve, 1980, he was downstairs watching television when the phone rang. He picked it up just as Beverly did upstairs and recognized Roger's voice.

Roger could tell from the dual clicks that someone else was on the line. "Hello, Stuart," he said in a sardonic voice. He went on to wish Beverly a happy New Year. "You are wonderful," he told her. "I love you."

The next day, Roger called Stuart. "It's a little strange to me that American husbands are so narrow-minded," he said. "They are so jealous. They always think that any relationship between their wives and other men is illicit. In Europe, things don't happen that way."

"You're not in Europe now," Stuart said.

———

That winter, Beverly and Stu virtually stopped talking. Without Stu ever actually saying so, Beverly came to realize that he had not expected her to move into the new house with him. He had thought that instead of moving, she would leave. He had not bought the house to save the marriage but to precipitate a breakup. At the end of winter, Stu left by himself to go skiing in Europe. When he returned, he had grown a beard and he acted younger—more decisive and vigorous. Almost immediately, he packed his belongings, moved into a condominium in north Richmond, and started divorce proceedings.

———

Beverly had been prepared to stay in the marriage, at least until all the children were out of the house, but she had anticipated his departure for almost two years, and when it finally came, she greeted it with relief. It was another indication of the new possibilities unfolding in her life.

She began spending more time with Roger. He was, she came to see, a genuine, if self-taught, expert on African art. He could distinguish works of the Urhobo tribe from those of the Bambara. He could identify the particular bend in the Ogun River that must have been the origin of a certain crocodile mask. Roger's knowledge of contemporary art was equally impressive. He hadn't actually purchased most of the paintings he owned. Instead, he studied art journals, visited galleries in Richmond, Washington, and New York, and when he saw work he liked, he called the artist and arranged to meet for a possible swap. He loaded his Dodge van with African pieces, drove to the artist's studio, whether it was in Virginia, New York, or New Hampshire, and tried to talk him or her into parting with some minor or earlier work in exchange for any African piece in the van.

Audacious as this sounded to Beverly, it often succeeded, due to Roger's ability to charm and to the press clippings he could show artists that established him as a prominent collector whose works had been exhibited in important Richmond galleries. Such exposure, Roger invariably pointed out, would enhance the artist's own reputation. It was important to Roger, who never used cash when he could trade, that no value be assigned to either work; this handily avoided the potential for misrepresentation—as well as the need to declare income and pay taxes.

Using this unorthodox scheme, Roger had over the years amassed a collection of more than four hundred contemporary paintings, primarily by mid-Atlantic artists like Sam Gilliam, but also including works from nationally known painters such as Alex Katz, Lowell Nesbitt, Sol LeWitt, and Les Levine. Some of the paintings, which ran the gamut from abstract minimalism to realistic landscapes, hung on the walls at Windsor. Others were stacked in the basement. Still more were simply piled up in an old toolshed. They were completely disorganized and unprotected. Field mice had gnawed the edges of the canvases. Beverly helped Roger catalog these pieces, photographing and indexing them and compiling biographical profiles of the artists. At Roger's urging, she also began calling artists to set up appointments and traveling in the art-laden Dodge van to New York to trade.

While at Windsor on the weekends, Beverly couldn't help but notice the dilapidated state of the property. Roger found farmwork tedious. He'd allowed the pond by the barn to silt up. Saw briers, honeysuckle, and poison ivy had enveloped the trees, visible from the house, that bordered the stream at the eastern edge of the property. Beverly arranged for the pond to be dredged and stocked with bass and bream. She and Roger hired two boys, and together they all pulled out the vines shrouding the trees.

Pulling saw briers was not how Beverly had intended to spend her summer. But once she started on a job, she stuck with it. The tough saw briers ripped their gloves apart, she came down with poison ivy, and they lost a few of the cedars, either from the drought that summer—it was so severe that even oaks were dying—or because by dislodging the vines they had disturbed the dirt around the root structure. But in the end, the result justified the labor. The vines had also covered the rocks around the stream, and now that they had been cleared away, it was an ideally tranquil place—the spring-fed water cascading down between the boulders into pools—to picnic and swim.

Roger's wife, Brigitte, never volunteered to pitch in. A polite, if cool and distant, figure, she was rarely visible on the weekends. Roger told Beverly that Brigitte had no interest in his projects. Beverly had the impression that while they shared the same house, they led separate lives. She was familiar with that situation.

———

Brigitte, however, was aware of Beverly. She was also aware of the many affairs Roger had had over the years, or if not of the affairs themselves, then of the fact that he was having affairs. The first one had occurred not long after their wedding, when they were living in Chicago, and Roger returned to Germany for a period of post-doctoral study. While he was there, he had gotten a young woman from Aachen pregnant. Upon his return to Chicago, Roger had made a full confession and Brigitte had decided to forgive him; the relationship had been a short one, and it had occurred far from home.

But a precedent was set, and eventually husband and wife reached an unspoken understanding: Roger could have affairs as long as they remained discreet, and did not threaten the family. Brigitte, for her part, would look the other way, pretend to know nothing, as long as Roger avoided embarrassing her. The arrangement had worked for almost twenty years. During that time Brigitte had watched a number of women visit Roger at Windsor. Some, like the former Philip Morris secretary, were ostensibly working for him, on real estate deals or bookkeeping details or art excursions. They even took trips with him. Brigitte could usually sense which ones were the mistresses. But as much as those women might covet the farm and her place on it, they remained respectfully unobtrusive, peripheral presences.

Beverly Monroe, however, was different. As she organized the clearing of the pond and the trees that summer, she seemed to Brigitte to be overstepping the boundaries and, in violation of Brigitte's understanding with Roger, encroaching on Brigitte's territory. Who was Beverly Monroe to take it upon herself to preside over the renovation of what was Brigitte's property and home? Brigitte began to feel imposed upon, and resentful. But she said nothing, certainly not to Beverly.

———

The dissolution of his marriage angered Stuart Monroe. What bothered him was less the loss of his wife than the disruption of his routine and the breakup of his family. He blamed Roger de la Burde. In the court papers he filed, Stuart accused Beverly of having an affair with Roger. He had taken with him the letters the theology professor had written Beverly, and he also introduced them as evidence that she had been repeatedly unfaithful. "The only things she wants," Stuart said in an affidavit, "is a marriage of financial convenience wherein [we] would share expenses but she would be free to do what she wants with respect to other men."

Angry at Beverly for going to work and warned by a neighboring housewife that when his children came home after school they had no "adult supervision," Stuart also claimed that Beverly was an unfit mother. The family court judge sent for the children individually to question them about Beverly before deciding custody.

Katie refused to go. She was angry at the world. She was a sixteen-year-old girl and her parents were messing up her life with this divorce. Her mother, she understood, was going through a selfish period where she was liberating herself. Some of the neighboring mothers thought that by having a job and being gone from seven A.M. until seven P.M. she wasn't being a good mother. They had poisoned her dad's mind against her mom. But her mom had been a great mom. Her dad's charges, and the nosy judge's questions, pissed her off. So what if Shannon came home from school to an empty house? She knew how to turn on the lights. So what if Katie and her boyfriend snuck off to the golf course to smoke cigarettes and drink Boone's Farm and then cruised the back roads in his Firebird? Whose business was that? When the judge reached Katie on the telephone, she shouted, "Fuck you!" and hung up.

———

In the end, the children chose the parent with whom they wanted to live. For Gavin, who by then had finished high school and was joining the army, the question was moot. Katie felt her father had acted like a jerk during the divorce, but she stayed with him because she wanted to graduate with her friends at Patrick Henry High in Ashland. Shannon moved with Beverly into a new house she built for herself on property Roger helped her buy in Chesterfield County, west of Richmond on Old Gun Road.

The lot was large—two acres—and wooded. Beverly got it cheap, because it was covered with construction debris and the trees were overrun with poison ivy. She hired a bulldozer to clear the debris and grade the land, but first she marked every tree on the site: wild cherries, cedars, a pear, a persimmon. She couldn't stand the thought of losing a single one. She paid another backhoe operator $50 an hour to move a row of huge cedars, which stood near an old fence line, to the front and sides of the property. There were twenty-five cedars in all, and they did it during one day—digging the holes, then digging a huge root ball for each tree, filling the hole with cow manure, dropping in the root ball, then tamping down the dirt and wiring the trees in place while a rotating group of neighbors constantly watered them.

When construction began, Beverly was at the site almost every day after work, overseeing the carpenters and clearing stones from the rock-pitted soil. The house, when finished, had cedar siding stained gray and a massive fireplace of rugged Maryland fieldstone. Big windows and sliding glass doors ensured that the interior was filled with sunlight. The trees that surrounded it, the trees she'd saved, provided a sense of seclusion and quiet rare in Chesterfield County. When Beverly and Shannon finally moved in, just before Christmas, 1982, she felt that for the first time since leaving the family farm in Leeds she was living in a place where she belonged.

CHAPTER IV

Drewry's Bluff

1

The day after Dave Riley's interview with Beverly, the investigator received a call from her. Riley was surprised. He hadn't expected his suspect to be phoning him. She immediately began talking about the guilt she felt over Roger's death.

"I was supposed to take care of him, Dave. I always promised him I would take care of him and I couldn't."

She began to sob.

"Beverly, quit beating yourself over the head," Riley said. He tried to convince her that Roger's death wasn't her fault. "He was a man that enjoyed controlling things," he said. "That's what it all boiled down to, the money and the art and the friends and the prestige, all was part of being in control. . . . And he could not stand the thought of not being able to have you and control the situation with Krystyna."

It was a curious state of affairs. Riley, who believed the suicide was nothing more than a story Beverly had concocted to hide a murder, found himself trying to persuade her how it would have been possible for Roger to have killed himself. But he was only doing it because he thought Beverly was trying to make herself seem more credible by pretending to be confused about it.

"I feel like I have to clear this up somehow," Beverly said.

"Well, I think you need to clear it up," Riley said. "The only person that I really feel you have any responsibility for . . . is Corinna."

"You told me that," Beverly said. "But I can't speak to her. I don't re-member exactly."

Riley felt he had to put a stop to Beverly's ambivalence. "Look, we re-solved one issue yesterday," he said. "Resolved issue was that the reason your behavior was so strange and inappropriate—even though you didn't realize it at the time—had to do with the fact that you were present. The polygraph and all that brought that out. We got that out in the interview. That issue has been resolved."

Riley described once again the scenario: how Beverly had fallen asleep, had been woken up by the gunshot, had seen Roger's body, had gone into shock and left. He told her she should not feel guilty about what happened. "Nobody's blaming you for leaving him there that night," he said. "No-body's blaming you. There wasn't a damn thing in the world that you could have done for him that night. He was dead the instant that gun went off."

Beverly complained that her memories were so muddled. "I wish I had that coherence in my mind," she said. "I really feel like I need to talk to someone."

"Well, if you feel that need, why don't you find a psychologist?" Riley suggested.

Beverly agreed that this might be a good idea. What she couldn't under-stand, she said, was the contradiction between her memory of what had happened and the facts as Riley had presented them. "I feel like my integrity has been questioned," she said.

"I haven't questioned your integrity," Riley replied.

"I know you haven't, but I just feel like—"

Riley interrupted her to repeat, even more forcefully, "I have *not* ques-tioned your integrity."

"I know you haven't," Beverly said again.

To reassure his suspect that the police did not doubt her story, Riley told her that the investigation was more or less complete. "All my questions are answered, as far as I'm concerned," he said.

Beverly asked about the other investigators.

"I think," Riley said, "we're pretty well on the same wavelength."

———

Beverly decided to take Riley's advice. She had never been to a psychologist before. She didn't even know anyone she could call for a recommendation. Going through the Yellow Pages, she saw an advertisement for a mental health clinic at St. Luke's Hospital. Beverly had taken Shannon to St. Luke's after she broke her arm. It was, if nothing else, a familiar name. She arranged an evaluation.

A nurse clinician named Marsha Alon saw Beverly first. She took some background information and then Beverly tried to explain what had happened, how she had apparently gone into shock after Roger's death and then suppressed any memory of it.

"Is this possible," she asked, "that someone can block something like this out?"

"Yes, it happens all the time," Marsha Alon said. "It's very common."

———

On Monday, March 30, more than three weeks after her father's death, Corinna had still heard nothing from the police about the status of the investigation, so she called Riley at his office.

The call, Riley felt, was fortuitous. He thought he had persuaded Beverly to confess to Corinna that she'd been present when Burde killed himself. But Riley didn't want Corinna blindsided by the confession. If that happened, Corinna might blow up at Beverly and accuse her of outright murder, and that could harm the smooth flow of the investigation, which depended on maintaining Beverly's cooperation. Riley felt it was time to bring Corinna into the investigative circle. He invited her to come up to First Division headquarters.

That evening, listening to Riley explain the police theory of the case, Corinna at first felt shocked and horrified. She was aware that the police considered homicide a possibility. But it had never occurred to her that Beverly could be a suspect. Corinna liked Beverly, who had always gone out of her way to make Corinna feel welcome and included. Beverly, Corinna had always thought, had a calming effect on her father, whom Corinna considered hyper. And Beverly was caring. In the last week or so, she had called Corinna a couple of times and left messages on her answering machine, checking in to see how Corinna was faring. The notion that Beverly might have killed her father was at first simply unthinkable.

But Riley explained that there was no other way to account for the facts. He even lay down on his side on the floor in his office to demonstrate how the position in which Roger had been found made it impossible for him to have shot himself. Corinna, who hadn't seen the death-scene photographs, was more than a little startled. She told Riley she actually had snapshots of her father napping in that very position.

Corinna didn't feel she was qualified to come to an intelligent conclusion on her own about what had happened. But she found herself forced to accept the idea that the woman she had known for twelve years, and who had seemed so devastated by grief, may well have murdered her father. She truly hoped Beverly hadn't done it, but from what Riley had explained, she was afraid that Beverly probably had.

When Riley asked Corinna if she would cooperate in the investigation, she agreed. Beverly, Riley went on, did not yet know that the police considered the death a homicide. He told Corinna she too needed to keep this fact a secret—not only from Beverly, but from everyone. Riley told her that Beverly would probably want to see her soon to explain how she had slept through Roger's suicide. When Corinna got together with Beverly, she had to appear neutral, friendly, and sympathetic and to do nothing that would raise Beverly's suspicions. "If you react adversely, it will shut her down," Riley said. "We want to play this out as long as possible."

Riley considered asking Corinna to wear a wire to the meeting with Beverly. But wires were fraught with problems. Remote transmitters had difficulties with reception and timing. Recorders often ran out of tape, or broke or accidentally got switched off. Besides, wearing a wire might make Corinna nervous, which in turn could trigger Beverly's suspicions. So Riley didn't bring it up. Instead, he told Corinna to listen closely to what Beverly said and then report back to him.

———

Corinna arranged to meet Beverly for lunch the following day, at the Marriott Hotel in downtown Richmond. Both of them were delayed by a parade through the city, but Corinna was waiting in the hotel lobby when Beverly arrived. It was a busy, noisy place, with a sunken conversation pit in the center. They made their way to the grill in the back, where a buffet lunch had been set up. They filled their plates with salad and found a small table in a relatively quiet area in the rear, with views through big windows of the Sixth Street marketplace. Neither of them felt like eating. Corinna seemed nervous and uncomfortable, but this was frequently her demeanor, so Beverly attached no significance to it.

Beverly had decided she was going to complete Roger's book as a tribute to his memory, and she and Corinna talked about that for a while. They discussed the questions the police had been asking Corinna about the allegations of fraud surrounding Roger's collection. Suddenly, Beverly said, "Corinna, I would like to talk to you about what happened that last night with your father."

She started crying and held out her hands to take Corinna's hand. She was there, she said, when Roger committed suicide. She described the dinner, the conversation, falling asleep, waking to a tremendous noise, feeling sick when she realized what had happened. She had visions, she said, of trying to get the gun out of his hand, but the visions were blurry. She didn't even remember driving home.

"Beverly, are you sure?" Corinna asked. Despite being prepared by Riley, she was absolutely horrified to hear these words coming out of Beverly's mouth. "You've been under so much stress. It's been a very difficult time for all of us. You're sure you're not imagining this?"

"No, I'm not," Beverly said. But it was all unclear, she added. She had been in a daze and she was unsure what exactly had happened. She was still struggling with herself to find the answers. She remembered a loud noise, she said, and she remembered trying to get the gun out of Roger's hand. But she thought she might be mixing up her memories of what happened that night with what happened the following morning, when she and Joe Hairfield discovered the body.

She also described the overwhelming sense of guilt that now plagued her, the feeling that she could have done or said something to stop him.

"Beverly," Corinna said. "You really need to get some help to deal with all of your guilt issues." Then to convince Beverly that she had known nothing of this in advance, she added, "And you really need to tell the police."

Beverly said she had already told the police.

At that point all Corinna wanted to do was get out of the hotel and away from Beverly, as quickly as possible. It wasn't so much what Beverly had said as the expression on Beverly's face, the way Beverly was looking at her, that convinced Corinna Riley was right: Beverly had killed her father. She told Beverly she had to go.

Beverly stayed to pay the bill. The people at the neighboring tables, she realized, had grown extremely quiet.

———

Riley called Corinna at home at nine o'clock that night. She recounted the conversation with Beverly. "I couldn't believe she said it," Corinna told Riley.

When Riley hung up, he had reason to feel satisfied. The commonwealth now had a witness outside the police force—a sympathetic, reliable witness—who could testify that Beverly had confessed to being with Roger at the time of his death. The pieces were coming together.

———

When Beverly reached her office the following morning, she too called Riley to report on the conversation.

"I just wanted to let you know that I did talk to Corinna yesterday," Beverly said. "And you're right—she is a wonderful girl."

"She took it a lot better than you thought, I guess," Riley said. He had no intention of letting Beverly know he'd already received a report on the meeting.

"I think so. It's a little difficult for her to comprehend, too, and difficult for me to explain, because I don't remember exactly."

"It's starting, though, I'm sure," Riley said. "It's starting to maybe come back to you a little bit now more and more."

"I guess."

They discussed Corinna's reaction to Beverly's disclosure.

"She didn't seem to hold it against you, did she?" Riley asked. "About this stuff that you just couldn't remember the fact that you were there. She didn't have a problem with that, did she?"

"No, she didn't at all. I think she really feels for me."

Riley asked if Beverly intended to talk to Joe Hairfield. He said he assumed that Corinna would now tell other people what had happened and that the story would get out.

"Well, I asked her not to," Beverly said. "I told her that I feel inadequate enough as it is."

"Okay," Riley said. He wondered if she had confided in anyone else. "I'm sure you told your own children by now, haven't you?"

"No, I haven't," Beverly said. She thought they were getting over their grief about Roger's death and that to try to explain her blocked memory to them, when she herself didn't even understand it, would only confuse and trouble them. They were worried enough about her as it was. "I don't want to stir anything up again."

"You think they'd understand, don't you?"

"Well, absolutely. I know they'd understand."

"It's none of my business," he said. However, he added, he did think she should talk to someone. "I'll feel better for you when you get the whole thing worked out in your mind and you remember, because eventually, eventually you'll remember everything."

"I know it'll have to come back."

———

At the end of March, Roger's will, which he had written in 1989, was probated in the Powhatan County Circuit Court. Roger left Windsor to Corinna but stipulated that Beverly would have the right "to reside in the main home for the duration of her life, with free access to all parts of the farm." Roger also stipulated that Corinna would be forbidden to sell or pledge the farm and that on her death, "Windsor shall pass by her Will to her most competent and accomplished, naturally born child, carrying the last name of de la Burde."

The will declared that much of the art had already been given away as an "annual tax free gift" to twenty named individuals, including Beverly and her three children and Krystyna Drewnowska. It created a "credit shelter trust" to be split between Corinna and Colette. Colette, however, was restricted to using her share of the principal only "for the purpose of educating her naturally born children on the condition that their father can be proven to be a college graduate. Special exception can be made to the above requirement if: The children are considered unanimously by the executors worthy of the de la Burde family tradition and if at the same time, they carry the de la Burde name."

The remainder of the estate, worth approximately $6 million once the taxes were paid and the debts settled, was to be divided up, with 20 percent going to Corinna, 20 percent to Beverly, 10 percent to various relatives and friends, including Benjamin—the son of his illegitimate German daughter, Sylvia—and Beverly's three children. The remaining 50 percent was to go to the creation of an education trust for the children of Corinna, Colette, Sylvia, and Beverly.

———

Arthur Hodges, the reporter covering the case for the Richmond *Times-Dispatch,* acquired a copy of the will. Since his first article on Burde's death, he had received anonymous phone calls from people with salacious anecdotes about the man's private life, and he had begun interviewing Burde's friends and acquaintances for a more detailed story.

Hodges's article, complete with the specifics of Burde's will, appeared on the paper's front page on April 7.

POWHATAN COLLECTOR LEFT LEGACY WRAPPED IN SMALL MYSTERIES

If Roger de la Burde loved anything, according to his friends, enemies, and associates, he loved order and control.

Putting together a book on his African art collection, the wealthy scientist and real estate developer insisted on making decisions on the smallest details. He offered friends inducements to learn German and French. He kept his Powhatan estate scrupulously clean.

But a legacy of de la Burde's untimely death at age 60—he was found shot at his home on March 5—may turn out to be one of the very things he most despised: a mess.

Powhatan authorities have not yet said whether de la Burde killed himself or was the victim of a homicide. They hope to make a ruling soon, said Capt. Vernon Poe of the Powhatan Sheriff's office.

———

The day the article appeared, Beverly received a phone call from a real estate agent she knew. Since, according to the *Times-Dispatch,* Beverly would be moving into Windsor, the friend said, did she want to put her own house on the market?

"I'm not planning to live at Windsor," Beverly said. "I like my house."

———

That same day, Beverly had her first appointment with her new therapist, Kathleen Westlake. Beverly, who didn't even like going to the doctor, was extremely uncomfortable with the process. Talking to a stranger about intimate matters felt wrong, and the session, she thought, was not particularly fruitful. Kathleen Westlake wanted to focus on the grieving process. She seemed to think Beverly ought to be angry at Roger. Beverly was frustrated by all the pointless emphasis on feeling.

"Is something going to happen?" she asked. "Is my memory gone? Will I get it back?"

"It takes time," Kathleen Westlake said.

Westlake didn't want to press Beverly on her memories. Marsha Alon, the nurse clinician who had done the initial assessment of Beverly, had diagnosed her as suffering from an adjustment disorder with mixed emotional features—a type of post-traumatic stress. Westlake believed that if a therapist tried to elicit memories prematurely from a post-traumatic-stress survivor, the stress of those memories could be overwhelming, causing a breakdown or dissociation. Westlake had seen patients who, when they were unable to cope with their memories, had gone right into another personality. So Westlake wanted Beverly to focus on ventilating her feelings about her boyfriend. That seemed to be the only place she was capable of going right then.

At the end of the session, Beverly appeared so weak that the therapist had to help her put on her coat and open the door. Westlake had never before seen a patient suffering from such a manifest inability to function that she couldn't even turn a doorknob.

———

Corinna called Beverly at the office, upset about the details of her father's will published in the *Times-Dispatch*. Was there any way, she wondered, to put a halt to all the publicity and speculation?

That afternoon Beverly called Riley and asked about the status of the investigation. Riley got the impression that Beverly was trying to speed the process along. The sooner the police wrapped up their inquiry and issued a finding of suicide, he figured, the sooner she would be able to claim her share of the Burde estate and move into Windsor. Riley assured her once again that the investigation was virtually complete.

Beverly described her session with the therapist. "I guess temporarily it helps to try to go through it and get it out of your system," she said. "I asked her yesterday if it's really better to remember fully or if it's going to be possible to remember. . . . She wouldn't say if it's better to remember or not remember."

"Whichever way it's going to be, I guess," Riley said. It had occurred to him that he might be able to make the suicide scenario Beverly had accepted even more incriminating. He suggested that she may have had some sort of physical contact with Roger at the time of his death. "Remember you said something about, you think you have this feeling like you tried to stop him or he touched you or that you touched him?"

"Right."

"That interests me," Riley said, "because I told you there were some things that trouble me, and I keep thinking that maybe that's what this is all about."

She had searched her memory, Beverly said, but the only thing she could recall clearly on that score was embracing Roger's body after she and Joe Hairfield found it the following morning.

"Do you think it's possible that you may have struggled with him," Riley asked, "trying to pull—"

"No, no, no," Beverly said firmly.

Riley, faced with resistance, decided it was best, as it could be sometimes with a fish fighting a hook, to pay out line. "I think it was over by the time you realized it," he said.

During that afternoon at First Division headquarters, Beverly had told Riley how her father too had committed suicide. Riley now suggested that she had reacted to Roger's death much as she had to her father's, when, during the drive down to South Carolina after getting the news, she had convinced herself that her father couldn't be dead. "That's just what you did that night," he told her. "You left the house knowing that was wrong, and then by the time you were home, you had forgotten all about it or put it out of your mind."

"I *had* forgotten."

"You have a feeling . . . subconsciously that people are going to blame you because you were there."

"Yes."

"You think, Well, they're going to think that I did it, or, They're going to think that I caused him to do it," Riley said. "You can't help having those thoughts."

"I guess," Beverly replied. "Will it make a difference if I remember or not?"

Riley, still thinking in terms of fishing, decided the time had come to give Beverly what he considered to be a little bait. By hinting that the prosecutor—not Riley himself, but the prosecutor—had some reservations about the case, he thought he might tempt her into elaborating on the incriminating statements she had already made. "Well, I have to tell you that there is only one person that's got any problem with this case, and it's not me and it's not Neal. It's the commonwealth attorney. I really don't believe he's overly concerned about it. He would like to know details. He's a little troubled that there aren't more details about that night."

"Give it time, I guess."

She hadn't taken the bait. Riley decided not to push it too hard. "Nobody's putting pressure on you," he said.

"I know."

Riley brought up the *Times-Dispatch* article. "Don't worry about what the newspaper says," he told Beverly. "I saw this thing in here talking about whether it's suicide or homicide."

"Yeah."

"Nobody from the newspaper has talked to the sheriff's department in almost two weeks."

The prying and the speculation, Beverly said, were distressing. Riley tried to reassure her that it would pass. "Right now I've got this thing written up as a suicide, okay?" he said.

"I know that," Beverly said.

"And I have written a report," he continued. "I have gone on to doing other things, but . . . I have not closed the case. It's just an open file. . . . At some point I suspect that you might remember more details, at which point I'll put it in there and I'll close the file out."

Beverly said she would continue trying to prod her memory, but she didn't want to push herself to the point where she imagined something that hadn't actually occurred. "You know, the power of suggestion is very strong and—"

"Don't do that, don't do that," Riley told her. "If you truly remember something, just call us. If you don't, just don't worry about it."

"That's exactly what I'll do," Beverly said. "I appreciate that very much, and I won't take up any more of your time."

"You're not taking up any of my time," Riley assured her.

Beverly described the progress she was making on Roger's book. "It will be a beautiful book and I'll make sure you get a copy, Dave."

"Well, that's really nice of you."

"I think you'd enjoy it very much."

"I really appreciate that."

———

Over the next few weeks, Beverly continued to see Kathleen Westlake. The therapist thought she was making progress. In her initial sessions, Beverly's description of her relationship with Roger de la Burde hadn't seemed to Westlake to be based on reality. Beverly would call Roger a soul mate but then simultaneously describe how he had betrayed her, cheated on her, and lied to her. While grief-stricken people often idealize the dead, Beverly seemed to Westlake to be suffering not just from idealization and memory lapses but from outright fantasies. In their most recent session, however, Beverly had begun to acknowledge how Machiavellian and manipulative Burde had been. Westlake considered it an important breakthrough.

From Beverly's point of view, all this excavating of emotions seemed a waste of time. But the therapist had told her that before she could recover her memories, she would have to work through her grief. She kept prompting Beverly to discuss her feelings about Roger. When she talked. As a rule, Kathleen Westlake didn't offer much feedback. On a couple of occasions, Beverly had the impression that the therapist had nodded off. If that was true, and it was only Beverly's impression, she didn't blame her. The therapist had to be bored, she decided, since all Beverly did during the sessions was cry.

She felt exhausted. Unable to sleep, she spent her long hours in bed at night straining to recall the maddeningly elusive memories. She believed there had to be some particular thing—an event or an object or an image—that would trigger the release of the memories, but she was unable to find it.

And the therapy just left her more exhausted and puzzled and uncertain. It made everything even more blurry, and added to the sense she had that her mind was disintegrating. The therapy wasn't costing much, only a five-dollar co-payment for each visit, since her insurance covered it, but Beverly decided that it wasn't worth the five dollars. It wasn't even worth the time it took to drive from Philip Morris to St. Luke's.

———

On sunny days, Beverly sometimes visited Roger's grave in Hollywood Cemetery. She cleaned up the twigs and branches that had fallen onto the grass and then sat for a while. Corinna and Brigitte had selected as a headstone a large, thick disc of polished black marble etched with an abstract African design. It was kind of garish. Beverly thought Roger would not have liked it at all. But he had liked the setting, which he had chosen himself. It looked across a wooded ravine. Wild violets grew scattered in the grass. A big cedar just up the slope provided afternoon shade and reminded Beverly of the huge spruce that stood near her father's grave in Marion.

——

Corinna kept in touch with Beverly after their lunch at the Marriott. She had by then gotten over the shock she had felt when Riley told her he thought Beverly had killed her father. And she had no particular qualms now about misleading Beverly. After all, she thought, Beverly herself was engaged in an elaborate charade, feigning grief and pretending to rack her brain for memories of the night her father died.

Corinna wanted to hear any new version of events that Beverly might provide. So she called Beverly regularly. One night, she even dropped by Beverly's house with her lawyer to ask for some help in figuring out her father's real estate investments. She also took Gavin out for his birthday, April 20, to a place on Shockoe Slip where they served a good white-cheese pizza. And she sent a card to Beverly, whose birthday was April 16:

> Beverly:
>   The card will probably be late, but I hope you have a happy birthday and a great year! I'll be thinking of you.
>
>   Corinna

2

As Dave Riley assembled his file on Beverly Monroe, he kept returning to one particularly vexatious discrepancy. Burde's publisher, Don Beville, had told the police that Burde called him shortly after ten o'clock on the night he died. If Beverly killed Burde, that meant she must have remained at Windsor past ten. But Beverly claimed that Gavin was in his bedroom studying when she got home around nine forty-five and could provide her with an alibi.

Riley, who hadn't interviewed Gavin or Beverly's daughters, decided he could resolve this discrepancy with a subterfuge. He would call Beverly and point out, as he had tried to do that afternoon after the polygraph, that she couldn't have come home at nine forty-five, if she had been present when Burde died. Gavin must be mistaken. Riley would ask her to have Gavin call him and explain it.

In response, he figured, Beverly would do one of two things. If she was being honest—that is, if she was innocent—she would say that had she arrived home at nine forty-five, she could not have been present at Roger's death and therefore must have only dreamed that she had been there. If, on the other hand, she had murdered Burde and now believed that she had successfully tricked the police into thinking he had killed himself while she was present, she would manipulate Gavin into changing his recollection. She would see Gavin's memory as a hole in her story, and either she would try to plug the hole or she would drop the story.

There was another advantage to the subterfuge. Should Gavin change his recollection, that would undermine his credibility if and when he did testify as an alibi witness for his mother.

———

On the morning of May 8, Riley called Beverly at Philip Morris.

"Look," he said. "I'm getting ready to send a report to the commonwealth attorney to finalize this thing and put it finally to rest."

"That would be good," Beverly said.

They chatted for a little while, then Riley said, "I've got a stack of reports on everything everybody said on this thing from day one, and I'm writing a summary and the title of it is suicide. . . . I've reread it to be sure I had everything lined up, and there's an inconsistency about something that's very minor and I just wanted to clear it up."

"Sure," Beverly said.

Riley pointed out the discrepancy between Don Beville's story and Gavin's recollection. "I can't imagine you getting home much before eleven or eleven-thirty or twelve that night, considering the circumstances," Riley said. "So I can't imagine how he could say that you were home at nine forty-five." He asked Beverly to have Gavin call him and clarify the matter.

"I don't know if he'll remember the time," Beverly said. "But I know that he'll remember that he was there."

"It's not a big deal," Riley said. "I just need about thirty seconds of his time."

———

That afternoon, Beverly met Gavin for lunch at a Ruby Tuesday in the Cloverleaf Mall in Midlothian. She was waiting in a booth under a stained-glass lampshade, nursing a glass of watery iced tea, when he arrived. He'd worked at the fitness center that morning and, with an afternoon class, was pressed for time. He ordered a hamburger.

When his mother told him she had been down to police headquarters to see an investigator named Dave Riley about Roger's death, Gavin was appalled. She'd been meeting with the police without an attorney present? He had seen enough cop shows to know that was something you didn't do. He asked why she hadn't told him before. Beverly said she'd just been trying to help the police and hadn't wanted to get him involved. His mother, Gavin thought, was off the wall.

He said they had to call Katie, but Beverly explained that she didn't want to involve Katie either. She said that detective Riley had told her she must have been present when Roger killed himself. Gavin argued that this was impossible, since Roger had died after ten o'clock and she had returned to the house before ten. He knew because he had been home, in his underwear in his bedroom, studying for a biology test. She had arrived less than an hour after he had gotten home, after working at the fitness center, around nine-ten. "Mom, you were home," he said.

Beverly replied that Riley insisted she was present at Roger's death. When Gavin took issue, she kept repeating herself, saying, He says I was there; he says I was there. Gavin got a little frustrated with her—it was like talking to a fence post—and finally gave up. He didn't like arguing. "Okay, fine," he said. "He says you were there."

Beverly said all Riley wanted to do was clear up the question of the time she got home. He seemed to have a problem with the idea that she was home by nine forty-five. He thought she must have returned later. It was the only thing preventing him from closing the case and ruling it a suicide. He wanted to discuss it with Gavin.

"Gavin, did you look at a clock?" she asked.

"No." He'd just estimated. He had felt fairly confident of his estimate, but since he had not actually looked at the clock, he did not, strictly speaking, know what time she had arrived home.

Beverly said that since she hadn't looked at a clock either, she herself couldn't really say what time she had gotten home. And it didn't really matter, she continued. What mattered was that they put this thing behind them and start to heal. She asked Gavin to call Riley and clear up the matter.

"I didn't look at the clock," Gavin said.

"Just tell him that."

———

After class, Gavin called the investigator. Riley adopted a businesslike manner. He asked Gavin for his full name and his Social Security number, and informed him he was taping the call.

"The reason I need to talk to you, I am getting ready to close this report, and I am calling it a suicide," Riley said. He explained that he was preparing a summary of the case and forwarding it to the commonwealth attorney, but he needed to clarify the time of Beverly's return.

Gavin said that he had gotten home shortly after nine o'clock, coming directly from his job at the fitness center, and that he had been studying for his biology exam when his mother arrived.

"Was it much later probably when your mother got home?" Riley asked.

There it was—the question. "I do believe so," Gavin said.

"Maybe close to midnight, would that not be stretching it?"

"Stretching it that way. I don't recall looking at the clock."

"But it was obviously much later," Riley said.

"Yeah, I would say at least ten o'clock or later."

"Could it have been as late as midnight?"

"Yes, it could have," Gavin replied. "I was studying for an exam. It's really hard to say."

"All right. So midnight would not be inconsistent?"

He hadn't looked at the clock, Gavin said again, so he couldn't be sure. His mother had come home, had gone back out for milk and sandwich meat, had returned and called Roger several times without success, and had then gone to bed.

"I appreciate your calling," Riley said. So, he reiterated a final time, it was probably around midnight when Beverly returned home.

"It was. I would say it was probably later."

Riley thought Gavin was now suggesting Beverly might have come back later than midnight. But the comment was ambiguous. He tried to push Gavin a little further. "It could have been after midnight?" he asked.

"It could have," Gavin said.

3

Ann Jones, the firearms expert in the division of forensic science, had been busy all spring. It wasn't until May 21, more than two months after promising Dave Riley that she could forensically re-create the death of Roger de la Burde, that she finally sat down in her laboratory and studied the evidence. She'd been given Burde's gun, the four cartridges that had remained in its cylinder, the bullet fragments the pathologist had removed from his brain, a box of the same ammunition taken from Windsor, and the pillows that had been on the couch alongside the body.

Jones test-fired several rounds from the cartridge box to see what sort of residue traces the ammunition would leave. It was, she thought, extremely dirty ammunition, some of the dirtiest ammunition she had ever seen in her eight years on the job. Dirty ammunition was a sign of cheapness on the part of the buyer, since it often came from used cartridges that had been reloaded by the manufacturer, who also then typically used inferior gunpowder. Jones held the gun one inch from the target and fired. The shot produced a four-to-five-inch spread of soot on the target's surface. From two inches away, the soot spread to seven or eight inches. Since the photographs showed little soot around the bullet entrance wound in Burde's forehead, she reasoned, the gun barrel had been held close to the skin.

Next, Jones tried to re-create the death scene. She studied the photographs taken by Greg Neal. They showed the charcoal-like smudges on Burde's fingers, the position of the two pillows—one plaid and one tasseled—on the couch, and the soot and spattered blood on the upholstery.

To replicate Burde's head, Jones formed some cotton padding into an ovoid shape. To replicate his right hand, she took a white glove of the sort she wore to avoid contaminating evidence and filled it with clay. She did not have the couch on which Burde died, so she used a box to serve as its backrest.

Jones then tried to arrange the gun, the clay hand, the ovoid head, and the pillows in a configuration resembling the one depicted in Neal's photographs. The bloodstained pillows had become stiff, and it was difficult to shape into them the exact curves she could see in the photographs. She did the best she could and then covered them with a white sheet. She slipped the muzzle between the fourth and fifth fingers of the clay hand—she had to spread the fingers considerably to do so—and angled the gun so it would reproduce on the white sheet the pattern of gunshot residue contained on the pillows underneath. Then she fired the gun.

The shot blew the ovoid head across the room. The clay hand toppled forward. On the fourth and fifth fingers, Jones observed, were soot marks similar to the ones on Burde's fingers.

She then filled a second glove with clay and placed it palm outward toward the gun, in the position Dave Riley had proposed when he said that Burde may have woken up just before dying and thrown his hand out to try to ward off the shot. She fired the gun again.

The blast from the cylinder tore through the glove down to the clay. If Burde's hand had been in that position it would have been injured. The photographs of Burde's hands, however, showed no such damage.

Ann Jones called Riley to tell him she had concluded the firearms test. The results, she said, were consistent with the theory that the murderer had slipped the gun muzzle between the fourth and fifth fingers of Burde's right hand, which had been clasped to his head, before pulling the trigger.

This was the news Riley had been waiting to hear. For all intents and purposes, he thought, Ann Jones's test eliminated the possibility that Roger de la Burde had killed himself.

<hr />

4

Dave Riley called Jack Lewis, the commonwealth attorney for Powhatan County. He said that the forensic results, together with Beverly Monroe's confession that she had been with Burde when he died, provided them with enough evidence to go before a grand jury and seek an indictment against her for murder.

Lewis wished, if possible, to avoid a trial. He had been the Powhatan County prosecutor for sixteen years. It was only a part-time job; he also had a private practice, doing mostly real estate closings and title examinations and handling loans for deeds of trust. Still, he represented the commonwealth on every case that came before the three courts—juvenile and domestic relations for family matters, general district for misdemeanors, and circuit for felonies—in the Powhatan County Courthouse. Frankly, he had his hands full. A murder trial was time-consuming and expensive. It was also risky, particularly in a case where the evidence was circumstantial. The jury could acquit, and the commonwealth would end up looking foolish. Lewis suggested trying to work out some sort of plea bargain with Beverly Monroe.

Riley knew he was the natural person to make this overture. He had the rapport with Beverly. However, he didn't think Beverly would agree to a plea. By doing so, she would destroy her reputation and forfeit her job at Philip Morris, since the company would automatically fire anyone who confessed to murder. That would be the end of her life as she knew it. No, Riley thought. If Beverly was charged, she would recant her confession, return to her original story, and insist on her innocence.

Riley was convinced that her insistence would fail. The officers and secretaries in the observation room had heard her say, during her interview at First Division headquarters, that she'd been present when Burde killed himself. She'd said the same thing to Corinna. Beverly, in Riley's view, was locked into the story. But that didn't mean she wouldn't try to wriggle out of it. She had no other choice.

Jack Lewis still wanted to avoid a trial. On the morning of June 3, after thinking over Riley's reasoning, he called the investigator.

"Let's see if we can get a confession," he said.

"She'll never do it," Riley told him. "She's going to go right back to square one."

Lewis urged Riley to try anyway. Riley said he thought the only way it might work would be if he, Riley, told Beverly that he was contacting her on his own, without the permission or knowledge of Jack Lewis or Greg Neal or anyone else on the commonwealth's team. He would tell her he was bringing her the inside scoop, which was that the rest of them believed she had committed first-degree murder and were inclined to indict her. Riley would appear as a friend and confidant, someone who was there to help Beverly by offering her a way out, the possibility of a lesser sentence, if she admitted killing Burde.

"Let's make one stab at this," Lewis said. "See if we can get her to confess."

"It isn't going to work," Riley told him, "but I'll try it."

———

As soon as he hung up, Riley called Beverly at Philip Morris. "Beverly, I need to talk to you," he said. "What does your schedule look like today?"

Beverly hadn't heard from Riley in almost a month. The last time they'd spoken he told her he was getting ready to close out the case and needed only to talk to Gavin. She was under the impression that the police investigation had come to an end and that the final report, with its conclusion of suicide, would be issued any day.

"Well," she said, "I'm busy, but I'm always available. What's the problem?"

"I think I need to talk to you in person."

Riley wondered if there was a place near Philip Morris, a park, for example, where they could go and talk. "I'd rather go someplace where there isn't anybody else around."

"That sounds ominous," Beverly said.

"Don't read too much into it," Riley said. "It's just to talk."

"All right."

"I don't want anybody else to hear the conversation." Riley had an idea. "I'm a Civil War nut," he told her. He suggested they meet at Fort Darling, a national park off Bellwood Road on Drewry's Bluff a few miles south of the Philip Morris plant. It overlooked the James River and was the site of a Civil War battle during which a Confederate battery drove back a flotilla of Union gunboats, led by the ironclad *Monitor,* that was trying to attack Richmond from the rear. Riley knew the spot well, having eaten many a bag lunch sitting in his car in the parking lot. It was usually deserted in the middle of the week. "I need to talk to you," he said again. "Need to talk to you in private."

"Okay."

"What's a good time?" Riley asked.

"I could be there in half an hour."

"I don't think I could make it that fast."

Riley suggested meeting at eleven o'clock.

Beverly agreed. She said she would be driving her dark blue Mercury.

"All right," Riley said. "I'll meet you there at eleven."

"Okay. Good. Thanks. 'Bye."

" 'Bye."

———

Riley reached Drewry's Bluff ahead of Beverly. Picnic tables were usually set up near the parking lot, but for some reason they had been removed. He got out of his unmarked police car and stood waiting for his suspect. The day was hot and slightly muggy. Riley expected this was going to be the world's shortest meeting. He would confront her with their suspicions, she would recant her confession, and they would part ways.

———

Beverly told Dee Shannonhouse she was taking an early lunch. She followed the Jefferson Davis Highway through a seedy stretch—passing a Tuffy muffler shop, a Wonder Bread discount outlet, the Deluxe Motel, and Hank's Bar-B-Q—down to Bellwood. She found the park entrance, a gravel drive disappearing into trees. She followed it through the woods to a circular parking lot. Riley's car was the only one there. He was leaning against its fender.

When Beverly pulled up next to him, Riley told her that because the tables were gone, they had no place to sit. He did not want Beverly in his car. He hoped to avoid any sort of situation in which she could later claim she had been in custody or at least felt she was in custody. That would raise Miranda issues.

"We can sit in my car," Beverly said.

Riley climbed into the passenger seat of the Mercury. He left the door open. He also pulled back his jacket and told Beverly he wasn't wearing a tape recorder. He was there, he explained, as a friend. "I've got bad news," he said.

A laboratory analysis by a firearms expert of powder-burn patterns, he went on, indicated that Roger could not possibly have shot himself. Someone else did it. That finding, together with her admission that she had been present when he died, indicated that she was the one who shot him. The commonwealth attorney was convinced she had killed Roger, Riley said, and so was he. But considering Roger's abominable behavior and his affairs with Krystyna Drewnowska and other women, he didn't blame her. What surprised him, he said, was that she had been able to tolerate the heartless monster for so long. "You should get a medal," he told her.

Riley's objective at this point was to commiserate with Beverly. By sympathizing with the suspect and blaming the crime on the victim's evil nature, you increased the chances for a confession.

Riley told Beverly that if she confessed, the prosecutor would agree to a lesser charge of second-degree murder. He would also be inclined toward leniency. He, too, was understanding. Who wouldn't be?

As Riley expected, Beverly vehemently denied killing Roger. Also as he'd expected, she said she'd begun to have doubts about being present when he shot himself. She was now convinced she had only dreamed about it. Furthermore, she said, she thought she might actually have proof that she was elsewhere. After coming home that night and talking to Gavin, she had gone back out to the grocery store. She always kept all of her receipts and she thought she could find the one she had been given then.

"Anybody can get receipts," Riley said. A person in possession of a receipt with a certain date and time on it was not necessarily the person who'd been given the receipt at the store. You could pick up receipts in a supermarket parking lot. And anyway, he told Beverly, it was extraordinary that if she had such a receipt she had never mentioned it before.

The evidence against her, Riley went on, was overwhelming and included signs of premeditation. He got out of the Mercury and went over to his car to retrieve a notepad. On it he had listed factors, in addition to her March 26 statement, that pointed to Beverly's guilt. Back in the Mercury, he read aloud:

• She might lose part of her share in Roger's estate if Krystyna had a child.

• She was a beneficiary of Roger's life insurance policy.

• She apparently owed Roger $155,000, for money he had put up to buy a lot in the exclusive Kanawha neighborhood, which had been acquired solely in her name.

• Her own father's suicide had not been investigated by the police, which may have led her to think Roger's would not be either.

• No one except Beverly had said anything about Roger's being suicidal.

• Roger was found dead on the visitor's couch, which suggested she had been there lying on the regular couch until he fell asleep.

• Beverly had reportedly been telling people the autopsy report put Roger's death somewhere between 11:00 P.M and 1:00 A.M., which, though the autopsy report did no such thing, would have provided her with an alibi.

• She had conspired with Krystyna's husband to break up the affair between Krystyna and Roger.

• Prior to talking to the police, she told someone Roger had been asleep on the couch when she left, which contradicted her official statement.

• Her behavior the morning the body was found was peculiar.

• She knew where Roger kept his gun.

• She said she and Roger had watched a show about Charles de Gaulle on PBS the night Roger died, but no such show had aired that evening.

What may have finally provoked her into a murderous rage, Riley then said, was overhearing Roger on the phone that night, planning to bring Krystyna to a lunch the following day with his publisher.

Beverly had grown very quiet. She seemed to Riley almost paralyzed. Finally, she said she couldn't conceive of having killed Roger. She loved him too much. But that evening had become such a blank, she went on, that she could no longer recall what had happened.

It became clear to Riley that he would be unable to elicit a confession. However, he thought, if he shifted his tactics slightly, he still might succeed in getting her to accept a scenario that, while seemingly innocent, in fact incriminated her. Riley thought he would try, as he had once before with Beverly, to dangle a little bait.

The commonwealth attorney had not authorized him to provide her with the details he had just revealed, Riley said. No one knew he was here. He had come because he sympathized with her and felt that Roger's behavior had been despicable. If she could somehow explain the forensic evidence, he went on, the commonwealth attorney would take it into consideration. The forensics suggested that someone had wiped off the gun before placing it in Roger's hand, he said. If the two of them could craft an explanation for this, he would present it to the prosecutor. That might prevent Jack Lewis from proceeding immediately with an indictment for first-degree murder. And in fact, he might not prosecute at all.

Riley began improvising. Maybe, he said, she had panicked when she was awoken by the sound of the gun going off as Roger killed himself, had picked up the gun, and then, in a state of confusion, had wiped it off and put it back. Riley explained that he was not saying she had done this, just that it was hypothetically possible.

Beverly said she couldn't remember what had happened, but she guessed it could be possible.

Riley was amazed by Beverly's reaction. She was once again accepting the she-was-there scenario, which she had repudiated only a few minutes earlier. He had brought her full circle. He asked what she would have used to wipe the gun.

If she had used anything, Beverly said, it would have been the long-sleeved sweater she was wearing.

Riley picked up the notepad and drafted a statement. He checked each sentence with Beverly before committing it to paper. Beverly refused some of his suggestions, forcing him to seek compromises in the language and tone. Composition of the statement was a halting process, but that may have been why, in the end, it had the lyric quality of free verse.

> I was on the sofa.
> Roger was on the other sofa.
> I was asleep.
> A noise made me jump.
> I don't recall getting up.
> I was standing over Roger
> who was on the sofa and seeing the gun.
> The above I remember clearly <u>but</u>
> I don't remember exactly what happened
> next, but I do know that having
> seen Roger in that curious trance my
> natural reaction would be (not knowing
> whether he was alive or dead at that instant)
> to try to stop him and that reaction would
> have been to take the gun away from him.
> My next reaction would be
> (upon realizing he was dead)
> to put back the gun. It would be
> natural to have put the gun
> back where I thought it
> had been or where it would
> appear it should have been
> considering the position of his body.
> It would have been natural for anyone
> realizing they shouldn't have touched the
> gun to have wiped it off before
> putting it back.

By the time Riley finished writing, he and Beverly had been sitting in the Mercury for two hours. Beverly read the statement.

"It sounds cold," she said.

Nonetheless, at Riley's urging, she signed both pages of the document in her deliberate, feminine handwriting.

> Beverly A. Monroe
> June 3, 1992
> 1:00 p.m.

"I'll give this to Jack Lewis," Riley said. "He's the one that's making the decisions. Maybe this will explain enough to sway him a little bit."

———

After Beverly signed the confession, she and Riley decided to go for a walk. Riley had left his gun in his car, since he had wanted to appear unthreatening. But on a previous occasion in the park, when he'd also left his gun in his car, he was almost mugged by two men, dissuading them at the last moment by displaying his police badge. Now he decided it would be a good idea to bring his weapon along. While Beverly was getting ready, Riley slipped his gun into his waistband.

A gravel path led through red oak, pine, and gum trees out to the eroded earthen parapets of Fort Darling on the bluff overlooking the river. Beverly and Riley sat down near the sole remaining cannon. Beverly did most of the talking. She seemed to Riley to have accepted the idea that she was going to be charged with murder and to have moved beyond the shock of that development to grapple with the question of what she should do next. She was concerned about the impact her indictment would have on her children. Riley thought he might be able to take advantage of these worries to get her finally to confess. "If you did this, Beverly, it's understandable considering the way Roger treated you in the relationship and how he was throwing you aside."

"I'm not a criminal or murderer," Beverly said.

"No, you're not," Riley said. "This is something you would never do again. This was something that was forced on you. It was irresistible. An irresistible impulse."

Riley described the "irresistible impulse" defense, a form of temporary insanity. It was a difficult defense to mount, he knew, since it required overcoming a reservoir of jury skepticism, but it was occasionally successful. He also told Beverly she might also want to consider a plea bargain.

"I know the commonwealth attorney would be more than willing to be very, very lenient in any sentencing against you," Riley said. "You know, the bare minimum. Maybe he would even go for a manslaughter charge, which would be a very short prison term. Maybe, if you're trying to save face, you know, you could not actually have to admit to guilt but acknowledge that there was enough evidence to convict you."

Such an acknowledgment, he continued, was called an Alford plea. If she was worried about how the publicity might affect her children, an Alford plea could work to her advantage. She could control the amount of information that was made public, and hence could limit the notoriety. In a public trial, the shrieking headlines and detailed articles would be horrendous. The commonwealth attorney would air every last sordid detail about her and Roger and Krystyna. He could paint her as deceitful, manipulative, and vengeful—"a black widow spider," Riley said, "that killed her mate."

Despite her anguish, Beverly seemed to Riley to be listening intently to everything he said. He felt sorry for her at that point; he truly did.

"I'm not a killer," Beverly said.

"Beverly, I know you're not a killer," Riley told her. He took out his gun and offered it to her, to show her how much he trusted her. "Here's my gun," he said. "I'd hand you my gun. I know you're not that kind of person. This was a onetime thing."

Riley held out the gun. He was willing to let her hold it.

Beverly was clearly taken aback by this gesture. "Oh no," she said.

"You're not afraid of guns, are you?" Riley asked.

"No, I'm not afraid of guns."

Riley put his gun back, and they walked out through the woods to the parking lot. As they were preparing to leave, Beverly turned to him with what seemed to the detective to be an expression of utter defeat.

"Do you know a good lawyer," she asked, "somebody that can help me?"

Riley could not believe that Beverly was asking him, the man who'd investigated her and who had just told her she was being charged with murder, for advice about a lawyer. It was too wild. "Beverly," he said. "I'm not the person that you should be talking to about this. You have a daughter that is a lawyer. You should be talking to her."

They got into their cars and left the park at the same time. Beverly followed Riley all the way up the Jefferson Davis Highway. Whenever he glanced in his rearview mirror, there she was in her blue Mercury. She finally turned off onto the Chippenham Parkway, and Riley pulled over at the first place he could find, the entrance ramp to I-95, and started making notes of everything he and Beverly had said.

CHAPTER V

Roger's Dilemma

Brigitte de la Burde had endured her twenty-six-year marriage with an air of stoic resignation. She had ignored her husband's extramarital affairs. She had stood by him when he was placed on trial for extortion. She had acquiesced when his illegitimate daughter showed up in Virginia and he began introducing her to their friends at the Farmington Country Club. She had watched silently as Beverly Monroe spent the summer clearing vines from the trees at Windsor.

But Brigitte had her limits. Once Beverly Monroe's divorce was final, she became a visible fixture in Roger's life. She was frequently at Windsor, helping Roger with his projects, attending his parties. Beverly and Roger played tennis together, inspected real estate, and traveled to New York to trade art. One day, caught up in another one of his enthusiasms, this time to renovate the house, Roger invited Beverly to accompany him and Brigitte to a bath-and-tile shop, to solicit her opinion on fixtures. Another day, he came home to announce that he had purchased a family plot in Hollywood Cemetery and that he intended Beverly to be buried there along with Brigitte and their two daughters. It was too much. Brigitte decided she had had enough—with Beverly, with Roger, with the whole situation. By 1984 her two girls, now grown, were no longer living at home. At the end of that year, she too moved out of Windsor and took an apartment in the west end of Richmond.

—

Initially, Burde was devastated by his wife's departure. The idea of family had always been important to him. He missed the formal structure that marriage gave his life, as well as, when his divorce became final, its tax advantages. But without ever moving into Windsor, Beverly Monroe took on most of Brigitte's wifely responsibilities, and gradually she and Roger, and their respective children, formed a new family. The two were in many ways ideally suited for each other. Roger needed someone who could share his enthusiasms, which neither his wife nor his daughters did. Beverly, who had boundless enthusiasm, had been waiting for someone to inspire her, and Roger, for all his devious qualities, had the gift of making people feel they were capable of much more than they had accomplished, if only they would listen to him.

Beverly acted as hostess at Roger's parties, for Polish friends and gallery owners, for curators and artists and Republican politicians, parties that involved tennis and chess, Roger's improvised dishes, Yugoslavian wine, and canoe trips down the James River. The two of them visited Poland and Switzerland, formed a German club, hiked through swamps inspecting land parcels, and bid for property at foreclosure auctions held on the steps of county courthouses. She called him Peacock. He called her Mouse or Angel. Demonstrative in his affections, Roger frequently appeared at Beverly's door with flowers. Once, when she told him she preferred ordinary broomstraw to supermarket tulips, he arrived the next day with a bundle of broomstraw he'd gathered from the fields at Windsor, and she kept it permanently on her kitchen counter in a terra-cotta vase.

Roger took a paternal interest in Beverly's children. He chided Shannon and Katie for dating the sons of farmers and squandering their summers working as lifeguards. He upbraided Gavin for his lack of ambition. Once, after a successful real estate deal, he slapped a huge roll of cash—more than $50,000—on the table in front of Gavin and shouted gleefully, "See? *This* is what you should be doing!"

But he was generous as well as demanding. He paid for Katie's French lessons. He arranged for Shannon to attend Trinity Episcopal by giving the school, in lieu of tuition, a large contemporary painting. He invited her to bring her friends to Windsor, to camp out along the boulder-strewn pools of Fine Creek. But his generosity, like everything else about him, was unpredictable to the point that he sometimes seemed, to Shannon, a little wacky.

One weeknight after dinner, when Shannon was still in high school and living with Beverly in the house on Old Gun Road, Roger showed up with a trunkful of fur coats in his car. There had been a sale at Thalhimer's department store and he had bought something like twenty furs—raccoon, fox, beaver, rabbit, just about every fur you could think of. He threw them all down on the living room floor and announced, "Pick the fur coat of your dreams!"

Shannon and her mom were laughing, because it was so bizarre and comical, but Roger was serious. "No, pick the fur of your dreams!" he said again. Beverly and Shannon didn't want fur coats, thank you very much. It was a nice offer, but they weren't fur-wearing women. Shannon wouldn't be caught dead in a fur. But Roger insisted. "Pick the fur of your dreams!" he kept saying. The man is totally bonkers, Shannon thought. So they made a game of it. They dressed each other up in these ridiculous fur coats, put one on Roger too, and stuck bananas in their ears and string beans in their noses and took pictures. They had so much fun that night. Still, it was very weird.

"Don't worry," her mother told Shannon the next day. "That's just Roger being Roger." It was how Beverly had taken to explaining a lot of the strange things he did.

2

By then, Roger had been working at Philip Morris for more than twenty years. In the early seventies, he and some of the company's other scientists discovered that by impregnating tobacco with liquid carbon dioxide and then converting it to dry ice and then rapidly heating the tobacco, they could expand the leaves without their retaining any harmful residues. The process became known as Dry Ice Expanded Tobacco, or DIET. Roger, like all the scientists employed by Philip Morris, had signed an employment contract giving the company the rights to any process he developed while working there, and in 1974 Philip Morris applied for a patent on DIET.

In 1984, Philip Morris sued the Brown & Williamson Tobacco Corp. for patent infringement, claiming, among other things, that it was using the DIET process without paying royalties. Roger, who had been receiving critical performance evaluations for several years, both orally and in writing, traveled to Macon, Georgia, to testify in the trial. It was an important case. The top Philip Morris executives were present, including Clifford Goldsmith, the head of operations, and Frank Resnik, the president of the American subsidiary, and they congratulated Roger on his testimony. Resnik, he said later, flashed a V-for-victory sign with his fingers and told him, "Great job!"

The following year, the trial judge found in favor of Philip Morris. In his ninety-page opinion, he calculated that between 1979 and 1985, the company had used the DIET process to expand some 200 million pounds of tobacco, which created a cost savings of $300 million. By the time the judge issued his opinion, Roger's supervisors were once again giving him unsatisfactory performance reviews. His project manager had even placed him on probation. Roger himself acknowledged that by then his attitude toward the company was "antagonistic."

When he was offered early retirement, he felt like he was being forced out, despite having helped Philip Morris save $300 million. Around that time, another Philip Morris scientist, who'd worked in the biochemical department, where sensitive research on smoking and health was conducted, left the company and then sued over contract violation. The gossip at the Richmond plant was that Philip Morris settled with him because it was afraid a trial might lead to the disclosure of confidential material. After Roger retired, still harboring a grudge against the company for what he felt was shabby treatment despite his brilliant scientific contributions, he decided he would file a similar suit, with the hope of reaching a similar settlement.

The complaint he filed claimed that in exchange for supporting the Philip Morris position during his testimony in the lawsuit against Brown & Williamson, Frank Resnik had promised him 1 percent of the benefits, royalties, and savings realized by Philip Morris each year from the DIET patent. In an act of "bad faith," Roger alleged, Philip Morris reneged on the agreement and instead "embarked on an intentional and malicious course of conduct to deceive, harass, persecute, and otherwise inflict emotional injury on Dr. Burde . . ."

Philip Morris' only purpose for entering into the contract with Burde was to eliminate his resentment and obtain his full support and cooperation in assisting patent attorneys to prepare and to testify in the pending patent infringement litigation so that a favorable result could be obtained; neutralize Burde's antagonism toward Philip Morris; satisfy Burde's concerns relating to future employment; and restore Burde's confidence as an employee, thereby reducing his emotional distress so as to restore his confidence in Philip Morris and Resnik, its President. There was never any intention to carry out the terms of the contract because, when Burde's involvement in the trial was completed Philip Morris resumed and continued its harassment and infliction of emotional injury upon Burde to bring about his early retirement, and refused to make the yearly payments under contract.

Roger asked for $12.5 million in losses and damages. Shortly after filing the complaint, his lawyer followed up with a letter to Philip Morris's counsel suggesting a compromise and warning that to pursue litigation could lead to the release of damaging confidential information Roger possessed about Philip Morris's research. But the lawsuit was a gross miscalculation. Unlike the other scientist with whom Philip Morris had reportedly settled, Burde was not working in a particularly sensitive area of research. The company's executives felt that the lawsuit, particularly when coupled with the letter, was a flagrant attempt at extortion. Rather than allow itself to be blackmailed and thus encourage similar suits, the company decided to make an example out of Dr. Burde.

In their response to his complaint, the Philip Morris attorneys denied the allegation that Resnik had tried to bribe Roger and pointed out that to do so would be illegal. They also noted that it was illegal to accept compensation in exchange for favorable testimony in a lawsuit, and therefore even if there had been an agreement between Roger and Resnik, it could not be enforced in a court of law. "Burde's claim for additional compensation in excess of the statutory witness fee is a malicious, unlawful attempt to extort money from Philip Morris," the attorneys wrote. By law, they said, Roger should be required, as a penalty, to pay Philip Morris four times the amount of money he tried to demand from the company—$50.4 million.

———

The legal hostilities created immediate problems for Beverly. Her supervisor at the time, Art Palmer, called her in and asked her what she knew about Roger's lawsuit. "Very little," she said. "I tried to talk him out of it. I couldn't. I don't think it makes sense. I don't like it any more than you do. But I have no part in it and I don't want any part in it." Art said he understood. But the company's management had to wonder where her true loyalty lay, with Philip Morris or with Burde. Beverly felt, with justification, that her position there was in jeopardy, and she became even more diligent and industrious than before.

During the next couple of years, however, she did not receive the routine promotions and salary increases typical for an employee at her level. When Art Palmer, a cigar smoker, died of cancer, his replacement as head of the patent department, Jim Schardt, told her, "Beverly, as long as you're with Roger, they're going to view you as a threat. You're not going to get anywhere in this company."

Schardt himself wanted to promote Beverly. The resistance came from above. The company lacked grounds for firing her. But it wasn't going to reward her for consorting with a man who, management felt, was trying to extort money from it. Roger told Beverly that if she lost her job because of his lawsuit, he would take care of her financially. But Beverly didn't want someone taking care of her. And unlike Roger, she genuinely enjoyed working for Philip Morris. It was a good company, with generous benefits, and while Beverly herself didn't smoke, she thought that people had the right to if they so chose.

———

Roger had hoped that Philip Morris would simply pay him some middling figure to settle the suit and be done with it. When he was summoned to Washington to talk with attorneys representing the company, he thought negotiations were going to commence. But he returned from the meeting terrified. He told Beverly that the attorneys had sent an investigator to Poland. The investigator had found that Roger's title of count was fraudulent. Roger was afraid that Philip Morris had set out to destroy him by whatever means possible. To protect himself, he bought the Smith & Wesson revolver. He also became convinced that his phone was being tapped, and he hired a local private investigator, Cecil Glunt, to check the lines. Beverly thought he was becoming paranoid.

Burde's fears of persecution heightened the eerie quality Windsor had always had. Shannon hated to go in the house; all those African carvings, especially at night, scared her. One friend of Burde's, a Polish woman named Joanna, had become convinced that a particularly grotesque statue, its smoke-darkened wood covered with hair and bones and dried berries, had brought a curse on Windsor. When, during a thunderstorm in the summer of 1989, a large oak crashed to the ground near the house, she refused to go back inside until Roger removed the offending piece.

At the same time, disturbing incidents occurred around the farm. Wild dogs began coming out of the woods to attack calves. Roger killed one with a rifle and the body remained in the pasture until Beverly buried it. The calves belonged to a tenant farmer, who paid Roger to keep his cattle in Windsor's pastures and also maintained the fences and barn. He was a cheerful young man, with a ponytail and a little son he brought with him when he came over to inspect his herd. Then one fall morning a SWAT team of U.S. marshals, wearing bulletproof vests and carrying automatic weapons, descended on Windsor and arrested him. Roger was working in his study when they arrived. The tenant farmer, they told Roger, was a large-scale drug dealer who had murdered his first wife. Confining Roger to the house, the agents searched the farm and seized all of the man's property. In the process, they took off the gates enclosing the pasture, allowing the cattle to wander into the woods.

Roger was alarmed that his tenant farmer was a drug dealer, but he was furious at the peremptory behavior of the marshals. It made him feel, he told them, as if he were back in Communist Poland. He watched with unconcealed rage when the marshals came back a few days later and impounded the man's cattle. But Roger also wondered what the tenant farmer and his friends, who'd come and gone on the farm as they wished, might have hidden there, and whether the friends would return to retrieve buried money or drugs. There were, he told Beverly, all sorts of people who could have reason to harm him.

———

Roger had always had such feelings. Listening to him talk about his childhood, Beverly had come to understand why. Life during the German occupation and then under the Communists had made him fearful and devious. Both systems were corrupt and brutal, intent on destroying him or at least crushing his spirit, and to survive, he'd had to learn to beat them, day after day. It became an instinct, one that remained with him after he came to the United States. He preferred cheating to honesty—even on the most minor occasions and even if honesty was easier. When he and Beverly and a Polish friend went to a Gauguin exhibit in Washington, he and the friend refused to buy tickets, sneaking in with a tour group instead. They thought this was a great accomplishment, far more important than seeing the paintings. They had an ingrained instinct, Beverly thought, to thwart authority and outfox the system.

Frank Vegas was another friend Roger enlisted in his escapades. Vegas was a tall, strapping man with shoulder-length blond hair, a handlebar mustache, and a gold tooth. Beverly thought he looked like a Viking. He worked as a stonemason but fantasized about becoming a sculptor. He knew he had the talent, but he'd never been able to get in touch with it until he met Roger. Roger directed him toward his talent, critiquing his work and promoting it among executives at Philip Morris, to whom Frank sold several pieces. Frank felt Roger had changed him so completely that without Roger he wouldn't be who he was.

Of course, Roger involved Frank in some crazy schemes. He suggested that Frank court a wealthy elderly woman Roger knew, with the idea of inheriting her money when she died. The woman was an alcoholic and had a vicious tongue and she was also fat, but she belonged to the Country Club of Virginia and thought of herself as a patron of the arts. She liked Frank's work, and sponsored it. He romanced her and for a time even moved into her house in west Richmond. Then Roger suggested Frank hide the digitalis the woman took for her heart condition. It was hard a lot of the time to tell when Roger was kidding. On this matter, Frank took him seriously. He thought about it, but morally he could not do it. It was not in his character.

From time to time Roger brought Frank photographs of, and precise measurements for, sculptures he wanted Frank to copy. He told the sculptor that the exercises would help him sharpen his talent. For years, the pieces sat outside the house at Windsor. Scoured by the weather, their stone began to age. Roger told visitors they were by two renowned modern sculptors, Fritz Wotruba and Andre Volten.

It was one thing to make an offhand claim about a work to a guest, another thing entirely to vouch for its authenticity in a financial transaction. But in 1989, faced with a cash shortage and a large tax bill, Roger realized he could enhance his reputation as a collector and reduce his taxes by making a donation to Radford University, which his daughter Corinna had attended. The university, in southwestern Virginia, agreed to create the Corinna de la Burde Sculpture Garden on the campus in exchange for seventy-two contemporary and African pieces.

Roger came to Frank with the specifications for a copy of another Wotruba. Frank had no reservations about copying the work of other artists to develop his technique, but he wasn't going to pass these off as originals. In fact, he carved his initials in the base of this new sculpture and videotaped himself making it. Roger didn't mind the initials—he thought of them as a private joke—but when he heard about the videotape, he told Frank to destroy it.

Beverly had gotten some inkling about the arrangement with Radford but didn't know exactly what Roger had in mind. When she saw a university catalog, published to celebrate the new acquisitions, she became worried. It contained a photograph of a sculpture by Wotruba that looked new. She'd seen real Wotrubas and they didn't weather well; they aged quickly. She pointed this out to Roger. He became irritated and told her he'd had it in storage.

The catalog also had pictures of some of the sculptures at Windsor, including two that Frank had done for Roger. Roger had attributed them to Wotruba and Etienne-Martin. Another piece, attributed to Andre Volten, consisted of some shards of slate stuck into cement. It was actually created by the son of one of Roger's neighbors, who had been playing at Windsor with leftover construction material. There wasn't any point to this deception. It was more in the nature of a joke. Frank Vegas had long ago accepted the fact that Roger just could not resist the temptation to put one over on someone.

———

Coincident with the opening of the sculpture garden, Roger also provided an elaborate account of his aristocratic lineage to *Radford Magazine*. "We come from a long line of scholars, royal notaries, and protectors of the royal seal," he told the interviewer. "Guillaume de la Burde I, who was overseer of the tradesmen in fourteenth-century Paris, was elevated to a post as ambassador of François I to Pope Leo X. He was admitted to the Chamber of the Counts in 1340. His son, Jean I, was a secretary to King Charles VI, the controller of the Chancery and a member of the Order of Malta. The important role of the family . . . lasted until the French Revolution."

During the Napoleonic Wars, he continued, the Burdes moved to Kraków. His father, Rudolph, was a lawyer and the "owner of major textile enterprises." After World War II, he said, the Communists seized the family's property. "We lost our palatial home. We literally had to sell our family jewels in order to live in a small two-room apartment in the city."

He began a political career, he claimed, and was elected vice-mayor of Kraków at the age of twenty-five, then, during a trip to East Berlin, escaped into the West. "I was picked up by the Americans, CIA and FBI, who tried to recruit me to return to Poland as their agent," he went on. "I refused to take on such an assignment. They threatened to put me on a plane and dump me by parachute into Poland. I said, 'If you do this against my will, I will go directly to the radio station and cite my treatment as a bad example of how Americans treat their refugees from Communism.' This seemed to persuade them and they left me alone."

When Beverly read the interview she almost became ill. Roger had told her about what had happened to him in 1976, when he published an article about his collection in *African Art* magazine. Susan Vogel, a curator at the Metropolitan Museum, in New York, had recognized some of the accompanying photographs as pieces taken from Nigeria in the 1960s. She'd confronted Roger, and at her insistence, he'd published a follow-up letter in the magazine advising scholars to treat his collection "with caution and with substantive independent research." Beverly now feared a replay of that scandal. After his death, when she learned from another article in the *Times-Dispatch* that many things Roger had told the interviewer were easily demonstrable falsehoods—François I had been king of France in the sixteenth, not the fourteenth, century; Charles VI had preceded him on the throne by 135 years; there was no record of Roger serving as vice-mayor of Kraków—she began to suspect that Roger was already becoming delusional in 1989, alternating between paranoia and grandiosity.

At the time, however, Roger's gift seemed a stroke of inspiration. In fact, it had been so easy to pass off Frank Vegas's copies as original works that in 1991, a year after the university sculpture garden opened and a year before he died, Roger invited Frank to Windsor to discuss a proposition.

Roger's money problems were getting worse. Frank had similar worries.

After passing up the opportunity to marry the art patron with the bad heart, he had married a younger woman and they now had three children. But his wife was in school full-time and they were struggling with their bills. Roger suggested that Frank move his family into the cottage at Windsor. He could live there rent-free, Roger said, and Roger would pay him $30,000 for a year if he would devote himself full-time to producing fakes.

Roger said he had lined up a buyer in New York City who could sell them in Europe for $50,000 to $75,000 apiece, a fee he proposed to split equally with Frank. It would be hard work—seven days a week for twelve months—but he had a standing order from the buyer for ten sculptures. He showed Frank some photographs of sculptures and a handwritten list.

FIRST CHOICES

1. Henri Gaudier-Brzeska
2. ~~Jacob Epstein~~ Andre Dernier
3. Zuniga
4. Max Bill
5. Wander Bertoni

Frank recognized the names. Francisco Zuniga was a renowned Costa Rican artist, whose pieces brought in a lot of money. Epstein was an English sculptor with work in the Hirshhorn. Bertoni, Bill—he'd seen their work in the big German-language art book Roger had encouraged him to study. Frank thought about the proposition. His share of the proceeds—at least $250,000, more money than he had ever had in his life—would solve a lot of his problems. But he couldn't help feeling that it would also create even bigger problems. He decided that forgery, like hiding the art patron's digitalis, was not in his nature. He told Roger that though he loved him like a brother, he'd pass.

3

That same summer, 1991, Roger's other preoccupation—his increasingly irresistible and tormenting desire for a son—overshadowed even his money worries. The fixation had first surfaced two years earlier. Alone at Windsor, having driven his wife away, having completely alienated one daughter and feeling disappointed in the other, he began thinking about the child he felt he deserved. He had acquired an estate and created an art collection that together formed a considerable legacy, he believed. But he had failed to father a child worthy of inheriting it.

He deserved a son, he decided, a young man who would assume and pass on the de la Burde name as well as the legacy. His friend Charlie Valentine had a talented son, little Charlie. Roger wanted a son like that. Or like Tomec Unrug, the handsome, athletic son of his friend Kot. Or like his nephew Sig Huber, a tennis player and premed student.

This missing son began to preoccupy Roger so much that he offered both Kot Unrug and his own sister, Monique Huber, several thousand dollars if they would change their sons' last names to de la Burde. When they refused—treating it as another one of Roger's jokes—he began thinking about hiring a surrogate mother to bear him a child, a "male heir." The more he thought about it—and the more he discussed it, with everyone from Beverly and her children to Frank Vegas and farm manager Joe Hairfield—the more appealing such a proposition became. It would be a straightforward financial transaction, work for hire, with none of the unpleasant complications or commitments of romance or marriage. It would also enable him to seek out a woman with the specific traits—looks, athletic ability, intelligence, breeding—he desired in a son.

———

In March 1989, while on a ski trip with Roger to Snowshoe, the resort in West Virginia where he owned a condo, Beverly overheard a couple speaking in Polish. She mentioned it to Roger, who struck up a conversation with them, and they all arranged to get together that evening for a drink in the ski lodge. Wojtek Drewnowska, an engineer at Hauni-Werke, which manufactured the machines that produced Philip Morris cigarettes, was in his early thirties, thin and mild-mannered. His wife, Krystyna, a biochemist at the Virginia College of Medicine, was five years older than her husband, blond, animated, and flirtatious. They enjoyed one another's company. When they returned to Richmond and Roger began inviting the younger couple out to Windsor, Wojtek felt as if he'd discovered a rich uncle.

Krystyna was taken with the farm. At Roger's invitation, she brought her sixteen-year-old daughter, Magda, out to ride the horses. She was also attracted to Roger himself, and he reciprocated the affection. That summer, while traveling alone in Europe, he wrote her from the French city of Dijon.

> Dear Krystyna,
>
> It's really hard to write about love when you have a full stomach. . . . It's very difficult because I have such a mess in my head. . . . I miss you very much. . . . Thank you so much from the depth of my heart for your feelings, for your thoughts. . . . I see you all the time in front of my eyes, ten times a day. Something is moving in my heart, which is empty at night. . . . I kiss you, both eyes, and I kiss your nose.
>
> > Bye, my love,
> > Roger.

Both Wojtek and Beverly became suspicious of the relationship between Krystyna and Roger. The following March, a year after they'd met, they all took another ski vacation, along with a Richmond ski club, to Sun Valley. Roger and Krystyna spent so much time together that it became a subject of gossip. One night, while Roger and Beverly were in their room dressing for dinner, Wojtek knocked on the door and demanded to speak to Roger. Beverly had just come out of the shower and was in her bathrobe. Wojtek warned Roger to stay away from Krystyna and from his family. Roger denied any impropriety, but in such an offhand manner that Wojtek felt his intelligence was insulted.

Wojtek told Beverly he was sorry. He had made a point of confronting Roger in front of her because he wanted her to be aware of the situation.

Beverly said it was fine. She thought it courageous of Wojtek, who was usually soft-spoken, to take a stand like this, and was glad he had brought the matter out in the open.

"Did you really hear what he had to say?" she asked Roger once Wojtek left. "Did you really hear him?"

Roger sat on the bed in silence, as if he had heard neither Wojtek nor Beverly.

———

Wojtek's concerns were hardly eased by the encounter with Roger. Back in Richmond, he searched his wife's belongings and found the letter Roger had written her from Dijon. It seemed undeniable proof that Krystyna was conducting an affair. When he confronted her with the letter, she admitted she was involved with Roger. It was a serious affair, she said, so serious that she wasn't certain whether she wanted to leave Wojtek for Roger or stay in the marriage. Wojtek decided that they should separate immediately. Since they lacked the funds to support two households, he moved his belongings into the first floor of their house on Mountview Crescent and left Krystyna the second story.

Wojtek also called Beverly. "There is something you need to know that I know," he told her.

"I know more than you think," Beverly said. She thought Wojtek was a nice man who didn't want to see her hurt. He was worried about his children, Magda and Bartek. He also really cared for Krystyna and didn't want her to leave him. Krystyna was truly caught in all of this, too, as Beverly saw it. But there was nothing Beverly could do to change that. It was, she thought, an awkward, stupid situation.

"I don't see much point in talking about this unless we can resolve something," she told Wojtek, "and I don't know that we can. We have no control over it. I'll make up my mind what I want to do and how I want to deal with it."

One way she dealt with it was to vent her frustrations in the bitter letter to Roger that Krystyna later found, copied, and turned over to the police.

————

Roger had told Krystyna, as he had most everyone, about his desire for a male heir. Krystyna decided in 1990 that she wanted to be the one to bear him a child. While still living on the second floor of the house she shared with Wojtek, she stopped taking birth control pills and, on periodic visits to Windsor, tried to conceive.

Initially, success eluded them. In February 1991, she and Roger visited Dr. Michael Edelstein at the Richmond Center for Fertility and Endocrinology. The doctor, who was under the impression that they were married, examined Krystyna. She seemed normal. He noted Roger's history of low motility from a previous semen analysis and the couple's infrequency of intercourse. He suggested they increase the frequency for a couple of months before proceeding with a complete fertility evaluation.

Krystyna began to worry about supporting a child if she did conceive. To clarify matters, she wrote up, by hand, on sheets of lined paper, an agreement spelling out Roger's relationship with her and how the child was to be provided for.

AGREEMENT

1. K. Drewnowska and R. de la Burde wish to have children, and assume joint responsibility for their appropriation, upkeep, and education.

2. Burde will contribute $600/month to an age of 0–10 years, and $1,000 a month for years 11–18, payable monthly at the residence of K. Drewnowska as long as her residence is not more than 30 miles from the capitol building in Richmond. . . .

3. Child/children will carry de la Burde name. This name cannot be changed until maturity or marriage.

4. D. and B. may wish [to] cohabit together, and may call themselves in writing or verbally a wife and husband. None of these acts . . . will be interpreted as being an act of marriage. If they do decide to enter into the marriage, this would be done by an execution of prenuptial agreement. . . .

5. In case of cohabitation/marriage and common children, B. obliges himself to provide house, food, and education for child/children and mother. . . .

6. D. obliges herself to help care and cater to R.B. in his advancing age.

Roger avoided signing the agreement. The document, he told Krystyna, was a work in progress and needed to be refined.

In May, the couple returned to see Dr. Edelstein. He reviewed Krystyna's temperature charts and again urged them to increase the frequency of intercourse. Roger at this point confessed that the real reason they had come to see him was for advice on sex selection. He wanted a male heir, he told Edelstein. The doctor didn't have a very high opinion of sex selection. He considered the techniques, having to do with variables like sexual position and the time of intercourse during the woman's menstrual cycle, unsuccessful and undocumented. Nonetheless, he recommended two experts the couple might want to contact.

———

Roger continued to insist to Beverly that Krystyna was merely a friend with whom he enjoyed a certain Polish camaraderie. He told Beverly *she* was the only woman who truly mattered. To demonstrate his commitment, he had spent $155,000 to purchase a wooded lot—which he put exclusively in her name—in Kanawha, the most prestigious residential neighborhood in Richmond. The city's legendary federal judge Robert Merhige lived across the street. Next door was Bobby Freeman, the president of Signet Bank. Roger and Beverly spent night after night drawing plans for the house—the dream house, grand in scale, Roger said, with upwards of 11,000 square feet, that they intended to build.

Roger admitted to Beverly that Krystyna had agreed to bear him a child, but she was nothing more than a surrogate mother, he said. The child would be conceived by artificial insemination. He showed Beverly a copy of the "baby agreement." In its dry details, it did seem to suggest a legal arrangement rather than a passionate affair. Since Krystyna had so far failed to conceive, Roger began thinking of other women who could carry the child, and even talked to one of his housekeepers about reversing a tubal ligation in order to serve as the surrogate mother.

Beverly thought the whole thing was insane. Knowing Roger and his temperament, it didn't make any sense at all. He was fifty-nine years old. He had little patience with children. He already had three grown daughters for whom he showed little affection. Why would he want to complicate his life with another child? Still, as Roger's determination hardened, Beverly decided she would be better off trying to facilitate his desire rather than obstruct it. She told him that if he was serious, they had to hire professional counselors, and that he and she and the surrogate mother all had to prepare for what would be an emotionally complex, and potentially fraught, transaction.

Katie also heard of Roger's plans. At first she thought it was just Roger being Roger. At some point it hit her that Roger was serious and that her mom was entertaining it as well. "Oh good grief, Burde!" she told him. "How could you? You suck as a dad. You're going to have another child that you're going to neglect and treat like crap and it's going to end up being as alienated as Colette and Corinna."

"Maybe you're right," Roger said.

Katie was also worried about a legal entanglement with the surrogate mother. She had just started working as a law clerk. One case before Judge Bernard Barrow involved a "Baby Doe." A surrogate mother had changed her mind about turning over the baby to the adoptive parents, who had already taken it and put their names on its birth certificate, and she wanted it back. It was a mess. The child was two years old and the court case was still going on, both parties arguing that Baby Doe rightfully belonged to them.

"Burde, if you're going to do this, let's keep it in the family," she told Roger. Katie ended up offering to have one of her own eggs clinically fertilized by Roger and then implanted in her mother. Roger latched on to that idea, and her mom started looking for clinics. If that was what they wanted, Katie thought she could do it. What the hell, she was game. An egg meant nothing to her. It was better than having Roger use a surrogate mother.

———

Krystyna thought of herself not as a surrogate mother but as Roger de la Burde's lover. In the summer of 1991, she decided to take an apartment for six months and wait for her future to come into focus. She might end up living with or marrying Roger if he left Beverly, who had a suffocating effect on him, Krystyna felt. Depending on his decision, she might end up alone. If that happened, she was thinking of returning to Europe now that her two children had graduated from high school. She was afraid of pressuring Roger—he had at times let her know that she was intruding in his life—but she felt entitled to some sort of clarity about their relationship. She wrote him a letter.

> Darling,
>
> I assure you in the first sentence, that this is one of the last, if not the last dissertation, I bring myself to write. The events or rather experiences of the last weeks, or maybe even days, forced me to put my thoughts on paper and share them with you. . . . I agree with you that since we spend so little time together we should not waste it on "heavy conversations." On the other hand, we both know well that it is time to make some binding decisions, laying out directions for the future. . . . I want to spend the future with you, offering you sincere and deep feelings, energy, willingness of collaboration in small as well as significant decisions and projects, devotion, loyalty, caring now and always, deep need to create a family together, as well as full support in rectifications of your shaky family relationships of long standing. . . .
>
> I would like to remind you also that if I ask you how did you spend an evening, for example, it is not because of my curiosity or an inclination of

"controlling" you, but only a need of participation in your life, sharing experiences, even those seemingly banal. . . . Be assured that I would not bother you, calling for example at night. What a pity, because it was a nice accent before sleep, when I feel really lonely but in my thoughts so close to you. [Un]fortunately "my thoughts" could not be switched off by hanging up (and now tears are falling from my left and right eyes).

Returning to the "decision." [W]hat I hear from you regarding the "future" would be the absolute priority for me. My dream is always to have children, children together with you, and to have a normal home and family life . . . I believe that, helping each other, we might be able to have it all.

I suffer very much, seeing you unhappy, being a witness of your impersonation into two so different personalities. "THERE"—intimidated, submissive, without your own opinion and freedom of thinking and acting. "WITH ME"—fighting, demanding, ambitious, but also charming, full of warmth, goodwill, and feelings, and . . . handsome! I love you very much in "my personality"! Time is running, life is passing in constant struggle and uncertainty. Let us be fair to ourselves and for others—this decisive step should be made (always better forward!).

I kiss you, always yours

Krystyna felt she had made it clear that Roger would have to choose between herself and Beverly. In an addendum to the still-unsigned baby agreement, she had written that she would "not accept any compromise/solution to the relationship of Roger and Mrs. Monroe."

4

Beverly, thinking Wojtek was entitled to know what Krystyna and Roger had in mind, gave him a copy of the baby agreement. To Wojtek, this represented the final outrage. His fellow expatriate had seduced his wife, stolen her affections, and was now arranging for her to bear him a child. In the summer of 1991, after Krystyna had moved into her own apartment, Wojtek decided to take action. The previous fall, Roger had sent Krystyna to New York to trade African carvings for contemporary paintings. Wojtek had been at Windsor with Roger when Krystyna called about a deal that had gone awry, angering a New York gallery owner who felt misled about the value of the pieces. Roger was extremely upset. As best as Wojtek could make out, Krystyna herself didn't know the pieces weren't legitimate; she knew nothing about art and had simply been following Roger's instructions.

So Wojtek called the state police. He told Colonel Carl Baker that Roger had been trying to pass off worthless African sculptures as valuable art. Since the activity apparently involved interstate transportation, Colonel Baker referred the matter to the FBI. An agent in Washington called Wojtek and promised to look into it. The agent directed Wojtek not to mention the investigation to Beverly; he was afraid she would tip off Roger. Wojtek agreed, and left the matter at that. He had done what he could to hurt the man he had initially regarded as an uncle.

———

That summer, around the time Frank Vegas rejected Roger's offer to go into business copying sculptures, Roger told Chuck Collins, a Powhatan County carpenter who did odd jobs for him, that he had a project he wanted Chuck to undertake. He showed Chuck some paintings and asked him to construct copies of the wooden frames. Some had odd shapes, but it was easy work. From time to time that year, an artist whose name Chuck didn't know appeared at Windsor. Chuck suspected that the artist was stretching canvas over the duplicated frames and then copying the original painting, but he never inquired about it. He didn't want to know.

———

Chuck's wife, Barb Collins, also worked for Roger, as an occasional housekeeper. Roger liked Barb. He called her late at night, which made Chuck jealous, and had even suggested that she move in with him, since he knew she and Chuck were having problems. He once told her that if they had a child together, it would be a great child. Barb thought something was loose in her brains when she heard that. Roger was also teaching her about art and to play the piano so that she could fit into his circle of bankers and other people at the parties he gave.

That summer, she saw him putting new paintings up on the roof of the house. He left them there for months at a time, rain or shine, to age them. Sometimes he buried them in leaves to make them moldy. Roger had told Barb not to go down into the basement, but her intuition, which was powerful—one of the reasons Roger wanted her to bear him a child was so it would have her powerful intuition—urged her to go anyway, and so she did. The place smelled of turpentine. Paint had been poured down the drain in the sink. Barb knew Roger was up to something. She considered him a great con artist.

———

One Saturday morning late in the summer, when Beverly was out at Windsor, Roger showed her some paintings lined up against the baseboard of the dining room wall. There were Lowell Nesbitts, a Ray Parker—supposedly. They didn't look right. They looked new. Roger said a friend had brought them from Poland. "Roger, get rid of these things," Beverly said. But he didn't, and they ended up floating around in his collection.

In September, *Style Weekly,* Richmond's alternative newspaper, published a cover story entitled "Just Who *Is* Roger de la Burde? Art Collector? Polish Count? Chemist or Alchemist?" In the photograph on the cover, Roger stared with glowering intensity into the camera. Despite the questions raised in the cover lines, the article's two co-authors accepted Burde's account of his life at face value. They also called him "one of a handful of serious collectors in the state." They compared him to Joseph Hirshhorn and cited his philanthropic gifts. They quoted his statements on contemporary paintings ("Not all contemporary art is good. Most is bad. That is the danger and challenge to the collector"); on art galleries ("They hold the buyer's hand. We don't need that"); and on existential freedom ("I believe you mold your own personal environment. That is what success is based upon. Most people are blinded by the routines of life; they never reach out to learn new experiences; they never go out and explore").

Roger, who was then being considered for membership in the Country Club of Virginia, loved the article. He made dozens of photocopies, combined them with copies of other articles that mentioned his collection, and insisted to Beverly that they drive around the streets near the country club late one night and slip the packets into mailboxes. Beverly thought the surreptitious publicity campaign would backfire. "This is old Virginia," she said. "You're really going to make them resent you." But Roger wouldn't listen, so she decided to treat the expedition as a lark.

In November, shortly after Roger received a letter from the country club rejecting his application—he had, a couple of years earlier, sued someone who turned out to be on the membership committee—he picked up a rumor of the FBI's inquiry into his art dealings. He called Beverly. He was in a panic like she'd never seen. He could barely talk coherently. He said something had gotten out about the suspiciously new paintings he had shown her. He needed a story that would account for them. He came up with the explanation that he'd made copies of paintings he already had to use in school exhibits, because he didn't want to exhibit the real paintings. Roger was afraid the FBI was going to call him in for questioning, but nothing happened, and after a couple of weeks it blew over.

———

Roger had a number of stress-related ailments that fall. He suffered from hypertension and esophageal reflex, the regurgitation of stomach acid. He had trouble voiding urine and was occasionally incontinent. He was so concerned that he had seen his internist, Dr. Bryan Wassermann, twice in six weeks. He was taking Maxzide, Kerlene, and Hytrin for high blood pressure and he often complained to Beverly about chest pains. His energy had dissipated. When he arrived for dinner at Beverly's house, he frequently went straight to the living room couch and lay down. He would ask Beverly to stroke his head; sometimes his face seemed so hot that it was boiling. She would check his blood pressure with a monitor she kept in the kitchen.

Roger was also bleeding periodically from his penis. The blood stained his underwear, and from time to time Beverly had to wash it while he was at her house. Roger's father had died of prostate cancer. He was afraid he might suffer the same fate, and this added to his worries, as did his inability to perform in bed. He would explain that he was tired, but Beverly could see that his failure bothered him tremendously.

Taken together, his symptoms reminded her of her father's symptoms before he killed himself. She had called Corinna every couple of weeks since Memorial Day to express her concern. Roger was becoming irrational, Beverly told her. He had feelings of hopelessness and despair. He would become distracted and forget what he had told her the day before. In January, Beverly told Corinna she was afraid that, like her father, Roger might kill himself.

"Beverly, that's crazy," Corinna replied. She saw her father only once a month or so, but he didn't strike Corinna as suicidal. He seemed to her to be the same controlling, moody, hyper person he had always been.

5

In December 1991, Krystyna was living by herself in an apartment. Three months earlier, Wojtek had filed a cross-bill for divorce, alleging that she had "willfully deserted" him and their children. Roger had still not made the decision she had hoped he would make about their future together. They had, however, continued to try to conceive a child, and that month Krystyna learned she was pregnant. The news, after a year and a half without success, took both of them by surprise. Since their relationship was so unresolved, neither of them was happy at first. The whole situation, Krystyna thought, was extremely messy.

—

After the New Year, Krystyna decided it was time to tell Corinna about the baby and asked her to lunch. Corinna had only met Krystyna a few times, but the woman didn't thrill her. She'd told Gavin she thought Krystyna was a phony. Still, Corinna agreed to meet. Over lunch, Krystyna talked generally about the plans for the baby. She wanted to know how Corinna felt about the development and whether she would accept a new half brother or half sister.

The idea of the baby frankly didn't thrill Corinna, either. She thought her father was too old to have another child. She was also afraid a baby would hurt Roger's relationship with Beverly. Corinna respected and trusted Beverly, who had a calming effect on her father. Krystyna had only come up rarely and briefly in conversation—it was as if the subject was to be avoided—and when she did, Beverly referred to Krystyna, rather dryly, as "the distraction." To be honest, Corinna had always been a little scared, the few times she was alone with Krystyna, that Beverly would walk in and think Corinna was on Krystyna's side.

On the other hand, the idea of a child had been on her father's mind for some time now. He wanted a male heir, who, unlike either her or her sister, would care about real estate and art and finance and social position. And regardless of what Corinna thought, it was her father's life, not hers.

—

Roger told his farm manager, Joe Hairfield, about Krystyna's pregnancy and how he hoped she would fulfill his desire for a male heir. Roger, carrying on about his male heir all the time, was beginning to sound to Joe like one of those olden-day English kings. As a way of pulling his boss's leg, he said, "What are you going to do if it's a girl, chop her head off?"

———

On January 12, a Sunday, Krystyna Drewnowska called the Chesterfield County Police Department to complain that someone was stalking her. Richard Reese, a patrolman, was sent to Krystyna's apartment. She told him that on several occasions a woman had been following her and loitering in the parking lot outside her apartment. She didn't give Patrolman Reese the woman's name, but she did have her license-plate number, HQP 741. When Reese ran the number, the computer reported that the car belonged to a Beverly A. Monroe on Old Gun Road West.

Around one o'clock, Patrolman Reese went to the address and introduced himself to Ms. Monroe, who invited him into the house. He told her of the nature of the complaint. She explained that she had known Krystyna Drewnowska for three years, that Krystyna had been to her house for dinner, and that they had even taken ski trips together. She said that she was seeing a gentleman and that Krystyna Drewnowska had become interested in the gentleman. Patrolman Reese understood. He thanked Ms. Monroe and left. No laws had been broken. There was nothing to investigate, no charges to bring. Back at headquarters, writing up his report, he categorized the incident as a "domestic-type situation."

———

In addition to his anxieties about an FBI inquiry into his art trades and his mixed feelings about Krystyna's pregnancy, Roger continued worrying about money. He had a balloon payment of $250,000 coming due on a large piece of raw land he hoped to sell to an industrial developer. He didn't have nearly that much cash available, and because of the slump in the real estate market, he could not liquidate any of his assets except at a large loss. He had actually put Windsor up for sale for $1 million, but no buyer had materialized. He tried to take out a loan from Signet Bank on the lot he and Beverly owned in Kanawha, but the bank turned him down.

Roger called his handyman Chuck Collins. He had loaned Chuck $5,000 and he wanted it back. Chuck said he thought Roger was rich. "Appearances aren't always what they seem," Roger told Chuck. "The farm requires running. There are horses in the field, the house looks great, but things are tight, and I need the money."

———

While hiding from Beverly the fact that Krystyna was pregnant, Roger continued to talk to her, she told her daughters and colleagues, about the possibility of the two of them getting married. They could sell Windsor, he said, and live in the house they would build on the Kanawha lot. Beverly had mixed feelings about that. She liked her independence and didn't believe Roger would be faithful. Also, Richard Thayer, the man with whom she had fallen in love while at the University of Florida, had contacted her a few years earlier. He was divorced and working in Texas in the oil industry, but he traveled to the East Coast on business, and Beverly had seen him a few times and even introduced him to Shannon, who thought he was great.

But Roger seemed so intent on their getting married that Beverly asked Jim Schardt how Philip Morris might react. It was a terrible idea, her boss said. Not only was Roger suing Philip Morris, but the suit involved the patent department. Jim reminded her that although he had never believed it possible, certain people at the company had always suspected her of stealing documents for Roger. They were still looking for an excuse to get rid of her. "Marry Roger de la Burde, and you'll seal your fate at this company," Jim said.

———

On February 14, Krystyna and Roger worked up yet another draft of the baby agreement, but it remained unsigned. Three days later, Krystyna took a test, recommended by her obstetrician for a woman her age, to determine if there were any chromosomal or biochemical abnormalities in the fetus. The test also determined the sex of the fetus. On February 27, a woman called from the office where Krystyna's doctor had sent her to have the genetic testing done. The results were in, the woman said, and everything was fine. She also asked if Krystyna wanted to know the sex of the baby.

"Yes," Krystyna said.

"It's a girl."

Krystyna decided not to tell Roger the news. She had received the information informally, over the telephone. Mistakes could happen. She decided she wanted to see the hard copy of the results and discuss them with her doctor. She did, however, call Roger to say the tests showed the fetus was normal.

———

Krystyna's thirty-ninth birthday was that Saturday. It was a special day for several reasons. She was pregnant, she had left her husband and was alone, and since she had been born on February 29, her true birthday came only once every four years. She had hoped Roger would celebrate it with her, but he told her he had a prior commitment that was impossible to break.

———

The masked ball took place that night. The next day, while Beverly was at Windsor helping him work on his book, she had gone into Roger's office and noticed a stack of papers on a shelf next to the computer. One sheet, typewritten, was sticking out from the pile. Beverly saw her own initials, written in Krystyna's distinctive Polish script, in the margin. She returned to the library and asked Roger about it. After some hesitation, he admitted that it was a revised version of the baby agreement and that Krystyna was pregnant. It was her idea, he said, and her fault.

"Wait a minute," Beverly said. "We both know that's not so." She pointed out that Roger had been talking about wanting a child for more than two years.

They sat down on the couch in the library, and Roger, with some difficulty, read the new baby agreement aloud to Beverly. Trying to remain practical, she asked Roger if he had shown it to an attorney.

"No," Roger said.

"You really should have somebody look at this document," Beverly told him.

They took a walk around the farm and talked about what they would do next. Roger asked Beverly not to leave him. She said she wouldn't. The unborn child, she pointed out, was a fact, and they would have to deal with it. She needed a little time, she went on, to think about how they could work it all out in some way that made sense.

———

The following afternoon, Connie Moslow, who lived next door to Roger at Oak Haven Farm, dropped by Windsor. She was collecting for the heart fund. Although she had only actually met Roger twice in the three years she and her husband had lived there, he greeted her warmly, invited her in, and offered her a cup of tea.

They talked for about an hour. Roger said it was a relief to have his book so close to completion. She told him about her five children, three of whom, after graduating from college, had gone to work for her husband. Roger seemed impressed with the family's cohesiveness. Before Connie left, he gave her $10. It was not the most generous contribution she'd ever received.

———

Barbara Samuels worked for Roger on Tuesdays and Thursdays. That Tuesday she arrived around nine o'clock. Roger described to her the ball and showed her the article and accompanying photograph in the *News Leader.* Studying the picture of himself, Roger said, "You know, I need a new tuxedo."

He asked her to look into prices. She called a few stores for quotes and relayed them to Roger. They were not cheap, and Samuels, who knew Roger was prone to save a nickel, mentioned that it was possible to buy a used tux from rental shops. Roger thought that sounded promising.

Later, she mentioned that she was going to Price Club after work. Roger said he needed an exercise bike to get into shape, and he asked her to price those as well.

———

Roger, who had seen Krystyna briefly on Monday night, went to her apartment for dinner on Tuesday. He arrived around six-thirty, bringing groceries with him. Krystyna cooked. After dinner, without telling Krystyna where he was going, he drove over to see Beverly. Avoiding any mention of where he had been, he complained about his heart and had her play her tape of Saint-Saëns's "The Swan" again and again. He told Beverly he was looking forward to their dinner at Windsor the following night. Then he drove home.

———

The next day, the department of human genetics at the Medical College of Virginia issued its final report on Krystyna's fetus, identifying the karyotype as XX, or female.

———

That afternoon, Hazel Bunch, who was Roger's occasional lover—one who made no demands—arrived for lunch at Windsor. They ate in the sunroom. Roger seemed in high spirits. He had solved all his problems, he said to Hazel. He had told Beverly about Krystyna and she had assured him that she would support whatever decision he made. He had decided he would marry neither Beverly nor Krystyna. But he would accompany Krystyna to Europe the next month so that she could introduce him as her husband and spare herself the shame of appearing to carry a fatherless child. When they returned, he planned to spend three or four nights a week with her. He wanted to help raise the child.

Hazel asked about the sex.

It's going to be a boy, he said.

As the lunch drew to a close, Roger asked Hazel to come back on Friday and bring a friend along. You don't have to do any talking, he said. I will do all the talking when you get here.

Hazel understood. The friend was to be someone whom Roger could persuade to go to bed with him.

———

At three o'clock that afternoon, Don Beville, Roger's publisher, received a call from Roger, who had an appointment to come to Byrd Press that afternoon and look at the most recent color plates. Roger suggested that they reschedule for the next day and have a late lunch afterward. He said he would bring a guest.

Roger also called Beville at home that night, between ten and ten-thirty. Beville, who was in training for the Boston marathon, had gone for a run, showered, and was watching the Democratic presidential primary debates on television with his son. Roger frequently called Beville at home, sometimes as late as two or three A.M. Beville endured these calls in the interests of client satisfaction. Roger could be impatient and unrealistic, in Beville's opinion. He thought tasks that took weeks could be accomplished immediately. He could also be suspicious, tightfisted, and easily angered. Just this past week he had written Beville a heated letter accusing him of overcharging for the color-systems work on the book's photographs. Some of Beville's colleagues had told him he should drop the project rather than endure Roger's abuse, but Beville was a patient man and had learned not to take the outbursts personally.

That night Roger's voice sounded peculiar—neither happy nor sad, just different—and their conversation was both brief and bizarre. "It's a new day," Roger said. He added that he was going to make some changes in his life. "The weight of the world is off my shoulders," he said.

Beville thought Roger's words were so odd that, to make sure he wasn't losing his own mind, he wrote them down—as he had done before when Roger had said something strange—on the first piece of paper he could find. It was the back of a Texaco receipt.

———

Sometime after hanging up the phone—possibly within minutes—Roger de la Burde died of a single gunshot wound to the forehead.

CHAPTER VI

Counsel

1

For the first two months after Roger's death, Katie Monroe had returned to Richmond almost every weekend. At times her mother seemed so grief-stricken, so inconsolable, that Katie worried for her sanity. Beverly frequently talked about her father's suicide, which she had never done before. Katie, who had grown up thinking her grandfather had died of brain cancer, realized that her mother was grieving for both men. But by May, Beverly had begun to recover her poise, and Katie, feeling less needed, stayed in Charlottesville on weekends. When Beverly called on June 3, after meeting with Dave Riley at Drewry's Bluff, Katie hadn't seen her mother in three weeks.

It was past five-thirty. Katie was alone in Judge Barrow's office, in the renovated old train station in Charlottesville, when the phone rang.

"Buggy?" her mother said, using her childhood nickname.

Right away, from the sound of her mother's voice, Katie became alarmed.

"Something terrible's happened," Beverly said. "They think I've done something terrible to Roger."

Katie almost had heart failure. Her mother hadn't said *murder.* She couldn't bring herself to use the word. But Katie knew exactly what she was talking about. Working for an appellate judge, she was aware that Roger's death might be viewed as a homicide. Or could even be a homicide. And if it were viewed as a homicide, her mom would be a natural suspect: She had motive, she was the last person to see Roger alive, and she was at the farm the next morning when the body was discovered.

Katie told her mother to drive up to Charlottesville. On the way back to her apartment, anticipating the need for fortification, Katie bought a large bottle of wine. When Beverly arrived and began describing the meeting that day at Drewry's Bluff, Katie, who knew nothing about any of her mother's conversations with Riley, flooded her with questions. What do you mean you're meeting with the police? Why were you meeting in a park?

For Katie to understand what had happened at Drewry's Bluff, Beverly had to explain her history with Riley. She ended up telling the entire story in reverse. When she got to the polygraph, Katie, for the first time in her life, wanted to punch her mother, actually hit her. It was a terrible feeling, but she did. She wanted to wring her neck. She couldn't believe her mother would be so dumb. "Why didn't you tell me what was going on?" Katie asked.

"You're an alarmist," Beverly said. "I knew if I told you I met with the police, you'd blow it into something that at the time I thought it wasn't. You would have done just what you're doing now."

Katie was so exasperated she wanted to scream. She knew that you never went to the police station to talk to the police. In the court of appeals, they regularly dealt with cases challenging the legality of police investigations. Katie knew the police asked you to come to the police station not to give background information but because they believed you were involved in the crime they were investigating. And even if you weren't involved, you didn't go to the police station without a lawyer, because the chances were so great that the police would accuse you of involvement. The police weren't *bad*—it was just that, in dealing with them, you had to know what you were doing. But her mom, for all her outward sophistication, had been raised in rural South Carolina. She'd been taught to defer to men, and to authority. She was brought up to believe that you could trust the police, that you could always turn to the police, that the police were your friends.

———

Katie called her boyfriend, Alan, who was a lawyer in Washington, D.C. Alan talked to some other lawyers and then called back to recommend Peter Greenspun, a criminal defense attorney in the Washington suburb of Fairfax. Katie reached Peter at home. He asked her to put Beverly on the phone for a confidential conversation. To give her mother privacy, Katie left the house and walked around and around the block. Her mother acted as if this were all just a misunderstanding that needed to be cleared up. Katie, however, had a feeling that it was going to require much more than simple clarification. The police seemed to have their minds made up. Her mother's situation was serious. If her mother didn't realize that yet, Katie did.

———

After work the next evening, Beverly and Katie drove up to Fairfax to meet with Peter Greenspun. The lawyer's office, in a brick town house, with a new Oriental rug on the floor, a leather sofa, and a fireplace that looked like it had never been used, was formal and businesslike. So was Greenspun himself, a crisp, prematurely balding man who often gave his clients the impression he was one step ahead of them.

As Greenspun listened to Beverly's story, her situation struck him, as it had Katie, as dire. Like Katie, he was appalled that Beverly had taken a polygraph and signed a confession without talking to a lawyer. His intuition told him that even if Beverly were willing to do so, the prosecutor would not let her plead down to manslaughter and a probationary sentence; there had been too much publicity, and the police both had too much at stake and seemed to think they had a strong case. A trial appeared inevitable, and Beverly Monroe was going to have to prove her innocence. Merely raising reasonable doubt wouldn't work.

Greenspun believed that in serious criminal cases, the presumption of innocence—the requirement that the commonwealth prove guilt beyond a reasonable doubt—was fairly dead in Virginia, anyway. Most juries accepted clear and convincing evidence, the standard in fraud cases, or even a preponderance of the evidence, the civil standard. Given that slipping standard—and given Beverly's statements to Riley—defending her would be an uphill battle.

Greenspun, who thought it was counterproductive and even dangerous to give a client false reassurance, told Beverly and Katie that there was a lot of work to be done, that they were going to have to do a great deal of it themselves, and that they had to get started immediately.

Katie liked Greenspun's aggressive and realistic attitude. At least in Greenspun her mother had someone who appreciated the true peril of the circumstances.

That night, Beverly wrote him a check for $10,000. It was after midnight when she and Katie set out for the two-hour drive back to Richmond.

———

The next day, concerned that the police might try to humiliate Beverly by arresting her at the office, handcuffing her in front of her colleagues, Greenspun called Jack Lewis, the commonwealth attorney. Lewis assured him that his client could relax—there was no irony in his use of the word—over the coming weekend. He would be presenting the evidence against Beverly to a grand jury on Tuesday. If an indictment was forthcoming from those proceedings, she could surrender voluntarily.

Back at work, Beverly talked to Jim Schardt about her situation. Powhatan, where the trial would take place, was a rural county, Schardt pointed out. Powhatan jurors might be ill-disposed toward an attorney from Washington. A local lawyer might fare better. Since she had a few days until her indictment, she might want to shop around before making Peter Greenspun her attorney of record. Schardt suggested she talk to Murray Janus, the most prominent criminal defense lawyer in Richmond. Aside from his impressive track record, he knew most every judge and prosecutor in central Virginia, and the value of his connections could not be overestimated.

———

Murray Janus had read the newspaper accounts of Roger de la Burde's death and was enormously intrigued by the mystery. It was Janus who had represented Burde back in the early 1970s, when the commonwealth charged Roger with felonious extortion—placing him in handcuffs at Philip Morris. Burde had given $3,000 to a young man to travel to Africa to purchase art, the young man had returned with neither the sculptures nor the money, and Burde had then made threats to the young man's girlfriend, which she caught on tape. The trial, however, was sort of a joke; the jury acquitted Burde after deliberating for only fifteen minutes.

Afterward, Burde had invited Janus to Windsor, showed him the art collection and the property, and regaled him with grandiose stories about the Burde lineage. Janus liked Burde—he was different, interesting, theatrical—but he didn't take him too seriously. He had turned down

Burde's request to represent him in the lawsuit against Philip Morris, since the facts involved arcane patent matters that lay beyond his expertise, and they had not talked since. Three weeks after Burde died, however, Brigitte had called Janus to ask if he could help her find out about the progress of the investigation. Janus had tried, but was able to learn nothing. Bringing the matter full circle, Janus now heard from Beverly Monroe, who wanted to confer with him.

Janus had hooded eyes and silver-streaked hair that he combed forward across his brow. He was soft-spoken and formal, addressing men as "sir" and women as "ma'am." The partners of his firm, Bremner, Baber & Janus, had included Robert Merhige, the federal judge who integrated Richmond's schools, and Leith Bremner. Bremner was possibly the greatest criminal defense lawyer in the history of Virginia, in Janus's view—a man who had tried more than three hundred capital cases without once having a client sent to the electric chair and who, curiously enough, had owned Windsor back in the fifties. Merhige was retired and Bremner was dead, and Murray Janus was now the firm's senior partner. In his nearly thirty years of practice, his clients had ranged from car thieves and petty drug dealers to Allied Chemical and Philip Morris. The rich, the poor, the guilty, the innocent, geniuses, fools—he'd defended them all.

Beverly appeared at the offices of Bremner, Baber & Janus, on the top floor of a Franklin Street tower overlooking the state capitol, on Friday afternoon. Janus ushered her into the conference room. He'd decided to avoid mentioning his prior association with the Burde family; it might just confuse things. While Beverly talked, he studied her. She was an appealing person, he thought, well-bred, pretty, demure. Her clothes were tastefully subdued. She would make a good witness.

Janus had a hard time thinking that the woman sitting across from him was capable of murder. On the other hand, he was well aware that all he had heard so far was her side of the story. Like most criminal defense attorneys, his practice was to have a preliminary meeting with the client, listen sympathetically to the protestation of innocence, and then go talk to the prosecutor. If the prosecutor said he had a videotape of the crime being committed, Janus would know what he was dealing with.

He told Beverly he would take the case for $150,000, and would need $50,00 up front. Beverly asked for the weekend to decide.

——

Katie, meanwhile, had been soliciting opinions from the members of the appellate court. She asked Judge Benton, Judge Moon, and her own boss, Judge Barrow, how they rated Janus and Peter Greenspun. No one had anything critical to say about either attorney. "Both are great," Judge Barrow told her, "but I have to say, if it was my mother, I'd want her in the hands of Murray Janus."

That weekend, Katie conveyed the judge's views to Beverly, who was already inclining toward Janus. Katie, however, wanted to see Janus herself before her mother made a final decision, and on Sunday she drove out to the lawyer's house in west Richmond. Their meeting was cordial. Katie described the detailed reconstructions and the witness lists that the family, at Peter Greenspun's request, had begun to compile. She told Janus she was a lawyer and had friends who were lawyers and that they were all eager to do whatever they could—research case history, gather exhibits, interview witnesses—to help clear her mother's name. Janus's reaction to this offer was pleasant but noncommittal. At the end of the meeting, he reached over and patted her hand. "Don't worry," he said. "I'll get your mother out of this."

Driving home, Katie felt vaguely disappointed. While Janus had been courteous and hospitable, he had failed to convey any sense of urgency, as Peter Greenspun had. He had come across, instead, as slightly complacent. He also seemed clearly if politely uninterested in her offer of help and had probably been put off by its presumption.

"He didn't move me," Katie told her mother the next day. "He's a nice guy, I'm sure he's a great attorney, but he didn't do a thing for me."

But Beverly had made up her mind. She called Peter Greenspun. She had decided, she said, to go with someone who had a little more gray in his hair. Greenspun was disappointed. He thought the case, while a tragedy of course for the Monroe family, contained fascinating legal issues and, given the element of mystery, the potential for incredible drama. It was a trial lawyer's dream. What was more, he felt he had instinctively grasped its dynamics and knew how to fight it. But he remained gracious and professional. He promised Beverly he would promptly return her retainer, minus a consultation fee.

———

Beverly then wrote out a check for $50,000 and brought it to the offices of Bremner, Baber & Janus.

"You've got to get this cleared up," Beverly told Janus.

She was still under the impression that the police were suffering from some misunderstanding. It did not occur to her that she might actually have to stand trial.

Janus patted Beverly on the hand. "I'll take care of it," he said.

2

On June 9, Jack Lewis presented the commonwealth's evidence to a grand jury, and it returned an indictment against Beverly Monroe on charges of first-degree murder and the use of a firearm in the commission of a crime. The following morning, Murray Janus picked up Beverly and Shannon in his silver-blue Mercedes sedan and drove them out to the Powhatan sheriff's office.

Beverly had rarely been to the village. It was inland from the James River, a good five miles south of Windsor, in a less affluent part of the county. Her lack of familiarity with this place, where everyone would doubtless know everyone else, intensified the dislocating sense of exposure she felt. At the center of the village, a cluster of old wooden stores on dusty streets faced a grassy courthouse square lined with ancient cedars. A few photographers and television camera crews waited by the door. "Don't say anything," Murray said, "but don't hide your head, either."

As Beverly and Shannon held hands, Murray led them through the jostling cameras and shouted questions. They went into the courthouse and down a flight of stairs. Deputy sheriff Neal, who had so sympathetically taken Beverly's statement the morning Roger's body was discovered, met them in the lobby. Saying nothing, he escorted Beverly into the back, gave her a numbered board, and positioned her in front of a flash camera. Just before he snapped the shutter, she reflexively smiled. Only after the picture was taken did she realize how idiotic her instinct had been. Smiling in her mug shot!

Next, Neal took her hand, grasped her fingers firmly one by one, rolling them on a violet ink pad and then pressing them into a square on a police form. He did the same with the fingers of her other hand. All ten of Beverly's fingers were stained. Neal gave her a towelette, but it didn't remove the ink.

A magistrate waiting in the sheriff's office set bail at $25,000. Beverly wrote the bail bondsman that Murray had retained a check for $2,500, then

Murray led her and Shannon, who had remained virtually mute the entire time, out through the cameras and back into the protection of the big Mercedes. As Murray drove off, Beverly looked at her ink-stained fingertips. What she had just gone through, she felt, was the most humiliating experience of her life.

———

The next day, Beverly's therapist, Kathleen Westlake, read about Beverly's indictment in the *Times-Dispatch* and called her. Beverly had missed a couple of her appointments and had only had her first real breakthrough, Westlake felt, in their last session. They hadn't even begun to get to the treatment plan, much less the possibly blocked memories. Westlake told Beverly that in light of what had happened, it was more important than ever for her to continue her regular sessions.

But for Beverly, the purpose of the therapy had been to uncover the supposed memories, and there was no point in trying to do that now. She told Westlake that she had hired a good lawyer but wouldn't be coming back for any more treatment.

———

Later in the week, Murray Janus invited Beverly back to his office to give him a more complete account of the events surrounding Burde's death. He asked his investigator E. B. Harmon to be present as well. A retired investigator for the U.S. Postal Service, where he had worked check thefts, burglaries of post offices, and postal fraud, E.B. was short and square-faced, with blazing white hair and a thick white mustache that hung down, walruslike, over his upper lip.

Being an old criminal investigator, E.B. leaned toward the prosecution most of the time when he was working a case. He kind of played the devil's advocate for Murray's office. There was more than one case in which he'd gone out, worked it, and come back and said, "Look, this guy's just guilty as sin." How Murray handled the case after E.B. investigated it was Murray's job. But at least Murray would know what had really happened.

As he listened to Beverly's story, some questions occurred to E.B. Why, he wondered, had Beverly driven all the way out to Windsor on the morning of March 5? She was on her way to work, but Philip Morris was in the opposite direction. The Windsor detour would add an hour to her trip. And her behavior once she got there seemed strange. She had knocked on the door but hadn't looked through the windows. She'd driven down to the barn but hadn't gone in. It was the behavior of someone who was confused, but Beverly at the time was not confused. She didn't yet know Roger was dead—she said. Also, it was hard to believe she'd been Roger's lover for twelve years but didn't have a key to his house. Maybe, E.B. thought, she did have a key. Maybe she had killed him and had returned the following morning to make sure he was dead, or to retrieve something incriminating, when Joe Hairfield caught her driving off. E.B. couldn't rule that out.

But then Beverly mentioned Dave Riley's name. E.B. had worked a couple of cases Riley had investigated. He knew about one instance in which witnesses to a murder claimed that Riley had tried to intimidate them when they wanted to change their testimony. E.B. didn't trust the man.

Beverly also mentioned that she'd told Riley about the receipt she'd gotten from the Safeway on the night of March 4. She kept all her receipts, she said; she had boxes of them.

"Bring them all in," E.B. told her. "Every last one."

After Beverly left, Janus asked, "Who keeps cash register receipts? Nobody saves them. Sounds like she's building an alibi."

"My wife saves those cash register receipts," E.B. said. "It's a thing some women do."

———

In early July, E.B. and Murray drove out to Powhatan. In a meeting at the sheriff's office, Jack Lewis, Greg Neal, and Dave Riley showed them the evidence they had collected so far. The irony, Janus thought as he listened to Lewis and Riley explain their case, was that the most compelling evidence—the only real compelling evidence the prosecution had—came from Beverly herself. Even if lie detectors were from time to time unreliable, the fact that she'd failed one undeniably cast doubt on her credibility. And then why did she make this truly bizarre admission that she might have been present when Burde killed himself? And why sign the even more bizarre "confession" saying that if he killed himself while she was there, she might have touched the gun, then wiped it off? Without these admissions, the police had absolutely nothing—*nothing*. Why make them? Janus wondered. Could his client—a woman with a master's degree in organic chemistry, who'd been married to a college professor and had a daughter who clerked for an appellate judge—actually be so naïve?

During the meeting, one of the commonwealth investigators said that someone had called the police the day after Roger's body was discovered and reported seeing a vehicle driving away from Windsor the night of the death. Neither Lewis nor Riley nor Neal volunteered the caller's name, however, and E.B. and Murray had the impression that the call was anonymous. Without the caller's name, they had no lead to pursue, so they didn't think much more of it.

To see what the reaction would be, E.B. mentioned the odd and troubling fact that Beverly did not have, or said she did not have, a key to Windsor. Neither Riley nor Lewis responded, but they did exchange a look, which made E.B. decide they were holding something back. He wondered if they would allow Beverly to take the stand and claim she'd never had a key, then prove otherwise. On the trip back into Richmond, E.B. said, "Murray, they got somebody who's going be able to testify that Beverly did have a key."

———

E.B. drove out to Windsor to interview Joe Hairfield. As a rule, he preferred simply to show up at a witness's house or place of work. Calling ahead and setting up an appointment only gave witnesses time to reconsider whether they wanted to cooperate. E.B. rarely taped his interviews, either. Mention tape to people and they tighten right up. So all E.B. had with him was a notebook.

E.B. found Joe Hairfield in the barn. He was pleasant but slightly cagey. He told E.B. what had happened on the morning of March 5. He said he couldn't remember whether or not he had touched Roger's gun. When E.B. asked about Beverly not having a key, Joe said there was a reason for that. Roger had girlfriends on the side, and he didn't want Beverly barging in unexpectedly while he was entertaining them.

So much, E.B. thought, for the key. Back at the office, E.B. typed up a memorandum of the conversation and mailed a copy of it to Joe Hairfield for his approval. E.B. did this after every interview, to make sure the witness was comfortable with what he had said. E.B. never wanted to be in the position where a witness denied on the stand something he'd told E.B. in an interview. That required E.B. to take the stand and contradict him, which made the witness hostile and confused the jury.

After Joe Hairfield got his copy of the memorandum, he called E.B. and said he didn't recall saying anything about Roger having parties at Windsor with other girlfriends. E.B. felt sure he hadn't pulled that one out of the air. Nonetheless, he considered it a minor detail and he wanted to keep the man happy. "Scratch it out in your copy," he told Joe, "and I'll scratch it out in mine."

———

Beverly gave E.B. a box of cash register receipts, including one from a Safeway store in Midlothian dated the night of March 4. The time on it was 22:40. The receipt also declared that the total price came to $29.11, and that the buyer had paid with a $75 check and received $45.89 in cash. E.B. thought Beverly should be able to produce the check, which would reinforce her alibi.

But E.B was most taken by the list of goods purchased.

CHEERIOS
AMER CHEESE
LIGHT WEINER
BNL CHK BRST
OATMEAL BRED
APPLE JCE
SPRING WATER
LETTUCE BSTN
LETTUCE GRN
STARKST TUNA
DIET COKE
BANANAS
APPLE GLD DL
GRAPES RED

It was nothing that could be argued in court, of course, but intuition told E.B that these were not the purchases that would be made by someone trying to establish an alibi. Particularly the grapes. Who the devil would think to buy grapes to establish an alibi? E.B. had faith in his intuition. Thirty-six years of working cases had given him a feel for the small but revealing truths buried in minor pieces of evidence. He began to warm to the idea that Beverly Monroe was in fact an innocent woman.

———

Around that time, Murray Janus received from Jack Lewis a copy of the notes Greg Neal had made on March 5, a complete set of the photographs he'd taken, and the recently completed fingerprint report on Roger's gun. These exhibits, and the investigative procedures that produced them, raised as many questions as they answered.

What had been in the fireplace? Janus wondered. Neal hadn't collected the partially burned material. Nor had he dusted the poker for prints. Even when Riley and Neal had returned to Windsor on March 10, at which point they considered homicide a strong possibility, they hadn't collected the material from the fireplace. Was there a new will that had been burned? Was there a letter? A suicide note that Roger decided to destroy? All the investigators had had to do was pull out the material with forensic forceps and send it to the lab. Maybe, among the burned magazines, there was a crucial document with a few legible words.

And then there were the Marlboro butts in the ashtray. With a DNA test, they could have determined whose saliva was on them. Neal had taken the trouble to photograph the butts but then hadn't bothered to slip them into an evidence bag. The more Murray thought about it, the clearer it became that he could use Neal's mishandling of the death-scene investigation to raise reasonable doubt.

Murray asked E.B. to review Dave Riley's notes and reports about his conversations with Beverly and make a summary. "Dave Riley is playing this woman like a fish," E.B. wrote after reviewing the material. "There was certainly nothing cunning about her." E.B. was particularly struck by Riley's account of the meeting at Drewry's Bluff. He wrote:

DAVID RILEY IS A MANIAC AND A VERY DANGEROUS MANIAC. I cannot believe this guy would actually do something like this and then put it down in writing for everyone to see. He doesn't just need to be fired. He needs a psychiatrist. I think both of them are insane, but I can understand Beverly going off the deep end if she really loved Roger. . . . Riley had been taping all other telephone conversations with Beverly. He didn't tape this one because he knew what he was doing was a violation of Beverly's Miranda rights. Riley has been around long enough to realize that he has a duty to advise a suspect of his or her Miranda rights.

Like Murray, E.B. brooded over the question of the cigarette butts. They seemed to him to hold the key to the mystery. He had checked into it and had verified that Beverly never smoked and that Roger smoked only rarely. When he did, he smoked Players and went outdoors. The cigarettes indicated plainly to E.B. that someone had visited Roger after Beverly left Windsor the night of March 4. But who? Krystyna Drewnowska, E.B. felt, was a prime candidate. That night, she had apparently tried to call Roger when Beverly was there, but Roger hadn't answered the phone and had said he'd call Krystyna later. And Riley had told the defense team that Krystyna had no alibi until midnight.

With this piece of evidence, E.B. began to speculate that perhaps Krystyna had tried to phone Roger again later that night, had found the line busy, and had driven out to Windsor, where she had confronted him over the terms of his support for the child she was carrying. Perhaps she told him it was a girl. Perhaps they argued. Perhaps, after she left, Roger felt his life was falling apart and killed himself. Perhaps Krystyna killed him. E.B. went to the Medical College of Virginia, where Krystyna worked, but she refused to see him. E.B. didn't take it personally; every witness had a right to talk and a right not to talk.

Krystyna was not the only possible suspect, E.B. decided. Roger had threatened to write Corinna out of his will. That was a motive. Riley had told them that Corinna had been in North Carolina that night, on a sales call for her company, 3M. E.B. tracked down the motel and calculated the distance to Richmond. Corinna, he figured, could easily have driven up to Windsor, killed Roger, then returned to the motel in time to check out the following morning.

There were plenty of additional candidates as well, E.B. found. There were the other women Roger was rumored to be sleeping with, like his housekeeper Barb Collins, and his part-time bookkeeper Hazel Bunch. There were Barb's and Hazel's apparently cuckolded husbands, and for that matter, there was Wojtek Drewnowska. There were business partners who felt cheated by Roger. There were disgruntled employees like Joe Hairfield. There were the partners of the drug-dealing tenant farmer. Roger himself had believed that Philip Morris had hired an assassin. If you got together all the people who might have a reason to kill Roger, E.B. thought, you could fill City Stadium.

Most of them could be eliminated, E.B. decided, by the fact that they couldn't have gotten into Roger's house undetected, and if they had, they wouldn't have known where to find the gun. But regardless of who killed Roger, what had become clear to E.B. was that this was a homicide. This was a deduction, one based on another hunch E.B. had about human nature. E.B. by now had no doubt in his mind that someone had come to Windsor after Beverly left—the person who had smoked the damn Marlboros. If the mysterious Marlboro smoker had not killed Roger, E.B. reasoned, he or she had no good reason to keep quiet about the visit. That person would have to be awful hard-hearted to allow an innocent woman to stand trial for first-degree murder when he or she could clear her by coming forward.

E.B. also pondered the fingerprint report, which said that only one print, belonging to Roger, had been found on the gun. This made no sense to him. Joe Hairfield had said that he couldn't remember if he touched the gun, but E.B. had talked to Dee Shannonhouse, Beverly's pretty little secretary, and she had said that Joe told her on the morning of March 5, when everyone was first gathering at Windsor, that he had touched the gun. She remembered, she said, because she had rebuked him for never watching *Perry Mason* or *Matlock,* and thus failing to obtain a grasp of the rudiments of police procedure. Hairfield, according to the police reports, also told one of the original troopers on the scene that he had touched the gun.

But if that was so, E.B. reasoned, Hairfield's prints should have been on the gun. E.B. called a friend, an old fellow who worked in the postal inspection lab. It was possible to handle a gun without leaving prints, the friend said, if your hands were dry. But if you'd just discovered a dead body, you'd be in such a high state of adrenaline that your hands would be secreting heavily and it would be next to impossible not to leave a print. What that meant, E.B. figured, was that someone had wiped off the gun after Hairfield touched it. He had no idea who that was or why they would do it, much less where this deduction led. But still—that someone had tampered with the crime scene was, in his mind, an unassailable conclusion.

3

The day after surrendering, Beverly had returned to work at Philip Morris. Footage of her walking into the Powhatan courthouse had appeared on the local television news the night before, and that morning the *Times-Dispatch* published a front-page photograph of the event. Entering the office, knowing that everyone in the building must be gossiping about her, she felt excruciating shame.

But their reaction was terrific. Jim Schardt said he didn't doubt her innocence for a second. Since she hadn't been convicted of anything, he added, it was the company's policy that, like any employee in good standing who was charged with an offense and presumed innocent until proven guilty, she could continue to work up to the trial. Secretaries stopped by to tell her how ridiculous they thought the whole thing was. Myles Waugh, who worked in the computer department, came into her office and said, "This is just a crock." Murray Bring, the general counsel, called from New York to assure her she had the company's full support.

Beverly understood, of course, that the situation was potentially embarrassing for Philip Morris. Out of gratitude, and to ensure that the company never regretted its support for her, she told herself that she was going to become a paragon of efficiency. In the days that followed, she never left the office until she had returned every phone call, written every letter and memo, and read and filed every abstract.

———

Philip Morris's attorneys were, in fact, worried that the company would be dragged into the case. An employee had been accused of murdering a former employee who was suing the company. Every article about the case mentioned Philip Morris. The police were interviewing Beverly Monroe's co-workers.

The company's executives, who felt they needed to know what these employees had told the police, had them interviewed by Hill Wellford, an attorney at Hunton & Williams, the Virginia law firm that handled much of Philip Morris's business. Wellford also listened to the tape of that strange call the plant's security desk had received, the weekend after Burde died, from the anonymous woman claiming that someone was going to try to blame Philip Morris for his death. Wellford called Dave Riley, whom he knew. He told Riley about the tape, and said he would send it along. Wellford also expressed discreet curiosity about the police investigation. Riley told him what he knew, which wasn't much beyond what the indictment contained.

For the litigation with Burde, Philip Morris's investigators had conducted an inquiry into his private life and business dealings, even contacting Beverly's former husband, Stuart Monroe. Wellford now shared some of this information with Riley. At the end of the conversation, Riley felt he had learned more from the lawyer than Wellford had learned from him.

———

Exactly one week after her indictment, Beverly arrived at work as usual and was walking through the patent department when she passed Jim Schardt's office. Jim's door was open. He asked her to step inside. With Jim in the office were Steven Parrish, one of the company's senior attorneys, and a woman from human resources. Jim seemed nervous. Steve Parrish and the woman were grave.

Parrish gave a short speech. It made no sense, either for her or for the company, for her to continue working. She needed time to prepare for her trial, so the company had decided to put her on administrative leave. She would continue to draw her salary, and they would of course hold her job. They all hated to do this, he said, but surely she understood the dilemma this posed for Philip Morris. Once the trial was over and she was exonerated, she could return to work.

Beverly, who wanted to continue working for the sake of her sanity—to keep her life as normal as possible—tried to make a dignified protest. She understood that the company was worried about its image, she said, and she could understand why. But she had been told a week ago that she would be able to continue working. The indictment had not affected her job performance in the slightest. She had a right to be considered innocent until proven guilty.

Much as he regretted the decision, Steve Parrish said, it was, they all knew, best for everyone.

The human resources woman accompanied Beverly to her office, two doors down from Jim's. Beverly was unsure what was to happen next. Should she finish her current assignments? Work for the rest of the week? The rest of the day? The woman told her she was to leave the premises immediately.

Beverly had all her personal papers and files in the office. She had brought them in during her divorce, when she feared that Stuart had been going through them, and she had gotten into the habit of keeping them there: tax returns, receipts, letters, bills, credit card statements, newspaper clippings, poems.

The company was going to keep everything, the woman from human resources said. The Philip Morris lawyers would go through it all item by item. Anything that was not company property would be returned to her.

The woman gave Beverly a box, which Beverly was allowed to fill with the photographs and mementos she kept on her desk. She asked Beverly to hand over her Philip Morris I.D. card, then locked Beverly's office and escorted her through the building. It was hideous. Beverly, carrying the box, tried to retain some remnant of dignity as she was led past the curious, tense people in the psychology and packaging departments—an open area with cubicles—out the metal doors at the rear of the building, and into the parking lot. The hundreds of cars glittered in the blinding sun. The woman from human resources stood watching as Beverly loaded the box into her Mercury and then, bewildered and numb, drove out through the plant gate for the last time.

————

In Charlottesville, Katie wondered if her job at the court of appeals might be in jeopardy. She was suffering constant body tension, but she tried to maintain her normal existence, to appear confident, to act as if the indictment were simply some bureaucratic error, like a miscalculated tax bill that had to be straightened out with the IRS. She knew she was the target of gossip. Judge Barrow's secretary, Linda, had told her that practically every other secretary had called wanting voyeuristic details about Katie's state of mind.

Judge Barrow himself had tried to be understanding, but he was not the most tactful or sensitive man in the world. He'd become irritated when Katie had taken some days off the week Roger died. It meant she missed a legal conference he had scheduled in Roanoke, and he wanted his clerks, who should feel privileged to work for a judge in the Virginia appellate court, there when he needed them. But he'd been helpful about the selection of an attorney for Beverly, and he'd tried to ease the awkwardness both he and Katie felt about her mother's situation by making light of it. The day after Beverly surrendered, Katie had come into work and found a copy of the *Times-Dispatch* on the couch in the judge's office. "Ah, so your mom made the front page," Judge Barrow joked.

Katie gave a feeble laugh. It was, she knew, an embarrassment for Judge Barrow to have her as a clerk. There was the notoriety, which made him a potential butt of jokes and threatened his judicial gravitas. There was also the conflict of interest. He was a member of the court to which Beverly would appeal in the event, incredible as it seemed, that her mother was convicted.

The humor, thin to begin with, soon evaporated altogether. The mood in Judge Barrow's office became grim. In July, the *Times-Dispatch* ran yet another long, embarrassing article, this one a profile of Beverly headlined GRIEVING LOVER OR GOOD ACTRESS? After Judge Barrow read it, he called Katie into his private office and said pointedly, "I expect that this won't affect your work." She resolved that it wouldn't. Her one-year clerkship would soon be over anyway. From then on, she and the judge made as little reference as possible to her mother's case.

———

Shannon's midterm exams at William & Mary had taken place the week after Roger's funeral. She had missed a few of them, and then, too upset to study, she had dropped out of half her courses. To catch up, she enrolled in some summer classes, but when, two days after her twenty-first birthday— the legal drinking age, but big deal, she didn't like to drink—her mother called to tell her about the impending indictment, she dropped out of summer school and drove back to Richmond.

Shannon had a generous mouth and her father's pale, freckled skin. She was a complicated young woman, moody, dreamy, easily disappointed, but also perceptive and intuitive. Of Beverly's three children, Shannon was the closest to her mother. After the divorce, when Gavin joined the army and Katie stayed in Ashland to finish high school and then attend Randolph-Macon, Shannon had moved in with Beverly. The two of them were used to being on their own together.

Despite what she felt was total chaos lingering, Shannon and her mom, like Katie in Charlottesville, tried to live a normal life. Gavin was around too, but school, his job, and his girlfriend, Michelle, kept him occupied. Shannon and her mom worked in the garden like crazy. They grew tomatoes, mowed the lawn, kept the chickweed in the driveway from getting out of hand. Her mom was still mourning Roger. She'd start playing the piano and then she'd break down. There was, Shannon thought, all of this underlying trauma.

They wanted peace and quiet, but the tabloid newspaper the *Star* had written a story about the case—MISTRESS ACCUSED OF KILLING MILLIONAIRE WHO DUMPED HER FOR YOUNGER VERSION—and the tabloid television program *Hard Copy* sent a team to Richmond. One Saturday morning, Shannon went downstairs to get her mom a cup of coffee. She was wearing only her underwear. A long-nosed Australian reporter, ignoring the NO TRESPASSING sign they'd put up, was standing on the lawn talking into a microphone. Beverly called E.B., who told her to call the Chesterfield County police. If he came over, E.B. said, it might get ugly.

That whole feeling of invasiveness seemed so threatening to Shannon. Cars and vans would pull in the driveway. From the road at night, you could see through the trees right into the house, and nobody could see you. Shannon felt like she and her mom were being watched twenty-four hours a day. "Why can't we just get blinds?" Shannon asked. But her mom loved the flow of light into the house and refused to get curtains on any of the windows.

They were also getting scary phone calls. Someone was calling and making threats. It was so creepy that Shannon wanted her mom to do something about it. But her mom could not believe that there might be somebody watching them or somebody who was serious about wanting to harm them. Somehow, it was not programmed in her to understand that other people could be evil.

Shannon felt she was getting sucked up into all of this weirdness. It became hard just to talk. People would ask her questions, and her voice would sound so meek and little whenever she tried to use it that she stopped saying anything.

She also had terrible nightmares. In one, her family was hiding her mom in the attic when she came up with a gun and realized she had to kill her mom herself. In another dream, there was a big SUV in their driveway with a wallet inside it and if she could just get the wallet it would have the name of a person who had all the answers. These traumatic dreams, in which she had to do these terribly irrational things, had to solve these horrible dilemmas, added to the surrealism of the summer. Her brain, she felt, was trying to make sense of the whole thing in whatever way it could.

4

A trial date had been set for late October, which meant the defense had four months to prepare. Beverly turned her bedroom into an office. She began making notes: of Roger's medical history; of potential homicide suspects;

of witnesses for E.B. to interview. She frequently called Murray Janus with suggestions and questions.

But Murray was always on the go, it seemed to Beverly, and he often sounded distracted, tired, and brusque. That may have been his manner, but she began to be afraid of irritating her attorney. When she did go to see him, she'd start to talk, and she knew she rambled, but he'd sit back in his chair—his suit jacket off, revealing that the white shirts he wore had short sleeves—and his eyes would roll back in his head and she couldn't tell if he was listening or asleep. Other times she felt he was berating her. "Why weren't you furious with Krystyna?" he'd ask. She'd say, "That's not me. That's not the way I react." He didn't seem to understand.

Murray did find aspects of Beverly's story puzzling. In addition to the odd claim that she felt no jealousy toward Krystyna, there were the troubling questions of why she had stayed with Burde all those years if he was so terrible to her and how Riley had convinced her that she had been present when Burde killed himself. Murray expected these two questions to be central to the prosecution's case, which meant that Beverly's ability to answer them to the satisfaction of the jury would be crucial to her defense.

At Murray's request, Beverly sat down at the computer in her bedroom and wrote a memo with her explanations.

Why was Riley able to make me think I could have been in that room when Roger did this, and why do I now know I wasn't?

I was devastated, depressed, and completely down on myself after Roger's death, for letting this happen to him after promising to take care of him. . . . All the regrets about my father came back. . . . The polygraph was completely confusing and unsettling, and Riley had this very knowledgeable and overpowering explanation and authority and experience to back up everything he said about the suicide and the trauma and shock, and I had nothing but my inability to remember any of this and all of this grief and feeling of inadequacy about myself to hang onto. I was exhausted and drained and not thinking, not able to understand but just feeling/believing something was wrong with me, with my memory. . . . As I look back on it, the whole feeling of his drilling this belief into me was one of hypnosis. . . . I still had some confusion in my mind and some uncertainty until I found that receipt and knew I had been right, that my memory was straight in the beginning.

Why did I stay with Roger if he was so terrible to me, etc.?

He wasn't, and although he did "betray" me in the usual sense of a re-lationship (and in his sickness and lack of control), except for his occa-sional temper (which was usually from stress and tension and pressure) he was a good and warm and sensitive person. He did have many problems and he always came to me for help, and comfort, for quiet and calming and for talking things out. . . . I have had the capacity to be objective and sensible and pragmatic about the relationship and about Roger for all of these years, even when I was very much attracted to him and in love with him at first, when I didn't see and recognize his faults and his severe prob-lems. For the last six years I have known all of these character and person-ality problems, and in the last year I watched them grow worse (I didn't know how bad, but what I saw was enough to know he was in or going through a crisis period). I had only two choices, to abandon him when he was in trouble and when he had asked for my help and my patience and my objectivity—or to stick by him and try to see him through the situa-tion. If he had had a dozen women pregnant, I would have still done the latter and tried to help him work the situation out <u>by facing up to it.</u>

Beverly had expressed herself as best she could in the memo, but after handing it over to Murray and listening to his still-skeptical questions, she became even more convinced that he didn't understand her, that he didn't *get* what had happened at First Division headquarters, that he didn't *get* her relationship with Roger.

As July turned to August and the humid summer days slipped by, Bev-erly began to feel increasingly frantic. Two months had passed, half the time until the trial, and it seemed that very little was getting done. When she called Murray and he didn't return the call, she would call again and again, five or six times a day. Murray was not ignoring Beverly, but he had other clients. He was often in conference or in court or traveling to bar associa-tion meetings.

What Beverly needed was reassurance. Murray, however, did not think it was his job to provide psychological counseling. Touchy-feely hand-holding, in his view, wasn't going to help her case. Indeed, time spent comforting Beverly, he felt, was time that could otherwise have been pro-ductively devoted to work.

When Beverly came to his office, he wanted to concentrate on preparing her for cross-examination by ferreting out the weaknesses in her story, even if that meant challenging and upsetting her. Instead, he often had to fend off her suggestions that E.B. pursue far-fetched leads and to listen to her discourse on the mistreatment she felt she had suffered under Dave Riley. Murray didn't think he could make the trial turn on Riley's behavior. Riley, he thought, had used every ruse in the book. Unfortunately, according to the law, he was allowed to do that, and Murray felt that complaining about it to the jury was not going to offset the weight of Beverly's confession. Murray had also had an independent examiner evaluate the polygraph Omohundro had given Beverly. He concluded that, for whatever reason, she had indeed tested deceptive. Murray began to worry that unless he treated Riley's interview with Beverly carefully, the results of the test might leak to the press or be introduced into evidence.

E.B., despite his conviction that Beverly was innocent, also found her wearying at times. Beverly could *talk*. If he didn't cut her off, he'd be in there three or four hours listening to Beverly. She'd be doing all this talking and he'd be feeling like he should be out looking for witnesses.

———

Losing faith in Murray Janus, Beverly quietly began interviewing other lawyers. All of them praised Murray and urged her to stick with him. Two of them actually used the same phrase: "You're in good hands." One told her that if she was serious about retaining new counsel, she should fire Murray first and then interview prospective attorneys; otherwise, they would be reluctant to talk to her. No lawyer in Virginia wanted to appear to be poaching Murray Janus's clients. He himself was so worried Murray would find out about the meeting that he asked Beverly to make out the $75 check for the consultation not to him but to his church.

Beverly realized that any lawyer she hired would have shortcomings. The three nervous men she had talked to certainly did. She decided to stick with Murray Janus.

———

On a hot August day, Beverly ran into Brigitte de la Burde in a dress shop in west Richmond. The two women were both standing in line at the checkout counter when they saw each other. Beverly had neither seen nor heard from anyone in Roger's family since her indictment. She had called

Corinna once, to insist on her innocence; Corinna had rather coolly said, "Fingers are pointing," and she didn't know what to believe; then she hung up. When Beverly saw Brigitte, she felt she had to say something, but because they were in a public place, surrounded by other customers, it was exceedingly awkward.

"I don't really understand how all of this has happened," Beverly said.

Brigitte nodded her head, murmured politely, then moved off.

5

By August, Dave Riley felt he had wrapped up most of his investigation on file no. 92-81-00-0224, as the case against Beverly Monroe was officially labeled. Since Beverly's indictment in June, he had made some additional discoveries. He had called Sheldon Gosline, a graduate student at the University of Chicago, who said that while he was staying at Beverly's house at the time of Burde's funeral, he heard her make several incriminating remarks about Burde's will and about the times she left and returned to Windsor. Gosline then wrote a long statement containing all the details and sent it to the investigator. Riley also found an unsigned draft of a new will on Burde's computer that left Beverly little more than the Steinway piano and the old Jaguar. It seemed further evidence that Burde was writing her out of the picture.

In the first week of August, Riley sat down and composed an overview of his and Greg Neal's findings for Jack Lewis, the prosecutor.

NARRATIVE OF OFFENSE

On the morning of March 5, 1992, the victim, Roger de la Burde, was found lying on his right side on a couch in the library of his home, dead from a single gunshot wound to his right forehead. . . .

The victim's long-time girlfriend, Beverly Monroe, now admits to being with the victim at his residence at the time of his death, however, in her first version of events, she said she went home during mid-evening, allegedly so the victim could call another girlfriend to break off an affair which Monroe had only days before confirmed, an affair which resulted in the other girlfriend, Krystyna Drewnowska, carrying the victim's child. . . .

When pressed about inconsistencies in her behavior and her original statement, Monroe changed her story and said she was actually present when the victim committed suicide and because she was in some sort of state-of-shock, she had blanked it out of her mind. She says she left his residence after the suicide, went home, and made the phone calls to his residence. This, of course, is totally incredulous [*sic*]. . . .

Monroe knew about Burde's gun. She took the opportunity to kill him when he took a nap on the couch with his back to her as she apparently lay on the opposite couch. When she was sure he was asleep, she got his re-volver and shot him in the forehead between the fingers of his right hand in which he was cradling his head as he slept. . . .

That this murder was pre-meditated is further evidenced by the fact that Beverly Monroe told the victim's daughter, Corinna, several weeks before the event that she was worried about the victim because his behav-ior was like her own father's just before he committed suicide years ear-lier. No one, except Beverly Monroe, says that the victim exhibited any tendencies toward suicide. To the contrary, everyone else said his total be-havior was absolutely the opposite of a person who might contemplate suicide.

I. MOTIVE

A. Jealousy and fear of being displaced in the victim's life by another younger woman who was pregnant with his child.

B. Immediate large financial gain from being a major beneficiary in the victim's current will and a large insurance policy.

C. Fear of a large future financial loss because the victim was in the process of changing his will and was also writing a document to financially take care of the pregnant girlfriend and the child.

II. MEANS

The victim's own gun which Beverly Monroe stated she had known of and its whereabouts ever since its purchase.

III. OPPORTUNITY

The victim and Beverly Monroe had been lovers for 13 years and spent a great deal of time together in each other's homes alone. Each would be comfortable napping in the other's presence.

IV. PROOF

A. The physical evidence concerning:

    1. The placement of the gun;

    2. Gunshot residue patterns on the right hand;

    3. Impression on the right hand of the gun butt, indicating the gun was placed there after death;

    4. Absence of gunshot residue on the left hand which would be necessary in a suicide in this occurrence.

B. Beverly Monroe changed her story from one where she was not present to one where she was present at the moment of what she alleged was a suicide.

C. Statements by Beverly Monroe both before and after the event that the victim was suicidal, which are totally inconsistent with the statements of everyone else with whom he had contact.

V. LOGIC

Since the victim's death was not a suicide, but homicide, and Beverly Monroe admits to being alone with him at the moment of his death, then the logical conclusion is that Beverly Monroe killed Roger de la Burde and staged his death to appear to be a suicide.

John Latane Lewis III was descended from one of the oldest families in Virginia. Raised in Williamsburg, where his father was director of personnel for the colonial village, he had moved to Powhatan County in the 1960s, when it had only two other lawyers, Billy Blandford and Leslie Longstreet Mason, Jr., whose firm he joined. Lewis was genial and easygoing. He competed with Peggy Palmore, the county historian, to see who would be the first to produce ripe tomatoes from their summer gardens; every fall he hunted deer with a bow and arrow. The people of Powhatan County liked him. They felt free to drop by unannounced at his small office in the village, in a dilapidated old house he had bought from Colonel Scaggs. In the sixteen years since he became commonwealth attorney, he had stood for election four times and been challenged only once.

Lewis brought Riley's memorandum with him on the vacation he and his wife and their four daughters took every August to Nags Head. Because the state police were involved, Jack had not tried to oversee the investigation into Roger de la Burde's death. He figured Dave Riley knew what he was doing. In fact, Lewis had done little more than glance at the material. When the forensic reports had arrived in the early summer, he had, as required by law, filed them with the court but had not studied them. He was occupied by other cases pending in all three of the county's courts.

Lewis spent most of his vacation in a rented beach house reading Riley's report. The man, he thought, had worked his tail off. In addition to composing his memorandum, Riley had supplied Lewis with three thick volumes of supporting material. He had subpoenaed Beverly's telephone and bank records. Among the photocopied items he'd included in his file was Beverly's canceled check to Murray Janus for $50,000. That was one hefty retainer. Riley had also acquired the records from Beverly's credit union at Philip Morris and even the records of the psychologist whom, at Riley's urging, she had been to see.

Then there were the witness reports. Riley had talked to everyone, it seemed, including one of Roger de la Burde's blood relatives, who said Roger's claim that he was descended from a French count was a complete fabrication. Roger had told his family he had invented the title of count to give himself cachet when he arrived in the United States.

Lewis had known Roger de la Burde slightly. They had had lunch once, to discuss real estate. In 1982, when Burde's neighbors the Armentrout sisters had charged Burde with trespassing and malicious damage to property, for cutting down two acres of their trees so he could have a view of the James River, Lewis had prosecuted the case.

There was something about the man, Lewis had always felt, that just made his skin crawl. Burde took advantage of people. And he was no more a count than Lewis's dog was.

During his years as commonwealth attorney, Lewis had tried some six murder cases. He had failed to win a conviction only once, in a case in which a hunter found the bones of a young woman who had disappeared two years earlier in Richmond. Lewis and the investigators believed they knew who had done it—a former boyfriend, the only one with a motive—but the evidence tying him to the crime was weak, and the jury acquitted him. By comparison, Lewis felt the circumstantial evidence against Beverly

Monroe was strong indeed. She had confessed she was there when he died. And not only had she failed the polygraph, but she had tested at close to the maximum level for deceptiveness, something like 22 on an outer parameter of 24.

Lewis still found it hard to believe that Beverly had agreed to take the polygraph. She did it, he decided, because she wanted to clear herself completely, to erase any vestige of suspicion, and because she believed she was smart enough to fool the examiner. She was a good actress, Lewis thought, what with all the public grieving she'd done—at the funeral, at police headquarters, in front of friends, family, and strangers. But she wasn't necessarily faking it. Lewis knew that when a wife killed a husband over a new girlfriend, it didn't mean the wife didn't love the man. To the contrary, the wife killed the husband *because* she loved him and couldn't stand to lose him. Which was, he thought, exactly what had happened with Beverly. She loved the man she felt she'd had to kill, and was mourning his death.

———

A couple of weeks later, when he'd returned from Nags Head, Lewis received a call from a woman in the Chesterfield County jail who identified herself as Zelma Smith. She had seen a newspaper or magazine article about the Monroe case, she explained, and she had recognized Beverly Monroe's picture. A year earlier, she said, Beverly Monroe had contacted her about purchasing an untraceable handgun.

Lewis thought: This is too good to be true. He told Dave Riley about Zelma Smith's claim.

"Bullshit," Riley said. He didn't believe it for an instant. He ran a check on Zelma Smith. He learned she had nine felony convictions for check forgery and fraud, had jumped bail last spring, been picked up in California and returned to Virginia, and was now awaiting transfer to the women's penitentiary to serve out a seven-year sentence. The woman was a career con artist.

Nonetheless, Lewis wanted Riley to talk to her, so Riley drove down to Chesterfield County on August 28. He returned with a story that, if it panned out, Lewis thought, would clinch the prosecution's case.

Riley said Zelma Smith told him in the spring of 1991 that she had been working as a bookkeeper out of her house in Henrico County. One Sunday she received a message on her answering machine from a woman identifying herself as Ms. Nelson. She called the number, and Ms. Nelson arranged to meet her at a Burger King on Parham Road. When Zelma, who was black, arrived at the restaurant, an attractive white woman in her fifties was sitting in the rear. She told Zelma she had decided to contact her because she knew Zelma had a criminal record. She wanted Zelma to find her an unregistered pistol small enough to fit into her handbag. "What do you mean unregistered?" Zelma asked. "You know, when you take the serial numbers off, file them off so they can't be traced," the woman replied. The woman gave her a $100 bill as a retainer and said she'd pay $800 for the gun itself. Zelma procured a .357 Magnum from a drug dealer she knew, called Ms. Nelson, and they arranged a second meeting, at the Greenwood Memorial Gardens cemetery just inside the Goochland line. It was a rainy weekday morning, two or three weeks after their first meeting. Ms. Nelson was wearing a beige raincoat. She told Zelma the .357 Magnum was too large, but paid her $480 anyway and asked her to keep looking. After that, she called Zelma a few times, irritated at Zelma's inability to find the right gun, but still polite, and then Zelma moved and didn't hear from her again. While she was in jail, she saw an article with a picture of Beverly Monroe and recognized her as Ms. Nelson. She couldn't remember the telephone number Ms. Nelson had given her. It might be in some of her old records, but they were in her car and the car had been stolen and was still missing.

Riley told Lewis he had gone down to the jail assuming Zelma Smith had made up her story. She had a criminal background, which meant she was prone to lying; she was obviously looking for some consideration in exchange for talking. But Zelma Smith impressed him, Riley said. She had little education, but she wasn't stupid, either. And the story she told had a persuasive ring to it. Riley said he had the feeling that Zelma Smith had been in Beverly's presence, that she had known Beverly or at least spent time in conversation with her. Beverly had an aristocratic way about her, an old Southern way of dealing with blacks that Zelma was able to convey.

When Riley asked Zelma if she'd take a polygraph test, she didn't balk, and this too impressed him. He had no intention of actually administering a polygraph, since career criminals almost always tested inconclusively, but Zelma's willingness to take the exam bolstered her credibility, Riley explained. So did the fact that, when he drove out to the cemetery where Zelma said she'd met Beverly, her description of the place—a mausoleum, a duck pond, and so forth—corresponded with what he saw. It was, basically, a white cemetery. Not a lot of black folks were buried there, and there was not a lot of reason for Zelma to be spending much time within its walls.

Jack Lewis liked what he heard. He now had a witness who could establish that Beverly Monroe had apparently been planning to murder Roger de la Burde a year before he died. Of course, Zelma's credibility was a problem, but if her story sounded persuasive to the jury, the problem was not insurmountable.

Lewis added Zelma Smith to the commonwealth's witness list. But Zelma told Riley she was worried that by taking the stand and declaring she had carried a gun out to the cemetery to give to Beverly Monroe, she could be prosecuted for illegal possession of a firearm. For a convicted felon, it was a potentially serious offense.

Riley brought Lewis down to the Chesterfield jail to allay her fears. Lewis told Zelma that if she took the stand, her words would amount to an uncorroborated confession, and in Virginia a confession uncorroborated by other evidence was insufficient to convict. "The only way you could be convicted was if Beverly Monroe got on the stand and testified that she tried to get you to get this untraceable gun," Lewis said. "And, Zelma, that's not going to happen."

———

When Murray Janus received the commonwealth's witness list, he was puzzled by the name Zelma Smith. He'd never heard of her, and Beverly said she hadn't either. Murray sent E.B. down to the Chesterfield jail to try to find out who she was. When the guards brought Zelma into the jail's interview room and she learned that E.B. was working for Beverly Monroe, she became the embodiment of moral indignation, refusing to talk, insisting that he leave, demanding to be returned to her cell. It seemed like an enormous act to E.B. Back at the office, he told Murray, "That's the lyingest bitch I ever met."

E.B. dug up Zelma's criminal history. This extensive record would give Murray Janus ample opportunity to attack her credibility, but even so, Murray did not have the slightest idea what Zelma Smith would say when she took the stand. That left him with no way of preparing to rebut her testimony. It was a position in which he hated to find himself.

———

In late September, Linda Newcomb, Judge Barrow's secretary at the court of appeals, received a call from David Riley of the Virginia State Police. Linda immediately thought something must be wrong with one of her children, but Riley said no, he needed to talk to her about Katie Monroe. The investigator arrived at the judge's Charlottesville office two hours later, while Judge Barrow was out. How had Katie acted the day before Burde's death? Riley asked Linda. What was Katie's reaction to the news of the death? How did Katie feel about Burde? Did Linda know if Burde had ever abused Katie?

Linda tried to answer the questions as candidly and carefully as possible. Katie had seemed fine the day before Burde died, Linda said, and she'd fallen apart after she heard the news. And while Roger may have abused Katie mentally by pushing her to go to law school, he hadn't, as far as Linda knew, abused her physically.

In exchange for talking, Linda insisted that Riley reveal the name of the person who had suggested he contact her. Riley said his source was Michael Beverly, a young lawyer at Hunton & Williams, the firm that represented Philip Morris. Michael had been Katie's predecessor as Judge Barrow's law clerk. Linda liked Michael, and they had remained in touch after his clerkship ended. When Roger had died, Michael told Linda that since going to work at Hunton & Williams, he had learned quite a lot about Count de la Burde. But if he told her what he knew, he said, he'd have to kill her. Joking, of course.

When Judge Barrow returned, he became irate after learning that Riley had questioned his secretary without his permission. In the future, he told his staff, any police officer who approached them should be referred to him.

Linda Newcomb called Beverly and Katie to tell them about the visit. That Riley, four months after her mother had been indicted and four weeks before the trial was scheduled to begin, apparently considered *her* a suspect seemed weird to Katie. By now she had heard her mother talk endlessly about Dave Riley, but she had yet to meet the man. He had never tried to interview her, or Shannon for that matter. But he had obviously spent time thinking about her and he had apparently formed opinions about whether she was capable of committing a violent crime. She sensed him circling her like a predatory animal in a dark forest, and she wondered where she would next catch a glimpse of him or if she would see him at all before he suddenly struck.

6

Even in the final weeks before the trial, Jack Lewis had been unable to devote himself full-time to preparing for it. He'd had other cases pending. An arrest had been made in two rapes that had occurred in the county the month before and the month after Burde's death, and the suspect, a Powhatan man who had been caught in Wingo County, West Virginia, was indicted at the session of the grand jury held on the second Tuesday in October, just two weeks before the start of Beverly Monroe's trial. Lewis had no associates or assistants to help him in any of this work; he and his secretary handled everything.

And the *Commonwealth of Virginia v. Beverly Anne Monroe* was by far the most complicated case Lewis had ever prosecuted. He had fifty-six exhibits. He had bewildering forensics. He had a lengthy witness list that he needed to pare down and organize, questions he had to frame for each of those witnesses, proposed jury instructions and opening and closing statements he had to write. It was a lot. It was, in fact, too much. Lewis started to feel like a golf ball lost in high weeds.

On Wednesday, five days before the trial was to begin, Lewis, for the first time in his career as a prosecutor, decided to ask for help. He called Billy Davenport, the commonwealth attorney for Chesterfield County, and asked if he could spare his deputy, Warren Von Schuch. Billy Davenport very graciously said yes, and that same afternoon Von Schuch drove up to Powhatan.

———

Members of the Virginia bar considered Warren Von Schuch one of the most capable prosecutors in the state. During the eighties, he had worked in the commonwealth attorney's office in Richmond, when the city had one of the highest per capita murder rates in the country. Drug wars, drive-by shootings, and gang feuds made those killings seem so casual and pointlessly random that some of the prosecutors jokingly reclassified homicides into murder, misdemeanor murder, and shooting into occupied clothing.

Von Schuch became Richmond's top homicide prosecutor. When Virginia re-enacted capital punishment, he tried the first capital murder case, against a man who had raped a singer in a Virginia Beach band called Bill Deal and the Rhondels and killed her husband and shot the lead guitarist. The guy got life. Von Schuch also prosecuted the Briley brothers, who were convicted of murdering eleven people in Richmond in a nine-month period and who then carried off the most sensational death-row escape in state history. But most of the cases he handled were routine dogs. Victim A would get killed by B, who would get killed by C, who would get killed by D, who would claim self-defense—with some justification. In one grim sixteen-month stretch, Von Schuch tried eighty such murders.

It got depressing. Von Schuch felt like all he was doing in Richmond was chasing bodies. So when his friend Billy Davenport was elected commonwealth attorney for Chesterfield County, Von Schuch joined him as his deputy and also traveled throughout the state helping local prosecutors on capital murder cases. In the process, he had put more defendants on death row than any other prosecutor in the state, a distinction that earned him the nickname the Executioner among capital punishment opponents.

At the time of Beverly Monroe's trial, Von Schuch was in his early forties, a broad-shouldered man who had played football at the University of Oklahoma. His eyes, behind rectangular wire glasses, were small and coldly observant. His voice, raspy in normal conversation, could swell to a declamatory boom. He had a dry wit and a detached, cynical outlook; the depravities he confronted every day in his work seemed to have engendered in him a state of perpetual disbelief. But he was familiar with the intricacies of blood spatter, fingerprints, and gunshot residue. And he had a flair for courtroom theatrics, an ability to summon forth scorn and indignation that witnesses found intimidating. Jack Lewis considered him a crackerjack attorney.

Von Schuch had not followed the Beverly Monroe case. The one article he had seen, in the *Times-Dispatch,* struck him as the kind of story he would find in *The National Enquirer* and he had tossed it aside after reading only the first few paragraphs. So he arrived at the Powhatan County sheriff's office pretty much cold. Lewis, Neal, and Riley were there, in a windowless conference room just past the receptionist's desk. Riley gave him a verbal report on the police investigation. Von Schuch went through the various forensics reports and looked at the autopsy pictures. Then Lewis showed him all this bizarre stuff: baby agreements, wills, love letters.

It seemed to Von Schuch that Lewis's strategy was misguided. In an effort to establish Beverly's motivation, Lewis was focusing on the romantic triangle between Roger, Krystyna, and Beverly. That was an element of the case, Von Schuch felt, but a potentially distracting one.

"Jack, you're trying this like a divorce case," Von Schuch said. "This is not a divorce case. What we have are forensics. We can re-create this. If you can't win it on forensics, you're not going to win it on the rest of this stuff."

Von Schuch took the witness list and on the chalkboard wrote out the names of all the forensics experts. He would conduct their direct examinations, he said, and he listed the order in which they would appear. Von Schuch also offered to handle Dave Riley's testimony. The investigator's account of Beverly's two confessions was central since, once the forensics experts had established that Burde's death was a homicide, all the commonwealth had to do was place Beverly with him at the time of his death. The rest of it, as far as Von Schuch was concerned, was incidental.

Von Schuch had tried cases with Murray Janus before. He knew that in cases involving confessions, Janus invariably attempted to put the police on trial by arguing that the confession was illegally obtained or that his client's will was overborne. He had enjoyed some victories against Von Schuch using just those tactics. But those had been with Richmond jurors, who tended to be black and who were more suspicious of the police. Von Schuch had tried cases all over the state. He knew rural juries were more likely to trust the authorities, particularly if they were state police; the local deputies sometimes made the citizens nervous. Von Schuch wondered if Janus would make the mistake of assuming that what worked in inner-city Richmond would work in Powhatan.

He also wondered what tactics Janus would use to get the jury to distrust Riley, and whether they would succeed. Von Schuch had never met Riley before, but he recognized the type: a beasty-eyed gumshoe, like every career state police investigator. You knew one, you knew them all.

———

The Sunday before the trial began, Murray Janus had Beverly spend the day at his office, reviewing her upcoming testimony. With him was David Hicks, a rising black attorney who had resigned his job as a city prosecutor that summer and come to work for Janus. At that point in his career, Murray had defended more than fifty murder cases. He was not one of those attorneys who kept a scorecard totting up his wins—one difficult victory meant more than ten easy ones, and many times a negotiated surrender in the face of overwhelming odds represented success. Much less was he one who went around claiming he'd never lost a case. Any lawyer who said that was shooting a line of bull, Janus believed. If you're doing it, and doing it regularly, you're going to take your lumps.

In recent years, he felt he'd been taking more than his fair share of them. Acquittals had become much more difficult to obtain. In the sixties, when Janus had begun to practice law, just after the Miranda decision in the heyday of the Warren Court, he had won case after case on illegal confessions and illegal searches and seizures. But the courts were now more conservative and the police were better-trained and more sophisticated. They knew their constitutional law. They knew where the line was and just how closely they could approach it without crossing it.

The police sophistication in Beverly Monroe's case made it difficult to construct a defense around violated rights, Janus felt. He would argue violated rights, of course, but he would have to argue other things as well: insufficiency of the evidence; an alternative theory of the forensics; other suspects if indeed the death had been a homicide. It was Janus's experience that murder cases like Beverly's were rarely won by an affirmative defense, one that unequivocally proved the client's innocence by establishing an alibi or demonstrating entrapment or self-defense. If such an affirmative defense existed, the case probably wouldn't have come to trial.

When Janus won a case, it was usually by preventing the prosecutors from proving his client's guilt beyond a reasonable doubt. So instead of staking a defense on a single theory of what had actually happened, his job was to present the jurors—who, despite the legal fiction that defendants were presumed innocent, tended to assume they were guilty merely because they were on trial—with a series of scenarios sufficiently plausible to raise doubt about the prosecution's version of the facts.

In Beverly's case, he would offer the old country lawyer's syllogism: I don't have a dog, but if I do have a dog, he didn't bite you, and if he did bite you, it was because you provoked him. In other words, he would argue that Burde's death hadn't been a homicide, but that if Burde *had* been murdered, someone else did it, and if in fact Beverly had pulled the trigger, that was because Burde was a philandering scalawag whose life wasn't worth much to begin with.

Janus never had any doubt about putting Beverly on the stand. It was a truism among trial attorneys that the defendant who refused to take the stand essentially conceded his guilt in the minds of most jurors. And Janus believed Beverly would make an articulate and appealing witness. The women, if they heard her soft-voiced account of life with Roger, might form a sisterly identification, a shared sense of female victimization. The men might find her pretty and touchingly vulnerable. But Janus still thought the jury might consider parts of Beverly's story—the absence of jealousy toward Krystyna, the lack of a key to Windsor—implausible. And on that final day of preparation, he felt he had to be tough, to ready her for what he was sure would be a grueling cross-examination.

Beverly found the Sunday rehearsal disjointed and frustrating. For hours she and Janus went over her story, with Murray at times calling a halt to speak to other defense witnesses. He challenged her, with an incredulous tone of voice, on every detail. The streets of Richmond, visible from Murray's fifteenth-floor conference room windows, were deserted. It was late October, and darkness settled in early. A small television sat on a table in a corner of the room. Murray, an avid football fan, had it tuned to the game the Washington Redskins were playing against the Minnesota Vikings in Minneapolis. The sound was turned down low. Murray merely monitored the game from time to time; he didn't allow it to distract him. Nonetheless, under the circumstances, Beverly considered his interest in this extraneous spectacle just one more small sign that her attorney had never quite regarded her defense as an all-consuming crusade.

CHAPTER VII

The Check Kiter
and the Egyptologist

Beverly's mother, Anne Duncan, and her three brothers, Steve, Bruce, and Stuart, believed from the outset that it was impossible for Beverly to have killed Roger. Stu Monroe, Beverly's ex-husband, also considered it inconceivable. A decade had passed since their divorce, the anger Stuart had felt at the time had faded, and, left with the fact that they had three children in common, they had become friendlier than either of them had ever expected to be. Even so, Stuart felt uncomfortable attending Beverly's trial. In the end, he decided to be present only for the testimony of his children—a choice Shannon found hard to forgive him for. But Beverly's mother and her three brothers and their wives planned to be there every day. Katie arranged lodging for them in motels near Old Gun Road.

Early on Monday, October 26, 1992, they gathered at Beverly's house. The skies were gray and drizzling rain. Murray Janus and David Hicks arrived in Janus's silver-blue Mercedes, E. B. Harmon following behind them in his Honda. The family loaded into their cars and set out—like in a funeral procession, it seemed to Katie—to the courthouse.

At the first intersection, where Robious Road crossed the railroad tracks, Janus, who was in the lead, began to pull out into the traffic and then came to a sudden stop. E.B., who was directly behind him, plowed into the rear of the Mercedes, crumpling the bumper, smashing taillights, and popping the lid of the trunk, where Janus had stowed all the trial documents. Murray was livid, but then had to admit that he'd halted a bit abruptly. They tied down the trunk lid with a bungee cord.

The incident, however minor, embarrassed the lawyers and jarred the family's already tense nerves. It seemed to everyone a bad omen. Only E.B. found the slightest humor in it. That was because, while the crash tore Murray's Mercedes all to pieces, it didn't hardly dent E.B.'s little Honda.

———

Television news crews and milling spectators waited under the cedars outside the Powhatan County Courthouse. As the Monroes parked and got out of their cars, Shannon noticed one of the TV guys puking on the courthouse lawn. What was his problem? Maybe she was trying to distract herself, but Shannon was fascinated by why that guy was puking.

The Monroes joined hands and walked up the rain-wet brick path. They passed the backpedaling cameramen and the obelisk honoring the Powhatan Troop of the Fourth Virginia Cavalry in Jeb Stuart's Confederate Cavalry Corps and entered the courthouse through a set of heavy double doors.

The pews in the courtroom were painted gray-green and had varnished wooden trim. The two front rows on the right side had been reserved for Beverly's family and friends. Since Katie, Shannon, and Gavin were to testify, they were not allowed to be in the courtroom during the trial proper, but they could watch the jury selection. That first morning, they joined their grandmother and aunts and uncles in the front pew. Just on the other side of the rail, Beverly, dressed in a blue blazer and skirt and a white blouse, sat between Murray Janus and David Hicks.

The courtroom was elegant, with tall mullioned windows and a high, crossbeamed ceiling from which hung a pair of globed chandeliers. But since local trials rarely attracted crowds, the room was also small, and every seat was taken. Powhatan people were there and reporters and curious spectators from as far as Richmond and Henrico County. Jack Lewis's wife sat in the first pew on the left side. In the rear of the courtroom were a group of unsmiling men in dark suits, who, Murray Janus explained, were attorneys for Philip Morris, there to watch out for the company's interests in a trial in which its employees were enmeshed and its confidential policies and practices would be discussed.

Promptly at nine o'clock, the bailiff called, "All rise!" and Judge Thomas Warren took his seat. The judge was a slender man, with close-cropped gray hair and thin lips. He had been the circuit judge, holding court in Dinwiddie, Powhatan, Amelia, and Nottoway Counties, since 1977, and had a reputation as a procedurally strict conservative. Both Murray Janus and Jack Lewis knew him. Lewis had been trying cases before him for fifteen years.

"Ms. Monroe," the judge said. "Stand and be arraigned."

The clerk read the two charges against Beverly: that she did feloniously kill and murder Roger de la Burde against the peace and dignity of the Commonwealth of Virginia and that she did unlawfully and feloniously use a pistol while committing the felony of murder.

"What is your plea, guilty or not guilty?" the judge asked on each of the counts.

"Not guilty."

"You may be seated."

Deputies ushered in the pool of potential jurors. The judge gave them a speech about civic responsibility and asked if any of them had any business dealings with any of the attorneys. One man raised his hand.

"Mr. Lewis has done some deed work for me."

"How long ago?" the judge asked.

"It has been a number of years."

"Would that have anything to do with your ability to be an impartial juror?"

"No, sir."

The judge allowed the man to remain in the pool. The voir dire proceeded briskly. One prospective juror admitted knowing Roger. Another said he'd already formed an opinion about Beverly's innocence. A third allowed he was more inclined to believe police officers because they had sworn to uphold the law. A fourth said he would find it difficult to convict a woman of murder. A fifth, a woman, said Beverly had to be innocent because if she was capable of murder, the person she would have killed was not Roger de la Burde but Krystyna Drewnowska.

None of these individuals were chosen. The final jury consisted of a mechanic, a teacher, a bookkeeper, an electrical contractor, a Philip Morris engineer, two housewives, employees of the Department of Motor Vehicles, the Virginia Correctional Center for Women, and Virginia Power, and one man who described himself simply as self-employed. They all lived in Powhatan County. Judge Warren informed them that because of the publicity the trial had received, they would be sequestered for its duration.

————

The lawyers then joined the judge in his chambers. Since Beverly's two statements to Dave Riley were central to the prosecution's case, Warren Von Schuch expected Murray Janus to move to suppress them by claiming that Riley had overborne Beverly's will. While Von Schuch didn't think Judge Warren would accept such an argument, concluding instead that the voluntariness of Beverly's statements was a matter of fact for the jury to decide, he nonetheless expected Janus to make it. To Von Schuch's surprise, Janus did not proceed down that avenue. Instead, he said he wanted to suppress both Beverly's verbal statements on March 26 and the written statement she had signed at Drewry's Bluff on June 3 on the grounds that she had been in police custody on those occasions but had not been informed of her rights.

Judge Warren decided to hear the testimony and arguments on this point in open court. Back in the courtroom, but out of the presence of the jury, Janus called Dave Riley to the stand. He admitted that on neither of those two occasions had he read Beverly Monroe her rights. Lewis, on cross-examination, pointed out that Wyatt Omohundro, the polygraph operator, had already read Beverly her Miranda rights on March 26. It was unnecessary, he tried to show, for Riley to do so.

"That afternoon at the state police headquarters," Lewis asked, "she was not under custody or arrest at that time?"

"Absolutely not," Riley said. "She brought herself there. She drove herself there. She drove herself away."

"And she left on her own on June third when the discussion was finally over in the park?"

"Yes."

Janus, calling Beverly to the stand, asked her about Riley's behavior when she and the detective were sitting in her car at Drewry's Bluff.

"Did he ever tell you, you were free to leave?"

"No."

"Did you think you were free to leave at that point?"

Roger de la Burde,
Christmas Day, 1991.

Beverly Monroe and
Roger attending a party
on a riverboat.

Roger and Beverly.

Beverly and Katie Monroe during a picnic at Windsor.

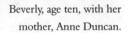

Beverly, age ten, with her
mother, Anne Duncan.

Roger and his daughter
Corinna at an art exhibit.

Shannon and Gavin Monroe.

The house at Windsor.

A view of the barn from the pond. The house is beyond the rise to the left.

The photograph that appeared in the Richmond *News Leader* of Roger dancing at the winter ball with Katharine Lee, director of the Virginia Museum of Fine Arts. (Copyright Richmond *Times-Dispatch*, used with permission.)

Beverly, accompanied by her daughter Shannon, arriving at the Powhatan County sheriff's office to surrender after her indictment. Her attorney Murray Janus is behind them. (Copyright Richmond *Times-Dispatch*, used with permission.)

Special Agent David Riley testifying during the trial. (Copyright Richmond *Times-Dispatch*, used with permission.)

Krystyna Drewnowska arriving at the courthouse with her lawyer. (Copyright Richmond *Times-Dispatch*, used with permission.)

During the trial, Ann Jones, the commonwealth's firearms expert, demonstrates her theory of how Roger de la Burde was killed as (from left) David Hicks, Beverly Monroe, Murray Janus, and Warren Von Schuch look on. (Copyright Richmond *Times-Dispatch,* used with permission.)

Katie Monroe on vacation in May 1997 after filing the state habeas petition.

Christmas 1998 at the Pocahontas Correctional Unit: Front row from left: Shannon, Beverly, Asher, Katie. Second row: Shannon's friend Alex, Andy Montague, Gavin. The photograph was taken by a guard.

"No, I didn't feel like that at all."

During the argument phase of the motion, Janus maintained that on June 3, when Riley told Beverly that the commonwealth had enough evidence to charge her and intended to do so, he also should have read Beverly her Miranda rights. At that point, he said, Beverly was for all practical purposes in Riley's custody and the conversation she had with him was in violation of her constitutional rights.

In response, Lewis pointed out that the U.S. Supreme Court had ruled in 1977 that the police do not need to read Miranda rights to every suspect they merely interview. Furthermore, he said, a defendant's subjective perception or feeling that he or she is in custody is irrelevant. And in any event, Beverly had been given her Miranda rights by Omohundro a relatively short period of time earlier.

"Two months?" Judge Warren asked sharply. "You call that a relatively short period? It was over two months."

"Well—" Lewis began.

The judge cut him off. "That's the short period of time you were speaking of?"

"It's not like five years two months," Lewis replied. "I would submit to the court, someone with her intelligence would clearly be able to remember two months down the road."

Despite his skeptical tone, Judge Warren agreed with Lewis. He pointed out that Beverly—a woman, he noted, of more than average intelligence and educational attainment—could hardly complain that Riley had failed to give her a Miranda warning on March 26, since she had just signed a waiver of those rights for Wyatt Omohundro. And the commonwealth was right, he went on, about the irrelevance of a suspect's subjective perceptions.

"The court," he said, " is not bound by suggestive ideas: 'I didn't feel too free'; 'I felt uncomfortable leaving'; 'I didn't feel I could.' "

Both statements, he ruled, were given voluntarily, without any violation of Beverly Monroe's rights.

————

After a late lunch, Jack Lewis rose from the prosecution table to give the opening statement for the commonwealth. Lewis was rangy and stoop-shouldered, his suit jacket hung on him loosely, and he had the gravelly drawl to which every country lawyer aspires. He had never tried a case before such a large audience; the deputies had been forced to turn some spectators away once all the seats were taken. Lewis was also aware of the pool television camera trained on him from the balcony.

Lewis was not like one of those egomaniacal attorneys who shoved people aside to get on camera. When Lewis saw a TV camera, his inclination was to slip out the back door. It made him a little apprehensive, all this attention, but when he reached the lectern in front of the jury box and placed his notes on its surface, he tried to ignore the spectators and the camera and simply focus on the jurors.

"The case you will be trying," he told them, "will be probably the most lengthy and in some respects the most complicated case that has been tried in the long, long history of Powhatan County. This case is going to test your physical stamina. It's a case that's going to test your mental stamina." He paused for effect, then said, "In spite of all the witnesses and complexity of the evidence, this is really a very, very simple case."

The narrative of the alleged crime that Lewis gave the jury hewed closely to the points in Riley's memorandum. It was a lengthy, complex story, but as Lewis proceeded, his confidence grew. He dwelled on Roger's numerous affairs. "Apparently," he said, "he believed in the European moral standards, or, I guess, by our standards, the lack of moral standards." He described the relationship between Roger and Krystyna and Beverly. He argued that Beverly reacted to Krystyna's arrival with much the same indignation that Roger's ex-wife Brigitte had shown at Beverly's appearance. He discussed witnesses who would testify about Roger's plans for the future and the inconceivability of his having committed suicide. He talked about Roger rewriting his will and Beverly's discovery of the baby agreement Krystyna had drafted.

"She knew she had lost the battle," he said in closing. "It's a question of 'Bye-bye, old will; hello, new will.' It's 'Bye-bye, Beverly; hello, Krystyna and the baby.' And finally she snapped, ladies and gentlemen. She couldn't stand what was happening to her financially. She couldn't stand losing the man she had captured for thirteen years to somebody else who was going to get him. She knew that. And when he went to sleep, took a nap on the sofa with his head cradled in his hand—you will see a picture of him sleeping in that position—she put the gun to his head, held it between the little finger and the ring finger, pulled the trigger, and killed him. There is absolutely no question, ladies and gentlemen, that Beverly Monroe murdered Roger Burde."

Lewis had been speaking for close to an hour. When he sat back down, Von Schuch leaned over and said, "Jack, I believe you know the facts of this case."

Coming from Warren Von Schuch, Lewis considered that a right good compliment.

———

"Mr. Janus," the judge said.

"May it please the Court."

Nodding to the prosecutors, Janus crossed the floor to the jury box. Jack Lewis, he felt, had inadvertently aided him by portraying Roger as an unregenerate scoundrel. This was what Janus himself intended to do—not only to force the jurors to question the value of Roger's life, if indeed they decided Beverly had taken it, but in order to advance the suicide scenario. The more outlandish Roger's life appeared, the more likely it would seem in the minds of the jurors that his myriad problems had combined to overwhelm him.

"The commonwealth has to prove its side of the case beyond a reasonable doubt," Janus told the jurors. "It's got to convince you of two things, really. Number one, that it wasn't a suicide. Number two, if it wasn't a suicide, that this defendant"—he turned and indicated Beverly, sitting beside David Hicks at the defense table—"is the person who did it. We don't think he will be able to satisfy you beyond a reasonable doubt."

After describing Beverly as a responsible divorced mother of three who was interested in art and music, Janus attacked Roger as a philanderer. "The evidence," he said, "will be that Roger had his affairs, his relationships with other women, because he was immoral. The fact that he was born in Poland or France or Europe or wherever is immaterial."

Roger de la Burde, Janus continued, was afraid he was going to be exposed for dealing in fraudulent artwork. He was narcissistic, obsessed, and paranoid. He suffered from heart problems, impotence, and depression. He was worried about bills and lawsuits. Philip Morris frightened him. And he regarded Krystyna Drewnowska as nothing more than a surrogate mother. His arrangement with her to bear him a child, Janus said, was a calculated financial transaction, like buying a used car.

Janus looked from juror to juror. "You may ask yourself why, if the evidence is anywhere near what Mr. Janus says it will be, why did this lady, this nice-looking lady sitting behind me"—again he indicated Beverly—"why did she put up with all this malarkey, this junk? Why didn't she say, 'I want out of here,' 'Hit the road,' 'Forget it, fellow'? And the answer is . . . she loved him, just as Brigitte had loved him before."

———

It was five o'clock by the time Janus finished, but Judge Warren, intent on moving the trial along as rapidly as possible, asked Jack Lewis to call his first witness. Joe Hairfield took the stand. He was clearly ill at ease. He described arriving at Windsor on the morning of March 5 just as Beverly was pulling out of the driveway. She told him she couldn't get into the house, he said, and had gone to the barn to use the phone there, but the barn doors were locked.

"Was the barn locked?" Lewis asked.

"No, sir. The barn is never locked."

"Was there any difficulty in opening the barn door?"

"No, there was not."

When Hairfield said this, Beverly began writing furiously on a yellow legal pad. She had never told Joe the barn door was locked, she wrote. She had driven down to the barn to see if anyone was there. The barn had been newly renovated; the doors were closed. It was obviously deserted. Late for work, and assuming that Roger was merely sleeping late, she had turned around without getting out of her car to begin the long drive to Philip Morris, and had then run into Joe out by the road. She tore off the sheet and passed it to Murray.

While the issue of whether or not the barn door was locked had no bearing on the central facts of the case, Murray Janus knew that Lewis would use Joe Hairfield's statements about it to suggest Beverly was not telling the truth. There was nothing Janus could do about that, since Hairfield seemed wedded to his account of the matter, but he thought he could make some headway on another point he knew Lewis hoped to use to discredit Beverly—the question of whether she had a key to Windsor.

"Sometimes women would be coming and going late," he asked Hairfield on cross-examination, "when Beverly was not there?"

"I don't know that," Hairfield said, adding primly, "By five o'clock I was home."

Hairfield, Janus thought, knew that Beverly had no key, and he knew the reason—because Roger had been afraid that she would catch him with another woman—but since Hairfield had asked E.B. to strike that item of information from E.B.'s report, Janus couldn't ask him about it directly. He could, however, allude to it.

"Beverly did not have a key that morning, did she?" he asked.

"No, she didn't."

"To your knowledge, you never saw her with a key?"

"No."

"Do you recall Roger telling you he didn't want her to have a key?"

"Something to that effect, yes, sir."

That was as far as Hairfield would go. Janus had hoped the man would volunteer something, but he didn't feel he should push him. He asked, "Would you summarize Roger as being a different kind of person, and unusual?"

"Absolutely."

"Very unusual?"

Hairfield murmured his response. Janus thought the jury hadn't heard him. "The last word—I don't want to belabor it—you sort of whispered *absolutely*?"

"Yes."

———

At the end of the long day, Deputy Sheriff Greg Neal took the stand. Lewis asked him to approach the jurors and pass around the seven photographs— of the library, of Roger's body from different angles and distances, of the gun, of items on the coffee table—he had taken at Windsor on the morning of March 5. The photographs, even the close-ups of Roger's face, were not particularly horrific. The jurors examined them soberly but, as far as Janus could tell, without an overt emotional reaction.

"There was no blood on his hands, was there, sir, to your recollection?" Janus asked Neal during cross-examination. It had seemed axiomatic to Janus that if Roger had been murdered by someone who slipped the gun barrel between his fingers, that hand would have been covered with the blood that had spattered onto the couch.

"I don't remember any blood on the hands," Neal said.

"You certainly don't have any photographs showing blood on the hands, do you, sir?"

"No."

Janus passed Neal one of the photographs the deputy had taken but had not shown to the jury—a close-up of the two Marlboro cigarette butts in the ashtray.

"Do you recall from eyeballing or from your memory whether or not lipstick was on any of the two Marlboros?"

"No, I don't recall."

"Were the two cigarette butts preserved?"

"They were not collected."

Janus passed Neal another photograph, this one of the fireplace.

"Can you tell us whether or not the charred paper in the fireplace was taken and preserved?"

"It was not taken. At a later time it was looked at right carefully."

By the end of the day, Janus felt he had accomplished much. He'd gotten a witness to explain why Beverly didn't have a key. He'd raised a question about the homicide scenario, suggested that Roger had had another—possibly female—visitor, and pointed out the inept crime-scene investigation. So far, he thought, the commonwealth's case was swimming in reasonable doubt.

<hr>

2

On the second day, Warren Von Schuch, who had spent the prior weekend closeted with the commonwealth's forensics experts, took over from Jack Lewis. Marcella Fierro, the deputy chief medical examiner at the time of Burde's death, was his first witness. She testified that the gunshot wound that killed Burde was in an unusual position for a suicide.

Fierro held up for the jury's scrutiny two photographs taken during the autopsy. While she was overseeing that procedure, she said, she noticed gunpowder residue on the fourth and fifth fingers of Burde's right hand. It indicated that at the time the gun was fired, the right hand had to have been between the muzzle and the wound.

However, the picture Greg Neal had taken of Burde's right hand showed an impression, caused by blood settling into the surrounding tissues after death, of a curved object. In Dr. Fierro's opinion, that curved object was the butt of the Smith & Wesson .38. Burde's death, she continued, was instantaneous, because the bullet severed his brain stem. That meant it was impossible for him to have switched the hand that held the gun after firing it. So while the gun somehow ended up in his right hand, he could neither have shot himself with that hand nor have shifted the gun from his left hand to his right after firing it.

Finally, she said, if the deceased had somehow managed to shoot himself with his left hand, gunpowder residue would have remained on that hand, and she had observed none on the day of the autopsy.

Von Schuch then called Ann Jones, the firearms expert at the Division of Forensic Science. She told the jury that the gunpowder residue around the wound was not in a circular pattern. The residue had spread up toward the deceased's hairline and down to his eyebrow, but not to the right or the left. What had impeded the even spread of the gunpowder, she said, were Burde's two fingers. She described how, by filling a white glove with clay, placing it next to an ovoid ball, and firing the gun between the fourth and fifth fingers, she was able to produce gunshot residue patterns that matched those on both the deceased's forehead and his hand.

Charles Pruitt, the fingerprint expert at the Division of Forensic Science, followed Jones. He said he had taken several latent fingerprints from Burde's gun. Only one had sufficiently pronounced ridge patterns for him to make a positive identification. It came from Burde's right index finger and had been found on the side of the barrel, next to the manufacturer's stamp.

———

During his cross-examination of Marcella Fierro, Murray Janus had gotten her to admit that she had seen some suicide wounds resembling Burde's. And he forced Ann Jones to concede that despite her elaborate reconstruction, she couldn't eliminate the possibility that Burde had killed himself with his left hand. Now, with Charles Pruitt, Janus felt he could raise the possibility, through forensics, that if Burde *had* been killed, there were other suspects—suspects the police had ignored.

Janus pointed out that Pruitt had received five latent prints from the crime scene but had only identified two, both belonging to Burde. He asked Pruitt if the police had given him lift cards, containing the prints of any suspects, in order to make comparisons with the three unidentified latents. "For example, from Beverly Monroe?"

Pruitt paused to check his notes. "No, sir."

"How about Krystyna Drewnowska? Were you given any fingerprints of hers?"

"No, sir. I wasn't."

"Wojtek Drewnowska?"

"No, sir."

"No one else?"

"No, sir."

———

These questions did not trouble Warren Von Schuch. Janus had succeeded in doing a little open field running, Von Schuch thought, but he had hardly impeached the commonwealth's forensics.

Lewis now moved on to the matter of Beverly's statements, calling four witnesses—Greg Neal, Wyatt Omohundro, and two police secretaries, Pat Dilettoso and Deborah Pollock—who had watched Riley's questioning of Beverly Monroe from the observation room at First Division headquarters.

Pollock, an eager, slightly anxious-looking young woman with shiny blond hair and a habit of cocking her head inquisitively when listening to a question, gave the most vivid description of the moment when Beverly suddenly thought she remembered Roger committing suicide. "After talking a little while about her mental stability at that time," she said, "as far as being confused and upset and possibly blocking it out of her memory, she seemed to change facial expressions and remembered that she was there at the time. . . . It went from a confused look, and she looked up, and as though enlightened said she suddenly did remember being in the room when it happened. . . . She thought at the time it was a dream, but then realized she must have been there."

David Hicks, to whom Janus delegated these witnesses, objected vigorously to the speculative characterization of Beverly Monroe's state of mind. He seemed so eager to interject himself into the trial that at one point he rose from his seat as if to speak, but then paused and remained standing silently at the defense table.

"Are you going to say something?" Judge Warren asked him. "If you are not, sit down, Mr. Hicks, please."

The attorney abashedly resumed his seat. He was, however, able to establish that Beverly's recollection, which Deborah Pollock had at first described as erupting almost spontaneously, had in fact come after repeated suggestion and prodding by Dave Riley.

"Isn't it a fact," he asked, "that Agent Riley told her it's not uncommon for people, when they have a traumatic experience, to block things out and not remember?"

"Yes, he did."

Hicks nodded. "He said it on more than one occasion, did he not?"

"Yes, he did."

"How many times did you hear Agent Riley say, 'You were there. You just don't remember because you blocked it out'?"

"I don't remember him saying those exact words."

"Words to that effect."

"Several."

"How many times?"

"I didn't count. More than once."

———

Once the trial had begun, Katie, Shannon, and Gavin Monroe were shown into a small room made available for defense witnesses. The room was furnished with nothing but a table, a few uncomfortable chairs, and shelves of law books. It made them feel strangely infantile, whispering or laughing awkwardly in this silent room as the adults carried on elsewhere with the grave matter of the trial.

Shannon had brought her journal with her—the same one in which she had recorded the dream she'd had about Roger the night before he died; a small hardback volume with paper the color of old ivory and a blue flame-patterned cover—and she spent much of that first morning writing in it.

Thinking of the jury—salamanders—people whom I will observe and will observe me—dissect me—misunderstand me—God please let them see through this conspiracy—To realize that these people have my mother's life in their hands whether they realize it or not!!!—It's as if Nathaniel Hawthorne resided somewhere amongst these pages of circumstance—of cause and effect—Yet this is not Salem—and to the naked eye there appears to be no scale on which to weigh the woman or the witch—except within the minds of 12 chosen for a box, solemnly sworn to exhibit what they each define as just.

Later that first morning, Shannon had ventured out into the courthouse. Exploring, she found an empty room with a pot of hot coffee and a plateful of doughnuts. She was famished, having had the appetite to eat only a small packet of Vance peanut-butter crackers at breakfast. Feeling slightly guilty, as if she were both trespassing and stealing, she helped herself to two doughnuts and a cup of coffee. They tasted great. When she returned to the room the next day and opened the door, looking forward to another snack, she found Dave Riley sitting inside talking to someone. He looked up, surprised. A deputy who was with him told her she was not allowed in the room and closed the door, with a click, in her face.

———

Late Tuesday afternoon, Von Schuch called Dave Riley to the stand. Von Schuch was not entirely comfortable with the way Riley had conducted himself during the investigation. Strictly speaking, Riley had done nothing unethical. Police officers were allowed, even trained, to mislead defendants, and as Von Schuch saw it, Riley and Beverly had each been trying to manipulate the other. Still, Von Schuch wished Riley had taped all his interviews. He believed that investigators should tape everything. It protected them from charges of coercion, and it prevented the witness from later denying certain statements, as Beverly Monroe was now doing.

Since Von Schuch expected Janus to make an issue of Riley's conduct, he wanted to limit what Riley said on the stand. Instead of questioning the detective, Von Schuch simply asked him to read the reports of his meetings with Beverly. Riley did, but he kept straying from the text of the report to explain things, to provide background, to speculate about Beverly's state of mind, to talk to Janus whenever Janus objected, and to defend his aggressive style during the taped portion of his March 26 interview with Beverly. "In listening to that phase of the conversation on the tape, not having heard the first part of it, it sounds as though I am the one saying everything and she is not saying anything," Riley explained to the jurors. "That's not a true picture—"

"I object to his comments on it," Janus said. "He can testify."

"I agree," the judge said. He looked at Riley. "Don't add anything."

"Yes, sir," Riley said.

Riley's demeanor was all wrong, Von Schuch thought. He was coming across as the typically overbearing police officer. It was driving Von Schuch nuts. Von Schuch had put the rascal on the stand to read specific things. But no matter how the court ruled or what questions Von Schuch asked, Riley was going to tell the jury what *he* wanted to tell them. He was forever sidetracking over here and wanting to add that and giving his opinion on this. Von Schuch tried to cork him. Even the judge tried to cork him on several occasions. But that rascal just wasn't going to be corked.

"Mr. Riley," the judge said, exasperated after yet another digression. "I have asked you, I think this is the fourth time, to read the statement."

"Yes, sir."

"I am not going to ask you anymore," the judge continued. "I will give it to the jury to read or let somebody else read it if you can't read it."

"Yes, sir," Riley said humbly.

———

Murray Janus had taken note of Riley's volubility and he thought he might be able to use it to his advantage. The next morning, on cross-examination, he asked the investigator to describe how he had convinced Beverly to accept the idea that she may have blocked out her memories of Roger killing himself. Riley, as if to convince the jury that while he had been deceptive with Beverly he had done nothing improper, continued to be remarkably forthcoming.

"I told her," he explained, "that my own father had committed suicide and I had blocked it from my mind, though that was not true. That's when she suddenly dropped her head and said, 'I'm starting to remember.' And I said, 'It's coming back to you now, isn't it?' And she said, 'Yes, yes.' And she started sobbing, crying. She said, 'Yes, yes. Now it's coming back to me.' And I said, 'Tell me what you remember.' And she says, 'I'm lying on the couch. He brought me a pillow and comforter. I had been lying on the opposite couch. I was dozing or asleep. He had apparently washed the dishes and had apparently come back in and was on the other couch. And I heard this loud crashing noise.' She never did say 'shot.' She said, 'This loud crashing noise.' And I said, 'The shot.' She said, 'Yes, apparently.' And then I said, 'What do you remember next?' She said, 'I remember—I don't remember getting up, but I do remember standing over him and looking down and seeing something shiny in his hand.' And I said, 'What was that? Was that the gun?' And she said, 'Yes, the gun.' And I said, 'What did you do next?' And she said, 'I don't remember what I did next.' . . . I tried to get her to remember events in driving home." Riley paused to explain. "I am helping her with this."

"Aren't you doing more than helping?" Janus asked. Aren't you, he continued, feeding Beverly Monroe a scenario?

"I am giving her things," Riley replied, "to see if that is what occurred." At that point, he went on, Beverly became upset at the thought that, having seen Roger shoot himself, she had not immediately called an ambulance.

Janus proceeded cautiously. He was worried—actually, he was white-knuckles scared—that he might inadvertently say something that would give Riley the opportunity to bring up Beverly's failed polygraph. Prior to the trial, the judge had ruled the results inadmissible in court, but he had warned Janus that if the defense allowed the test in through the back door—by accidentally referring to it—the commonwealth could pursue the topic.

"Mr. Riley," Janus said. "Didn't you tell her, 'The reason you blocked this out is because you feel guilty that you didn't call anyone'?"

"I may have, yes, sir. I may have very well said that."

That conversation was unrecorded, Riley explained, because when he had gone back into the interrogation room after Wyatt Omohundro told Beverly he thought she was lying—Riley also was careful to make no mention of the polygraph, though he wondered what the jury would think was the basis for Omohundro's conclusion—he had forgotten that Omohundro had told him he needed to turn on the tape recorder. Only after she made the confession, he said, did he realize his mistake.

"When I slid away from her, in a sort of relief-type situation, you know, that we had gotten this far," he recounted, "I remembered what Omohundro had said to me before she ever arrived, and I thought, 'I hadn't recorded this.' . . . I reached over and flipped the switch on. And then I slid back in front of her again. And I immediately grasped her hand again, and I said, 'Beverly, let's go over this one more time.' "

"*That* was recorded?" Janus thought the sarcasm in his voice conveyed to the jury his disbelief of Riley's story. He played the fifteen-minute tape for the court. While Riley's voice came through on the recording as clear and strong, Beverly's was almost inaudibly weak. She sounded emotionally drained, and was at times incoherent.

"Have you made any analysis," Janus asked, "of what percentage of the conversation David Riley is talking and what percentage—"

"Absolutely," Riley interrupted. "David Riley is talking most of the time here. I am trying to get her to repeat what she had already said. When I slid back in front of her, she had a look of surprise like, 'What do you need to know this again? I have already told you.' And at that point, she was very hesitant, very reluctant to say or repeat anything she had already said."

Janus was pleased. Riley had effectively admitted that he had suggested the entire scenario to Beverly, then failed to get her to articulate it on tape.

"At no time in that interview," he asked, "did Beverly Monroe ever tell you that she shot Roger Burde, did she?"

"Absolutely not."

Janus was surprised at how eagerly Riley acceded to all these points. "Isn't it true, sir," he asked, "that you found Beverly Monroe to be naïve?"

"No," Riley said. She was not, he explained, an intrinsically naïve person. But she had been naïve in her assumptions about what she, as a criminal, thought she could get away with. He added, "She is naïve about not getting an attorney, if that's what you mean."

"Did you take advantage of her because of that naïveté?"

"I certainly did," Riley said, "because that's what I am paid to do."

Riley's acknowledgment was so emphatic that Janus felt he didn't need to hammer on it. He moved on to ask the investigator why he hadn't taped the meeting at Drewry's Bluff. Undercover police officers, he said, often wear body transmitters, which pick up the voices and transmit the signal to a second unit in a nearby vehicle. "You ruled that out because you—"

"—couldn't anticipate where the meeting would take place."

"But *you* set the meeting up, didn't you, Mr. Riley?"

"I called her to set up the meeting," Riley acknowledged. But he had scheduled it on such short notice—to avoid giving Beverly the opportunity to change her mind—that he hadn't had time to arrange to wear a body transmitter. And he hadn't worn a portable tape recorder, because the weather was hot that day. He anticipated taking off his jacket, and he wanted to show Beverly that he wasn't wired.

"Didn't you tell her you were there as a friend?" Janus asked. "Mr. Lewis didn't even know?"

"That's right," Riley said. "I told her that I could understand her reason for killing Roger Burde. And again, I was blaming the victim."

"It's another technique."

"Another technique," Riley agreed.

But, Janus asked, hadn't he also used an utterly different technique as well? "Isn't it true that you told her that you could make her out to be a sympathetic person who killed someone who was bad, or you could make her out to be the black spider woman of all time?"

"No, I didn't say that in that context."

"Well, tell us the context in which you did say 'the black spider woman.'"

"I said I viewed her as a sympathetic person, considering the way Roger was," Riley explained. What he had told Beverly, he went on, was that if the matter came to trial, the less sympathetic aspects of her story could be introduced as evidence against her. "The jury might hear things she might not want heard. She could be viewed in a darker light—black widow spider, I guess, would be the term."

Janus had one final matter. The day before, during direct examination, Riley had read a list of nineteen circumstances pointing to Beverly's guilt that he said he had enumerated to her at Drewry's Bluff. These ranged from Roger's rewritten will disinheriting Beverly to the absence of a suicide note to Beverly's conflicting statements. It was on the basis of this overwhelming evidence, Riley had said, that Beverly signed the confession he wrote out for her in the car. When Riley started to read the list, Janus had objected, since Beverly had told him Riley had not in fact read a list but had merely mentioned a few circumstances, some of which had turned out to be untrue. But Judge Warren had ruled the list admissible.

"Yesterday," Janus said, "you read in verbatim nineteen different circumstances that you thought were very suspicious in pointing to Beverly's guilt. Is that correct?"

"That's correct."

"Were all of those true, or were some of those tactics or techniques, part of a plan?"

"Well, I told her all these things thinking they were true at the time," Riley explained. "Some of these things I later learned not to be exactly accurate."

Janus left it at that. Beverly had told him that the inaccuracies Riley was now admitting proved he had been lying all along. She was particularly incensed about the Charles de Gaulle show on PBS. Riley had succeeded in causing her to doubt her memory by insisting no such show had aired that night when in fact it had. Beverly was convinced Riley knew all along that this was untrue. Maybe it was. But Janus felt that since he couldn't prove Riley was lying, drawing the investigator out on which circumstances were untrue and why he had believed them to be true at the time would only weaken the defense. As Janus sat down, he felt satisfied with his morning's work. He thought he had succeeded in demonstrating that Riley was an overzealous, unchecked officer who had jumped to conclusions about the cause of Roger's death and the identity of the murderer, then misled and bullied a grieving woman. Janus had won acquittals with flimsier defenses.

———

Katie and Shannon had both started smoking that week. What the hell—so had their granny, and she had heart trouble. Venturing out of the little witness room, they cadged cigarettes from deputies and loitered on the courthouse steps sucking on these nasty Pall Malls and joking with some of the very same fellows—okay guys, actually—who'd been at Windsor the day Roger died. It was a weirdly ironic situation, they felt, but what else were they supposed to do?

The only time they saw their mother was during short breaks and at lunch. Around noon, the courtroom doors would suddenly open, and the spectators would spill out into the square, followed by the attorneys and Beverly. They would all walk across the street to the one restaurant in Powhatan, a family-run placed called the Crackerbarrel. It had a cow theme and its slogan—which they agreed was the absolute worst pun ever coined—was "Udderly Delicious." The spectators, the deputies, the reporters, the lawyers, and the defendant all ate there every day, leaning across the tables to talk, ordering the presweetened iced tea and not-bad barbecued pork sandwiches that were the house specialty.

Janus and Hicks were upbeat. The commonwealth's case, they told the Monroes, was transparently weak. Katie's boyfriend, Alan Block, who was sitting in the courtroom, also thought it was going well. During Riley's cross, he said, Murray had gone after him like a bulldog, highlighting every single outrageous thing the cop had done.

But Shannon had become convinced that her mother was going to be convicted. It seemed that all year, the worst that could happen *had* happened, and she just had this deeply rooted feeling that it would go on like that. Her mother was damned.

After lunch the third day, when everyone had gone back into the courtroom and she and Katie were looking for a bench to sit on and smoke an extra-long menthol they'd mooched from a commonwealth witness, they saw an old black woman on the porch of a little ramshackle house across the street. They went over to talk to her. The woman's name was Annie Palmer. She was tiny and wizened. She wore a housedress, had skin the color of faded iron, and her gray hair, under a black polyester cloth, was pulled back in braids. She hadn't been in the courtroom, she said, but she had been following the trial on television and she had no doubt that Beverly was innocent. She told Katie and Shannon she would pray for their mother that night. "Prayer is the key," she said, "but it's faith opens up the door."

3

Once Dave Riley stepped down from the witness stand, Jack Lewis began calling the witnesses who would explain Burde's life in the days and months prior to his death. Von Schuch had dismissed these witnesses, and the story they would collectively tell, as more suited to a divorce case, but since the evidence against Beverly Monroe was circumstantial, Lewis felt it essential first, to establish motive, and second, to demonstrate that Roger de la Burde, far from feeling suicidal, was making plans for the future right up through the day he died. If the testimony proved lurid and the jurors came to feel that Burde was a loathsome individual, that would only make it easier for them to believe that Beverly had murdered him.

The first witness Lewis called was Corinna de la Burde. Roger's daughter appeared awkward and uncomfortable as she settled into the witness chair. She sat hunched forward and ran her fingers through her dark hair, pushing it off her narrow, olive-complexioned face. She answered Lewis's first few questions in such a low voice that Judge Warren asked her to speak up.

"Are you nervous this morning?" Lewis asked.

"Very."

That was fine with Lewis. Nervousness in a witness could be appealing to jurors, most of whom would also feel nervous in that situation. "Try to relax and do your best," he said.

Lewis in fact considered Corinna one of his most important witnesses. Sympathetic as the innocent and victimized daughter of the deceased, she had also initially been Beverly's ally—a fact that Lewis quickly established.

"Corinna, what was your relationship with Beverly?"

"I considered her my friend," Corinna said. "I liked her, I respected her, and I trusted her."

"How did you view your father's relationship with her?"

"I thought they did well together. He was really hyper, jumping from project to project and whatnot. She had a calming effect on him. I liked that. I thought she was good for him."

Lewis asked Corinna if she preferred Beverly over Krystyna Drewnowska as her father's companion.

"No question. I was committed to Beverly to the hilt."

Having demonstrated Corinna's feelings for Beverly, Lewis set out to reveal how Beverly had callously exploited the younger woman's trust by going to great lengths to convince Corinna that her father was suicidal. At his prompting, Corinna told the jurors about the repeated telephone calls she received from Beverly in the year preceding Roger's death, calls in which Beverly worried aloud about his depressions, despair, and irrationality.

"Did you observe any symptoms of depression and forgetfulness and irrationality described to you by Beverly?"

"No," Corinna said. "In the beginning, I was a little concerned. I tried to confirm it. But my dad didn't express any depression at all. He was just kind of like my same old dad." She paused, then added, "But then again, I wasn't there all the time."

During her pretrial interview with Riley, Corinna had described two incidents involving Beverly that Lewis thought would advance the commonwealth's case immeasurably. He now proceeded to the first, asking Corinna about her arrival at Windsor the day her father's body was discovered.

"When I walked in—Gavin is her son, he grabbed me. He hugged me. And the next person was Beverly. And she grabbed me and hugged me. And then she looked up at me and said, 'She is pregnant.' "

Lewis paused for a moment. He wanted the jury to dwell on this flash of apparent jealousy by Beverly Monroe, who had always maintained that she felt no hostility toward Krystyna Drewnowska.

"Did she say anything to you at that meeting other than 'She is pregnant'? Did she try to console you?"

"Not at that point. That was the only comment made. And there were other people to hug."

Lewis then moved on to the second incident Corinna had mentioned to Riley. He asked Corinna about the lunch she had with Beverly on April 1 at the Marriott. Corinna told the jury how Beverly had suddenly confessed that she had been present when Roger killed himself.

"She started talking about the guilt and whatnot," Corinna said. "And she also said that she wanted to tell me before. And she asked me if I remembered that day in the kitchen, after the funeral, when I asked her if she felt like my dad had really committed suicide. And I said, 'Yes, I remember that day.' And she said, 'I wanted to tell you then, but I didn't know just what to say.' "

"That was on the Monday night after your father's death?"

"Right."

Murray Janus could carry on for the rest of the trial about how Beverly Monroe's will had been overborne by Dave Riley, Lewis thought. In Corinna, the commonwealth had an unimpeachable, eminently trustworthy witness who could connect Beverly's memories of waking up when Roger pulled the trigger to a moment in time more than two weeks prior to Beverly's first meeting with Riley. How, if the investigator had suggested the whole thing to her, could that have happened?

———

Beverly passed a note to Murray. She had not told Corinna the day they discovered Roger's body that Krystyna was pregnant. Beverly knew that Corinna already knew about the pregnancy, since Roger had told Beverly about Krystyna's lunch with Corinna. And what she had wanted to tell Corinna the day of the funeral was not that she had witnessed Roger's suicide but that she had wanted to explain how guilty she felt for failing to anticipate and prevent Roger's death. Corinna was jumbling parts of a long conversation. Janus read the note and folded it. Beverly might well be right, but unless Janus could discredit Corinna's version, it didn't pay to have her repeat it.

———

Lewis asked Corinna to produce a photograph she had brought with her. It was taken in the summer of 1988, out by the pond at Windsor, and showed Roger asleep.

"Corinna, why did you snap that picture?"

"He's kind of cute. Kind of peaceful and restful-looking."

Lewis passed the photograph to the jurors. They had already seen the pictures of Roger's body lying on the library couch. Greg Neal had taken one of them from almost the same angle as Corinna's snapshot. In the two pictures, Burde was lying in virtually the same position, resting on his side, with his knees drawn slightly up and his hands cupping his head. The jurors soberly studied the picture. Even without Lewis pointing it out, which he would do in his closing argument, they could hardly miss the similarity.

Lewis had one more point he wanted this witness to make. It was un-planned, a matter of serendipity. When Dave Riley was trying to confirm Zelma Smith's story about Beverly's attempts to buy a handgun, he had called Corinna to see if, as Zelma claimed, Beverly owned a tan trench coat. Corinna had said that indeed she did.

It had rained every day so far during the trial, and, like so much else in the case, the bad weather played into the commonwealth's hands, for Bev-erly had shown up in court wearing a tan raincoat, which was draped over the back of her chair.

"Corinna, are you familiar with a type of coat that Beverly Monroe might wear," Lewis asked, "in rainy or inclement weather?"

"I am familiar with two coats of hers—"

Before Corinna could go any further, Janus cut her off. "Judge, I don't know the relevance of this."

Judge Warren turned to Lewis. "Mr. Lewis, can you proffer that that is relevant?"

"Yes, sir. It is, quite."

"Okay," the judge said.

Lewis asked Janus to pass him Beverly's coat. He held it up in front of Corinna and asked if this was in fact Beverly's raincoat.

"I don't know," she said, "but that's definitely the type of thing she wore for years."

Lewis told the judge that the commonwealth would like to introduce the coat as evidence. Since it was raining, he said, he would return it to Beverly if the court would direct her to bring it back.

"Well," Judge Warren sighed, "let's just get it for identification. It's not relevant at this point."

"I understand it is not relevant at this point," Lewis told him. "But it will *become* relevant."

———

That afternoon, Gavin ran into Corinna in the courthouse hallway. God, it was the hardest thing in the world to find a true friend—someone you could always count on, someone who was there for you—and that's what Corinna had been to him. He had loved her to death. So had his mother. She was nothing but grand to Corinna. After his mother's indictment, Gavin had called Corinna and left messages, but she never called him back. And then he learned that his best friend was cooperating with the police and had refused even to be interviewed by his mother's investigators.

At first, Gavin was going to walk past Corinna, but then their eyes met and he decided to go up to her.

She seemed nervous. She asked him how he was doing, as if they were still friends and had just happened to bump into each other.

"Corinna, what is going on?" Gavin asked. "Why are you doing this? Why didn't you call me and talk to me about this?"

Corinna's eyes welled with tears. She told him *he* never called her.

"I left you messages," Gavin said.

"What messages?" she asked.

Then Katie came over. She had seen Gavin and Corinna about to indulge in this mutual sob fest, and she wasn't going to allow that to happen. "Come on, Gavin, let's go," she said, and led him away.

Gavin told his sister he had been trying to find out what Corinna's thinking was. She seemed brainwashed. "That's not the Corinna I knew," he said.

"She's a cold individual now," Katie said. "Cold and hard."

Gavin was reflecting on that when he realized this was the only time he'd ever seen Corinna cry.

———

Krystyna Drewnowska's daughter, whom she named Victoria, had been born two months earlier. The occasion had warranted a brief report in the *Times-Dispatch*. "Millionaire homicide victim Roger de la Burde's fervent desire for a son will remain unfilled. The woman who claimed to be carrying his child gave birth yesterday—to a girl." But as Krystyna crossed the courtroom well that afternoon with a rolling, wide-hipped gait, she looked trim and stylish, her neck-length blond hair parted sharply on the side and swept across her wide brow.

Speaking with a thick Polish accent and occasionally mangling her syntax, Krystyna acknowledged that a recent DNA test had established that Roger was indeed the father of her new baby. Jack Lewis asked her about the evolution of their affair. It was, she said, a serious emotional relationship that evolved gradually. "I didn't have in mind to leave my husband or leave my family, so it really took a much longer time to come to the point that I was sure that I am very much in love with Roger and he was the same thing to me."

Warren Von Schuch, who had not known what Krystyna's testimony would be, listened with mounting incredulity to her story. The feminist movement would not be pleased, he decided. Beverly with her master's degree and Krystyna with her Ph.D. in biochemistry and they're fighting over Roger de la Burde. Twenty-five years of feminism and this was as far as they'd gotten.

On the stand, Krystyna said she and Roger had talked about having a child together since the summer of 1990. At Lewis's request, she read the jury the baby agreement. She explained how, when she and Roger had visited the fertility clinic and had asked Dr. Michael Edelstein about techniques for sex selection to ensure that the child would be a male, she had registered her disapproval. "When we left his office, I made it clear to Roger that I am not interested to have the child if this is in his mind," she said. "I made it very clear that this is not moral and not ethical."

At that point, Von Schuch leaned across to the defense table—since the courtroom was so small, the two counsels' tables were practically touching—and whispered to Murray Janus, "Well, I'm glad she draws the line somewhere."

Janus choked back a laugh.

———

Von Schuch had been joking, but his point, Janus thought, was nonetheless a telling one. After lunch, on cross-examination, he picked up the theme.

"You mentioned early on," he said to Krystyna, "you thought it was immoral to have predetermined the sex of the child."

"Yes," Krystyna replied.

"Did the thought ever occur to you, Dr. Drewnowska, that this might be immoral, what you were doing with Roger de la Burde?"

"Yes, it did. I was very uncomfortable with the situation. That's why I made the decision to leave my husband."

Janus tried, discreetly, to present Krystyna to the jury as someone with a motive to kill Roger. He got her to acknowledge that under the "pretermitted heir statute," her daughter Victoria stood to inherit a portion of Roger's estate equivalent to those received by Corinna and Colette. She also acknowledged that Wojtek had filed a cross-bill of divorce accusing her of willfully deserting him and their children. She admitted to having a key to Windsor, to sleeping at the farm from time to time, and to knowing where Roger kept his gun. But she denied discussing with him the possibility of having an abortion if the fetus was a girl, and she insisted that Roger wanted the child regardless of its sex. She explained she hadn't told him its sex when she learned of it because, first, she had only been informed unofficially over the phone and, second, because she didn't want him to refer to the still-unborn child in the dedication to his African art book, as he intended to do.

Janus showed Krystyna the medical lab's official written report. It was dated March 4, 1992. She must have received the report, which presumably would have meant she could no longer conceal the sex of the fetus from Roger, on the very day he died. Krystyna professed bewilderment at the document.

"I have never seen this page," she said. "I have no explanation what this means."

To Janus, this seemed clearly implausible and he assumed the jury would agree. In any event, he pointed out, Roger had learned one week earlier that she had received the informal results. "Are you saying that he wasn't curious? Didn't ask you, 'What's the result, Krystyna?'"

"He didn't ask me."

There was one final question Janus considered asking Krystyna: whether or not she smoked. But since he had heard conflicting reports on the matter and since he didn't want her declaring to the jury that she never smoked unless he could prove otherwise, he let the matter stand.

———

Lewis called Dennis Belcher, the attorney handling Roger's estate. Belcher estimated the estate's total value—the cash, the real estate, the mortgage notes from people, including Krystyna, who owed Roger money, and the stocks and bonds—to be between $5.5 million and $7 million. Beverly's portion of this estate, he said, included her lifetime right to reside at Windsor, a 20 percent interest in the balance of the estate once all taxes and debts had been paid, half of a $100,000 life insurance policy Roger had through Philip Morris, and the Jaguar. Altogether, Belcher estimated, her share was worth between $500,000 and $900,000. Under the new will, he continued, the one that was unsigned and found in Roger's computer after his death and thus had no legal validity, Beverly stood to inherit no more than $150,000.

According to commonwealth law, the prosecution was not required to try to prove motive. Jack Lewis had tried some cases where he'd been unable to get into motive at all, offering as evidence little more than a corpse, a weapon, and a witness. But in this case, he felt he had enough motive for five trials. Looking pointedly at the jurors, he asked, "Under Virginia law, Mr. Belcher, if a named beneficiary under a will murders the testator, does that person inherit?"

Murray Janus objected that the question was irrelevant.

"I think it's the law," Lewis said, "the very element that goes to motive in this case, Judge."

Judge Warren agreed.

"Virginia has a statute called the slayer's statute," Belcher explained, "so that if someone is convicted of murder, they do not inherit under a will or under an insurance policy."

———

Brigitte de la Burde took the stand at the end of the day. Dark circles ringed her eyes. She gave the impression of someone who was profoundly tired. Jack Lewis's primary objective in calling Brigitte was to impugn Beverly Monroe's character. To do that, he had to impugn Roger de la Burde's character as well. This meant potentially embarrassing Brigitte, but she had said during her pretrial interview that she was willing to testify about her ex-husband's infidelities.

"During the time that you and your husband were married," Lewis asked, "is it a fact that he had various affairs with various women?"

"That is correct." Brigitte spoke with a pronounced German accent.

"Was that something that caused you pain?"

"In the beginning it did, and then later we had kind of an agreement to keep the family together."

"These affairs that he had through the years, would these be considered discreet affairs that did not cause you public embarrassment and humiliation?"

Brigitte nodded. "They were discreet. While I was actually not supposed to know, I knew what was going on."

Roger's affair with Beverly Monroe, she explained, was different.

"Did she seem to flaunt her position with your husband?" Lewis asked.

"Yes, she did."

"And she didn't seem to care one iota how much it embarrassed—"

Janus interrupted, accusing Lewis of leading the witness, and Lewis backed off. He felt he had made his point.

Janus knew he had to tread carefully during cross-examination. If he treated the sympathetic, obviously victimized woman harshly, he could alienate the jurors. He got Brigitte to admit that two other women with whom Roger had lengthy affairs had visited Windsor and traveled with Roger. Even so, she was clearly less troubled by those relationships.

"Were you aware, Dr. Burde, that he continued to have other affairs with women other than Beverly from 1984 to 1991?"

"No," she said. "I had not much contact with him after I moved. I did not want to."

"Did you know of a cockamamy scheme he had in 1990 to have a child by—?"

"He told me," Brigitte said.

"What did you think of that?"

"I thought he was crazy."

"Nothing further."

Judge Warren was clearly pleased with the tactful way the two lawyers had treated Brigitte. As she stepped down, he told them, "I am proud of both of you."

4

It continued to rain throughout the week, a fitful, dreary, chilling rain that knocked the leaves from the trees and left muddy puddles on the court-house sidewalks. The bad weather did nothing to discourage attendance at the trial. Many people who lived in Powhatan, even those with jobs, made a point of stopping by to listen to at least a few hours of testimony. Some elderly women attended every day. The husband of one of the jurors brought their two children most afternoons after school was out, and they waved to their mother and held up their artwork.

Every day, Beverly's family and supporters—from friends at Philip Morris to Katie's high school classmates and Gavin's fraternity brothers—filled the first two rows on the right side of the gallery. Now that they had testified, Krystyna Drewnowska and Corinna and Brigitte de la Burde all sat in a group on the left. Pretty ironic, Gavin thought when he saw them together. Corinna used to tell him what a phony she thought Krystyna was. Now, drawn together by hatred of his mother, they had formed a clique.

While Katie, Gavin, and Shannon were still unable to sit in the court-room, Katie's boyfriend, Alan, brought out encouraging reports, and Katie did not feel things were as bleak as Shannon felt. Nonetheless, when she awoke every morning, her stomach seized up with dread. She couldn't show it. She needed to give her mother strength, and that meant holding her head high, appearing unfazed and proud, but the uncertainty about how the trial would end—and the exposure of her family's private affairs—made her sick.

Katie was also frustrated. She felt she knew without a doubt what had happened—that a depressed, unstable sixty-year-old man, saddled with the prospect of a child he suddenly realized he didn't actually want, had killed himself—but she had been denied a chance to explain this to the prosecutors or the police. And she was exhausted. She had taken charge of managing the family. She saw to it that Shannon and Gavin dressed appropriately for court, even if that meant lending Shannon one of her dark dresses and buying her a pair of cheap black shoes from Kmart. She wrote exhortational slogans—BE PROUD! BE STRONG! WE WILL WIN!—on posterboard and hung the signs in her brother's and mother's rooms. She called her mother's supporters to ensure that they would attend, and saw that everyone arrived at court on time and took their places on the front benches.

The days, she felt, were endless. Judge Warren, aware that the trial was proceeding more slowly than anticipated, kept court in session until six o'clock at night, by which time it was completely dark outside. One evening, sitting by herself in Alan's car as the trial dragged on, staring through the wet darkness at the illuminated windows of the courthouse, Katie began to wonder if this was really happening to her, if the courthouse and the trial, Roger's death, everything, would simply disappear if she blinked her eyes. It was all so unreal. It occurred to her that the most intense feeling she had about the trial was one of unreality, as if it were an extended out-of-body experience. She wondered whether it all seemed so unreal *because* it was un-real or whether this overpowering sense of unreality was a defensive tactic adopted by her mind to keep her from falling apart.

———

As the commonwealth wrapped up its case on the fourth day of the trial, Jack Lewis produced a string of witnesses who testified to Roger de la Burde's frame of mind just before his death. Barbara Samuels, his secretary, took the stand, and so did Don Beville, his publisher, and so did James

Whetstone, a real estate agent, who said Roger had called him on March 4, the day he died, about a prospective land purchase. "It was almost childish, his desire to buy this property." Jay Kauffman, one of the attorneys representing Roger in his lawsuit against Philip Morris, told the jury that while nothing had been put into writing, he believed the company was close to settling the case for approximately $500,000. Although Roger had begun arguing with his lawyers about how much of that would go to them—they had initially agreed to take 40 percent, but because they had invested more time in the case than expected, they now wanted 50 percent—he was nonetheless upbeat, Kauffman said.

Hazel Bunch, who had worked as Roger's bookkeeper, took the stand. Her bleached white hair and the reading glasses dangling around her neck gave her a matronly air. She described the lunch she'd had at Windsor with Roger the day he died. He was going to marry neither Beverly nor Krystyna, he'd said, but would spend several nights a week with Krystyna helping her raise the baby. Beverly had told him she would go along with whatever decision he made.

Murray Janus wanted to counter the positive, resolved, forward-looking portrait of Roger de la Burde that the commonwealth's witnesses had given and portray him instead as someone who was physically ill and so debauched that the jurors might question his sanity, or at least feel the world was well rid of the man. He believed he could do this by exploring in detail Hazel Bunch's relationship with Burde. Since she was a local woman, there was a risk this would backfire among the jurors, some of whom probably knew her. But Janus felt the benefit outweighed the risk.

"There came a time when he—let me see how to phrase this." Janus hesitated, seeking just the right words. "Excuse the vernacular, but, 'put the moves' on you. Is that—excuse the terminology—is that a fair statement?"

"Yes."

"And then you started having a sexual relationship with him, isn't that correct?"

"It's hard to classify it as a sexual relationship."

Janus tried a bald statement. "Roger Burde and Hazel Bunch had sexual intercourse. Is that true?"

"Not in the . . . not in the . . . " Hazel Bunch was having trouble completing the thought.

"True sense of the word?" Janus offered.

"True sense of the word."

"The reason you are having difficulty is because Roger tried but he was impotent. Isn't that correct, Mrs. Bunch?"

"Yes."

"And despite trying," Janus continued, "because of those problems, he couldn't consummate what he was trying to do."

"Yes."

"And that would get him upset and frustrated."

"No." Hazel Bunch suddenly seemed to overcome her embarrassed reluctance. "That always surprised me about him," she volunteered. "It really never seemed to bother him. . . . It was like, 'Okay, it happens,' or, 'Okay it doesn't happen,' you know?"

"Ma'am, I don't mean to delve into your private life, but that's what happens in a court of law," Janus said. "The two of you would be in bed, unclothed. He would be attempting to have intercourse with you. He couldn't do it because he was impotent. And it didn't bother him? Is that what you are telling the ladies and gentlemen of the jury?"

"That's exactly the way it was."

Someone in the gallery tittered. Judge Warren glowered at the spectators.

"Well, ma'am," Janus continued. "There came a time when you observed blood in his semen, isn't that correct, Mrs. Bunch?"

"He told me that he was having some prostate trouble, and it was not really . . . " She paused, clearly flustered. "It was not a natural relationship in that he mostly masturbated."

One Powhatan woman sitting through the trial saw the two ladies next to her, ladies who'd come all the way from Amelia County, jab each other in the ribs and exchange disbelieving, voyeuristically excited smirks.

"At the time when he masturbated, you observed blood in his semen?"

"Yes."

"That upset him, isn't that correct?"

"It didn't really upset him," Hazel Bunch said. "He told me that . . . it had happened before."

Janus asked, "You and Mr. Burde engaged in other sexual activities other than sexual intercourse, isn't that correct?"

"Mostly what I have said."

"Mr. Burde . . . suggested to you having sexual partners at Windsor, inviting other people to join you, isn't that correct?"

"No."

Suddenly Jack Lewis interrupted, telling the judge he needed to take up a matter outside the hearing of the jury and the witness. When they had all left the courtroom, Lewis said, "Your Honor, I think professional ethics dictate that I must inform the court that in my conversation with Mrs. Bunch, she told me that she had been asked by Roger Burde to arrange sexual encounters with another female, at a subsequent time. And this was shortly before the time of his death, and it never came to fruition. . . . She may be answering truthfully, Your Honor, but it's not what I recollect her having told me."

The judge was unfazed. "Well," he said, "maybe she tells you something one time and something different on the stand. That is really not unusual."

Before calling the jury back, the judge advised the lawyers to exercise caution. "I do want to try to eliminate any continued sort of titillating information that is only that, only titillating and not really helpful to the jury in deciding the question," he said. "I don't want to embarrass or humiliate this woman any more than she probably already is."

Janus responded that he had asked only the questions he thought were necessary and that the subjects they explored were beyond his control. "I didn't write the script, Judge Warren."

"I understand," the judge said.

When Hazel Bunch returned to the stand, Janus got her to admit that in the summer of 1991, well after Roger's affair with Krystyna had begun, he had talked to her about finding a woman in Powhatan County—someone intelligent, with a college education; Roger had given her an entire list of criteria, she said—who could bear him a child. Hazel Bunch also acknowledged the liaison Roger had urged her, on the day of his death, to arrange.

"It would be a sexual situation?"

"Not with me," Hazel said.

"With the friend."

"That's what I gathered."

At that final lunch, Janus asked in conclusion, when Roger felt he had resolved his problems and was looking forward to raising a child with Krystyna, didn't he think it was going to be a boy?

"He thought it was a boy."

———

Later that morning, after Hazel Bunch had left the courtroom, everyone heard the sound of an ambulance siren. It grew louder as the vehicle approached the courthouse, then faded. At the mid-morning break, a deputy informed Jack Lewis and Warren Von Schuch that after her testimony, Hazel Bunch had gone home and swallowed a handful of pills. The ambulance had been summoned to take her to the hospital.

Jack Lewis was furious. The poor woman had been so mortified by what Murray Janus had forced her to reveal in front of her friends and neighbors and fellow church members that she'd tried to take her life. Lewis wanted to confront Janus. Von Schuch, who was afraid Lewis would say or do something rash and possibly prompt a mistrial, talked his colleague into letting him speak to Beverly's lawyer instead. Outside the courtroom, he stopped Janus.

"You went too far," Von Schuch said. It had been unnecessary and cruel, he added, and it had angered Jack Lewis.

But Janus felt he couldn't afford to worry about either angering Jack Lewis or protecting the feelings and reputations of witnesses. He was defending a woman who could be sentenced to life in prison if found guilty and he had to seize every opportunity to prevent that from happening.

"Warren, this is a murder case," he said. "I'm going to do what I have to do."

Having made their respective points, both attorneys backed off and remained civil. After the break, Von Schuch asked the judge to allow Janus's forensics expert, Herbert MacDonell, to testify out of order because of a scheduling conflict. A well-known independent consultant from Corning, New York, MacDonell had testified in a number of high-profile cases, such as the police shooting of the Black Panther Fred Hampton and the assassinations of Robert Kennedy and Martin Luther King, and was the subject of a flattering book, *The Evidence Never Lies,* which described him as "a modern Sherlock Holmes." Janus had a high regard for MacDonell. In fact, he had always wanted to hire him, but until Beverly Monroe came along, he had never had a client who both needed a forensics expert and could afford to pay for one.

MacDonell had a salt-and-pepper beard and spoke in ponderous, elaborately qualified sentences. After conducting his own tests, he told the jury, he had concluded that the black marks on the fourth and fifth fingers of Roger de la Burde's right hand had come from gunpowder discharged out of a gap between the breech end of the gun's barrel and the front end of its cylinder. What he believed Burde had done, he told the jurors, was hold the gun upside down, with the fingers of his right hand clenching the barrel and the cylinder frame, and then pull the trigger with his left thumb. "This is not at all uncommon in suicides," he said, "because of a wish to steady the revolver in some fashion."

However, when Janus asked him what he as a professor of forensics made of the evidence, he could not eliminate the possibility that someone had killed Roger. "I concluded it was a suicide, but I certainly would not say that it was impossible, absolutely impossible, that someone else might have used the revolver in a most awkward fashion, reaching over a fifteen-inch back of a sofa. It seems almost an anatomical impossibility, but I don't use the word *impossible*." He added, "I cannot categorically say it was impossible that it wasn't even an accident."

Von Schuch was struck by MacDonell's tentativeness. If he himself were paying an expert thousands of dollars, he would expect a more aggressively rendered opinion. Von Schuch knew MacDonell's work. He was, in Von Schuch's view, one of the top fingerprint experts in the country. But Von Schuch did not believe that MacDonell's expertise was as extensive in matters such as gunshot residue and blood spatter. There were definite weak points, he thought, in the professor's testimony.

On cross-examination, Von Schuch forced MacDonell to admit that in his test, he had used a slightly different model revolver from Burde's Smith & Wesson. MacDonell also acknowledged that he had conducted his test with fingerprint powder instead of gunpowder. Von Schuch hoped that since Powhatan was a rural county, there were one or two hunters on the jury who would find that an important distinction. He had the professor describe how he had plugged the cartridge, filled with fingerprint powder, with a cork; how he had not, when firing the gun, wrapped his hand around it to duplicate the technique he claimed Burde had used; and how he had not attempted to re-create, as Ann Jones had done, the gunshot residue patterns on the pillows or around the wound.

Sitting down, Von Schuch felt that he had neutralized the man. Mac-Donell, it seemed to the prosecutor, had strengthened rather than undercut the commonwealth's forensics. For the kind of money Murray was paying MacDonell, Von Schuch thought, he himself could have done a better job.

———

Von Schuch and Lewis had taken to eating lunch in the conference room in the sheriff's office, beneath the courthouse, where they discussed their strategy in private. That Thursday, on the way to lunch, Von Schuch saw a broad-shouldered black woman sitting in one of the small courthouse waiting rooms. She was smoking a cigarette and drinking a Pepsi.

The woman's name was Zelma Smith, Lewis explained. He told Von Schuch how Beverly Monroe had tried to buy an untraceable gun from Zelma in the spring of 1991. Zelma's testimony would prove, Lewis said, that Beverly had been thinking of murdering *someone*, maybe Roger, maybe even Krystyna, a good year before the crime had taken place.

Von Schuch was instinctively skeptical. "Come on, the story's a little bizarre," he said. "Beverly met this woman on a rainy day in a cemetery and asked for a gun?"

Lewis said he was convinced Zelma was telling the truth because of her accurate description of Beverly's tan raincoat. But half the women in the country, it seemed to Von Schuch, had tan raincoats. What other color raincoats did they wear? Von Schuch thought Zelma Smith's tale was something Dave Riley had sold Lewis. She was not, Von Schuch felt, going to go over well in the courtroom. "Whether she's telling the truth or not," he told Lewis, "let's look at the makeup of this jury and what this is about. Do we really need this?"

But Lewis was adamant that the commonwealth call Zelma Smith. Returning to the courtroom, Von Schuch feared that Smith's lack of credibility—she was a career con artist, a check kiter—might taint the commonwealth's entire case. But it was Lewis's call, he thought. It was Lewis's jurisdiction and Lewis's witness.

———

Beverly watched with a strange feeling of anxious curiosity as Zelma Smith took the stand. Everything about her was *big*—her hips, her shoulders, her head. She had a wide mouth and spoke, Beverly thought, in an accent that was more rural than urban.

Lewis brought out what he referred to as her "rather extensive criminal history." She acknowledged all nine of her felony convictions, modestly responding, "Yes, sir," as Lewis asked her about each item on the list. Then she explained how, in 1991, while operating her tax filing and bookkeeping service, Zelma Smith Enterprises, she had received a telephone message from a Ms. Nelson and had called her back only to have a man answer the phone.

"He said, 'Hello.' I said, 'May I speak to Ms. Nelson?' He said, 'Who?' I repeated myself. I said, 'Ms. Nelson.' And he said, 'Ms. Nelson don't live here.' But then he said—I heard a voice in the background—and he said, 'Wait a minute.' And it was like he put his hand over the receiver. And then a woman came on the phone, and she said, 'This is Ms. Nelson. I can't talk now,' after I identified myself. She said, 'Let me call you right back,' and hung up."

When Ms. Nelson returned the call, Zelma continued, she suggested meeting at a Burger King on Parham Road at one-thirty the following Tuesday. Since Zelma had a business appointment over there that day anyway, she agreed. At the restaurant, she said, Ms. Nelson offered to pay her $800 for a small handgun with the serial numbers filed off, and gave her $100 for expenses. Once she'd located a weapon, she continued, she met Ms. Nelson again, this time at a cemetery on Patterson Avenue.

"Was she already there when you arrived?" Lewis asked.

"Yes, sir, she was there," Zelma said firmly. "She was sitting on a little bench in front of a pond with some ducks in it."

At this second meeting, she went on, she gave Ms. Nelson the gun, a .357 Magnum. "Well, she looked at it," Zelma said. "She said that wouldn't do at all. That's what she said."

"Did she pay you any money that day for your expenses?"

"Yes, sir. She paid me four hundred and eighty dollars for my expenses up to that point."

"What was supposed to happen afterward?"

"I was supposed to keep looking."

"Did you keep looking some more?"

"No, sir."

Lewis pointed at Beverly Monroe. "Look at her closely," he said. "Is there any question in your mind Ms. Nelson is actually Mrs. Monroe?"

"No, sir. No doubt in my mind."

"The day you met her out at the cemetery," Lewis asked, "do you recall what the weather conditions were?"

"Yes, sir. It was drizzling."

"Did she have . . . anything to protect her from the rain?"

"Yes, sir. She had an umbrella and she had on a trench coat."

Lewis had Beverly's umbrella and trench coat with him. He held up the umbrella. "I show you this umbrella," he said. "I don't know if that made any impression one way or the other."

"No, sir."

The answer spoke to Zelma's credibility, Lewis thought. If she was lying about meeting Beverly, he figured, she would have said she recognized the umbrella. He picked up Beverly's raincoat. "I show you this trench coat, is that—?"

"Yes, sir, that looks just like it."

———

David Hicks handled the cross-examination of Zelma Smith. She was the sort of career criminal he had become accustomed to questioning while working in the Richmond prosecutor's office, and several aspects of her story seemed to beg for withering sarcasm. He began with her selective memory. "What month was it that this person called you?"

"It was in the springtime," Zelma said.

"What month?" Hicks asked again. Zelma had said the meeting at the Burger King took place on a Tuesday. If she would tell them the month it supposedly occurred, Beverly could check her appointment book. Since she had been working then, she might well have an alibi for every Tuesday afternoon of whatever month Zelma specified.

"I can't remember the exact month," Zelma said, "but it was in the springtime."

"You can remember the exact raincoat, but you don't remember the month?"

"Yes, sir."

Hicks turned to the question of Zelma's remuneration. "So a person who you never met before gave you five hundred and eighty dollars, in a short period of time, and you had this person's telephone number, didn't you?"

"Yes, sir."

"You never called that person again?"

"For what reason?"

"You got five hundred eighty dollars for doing nothing, ma'am. You wouldn't call that person again to see if there was any more?"

Zelma's answer was a confusing nonsequitur. Hicks tried again to get her to respond to the question, but she wouldn't, so he gave up. "What was the telephone number that you called?" he asked.

"I do not remember."

"You didn't keep it?"

"I kept it. It was in my automobile with some paperwork, but my car was stolen."

Hicks glanced at the jury, as if to say, Convenient, wasn't it? "How did you find out about the case, Ms. Smith?" he asked.

"Actually, in a . . ." She faltered. "A article."

"In the newspaper."

"It may have been, but I doubt it. I think it was *People* magazine." She saw the article in June, Zelma said, when she was awaiting sentencing. But she didn't call Lewis, she explained, until August, *after* she had been sentenced to seven years in prison for passing worthless checks and jumping bail.

"Has Mr. Lewis offered to help you out a little bit with your time if you come on in and testify today?"

"No, sir."

"You had no thoughts, whatsoever, ma'am, that calling Mr. Lewis up in August, after you got final disposition of your charges and saying, 'I might have some information to help you'—you had no idea that that might help you out with your current situation?"

"No, sir."

Hicks sat down. Janus gave him an approving nod. It was, Janus thought, about as thorough a demolition as could be accomplished by imputation alone.

———

For the commonwealth's last witness, Lewis called Sheldon Gosline, the aspiring curator who had lived at Windsor for a few months in 1989 while helping Roger catalog his African art collection. Sheldon wore tortoiseshell spectacles, a striped shirt, and his blond hair brushed back off his brow. Beverly Monroe always thought he looked as if he had just come off an English cricket field.

Speaking with a plummy accent, Sheldon told the jurors that it was inconceivable that Roger, who was excited about the long-awaited completion of his book, would have killed himself. However, he said, Beverly had invested a great deal of time during the funeral trying to convince everyone that the death could only be a suicide. Furthermore, he said, Beverly had a key to Windsor. He knew this because she told him during the funeral that the caretaker, Joe Hairfield, had called her at eight-thirty on the morning of March 5 to come and unlock the house.

Sheldon next insisted that Beverly had a copy of Roger's will, which she produced when Katie, in Sheldon's presence the day after the funeral, questioned her about it at the house on Old Gun Road. "Beverly said, 'Well, why don't we just go and look at the will?' And Katie said, 'Oh, you have a copy?' Apparently she did not know that. And Beverly said, 'Yes, it's upstairs in my room in my drawer.' And they then left. We were in the kitchen at the time. They went upstairs to Beverly's room and got out the copy of the will and started looking at it. I then walked into the living room–dining room area and I saw them looking over the will and overheard some discussion as to its contents, from below."

Gosline had one other damning recollection, which contradicted a key part of the story Beverly had told everyone else—from Dave Riley to Murray Janus—about what had happened the night of March 4. According to Sheldon, Beverly had originally explained to him that she came home that night at eleven o'clock, but then, on Katie's advice, changed it to nine-thirty. "Katie told Beverly, '. . . Mother, I don't think that you should say that you left at eleven. You should say you left at nine-thirty.' And Beverly said, 'Why?' And Katie said, 'Come over here, I have something to tell you.' "

———

Throughout Sheldon's testimony, Beverly Monroe had been writing notes on her yellow legal pad. This is *not* true, she wrote, this is *all* wrong; Sheldon was confused about everything. He said Roger's niece Dita Huber was Sig Huber's girlfriend when in fact she was his sister. Sheldon said Beverly had told him she drove to Windsor in ten minutes when it never took less than twice that long.

But those were small details. He was also confusing what she, Beverly, had told him with what Barbara Samuels must have told him. It was Barbara whom Hairfield had actually called at eight-thirty on the morning of March 5, because he wanted someone to unlock the door to the house. And Sheldon was confused about the will. Corinna had been looking for Roger's will. Sheldon had garbled a recollection of hearing Beverly and

Katie talk about where the will might be and checking through her own papers to see if she had a copy. And she had never told *anyone* she had come home at eleven o'clock on the night of March 4. Sheldon was confusing the time of her return from Windsor with the time of her return from the Safeway, which had been around eleven. He had jumbled his memories, just as Corinna had.

Janus looked at these notes. He didn't see how they would help him in his cross-examination of Gosline. To go over Gosline's assertions would simply give him an opportunity to repeat the charges without really allowing Janus to rebut them. He had faced the same problem with Corinna's incriminating but apparently confused recollection of what Beverly had said to her the day of the funeral. If you couldn't disprove a claim, you were better off ignoring its substance and going after the witness in some other fashion. Janus thought the best way to impeach Sheldon Gosline's testimony was to attack his credibility.

Forsaking the pleasantries with which he usually greeted witnesses, Janus walked over to the witness box and asked abruptly, "Who is Eshu?"

"Eshu is an Egyptian deity," Sheldon replied.

"Egyptian or Nigerian?"

"A Nigerian." Sheldon, clearly embarrassed, apologized for the mistake.

"Roger was a follower of Eshu, the deity, the god, isn't that correct?"

"Well," Sheldon said, "I would say that to an extent, Roger's life was ruled by Eshu." He saw an opportunity to recover his dignity and score a point off Murray Janus. "You see," he added pedantically, "I was a little bit thrown off by your pronunciation of the word, because it is *E*shu."

"*E*shu? I apologize for the mispronunciation."

A ripple of laughter spread through the courtroom. It was contagious. Even the judge gave a dry chuckle, and Warren Von Schuch, at the prosecution table, felt the urge to laugh rise up in his gut. He had been sitting there for days listening to the most bizarre testimony, about baby agreements and sex selection and serial adultery and meetings in cemeteries, and it had all come down to this, an argument over the pronunciation of the name of a Nigerian deity. Von Schuch looked over at David Hicks. Hicks was also fighting down laughter, and so was one of the jurors. That was when Von Schuch lost it. The laughter came welling up. He ducked his head below the table, laughing so uncontrollably that he felt tears rolling down his cheeks.

Murray Janus, not displeased by the stir among the spectators, pressed ahead with his line of questioning. "Eshu, the god, committed suicide, isn't that correct?"

"I am sorry, sir, deities do not commit suicide."

"But in mythology, this deity, this Nigerian god, committed suicide, didn't he?"

"Well, if you didn't consider Eshu to be a true deity, then I guess you could say that."

Janus asked Sheldon what he meant by saying that Roger's life was ruled by Eshu.

"I used that expression metaphorically, that his life was ruled by the order of chaos," Sheldon replied. "Confusion was security for Roger."

Sheldon, unprompted by Janus, then brought up the subject of Krystyna Drewnowska. "I considered her to be a gold digger in the true sense of the word."

"You didn't trust Krystyna one bit, did you, sir?"

"I did not." Gosline leaned an elbow on the witness-stand box front and gestured with his other hand. "I felt she was only after Roger for his wealth, and I thought that it was unwise for Roger to be associating with her. And I advised against the association." But Sheldon acknowledged that Roger, rather than succumbing to the manipulations of others, was much more likely to be the one doing the manipulating, in both his sexual and his business relationships. "Roger was very hardened as a businessman," he said, "and made enemies with other hardened businessmen, whom he outsmarted." Sheldon also reiterated his conviction that Roger would not have killed himself.

"That's your firm belief?" Janus asked.

"Yes."

"And if it was a homicide, you want to see someone convicted, isn't that a fair statement?"

"I guess you could say that, yes."

Murray Janus's imputation annoyed Jack Lewis. Rising to question Sheldon on re-direct examination, he asked, "In response to Mr. Janus's question, if he was murdered, you would like to see his murderer punished?"

"Yes," Sheldon said. "There should be justice."

"You would not commit perjury against someone to see they were convicted if they didn't do it—"

Murray Janus cut Lewis off by objecting, and Judge Warren ordered Sheldon not to answer the question.

"I was only addressing what Mr. Janus was implying," Lewis said, "that he might be perjuring himself to see that somebody gets punished for murder."

Judge Warren started to frame a question, but Sheldon interrupted him. "May I say something?" he asked.

"No, you may not say anything," the judge snapped.

At the prosecutors' table, Warren Von Schuch watched this haggling with disbelief. Sheldon Gosline seemed like a complete goofball. Von Schuch liked to end a murder case by directing the jury's attention back to the gravity and tragedy of the crime. It was, he thought, best to conclude with something that unmistakably pointed to the defendant as the perpetrator of the crime, or, at the very least, with a sobering witness. Corinna de la Burde would have done the job more effectively than the duo of Zelma Smith and Sheldon Gosline—the check-kiting bail jumper and the Egyptologist goofball.

When Lewis sat back down, Von Schuch leaned over and whispered, "That's a hell of a way to end a case, Jack."

5

Once the prosecution's case was complete, Beverly wondered whether Murray Janus should move for a mistrial. Lewis, she felt, had lied to the judge and the jury. He had asked one witness if he knew that Beverly had hired a detective to trail Roger, that she had spit on Roger at a restaurant and tried to choke him at Windsor, and that she had told someone at the funeral, "I'm glad the bastard's dead, I hated his guts." Lewis had *promised* to produce witnesses to testify about these allegations, and when Judge Warren had pressed him, he had reiterated the promise. Yet no witnesses had ever appeared. The vicious allegations had been allowed to remain in the record, and in the jury's memory, unsubstantiated but unchallenged.

Janus, however, decided against asking for a mistrial. Every case and every defense had its loose ends. Lewis could probably offer Judge Warren a plausible explanation for why he decided not to or was unable to produce the witnesses responsible for the allegations, and the matter would end there. Also, Janus felt the momentum of the trial favored Beverly. Even before putting on the defense, he thought that the prosecution's case left ample room for reasonable doubt, and he didn't want to have to start over with a new jury. He believed the details of the forensics were probably lost on the jurors, who, he hoped, had been left with the impression that Herb MacDonell's suicide theory offset Ann Jones's homicide theory.

Janus began the defense by calling Sylvia Beckner, a florist and friend of Roger's, who testified that he had become so depressed and disoriented in the past year that he had shown up at her shop one day wearing a business suit and bedroom slippers. Chuck Collins, the electrician who had done work at Windsor, testified that Roger was so desperate for money that he had asked Chuck for early repayment of a $5,000 personal loan. He also said that he suspected his ex-wife, Barb, had been having an affair with Roger and that she smoked Marlboros, had a temper, had a key to Windsor, and knew how to shoot a gun. Barb Collins, who followed Chuck, told the jury that Roger had discussed having a child with her and had shown her documents that he said had been stolen from Philip Morris. Beverly Monroe, she said, did not have a key to Windsor. Shannon and Katie testified that in the last six months of his life, Roger had seemed tired and lethargic and had complained about his health.

By that time, Murray Janus was feeling drained. Night had fallen; the windows were black. He had risen before dawn to prepare, and had been in the stuffy, overcrowded courtroom for the better part of eight hours. Much of that time he'd been on his feet. He had examined or cross-examined sixteen witnesses. He had argued with some of them, had apparently driven one to attempt suicide, and had faced off with Von Schuch over his tactics. He had skipped lunch, his voice was hoarse, and his head throbbed.

"Judge Warren, with all due respect, I have a splitting headache," he said. "Would this be an appropriate time . . ."

The judge, a former trial lawyer, nodded. "You've got all the reason in the world," he told Janus, and then struck the gavel solidly, bringing the day's proceedings to a close.

———

Instead of going home, Janus returned with David Hicks to their office. The building was largely deserted; a security guard let them in through the locked front door. Murray's secretary told them that an anonymous caller had threatened revenge against Janus for what he'd done to Hazel Bunch.

Janus shrugged it off. All trial lawyers received such calls from time to time. The secretary also said that a Dennis Barden had called to say he could provide an alibi for Beverly Monroe.

Janus called the man. Barden told him that when he had seen pictures of Beverly Monroe on television he recognized her because, on the night of March 4, he and his son had been standing in line at the Safeway. Beverly was behind them. She had knelt down to comfort his little boy, who'd been crying. When they fell to talking, Barden told Beverly he was looking for work as a carpenter and gave her his business card. Barden said that he'd be happy to testify and that, in fact, he had called the commonwealth attorney with his story but his call had never been returned.

Dave Riley, Janus thought, had disparaged Beverly Monroe's claim that she had been at the Safeway around the time Roger died. But if, as Don Beville had testified, Roger had called him shortly after ten o'clock, and if, as Gavin Monroe would testify, Beverly had come home around ten, gone out to the grocery store, and come back around eleven, and if both Beverly's Safeway receipt and Dennis Barden's testimony put her at the supermarket at ten-forty, her alibi seemed close to seamless. Janus now had his own surprise witness who could clinch his client's defense. He still had a splitting headache, however.

———

The experience of testifying left both Shannon and Katie exasperated. Shannon had wanted to stand up and scream. She'd built this whole speech in her mind, but instead of being able to tell the jury what she thought, she'd had to simply answer the questions put to her by Murray Janus and Jack Lewis. "You love your mother, do you not?" Lewis had asked. It was practically the only thing he *had* asked her, as if to show the jury that since she did love her mother, they could dismiss anything she said as biased.

But at least Shannon and Katie were free now to join Beverly's supporters in the courtroom on the fifth day of the trial, when Beverly was scheduled to testify. So many spectators had squeezed into the courtroom that morning that they outnumbered the seats. As the proceedings began, many of them were still searching for places.

"If you all can find a seat, that's fine," Judge Warren informed them. "If you can't, I'm sorry but you will have to leave."

The deputies escorted a few unlucky people from the overcrowded room. Janus called his client to the stand. Beverly, wearing a navy suit and a white shirt, tried to make herself comfortable in the witness chair. It was an unnerving moment. Beverly always felt uneasy being the center of attention. She sensed the avid curiosity of the jurors and the spectators. Murray had told her he had no hesitation about putting her on the stand. She would make a good witness, he had said; the jury would believe her. He had intended to be reassuring, but it was frightening to think that the verdict might depend on whether or not the jurors *happened* to believe her. What if for some reason they didn't?

"Did you kill Roger Burde?" Janus asked.

"Absolutely not."

"Were you present when he was shot?"

"No, I was not."

All morning, Janus led Beverly through her story. She described her history with Roger, his difficulties with his children, his health problems and money worries, the affair with Krystyna, and his numerous compulsions. "It was like living with an alcoholic," she told the jury.

Janus thought such an explanation was inadequate. He found it hard to believe that Beverly, as she claimed, had never felt jealous of or threatened by Krystyna Drewnowska. He was afraid the jurors would be similarly skeptical. If they decided that Beverly was being dishonest about her true feelings toward Krystyna, they could easily conclude that Beverly was lying about everything else as well, since the threat Krystyna seemed to pose to Beverly's relationship with Roger was at the core of the commonwealth's theory of motive.

Janus, hoping to draw from Beverly a more personal reaction to Krystyna, hoping to make his client seem understandable and human and sympathetic, asked how she felt when she discovered the baby agreement Krystyna had drafted.

"I was concerned about the legal complications," Beverly said.

That was not the direction Janus wanted Beverly to take. "Ma'am," he said. "Beside the legal complication, what about the moral and the ethical complications?"

"The moral also," Beverly said. Murray had told her to keep her answers as brief as possible and never to digress or volunteer unnecessary information, and she was trying to follow his instructions.

Janus, however, waited for her to continue. When she said nothing further, he prompted her. "What were your thoughts on that?"

"I tried to tell Roger that it wasn't the right thing to do for the child."

This wasn't what Janus wanted, either. He tried again to elicit something personal. "Beverly, aside from the child, what were your thoughts on him having sexual intercourse with Krystyna Drewnowska in order to produce this child?"

"He told me at the time that it was going to be an artificial insemination," she said, adding, "I didn't believe that, of course."

Beverly, Janus realized, was just not going to deliver emotionally on this particular point. But she became more persuasive as she proceeded with her story. She denied knowing Zelma Smith, explained that she was mystified by Sheldon Gosline's statements, identified the Safeway receipt she'd received the night of March 4 and the check she'd written for the groceries, and described her grief and horror when she saw Roger's body. It was the first time, she said, she'd ever seen a corpse. When Dave Riley interviewed her at police headquarters on March 26, she said, he had sat so close to her and repeated his scenario—that she'd been in the room when Roger shot himself—so many times and with such conviction and forcefulness that she felt she was being hypnotized.

At the Drewry's Bluff meeting, she recalled, Riley had told her he had boxes of files on her case, all containing evidence about the circumstances surrounding Roger's death. "He said, 'I can take these circumstances and twist them in any way I want.' . . . He said that he could charge me with first-degree murder and that nobody would believe me. . . . He just went on and on about all the terrible things he could do to me and my children. . . . I was stunned, frightened. I couldn't think of anything to say." She described how she had told Riley she had the Safeway receipt. "He sort of laughed and he said, 'Anybody can get receipts. You know nobody is going to believe you.' . . . If he could just take Mr. Lewis a hypothetical explanation, he said, there probably would be no charge. It would all go away. He looked at me, and he said, 'Do you understand what I mean? Do you understand what I mean?' He was yelling at me. What I understood was that if I didn't do what he said, he was going to arrest me right there on the spot. . . . He started going through this hypothetical explanation of things. . . . And I would tell him, 'I don't remember that.' And then he would write it down anyway."

"You signed it?" Janus asked.

"Yes, I signed it. He said I had to sign it."

———

During the lunch break, Beverly went into the women's bathroom, down the hall from the courtroom. Among the women at the mirror checking their makeup were Brigitte de la Burde and Fanny, the Burdes' longtime maid. The bathroom grew suddenly quiet. All the other women were watching them. Beverly wasn't going to ignore Brigitte, she decided, and she wasn't going to leave, either. She walked up to her and said, "You surely know that I didn't do this to Roger."

Brigitte seemed to blanch. "I can't really talk to you," she said, and left.

When Beverly had run into Brigitte in the dress shop two months earlier, she had sensed, though Brigitte had said nothing explicit, that Roger's ex-wife believed the charges against her were wrong. But whatever Brigitte may have thought back in August, Beverly realized that she had now clearly come to accept the prosecution's version of the facts. There was no use in trying to talk to her.

———

Jack Lewis had decided that Von Schuch, the more experienced homicide prosecutor, should conduct the cross-examination of the defendant. When the court reconvened after lunch, Von Schuch stood up, buttoned the front of his suit jacket, and crossed the well. Beverly Monroe, who had returned to the witness chair, watched him tentatively.

"Good afternoon, Mrs. Monroe," Von Schuch said. "Let me tell you at this point I know Mr. Janus had you on the stand for a period of several hours this morning, and I understand it was a grueling experience. I would like you to know I don't intend to keep going that long."

Having reassured Beverly—and established, for the jury, his own sympathetic side—Von Schuch had her acknowledge her intelligence, her education, and her familiarity with legal work. After dwelling on the intellectual challenge of obtaining a master's degree in organic chemistry, he turned to Beverly's job at Philip Morris.

"Do you work with lawyers?"

"Yes. There are two attorneys there."

"Do you work with other research scientists?"

"Yes, I have contact with them."

"Some of them with Ph.D.s or doctorates, things of that nature?"

"Yes. We rely on them."

"And those are people that also have a great deal of education and experience in very difficult areas, like science, math, physics. Is that a correct statement?"

"Yes."

Once Von Schuch had demonstrated Beverly's intellectual sophistication, he asked a series of questions designed to reveal how intimately involved Beverly was in the details of Roger's life. She had known Roger for thirteen years, she said. She visited Windsor one, two, or three times a week, sometimes spending the night. She and Roger had jointly invested in some half-dozen real estate ventures. She had written articles for him and helped edit his book.

"Did you know, Mrs. Monroe, that prior to Roger's death he hadn't finished his art book?"

"Yes."

"Did you know that prior to his death, he hadn't finished his new will?"

"Yes."

"Did you know prior to his death he had . . . Mrs. Samuels go buy him an exercise bicycle?"

"No, I didn't know that."

"You didn't know that." Von Schuch knew how to use inflection to convey disbelief or outright scorn, and he now allowed a skeptical tone to color his words. He pointed out that in Roger's new will, the unsigned one, Beverly's share of the estate was seriously diminished. "Do you have an explanation why he was reducing your part and your involvement in his . . . financial empire?"

"Honestly, Mr. Von Schuch, I am not really aware that he was."

Von Schuch, feeling he didn't need to argue the point but merely to introduce it, turned to Roger's relationship with Krystyna Drewnowska. "Now, Krystyna was much younger than you at the time?"

"Yes."

"I apologize for having put that that way. She is a younger woman."

"That doesn't bother me."

"She is an attractive woman."

"Yes."

"And Krystyna, she is an intelligent woman."

"Yes, she is."

"Much like yourself, correct? She has got a Ph.D. in biochemistry, almost the same kind of scientific training you have, correct?"

"Yes."

"And she is going to bear the child that he is going to raise and mold into his own image, isn't she?"

"If it were a son, I think so, yes."

"Roger was willing to accept a son or daughter, wasn't he?"

"He wanted a son."

"But the agreement called for the same thing regardless of sex, didn't it?"

"That was in the agreement."

Von Schuch pointed out that in the thirteen years Beverly was involved with Roger, he had not made such a serious contractual commitment to any other woman. "You . . . became involved in Roger's life when Mrs. de la Burde had not yet departed the house, is that correct?"

"Yes."

"And you heard, and you recall her testimony, that she was trying to hold the family together?"

"Yes, I heard that."

"And she left because she complained that you were squeezing her out, that you were being more aggressive than the others and she couldn't take it anymore. Do you recall that?"

"I recall her saying that, yes."

"Well, isn't that exactly what was happening to you? Wasn't Krystyna squeezing you out? The baby. The agreement. The commitment. The financial support."

"No, it wasn't like that. No."

Beverly wanted to explain that whatever Roger may have led Krystyna to believe, the truth was that he considered her nothing but a surrogate mother and had in fact been simultaneously talking to other women about bearing a child for him, but Von Schuch wouldn't allow it. Instead, he asked her to read from the letter she had written in 1990, which Krystyna had found, copied, and turned over to the police. He pointed to a specific passage. Beverly began to read, but her voice was almost inaudible.

"Ma'am, I'm sorry," Von Schuch said. "Would you please speak up?"

Beverly, growing confused, lost her place for a moment and then started over. " 'If you had ever actually asked and planned for me to marry you, which you haven't—' "

"All right," Von Schuch said, cutting her off. He pointed out that this contradicted her claim, to Greg Neal and to Dave Riley, that Roger had frequently asked her to marry him.

"Roger asked me so many times, both to live with him and to marry him," Beverly said, "but never did he meet my condition for that kind of commitment."

"When you say 'actually,' then, you don't mean it?"

"When I say 'actually,' I mean according to what I understand marriage to mean."

It was a weak distinction, Von Schuch thought. "Were your grandparents involved in the funeral business?" he asked.

Beverly admitted that her grandparents and one of her brothers had operated a funeral parlor.

"Were you considering that when you answered Mr. Janus's question about the fact you had never seen a dead body before?"

"I think," Beverly said, referring to the discovery of a loved one's body, "Mr. Janus's question was directed towards my finding and experiencing *that* kind of scene."

It was a second weak distinction, Von Schuch thought. Either you've seen a dead body or you haven't. He now raised the issue of Beverly's disputed confession to Dave Riley. Beverly at first denied that she had confessed, contradicting the testimony of Greg Neal, Wyatt Omohundro, and the two police secretaries. She then explained that what she had done instead was merely agree with Riley's repeated suggestions that she had been present when Roger killed himself. It was, Von Schuch thought, the third weak distinction she'd tried to make. Once could be an accident and twice a coincidence, but the third time something happened, you had a pattern—in this case, of disingenuous hair splitting.

"Why would you agree with Mr. Riley?" he asked.

"Mr. Riley was so convincing, and so convinced himself," Beverly said. "He told me that he knew, he really knew, that I had to have been there. I kept telling him, 'I can't remember that.' 'I can't see it.' 'I don't remember at all.' He would talk over my voice. 'Yes, you remember. Don't you remember? Give me that much.' And I would say, 'I can't remember.' It went on and on. I became exhausted, I know."

Von Schuch ratcheted up the skepticism in his voice as he bore in on the one claim by Beverly that he thought the jury, and most of the people in the gallery, would have the greatest difficulty accepting. "Mr. Riley, a state police investigator, convinced you, a woman with two college degrees, who speaks two languages, to agree with him when he makes a suggestion that was totally inconsistent with your knowledge of what happened that night, correct? Is that what you are telling this jury?"

"I am telling you Mr. Riley convinced me he was right and I was wrong."

There it was, Von Schuch thought, the central implausibility in her story, reduced to its most simplified form. He asked about the vision she had told Corinna she'd had of trying to wrest the gun from Roger's hand. "Did you tell that to Corinna?"

"I still have, have visions . . . " Beverly's voice faltered as emotion overcame her.

Von Schuch, thinking she had said all she was going to say, asked again, "Did you make the statement to Corinna?"

"Wait," Judge Warren interrupted. "I don't think she finished."

"I'm sorry," Von Schuch told him. "I thought she did."

"*I'm* sorry," Beverly said. "I just couldn't get it out."

"Mrs. Monroe, take your time, please," Von Schuch said.

After a moment, Beverly continued. "I still have visions and dreams about trying, trying to do something to stop Roger. And I also have dreams about my father. I still have them. But if I had been able, if I had been able to be there—"

"Mrs. Monroe, my—"

"—if I had been able to be there, I could have done something." Beverly stopped again, once more overcome with emotion, and this time she began sobbing.

Von Schuch looked over at the jurors. One of them seemed to roll his eyes. The overt display of disbelief surprised Von Schuch. He had been unable to trick Beverly into contradicting herself or to get her to admit anything she hadn't already planned on admitting, but he now felt he had maneuvered her into a position in which she seemed to the jurors to be acting. He had asked a straightforward factual question, and she had wandered off onto the subject of her father's suicide, as if she were reminding herself of this tragedy in order to force herself to cry. It looked to Von Schuch like a transparent play for sympathy, and at least one of the jurors seemed to agree. Beverly had not opened herself up factually to impeachment, but she had begun to lose credibility. Von Schuch told Beverly he had simply asked if she recalled making the statement about visions to Corinna.

"I understand the question," Beverly said.

"Would you prefer to answer the question?" Von Schuch asked. "If you didn't go off, it might not be so painful to you."

As he wrapped up his cross-examination, Von Schuch had one final objective. Murray Janus had wasted no opportunity to disparage Roger de la

Burde. Von Schuch wanted to raise a question: If Burde was so despicable, what should the jury make of the woman who had been his collaborator, partner, and consort? The maneuver, which Von Schuch had used in other trials, required a setup.

"Roger has been described," he said, "as having two personalities. . . . The first personality was a kind personality, a person who wanted to be good, a person who would make the kind of statements that he made about Corinna, his loving daughter, when he expressed his love eloquently in his will. He was capable of being that kind of man, correct?"

"He was capable," Beverly answered. "That was not his primary personality."

"Was the primary personality the ruthless one, the immoral one that we have heard described here all week?"

"Yes, the ego-driven one, yes."

"This was the man you had become sexually involved with, correct?"

"Yes."

"This was the man you worked in business with and helped with his art, his hobbies and art collections and things like that, is that correct?"

"Yes."

"This is the man that you devoted thirteen years of your life to?"

"Well, not quite thirteen years, but it was a goodly time."

"A good portion of it, is that correct?"

"Yes."

Von Schuch liked, if possible, to close a crucial cross-examination with a little surprise, something tantalizing that would linger in the minds of the jurors. The forensics had indicated that whoever killed Roger de la Burde would have had a much easier time of it—since it involved leaning over the couch in an admittedly awkward position—if he or she had held the gun with his or her left hand.

"I have just one last question, Mrs. Monroe. Are you right-handed or left-handed?"

"I do some things with both hands. I—"

Von Schuch interrupted. "I saw you taking notes with your left hand."

"That's right. I write with my left hand and I place things with my right hand."

"Thank you."

During the next break, Von Schuch went out to use the bathroom. In the hallway, he saw Katie Monroe and her boyfriend. Von Schuch had been aware of Katie from the beginning of the trial. He had seen her striding around the courthouse in her clicking black high heels, organizing Beverly's family, ushering supporters into the gallery at the beginning of each session, pushing through the doors at every break to comfort her mother. Just before she testified, he had a recollection that she had been in the court during the early part of the trial, and he had protested to Judge Warren, pointing out that one of the reasons he remembered seeing her was that she was an attractive woman and therefore hard to forget. The judge, after questioning Katie, had allowed her to testify when she denied sitting in the court while it was in session.

Katie, with her long black hair, pale skin, and gray-green eyes, *was* an attractive woman, in Von Schuch's view. He was only doing his job in the courtroom, but every time she saw him, she gave him a baleful, hateful stare. She practically quivered with hostile fury. While Beverly had struck Von Schuch as an essentially weak person, Katie seemed a hell-for-leather spitfire—enraged, steely, vengeful.

Now, as he came out of the courtroom, she raked him with another dire glare. Noticing that he was headed for the men's room, she nudged her boyfriend to follow him in, apparently, Von Schuch gathered, to see if he could overhear any conversation the prosecutor might have and report it back to her. The boyfriend did indeed take the urinal next to Von Schuch. As he was finishing up, Von Schuch, who hadn't engaged in any conversation in the bathroom, much less talked strategy, looked over and said, "If you marry that woman, you sleep with one eye open."

Then he walked out.

——

Despite Von Schuch's cross-examination—which Murray Janus had to acknowledge was highly effective, even impressive in its pacing and theatricality—Beverly's attorney believed her defense was proceeding without much hindrance toward an eventual acquittal. He was about to present to the jury two authoritative experts who could explain why Beverly had made the incriminating statements to Dave Riley. And he was going to provide a thoroughly documented alibi.

Roger Shuy, a professor of linguistics at Georgetown University, had studied the tape of Riley's March 26 interview with Beverly. Riley interrupted Beverly forty-seven times in less than twenty minutes, Shuy told the jurors, in an effort to dominate the conversation and force her to accept his proposition that she was present when Roger died—a proposition that, on the tape, Beverly never accepted. James Corcoran, a forensic psychiatrist and professor at the Medical College of Virginia, had listened to the tape as well and had also interviewed Beverly. He declared that on March 26, Beverly was grief-stricken and highly suggestible. She was troubled by the emergence of guilt about her own father's suicide, which had been provoked by Roger's death. She wished to please the individual in authority who was interrogating her and who had taken pains to point out similarities between her experience and his.

Five separate witnesses supported, directly or indirectly, Beverly's alibi. Rob Richmond, an assistant manager at the Safeway where Beverly bought the groceries the night Roger died, identified the receipt as coming from his store. He said the check Beverly had written for the groceries, with her signature on it, had indeed been cashed there that night. Dennis Barden described how, while standing in line at the Safeway that same night, he had given Beverly his business card after she said she needed a carpenter to do some deck work on her house. Dee Shannonhouse, Beverly's secretary, told the jury how she and Beverly had searched through the batch of old receipts and found the one for March 4.

Next, Lisa Stone, Gavin's supervisor at the Riverside Wellness and Fitness Center, produced Gavin's time card, which showed that he punched out at 9:01 the night of March 4. Gavin himself testified that he arrived home around 9:10, that his mother returned shortly before 10, left for the grocery story some twenty minutes later, returned again some twenty-five minutes after that, around eleven o'clock, then went upstairs and went to bed. The following day, he said, he was at Windsor when Corinna, whom he had loved and defended to Roger, arrived. He met her, hugged her, and led her to his mother. Beverly, he said, never told Corinna, "She's pregnant."

"All they did was hug and cry."

"A lot of crying," Janus said.

"Yes, sir."

Trying to pre-empt Lewis, whom he knew would attack Gavin's credibility for telling Riley that Beverly may have come home much later than ten o'clock, Janus got Gavin to explain the circumstances of that conversation. But this did little to blunt Lewis's cross-examination. When the prosecutor repeatedly questioned Gavin on his acknowledging to Riley that his mother may have come home as late as midnight, Gavin insisted that all he could remember telling Riley was that he hadn't looked at the clock.

"I ask you one last time," Lewis said. "Did you not tell Officer Riley that your mother might have gotten home as late as midnight?"

"I could have said *'probably,' "* Gavin replied. "But I said I didn't look at the clock."

Janus concluded his defense with Roger's friend Frank Vegas, who described Roger's reaction to Krystyna's pregnancy. "He didn't know what to do," Vegas said. Roger had initially thought Krystyna would simply give him the child and walk away, Vegas explained, but not after she actually became pregnant. "He knew that wasn't going to happen."

Lewis asked Vegas a few desultory questions about the sculptures he had produced for Roger, then dropped the topic. "I don't think any of this is germane," he told the judge.

"Your Honor," Janus said. "The defense rests."

———

Warren Von Schuch believed that since people remembered more vividly and precisely what they saw than what they heard, anything he could demonstrate visually during a trial always had a much greater impact than verbal testimony. On Saturday, when the prosecution had the opportunity to present rebuttal witnesses, he re-called the commonwealth's firearms expert, Ann Jones.

The ostensible purpose of her testimony was to rebut the defense's forensics expert, Herb MacDonell. MacDonell had said in his written report and in his testimony that the primers in bullet cartridges have no great explosive force by themselves. That was why, he argued, the gunpowder marks on Roger's fourth and fifth fingers were minor.

"Is that consistent with your expertise and your knowledge of primers?" Von Schuch now asked Ann Jones.

"In my opinion, primers can be very dangerous," she said.

To demonstrate that danger, Jones held up a Smith & Wesson double action revolver similar to Roger's. It contained, she said, a cartridge with the bullet removed but the primer still intact in the cartridge butt. She then held up a square of white cloth and wrapped it around the cylinder. Pointing the gun at the ceiling, she fired once. Everyone in the courtroom expected the shot, but the sudden explosion in the small, enclosed chamber was nonetheless startling. Even Judge Warren blinked.

Jones passed the white cloth, now extensively burned, across to the jurors. Von Schuch watched them scrutinize it curiously. He then asked Jones to produce the rest of her exhibits for the jury. She held up another revolver, a tattered white glove, and MacDonell's photograph depicting two hands clenching an upside-down revolver. McDonell had described on Thursday how he thought Roger had killed himself: by holding the gun upside down, grasping the barrel and cylinder frame with his right hand, and pulling the trigger with his left thumb. Ann Jones said she had tried to duplicate his experiment. But instead of using fingerprint powder in a cartridge capped with a cork as MacDonell had done, she'd used real ammunition. She'd also wrapped the fingers of a clay-filled white glove around the cylinder. At Von Schuch's urging, she now held up the glove. The blast from the cylinder had torn through the fabric down to the clay. "This is what the hand of the shooter would have looked like," she told the jury.

Murray Janus managed to get in the last word. "You cannot exclude the possibility that this was a suicide, can you, ma'am?" he asked.

"Not based on my evidence," Jones replied. "No, sir."

But as Von Schuch listened to Judge Warren inform the jury that they would need to remain sequestered through the weekend, he was unfazed by that last minor capitulation. What was going to stay with the jury for the next day and a half, he thought, was the startling sound of that gunshot and the sight of the torn and blackened glove.

———

Judge Warren finished his admonition to the jury and gaveled the day's proceedings to a close promptly at one o'clock. Although this was known by neither the jurors nor the defendant, the timing had been set by prearrangement. The judge was an avid University of Virginia football fan, as were Murray Janus and Jack Lewis. Back in the summer, when the lawyers had sat down with the judge to set the dates for the trial, Lewis estimated it would last a week, and he proposed a late-October date. That's fine, Janus said, but that Saturday Virginia's playing Florida State, the best team in the country, and I'm going to be in Charlottesville. And the judge said, Well, I'm going to be there with you. So they all had an agreement that on Saturday they would quit at one o'clock so everybody could go to Charlottesville for the game.

6

Monday, November 2, was the seventh and final day of the trial. The skies once again were leaden and wet. Inside the courtroom, people sat with their raincoats bundled on their laps and their umbrellas hooked over the pews in front of them. The rain gear made the room feel damp, but the packed rows of spectators rustled with excitement. Everyone seemed to be talking—Corinna, Brigitte, and Krystyna over on the left near the jury box, the Monroes and their supporters on the right, near the two counsels' tables. The reporters, with their newspapers and notebooks, compared theories. The dark-suited Philip Morris lawyers murmured among themselves. It was, Katie thought, like being at the opera before the lights dimmed.

At nine o'clock Judge Warren—formal and austere in his black robe—entered from the door behind his bench, and took his seat.

"Good morning, ladies and gentlemen," he said to the jurors.

"Good morning," they replied in unison.

Katie studied the jurors. She found it hard to believe that these people were going to decide her mother's fate. Some of them seemed frankly incapable of deliberation. One of them had asked, during voir dire, what *sequestered* meant. In the time since Katie's testimony, when she had been allowed to sit in the courtroom, she had seen another juror, a woman in her seventies, sleep through long portions of the proceedings, her head toppled over onto her shoulder and her mouth agape, dead to the world. Two other jurors, a pair of younger guys with mustaches, who resembled the two main characters in *Dukes of Hazzard,* Bo and Luke Duke, were true Von Schuch fans, always nodding along with the prosecutor. One of them had actually leaned out of the jury box and tried to talk to Krystyna Drewnowska when she finished testifying—chatting her up in front of the judge.

Nonetheless, as the trial reached its conclusion, Katie felt her spirits lift and her confidence grow. The evidence against her mother had been shown to be so flimsy, she and Alan agreed. It seemed to her almost inconceivable that the jurors would buy the idea that her mother, who had never even had a traffic violation, had killed Roger and then carried out a convoluted subterfuge to convince the world the murder was a suicide.

Fourteen people sat in the jury box throughout the trial, two more than needed. Judge Warren now drew at random the names of two of the fourteen, excused them, and began to read his instructions to the remaining twelve. The defendant had been charged with murder in the first degree, he explained. The commonwealth had to prove beyond a reasonable doubt that the killing was malicious, willful, deliberate, and premeditated. It was possible to convict the defendant on circumstantial evidence alone. But it was not sufficient for those circumstances to create a suspicion of guilt or even a probability of guilt. The evidence as a whole needed to exclude every reasonable theory of innocence.

Katie thought those words served as a virtual instruction to acquit. She watched Jack Lewis cross the courtroom floor to present his closing argument. He had seemed to her at times inept. He stumbled over words, was slow in his presentation, and had been frequently reprimanded by Judge Warren for leading witnesses or nodding along with them. Maybe he was, compared to Murray Janus, just a country lawyer, but this was his country. Would the jurors, Katie had wondered for months, implicitly trust someone whom they considered one of them?

When he began his closing argument, Lewis, as if playing to a strength, seemed to become even more countrified, so folksy and homespun that Katie half expected him to pull out a stick and start whittling. "Who on God's earth," he asked, "would lay on a sofa with his head on the back of the sofa and in some convoluted way try to kill himself? I don't believe you need to be a rocket scientist to realize just from that fact alone that this was murder, not a suicide."

Lewis urged the jurors to believe Sheldon Gosline and Zelma Smith. "Sheldon Gosline would be categorized as a flake, a certifiable flake," he said. "And Zelma Smith is a convicted felon. But, ladies and gentlemen, that doesn't mean a flake and a convicted felon should not be believed." Sheldon, he continued, had no motive to lie. And Zelma Smith, whose story proved that Beverly had been planning to murder Roger or Krystyna for a year, had demonstrated her credibility. Lewis crossed the room again and held up Beverly's raincoat. "The proof of the pudding is the proof of this raincoat," he announced. "She could not, ladies and gentlemen, have made up this business about this tan trench coat that Beverly Monroe wore to the cemetery that rainy day."

Lewis spoke for almost an hour. He reviewed the witnesses he'd presented. He explained away Beverly's alibi by saying she could easily have killed Roger before or after she'd gone to the Safeway, which she'd done solely to establish an alibi. He ridiculed her claim that Riley had manipulated her into acknowledging she might have been present when Roger committed suicide. "Ladies and gentlemen, bull, bull, bull," he said. "It's totally unfeasible. It's totally unrealistic. And it just didn't happen. She was there and she killed him."

When Lewis sat down, he thought he had covered all his points thoroughly. His one regret was calling Sheldon Gosline a flake. He could have bit his tongue off the minute he said it. Sheldon may have acted flaky as the devil, but still, you didn't do that to a cooperating commonwealth witness. Sometimes the mouth gets in gear before the brain does.

———

The judge declared a ten-minute recess. Then, when the court reconvened, he asked Murray Janus to make his closing argument. Warren Von Schuch had left the jury with one memorable visual demonstration and now Janus intended to do the same. He asked the marshals to bring Roger's couch into the courtroom and drape it with a sheet. He asked David Hicks to lie on it in the position in which Roger's body was found, then invited the jury to stand and watch as he showed them how it was almost anatomically impossible for someone, whether right-handed or left-handed, to lean over the back of the couch, holding the gun upside down, wedge it down in the pillows beneath Roger's head, thrust the barrel between his fingers, and fire. Janus pointed out that since Roger was lying on his right side and the bullet had traveled from the right to the left side of his brain, the gun would have to have been both lower than Roger's head and pointing slightly upward. For a murderer to have chosen to kill someone from such an impractical and awkward angle—one that also risked waking the victim—was almost inconceivable. "You can't do it without being a contortionist," he said. "To a light sleeper, you can't do it."

The jury, Katie thought, studied this demonstration intently.

"Mr. Von Schuch," the judge asked, indicating the couch when Janus was finished with his demonstration. "Do you want that on your rebuttal?"

"I don't think Mr. Hicks will go down there again for me," Von Schuch replied.

Almost everyone in the courtroom broke into laughter, including several jurors. Even Beverly managed a small smile. Nonetheless, Von Schuch's joke threatened to make light of the entire demonstration and Janus tried to restore a tone of gravity. He began to discuss the case, but it had so many facets—art fraud, baby agreements, bloody semen, wills, pregnancy tests, tan raincoats, cemeteries, gunpowder stains, missing cigarette butts, balloon payments, ménages à trois, lawsuits—that he began to wander, throwing in his comments when they occurred to him without regard for logic or sequence. Good God, Katie found herself thinking, get to the point.

Janus himself realized the problem. "Excuse me if I seem disjointed," he told the jurors, "but there is so much I want to tell you." A short while later, again becoming sidetracked, he said, "I don't want to bore you. It's tedious, I know that. But I am so afraid I will miss something." And so he persisted, eventually spending almost two hours on his feet, talking without interruption the entire time. He concluded, as he had done in his opening argument eight days earlier, by declaring that Beverly Monroe was a naïve woman guilty only of loving a disreputable man. "If one single one of you has a reasonable doubt," he told the jurors, "if one single one of you has the courage of your convictions, you can't convict her, because she is innocent."

———

By then it was after twelve noon. Judge Warren asked the jurors if they wanted a break. They looked at one another and shook their heads. The judge invited Von Schuch to give the rebuttal. The courtroom was intensely quiet as Von Schuch made his way over to the jury box. He felt that after Jack Lewis's antics with the raincoat and Murray Janus's urgently rambling discourse, the jury would welcome simple words, spoken in a calm, quiet, reassuring manner.

"The most important evidence in the case," he said, "is the forensic evidence. And do you know why? Because you can touch it. You can see it. You can feel it. It can't skip town. It doesn't forget. It doesn't have a motive. It can't lie. That's why it's important. It's a measuring stick that you can rely on and trust and take through the testimony of witnesses when you are trying to determine who is telling the truth."

The forensic evidence, he explained, proved that Roger de la Burde could have killed himself with neither his right hand nor his left hand. And because he couldn't have killed himself, it didn't matter how suicidal he may or may not have been. Beverly Monroe killed him, Von Schuch went on. She now claimed that Dave Riley had tricked her into confessing she'd been with Roger when he committed suicide. Riley *had* been trying to trick her, Von Schuch said. But *she* had been trying to trick Riley—into believing the death was a suicide. She even enlisted her son in her scheme, persuading him to lie to Riley about the time she got home on the night of March 4, and then, when he took the stand on Saturday, to revert back to his original story that she had arrived home around ten o'clock.

"Gavin Monroe will lie for his mother," Von Schuch said. "Thank heavens. It's the most refreshing thing I have heard all week. I have sat here and I have heard about baby agreements, I have heard about forty-year-old women leaving their husbands to create a baby someone can mold in his image, I have heard about daughters and mothers giving eggs and sperm to create another one as a countersolution to that. I heard about Eshu, the Nigerian god of chaos and confusion. . . . I sat here and I asked myself, Am I the only normal person here?"

Von Schuch looked carefully at the jurors. He was sure they felt the same way. The juror in the front row who had rolled his eyes during Beverly's tearful cross-examination seemed almost imperceptibly to nod.

"There were two things that were refreshing here today for me," Von Schuch continued. "One of them is that Gavin would lie for his mother. My gosh, who wouldn't? The second thing was when Mr. Lewis asked Corinna a question that caused her to remember her father, and she started to cry. She turned from you and wiped away the tears." He paused. "Two children who love their parents. And I don't know whether either one of them deserved it."

Von Schuch pointed across the courtroom at Beverly Monroe. He told the jurors that when they asked themselves if she was capable of murder, they should consider the fact that she was someone who was intimately involved with Roger de la Burde and his real estate deals and art trades for thirteen years.

"It is a desperate act," he said. "It is a cruel act. But, ladies and gentlemen, it is an easy shot for Beverly Monroe, who uses her left hand."

———

The jury retired at twelve-forty to begin deliberations. Judge Warren had told them he would have the sheriff bring them sandwiches. Assuming they would require hours merely to sift through the exhibits and listen to some of the tapes, the judge had advised them to take their time. If by the end of the day, they were feeling frustrated, they could go back to their motel for the night and return the next day refreshed. If on the other hand they felt they were making progress, he and the lawyers were prepared to stay at the courthouse late into the night.

Most of the spectators drifted across the street to the restaurant. Beverly and her family and supporters, none of whom had much appetite, stayed in the courthouse. Katie went out to the hall at the back of the courtroom, and at the top of the stairs down to the sheriff's office, she ran into Warren Von Schuch.

"I'm sorry I had to say what I said about your mother. I'm sure she's a very nice lady," Von Schuch told Katie. "I was just doing my job."

Katie was so stunned she couldn't even think of a reply. She returned to the courtroom and sat on the defense table, near her mother, who was sitting in the chair she'd sat in all week. No one had much to say. After a while, David Hicks came in with the information that the jury had asked to see the couch. It was the only exhibit they requested.

Next, the jury sent out a question, relayed by a deputy to the clerk of the court, asking for the definition of premeditated murder. Janus saw the request as an extremely bad sign. It meant, in his mind, that the jury had already decided Roger had been killed and that Beverly had killed him and was now wrestling with the question of whether to convict her of first- or second-degree murder. The judge called the jurors in and read them the written version of the commonwealth's Instruction 1 supplement, then sent them back to continue deliberations.

Katie went out with Alan to stand on the courthouse steps. Rainwater dripped from the ancient cedars onto the muddy brick sidewalks. The cold, wet air quickly chilled her. She felt small and vulnerable and rigid with tension. When she went back inside, she caught sight of Dave Riley at the end of the corridor. He too was there, waiting.

———

Since his part in the trial was over, Von Schuch returned to his office at the Chesterfield County courthouse. Jack Lewis went home for lunch. Assuming the jury would deliberate at least through the afternoon, Judge Warren, Murray Janus, and the clerk of the court, William Maxey, all drove down to a barbecue place on Route 60, where they discussed UVA's 13–3 loss to

Florida State on Saturday. At two o'clock, Maxey received a call on his cell phone; the jury had reached a verdict. The news shook Janus. The deliberations had lasted little more than two hours, which meant the jurors had not even bothered to look at the dozens of exhibits. Most of them must have gone into the jury room with their minds made up. The judge told Maxey to say that they would arrive as soon as they had finished their coffee.

———

Word sped through the courthouse that the jury had reached a verdict. The spectators excitedly retook their seats in the pews. The attorneys arrived, and then Judge Warren. "All right, bring the jury in," the judge said.

The jurors filed into the room. To Katie, two of the women looked distraught and red-eyed, as if they had been crying. The clerk passed the judge the verdict.

"On the murder indictment, you find the defendant guilty of first-degree murder as charged in the indictment—"

"Witch trial!" shouted Shannon. Katie cried out, and several of Beverly's supporters groaned loudly. Among the people sitting on the left, there was an exultant stir. Beverly's brother Stuart, glancing over, saw Corinna and Brigitte give each other a high-five hand slap.

The judge glanced up sternly, then continued reading. "And you fix her punishment at twenty years in prison. Signed by your foreman. On the use of a firearm in the commission of a murder, you find the defendant guilty and fix her punishment at two years. Signed by your foreman."

Katie looked at her mother. Beverly was stiff and pale as she stared at the judge. While the judge polled the individual jurors, Beverly's mother, Anne Duncan, started sobbing. She had been so devastated by her daughter's indictment that during the fall, she'd developed congestive heart failure. Katie worried that now, under the shock of the verdict, her grandmother's heart might suddenly give out altogether.

The judge set a sentencing hearing for December. At that time the defense could argue for a reduced sentence. Janus requested that Beverly be allowed to remain out on bail until the official sentencing, which would follow the hearing. "She has never been in any difficulty with the law before," he said. "She owns real estate in her own name. She has three children. She is not a threat not to appear."

"Mr. Lewis?" the judge asked.

"If it please the court, I don't believe she is a threat to leave, and I don't think she is a threat to hurt anyone else. It is rather unusual on a murder charge for it to be granted, but if the court is so inclined, the commonwealth wouldn't oppose it."

The judge agreed to grant the motion. But he told Beverly that she should not assume his leniency on this matter would affect the ultimate disposition of her sentence. And he reminded her that her status had now irrevocably altered. "You have now been convicted," he said. "You are no longer presumed innocent."

———

Shannon held her mother's hand as they left the courtroom. Janus was in front of Beverly, protecting her. Outside, the rain had begun again. The camera crews were going crazy, crowding around them. Shannon saw the guy who'd been puking the first day of the trial. She watched as Gavin's girlfriend, Michelle, pushed the cameras out of the way, literally putting her hands over the lens like they do in the movies, that whole stupid scene.

They made it to their cars. Janus told the Monroes he'd see them in his office tomorrow, then he and David Hicks drove off. Katie, Shannon, Beverly, Gavin, Beverly's mother, and Alan climbed into Beverly's Mercury. Gavin drove. He was so distracted that from time to time he forgot he was driving and took his foot off the accelerator and the car slowed. Nobody spoke. There just wasn't anything to say.

Back at the house, Katie started screaming and crying. Shannon could see that her sister was absolutely traumatized. Even more than Shannon, she was crushed. Katie ran out in the yard, in the rain. She was bawling; then she disappeared. Shannon was really worried about her. She ran after her, trying to find her, but she couldn't find her. Katie was gone. Everybody was screaming. They were all standing in the yard in the rain. Everywhere Shannon turned, everybody was in so much pain. And Shannon thought: Mom. Where is Mom? Shannon wanted them to grab their mom and run for their lives, because she knew it was all over.

CHAPTER VIII

Goochland

1

The day after the verdict, Beverly received a brief, formal letter of termination from Philip Morris. Later, she and her children drove up to see Murray Janus. He had bad news. The attorney general had read the newspaper story about Judge Warren's decision to allow Beverly to remain out on bond until her sentencing. He had called Von Schuch and pointed out that under the Virginia statute, someone convicted of first-degree murder could not remain free on bond between the time of the verdict and the time of the sentencing. After sentencing, however, it would be possible to file a petition to stay free on bond until an appeal was decided. Von Schuch had passed this information on to Judge Warren. At first the judge had demanded that Beverly surrender within twenty-four hours, but then, after Janus pleaded with him, he had relented and allowed her until the following Monday to get her affairs in order.

———

Shannon felt sick and nauseous all week. Katie was a mess. Shannon got the impression that Katie thought they should take their own lives. Katie wasn't offering the means to do it, but her attitude seemed to be: What's the point in going on, this is it, they've destroyed us all. But their mom, Shannon felt, had kicked into her survivor mode. She was alive, and she was going to face whatever it was she had to face.

Beverly decided to transfer all her assets—her mortgage notes, stocks, bonds—into Katie's name. She and her children took her papers out of the safe-deposit box at her bank. They calculated the estimated taxes she would have to pay at year's end. They packed the cardboard box with the possessions Beverly was bringing to prison. All these chores kept them busy and distracted until Monday morning, when they drove up to the sheriff's office. Then Katie, Shannon, and Gavin followed the police car out to the prison and watched as Beverly, carrying her cardboard box, disappeared inside.

2

Several days passed, and then a week. Since Beverly's children couldn't call her and she was not allowed to call them, they had no idea how she was faring. Was she suffering? Was she in pain? Was she dying in there? Katie called Murray's office to see if he could find out anything about their mother's condition. Murray's secretary explained that the attorney was in Acapulco. Acapulco! While her mother was in prison, unable even to communicate with anyone, her mother's attorney was lying on a beach in Acapulco. Just thinking about it made Katie furious.

———

Janus had gone to Acapulco to attend a meeting of the Virginia Bar Association. Peter Greenspun, the Fairfax County attorney Beverly had initially contacted before deciding she needed a Richmond lawyer, was there as well. Greenspun knew Janus, respected him, and in fact felt close enough to him to be able to joke that because both of them were unusually short, each was the only member of the Virginia bar whom the other could look directly in the eye.

Greenspun had also been following the Monroe trial, reading faxed copies of the *Times-Dispatch*'s daily stories, and one afternoon the two attorneys sat by the side of the pool at the Princess Hotel, their feet dangling in the aquamarine water, and discussed what had happened. Janus looked exhausted. He also seemed devastated by the verdict. Janus told Greenspun he thought the trial had gone well. He said there had been reasonable doubt from start to finish. In addition, there had been actual evidence of Beverly Monroe's innocence. Powhatan County, he added, was simply a tough place to try a case. The jurors had favored the prosecution so heavily that they hadn't even looked at much of the evidence he had presented.

Greenspun had thought from the beginning that the trial would turn on the matter of Beverly's statements to Dave Riley. It had seemed to him, after his one meeting with Beverly, that it would be necessary for the defense to ask the judge to declare the statements inadmissible on the grounds that they had been involuntarily given. Greenspun, thinking this could provide the basis for an appeal, asked how the judge had ruled on the question of voluntariness. Janus said he had not raised the issue. Surprised, Greenspun asked why.

"I missed it," Greenspun would later recall Janus saying. "I blew it."

———

Janus only spent a couple of days in Acapulco. When he returned, E. B. Harmon, who remained convinced that Roger de la Burde had been murdered, but not by Beverly Monroe, showered him with thoughts on how to find the real killer. Under Virginia law, the defense had twenty-one days to present new evidence to the judge to overturn the verdict. Murray told E.B. it was a waste of time, but the investigator continued to pester him with memos.

"Murray," he wrote a week after the trial. "I know you told me to leave this thing alone, but this morning at 3:00 A.M. I woke up with a brain storm." He wanted to contact Dr. William Jefferson, who had conducted the autopsy on Roger's body. Jefferson, he said, might reveal that Marcella Fierro had not actually supervised the procedure, and may not even have been in the room. That in itself, he thought, might be sufficient cause for Judge Warren to void the verdict.

E.B. also thought the unidentified prints picked up in the library at Windsor could yield the identity of the real murderer. But what most intrigued E.B. were the missing Marlboro cigarette butts. E.B. had wondered all along if the police had in fact collected the cigarette butts from Roger's coffee table and then simply failed to produce them. E.B. had repeatedly told Murray Janus that it made no sense for Neal to take photographs of the cigarette butts, an act that proved he was aware of their potential evidentiary value, unless he was going to collect them. After all, the only reason to photograph them was to show a jury their location at the crime scene before they were collected. "Why else would he take the pictures?" E.B. had asked over and over. "What would be the point?"

Now that Jack Lewis had his conviction, E.B. thought, the prosecutor, who at the end of the trial hadn't seemed particularly eager to send Beverly Monroe off to prison, just might discreetly slip the cigarette butts to the defense—if he had them. Janus, who knew that police investigators were capable of withholding evidence that hurt their case, agreed. It was a long shot, he knew, but he decided to write Lewis a letter.

In the letter, Janus complimented Lewis on the job he'd done and expressed his surprise and disappointment with the verdict. He said he still had a nagging feeling that something was amiss and suspected that one or more people on the jury had information that Beverly had taken a lie detector test and flunked it. He had no evidence of this, he said, but he did know that there was a rumor to that effect among the spectators at the trial. He told Lewis he would appreciate it if the prosecutor looked through his files again, just to see if he missed anything by way of exculpatory evidence that the defense should have had. In particular, he said, if the cigarette butts were preserved, he would like them sent to a lab for analysis. "I really do have this horrible feeling of the possibility that an innocent person is going to the penitentiary, and I know you do not want that to happen any more than I do." Nonetheless, he congratulated Lewis on his victory. "It was a hard fought battle, but I would like to think it was done by and between gentlemen and we kept it on that high plane throughout."

Lewis called Janus after receiving the letter and thanked him for sending it. Unfortunately, he said, he didn't have the cigarette butts. He did tell Janus that a couple of the jurors had come by to see him after the trial. While they were sequestered, one of them had tried to re-enact the suicide on his motel couch. The juror had decided on his own, and then persuaded the others, that it would be almost impossible to kill yourself in that position. Once the jurors, based on this experiment, had eliminated the possibility of suicide, they took up the fact that Beverly had changed her story and told the police she'd been there when Roger de la Burde died, put the two together, and concluded she was the murderer. They hadn't really bothered with any of the other issues or evidence, which was why they had deliberated as briefly as they had.

It was, Janus thought, a hopelessly simplistic approach to a complex case.

On the other hand, he had told Beverly back in July that there was a good chance the trial could boil down to precisely those two issues.

3

Beverly Monroe's day began with morning count at five A.M. A prisoner, accompanied by a guard, brought her meals. Breakfast was a cold hard-boiled egg or cold oatmeal and a cup of tepid coffee. Lunch was the main meal, cold canned greens accompanied by a hot dog or meat loaf or mackerel cakes that smelled so fishy Beverly had to open the window and sit by it until the uneaten food was removed. Dinner was a bagged sandwich.

The prison, which had seemed so quiet when she first arrived, turned out to be a place of relentless, jarring noise. The doors opened and shut with a loud electric buzz. The inmates looked out their windows and shouted at anyone walking by. Some of them seemed deranged. One black woman, goaded on by her neighbors, who called her Colt 45, sang for hours or went on long obscenity-strewn rants. People kept up the yelling even at night. Guards walked up and down the corridor, their radios spluttering, and sometimes roused everyone for unexpected midnight counts.

Watching through the slot in the door, Beverly saw that the inmates in all the other cells, except for hers and the one directly opposite hers, were let out three times a day for meals. She started talking to the two women in the opposite cell. They explained that this was Cottage 3, for inmates who were violent or unstable. However, their cell and Beverly's cell were rented by the Powhatan County sheriff's department to house overflow prisoners. Until the court order came through remanding them into the control of the state prison system, they were all technically still in the sheriff's custody. Consequently, prison officials considered them 24-7, confined to their cells twenty-four hours a day, seven days a week.

After she had spent a week in the cell, Beverly was escorted by a guard to the dining room, where she was allowed to buy some crackers at the canteen and to retrieve her possessions. Once she had her things, Beverly was able to establish a routine. She woke early, before the morning count, and ran back and forth between the door and the window, leaned against the wall and did press-ups, and then lay down on the bed to do leg lifts. When the sun rose, she sat by the window, which a guard had helped her fix, and wrote in her notebooks. Then she read and reread the books she'd brought, especially *A Year in Provence*.

By kneeling at her door and lining up the food slot with the window in the exit door at the end of the hall, she could see the tree line of the James River. She calculated she was about four miles from Windsor. Sensing how easy it was, in this sort of isolation, to lose connection with the outside world, she spent part of each morning systematically thinking about the life she had left behind. She thought about her Mercury. Did Gavin need to replace the clutch? She thought about her house. Did the kids remember to open the damper when they built fires in the fireplace? She thought about Philip Morris, too. Worried about it, strangely enough. Who was doing all the work she had done? Were the patent applications being filed by deadline? Was the database kept up-to-date?

———

At the end of the third week, when her quarantine was officially over, she was able to make her first call to her children. Three weeks after that, they were allowed their first visit. Shannon felt she had to get herself into an almost Zen-like state just to go into the prison. The guards were so upsetting. They were totally jerky, with their crackling walkie-talkies and big guns on their hips. They either stared at you coldly or smiled as if it were all a joke at your expense. And they frisked you, looking for every reason not to let you in.

Beverly had yet to be processed into the general prison population and evaluated as a security risk, so, taking no chances, the guards locked her in a booth in the visitors' room and allowed her to speak to her children only through a Plexiglas window with a small round ventilation hole. Shannon put her hand on the glass and her mother put her hand up on the opposite side and they leaned down to talk through the little hole. Her mom was totally supportive, only concerned about Shannon's welfare, calling Shannon her little braveheart, insisting everything was going to be fine, asking about Butterscotch, the cat, telling Shannon to sing her a song. Shannon had made up her mind that she was going to be exceptionally strong and not cry through the visit. It was hard, but she did it.

She cried afterward.

———

As the date for Beverly's sentencing hearing approached, Murray Janus decided he had to explore what he believed could be a mitigating circumstance in her case. It was an extremely delicate matter. Despite his vigorous advocacy of the suicide theory during the trial, Janus had never been able, in his own mind, to rule out homicide altogether. In fact, he felt, there were certain maddeningly inexplicable aspects of Beverly's behavior that made sense only if Burde had been killed and if either Beverly was the murderer or was covering up for the murderer.

Why, for example, had Beverly always pretended to be so serenely indifferent to the threat Krystyna clearly represented? Why had she driven out to Roger's house the morning his body was found when her office was in the opposite direction? Why had she bought Riley's story if, all along, she knew she had the Safeway receipt and her own son's account of the time of her return to prove that she couldn't have been at Windsor when Roger died? Why had this sophisticated, educated lady agreed to take a lie detector test and then signed that confession at Drewry's Bluff when all she had to do before taking those fatal missteps was to call her daughter the lawyer? This behavior was contrary to human nature as Murray Janus had come to understand it, and in the decades he had spent practicing criminal law, he felt he had acquired a pretty firm grasp of human nature.

That same knowledge made him doubt that Beverly Monroe herself was the killer. She lacked the steel to take a human life. So did Beverly's daughter Shannon, a quiet, sensitive college student, and her son, Gavin, whom Janus considered a somewhat weak personality. Katie Monroe, on the other hand, was decisive, opinionated, emotional, and slightly arrogant. Janus believed she had the balls to kill.

Riley, Janus knew, had considered Katie a suspect. And Sheldon Gosline had essentially testified that Katie conspired with Beverly in a cover-up alibi. In the notes Greg Neal had written during his interview with Beverly the day Roger's body was found, he had said, "daughter came home at midnight." Beverly had always maintained that Neal had mistakenly attributed this comment to her when in fact it came from Krystyna. That was possible. But it was also possible that Katie had in fact come back to Beverly's house that night.

This possibility was supported by a disturbing discovery Murray Janus and David Hicks had made. The night before the trial began, while they were in the office conference room preparing for opening statements, David had suddenly cried out, "Oh my God!" and passed Murray Janus a copy of Beverly's phone records, which showed that at 6:05 P.M. on

March 4, a long-distance call had been placed from Beverly's house to Katie's Charlottesville apartment. The two lawyers wondered if Beverly had called Katie to say that Roger was leaving her for Krystyna, if Katie became enraged, drove to Windsor and killed Roger, then appeared at Beverly's house at midnight and confessed to the crime.

Janus had never mentioned their suspicions to Beverly. But during and after the trial, he had never been able to banish them entirely from his mind. And now, he thought, the time had come to broach the matter. If the scenario was true, it could be used to argue for a reduced sentence.

Janus drove out to see Beverly at what he called the women's farm at Goochland. Beverly was wearing one of those depressing prison-issue jumpsuits and it was about five sizes too large for her. At first Janus tried to be circumspect.

"Beverly," he said. "Now is the time. If you're covering for anybody else, you've got to tell me now. Your sentence is coming up; you're looking at twenty-two years."

"Murray, what are you talking about?"

"If you're covering for anybody else, please say so."

"I don't know what you mean."

She was, he felt, forcing him to spell it out. But she was his client. It was his job to represent her as aggressively as possible, whatever the consequences were for her daughter.

"Katie," he said. "Are you covering for Katie?"

"Absolutely not."

Janus detected no hesitation in her voice. If Beverly Monroe *was* covering for her daughter, she had no intention of stopping now.

———

Katie often thought about the female juror who had seemed to be crying when the jury had trooped in to announce the verdict. She suspected that the woman had been browbeaten by the men into voting for a conviction. Maybe they had agreed to give Beverly the minimal sentence if the woman voted for a verdict of guilty. It was a solution that trial lawyers, in deference to Solomonic wisdom, called splitting the baby. To Katie, nothing else could explain the combination of the harsh verdict and the relatively mild sentence. After all, if all twelve jurors were convinced that Beverly had committed first-degree murder, wouldn't they have sentenced her to life imprisonment?

Katie shared her thinking with her grandmother, Anne Duncan, who wondered if the woman juror could be persuaded to come to the sentencing hearing and explain her apparent unhappiness with the verdict. Anne tried to call the woman, but when she identified herself to the man who answered the telephone, he hung up on her.

———

The sentencing hearing took place on December 22. Dressed in the wrinkled skirt she had worn when she surrendered, Beverly was driven the twelve miles from the prison to the courthouse. The hearing seemed pro forma. Murray Janus presented no witnesses on her behalf. Warren Von Schuch argued that Beverly had already received the most lenient sentence possible for someone convicted of using a firearm in a premeditated murder. Judge Warren agreed and officially set the sentence at twenty-two years. The marshals escorted Beverly back to the waiting van.

Outside the courthouse, Anne Duncan saw Von Schuch walking toward his car. Enraged at the man she felt was responsible for putting her daughter in prison, she pulled at his arm to stop him and tell him what she thought of him.

Von Schuch couldn't understand what this little old lady was doing. Was she trying to attack him? Grab his car keys? Whatever it was, he didn't need the grief. "Get her out of here before she gets in trouble," Von Schuch said to Gavin, who pulled his grandmother back.

———

After the hearing, Katie called Hicks and Janus repeatedly to try to get them to visit her mother, just to reassure her. The lawyers would promise to make the trip, but other matters intervened and for weeks it got postponed. In late January, Hicks finally went out and saw Beverly. By way of consolation, he pointed out that she'd be eligible for parole after serving one sixth of her sentence, which meant she could be free in as few as four years.

"Nothing to it but to do it," he said.

Hicks's casual tone, his offhand, rhyming pep talk, astonished Beverly. Nothing to it but to do it? she thought. Easy for you to say, Dave.

4

On February 5, 1993, six weeks after Beverly Monroe's sentencing hearing, Judge Herbert Gill of the Chesterfield County Circuit Court held a sentence-reduction hearing for Zelma Smith. It took place at the instigation of Zelma's lawyer, Louis Rosenstock, who had filed the motion requesting it on November 7, five days after Beverly Monroe's conviction. "Zelma Smith voluntarily came forth and provided valuable information to the Commonwealth in the case of Commonwealth vs. Beverly Anne Monroe," Jack Lewis wrote in a letter of recommendation to the judge. "Not only did she provide the information but she was a compelling witness at trial."

The hearing was held privately, in Judge Gill's chambers. Zelma Smith, Rosenstock, Dave Riley, and Warren Von Schuch were all present. Riley told the judge that without Zelma Smith's testimony, Beverly Monroe would not have received the sentence she had. Judge Gill asked Von Schuch for his views.

Under these circumstances, Von Schuch usually liked to make a few ingratiating remarks, describing the burden the witness had undertaken in coming forward, his or her candor, and the degree to which this cooperation had aided the commonwealth. But after hearing Zelma Smith give her story on the witness stand, Von Schuch had felt like he needed to go home and take a shower. He wasn't going to get into that with Judge Gill. Zelma had always been Jack Lewis's witness, and Lewis thought she deserved time off. But Von Schuch would state the matter as baldly, and as unenthusiastically, as possible—that what the commonwealth had with Zelma Smith was an arm's-length business deal.

"I think it's a situation where she's entitled to some relief," Von Schuch told the judge. "The commonwealth looks at it as the cost of doing business. You know it, she knows it, we know it. It's a tit-for-tat kind of thing."

Von Schuch looked at Zelma. She had been all smiles on the way into the judge's chambers, but she wasn't smiling now.

"Miss Smith," the judge said. "The court is not unfamiliar with the commonwealth's term *the cost of doing business.* I look at your record and I understand that you're familiar with the cost of doing business. . . . You know the system as well as I do, and as well as the lawyers that are here, and as well as Mr. Riley, who testified on your behalf." He continued, "You seem to think that this is a way of life. You seem to think, I get in trouble, I work myself out of trouble, I get in trouble, I work myself out of trouble. This is a dangerous pattern."

Nonetheless, he said, because she had testified against Beverly Monroe, he would reduce her sentence from seven years to four years. "But let there be no misunderstanding between you and I," he added. "I don't like your pattern."

———

How do we get her out of this? Katie, Gavin, and Shannon asked each other every time they talked. Shannon and Gavin implicitly expected Katie, the lawyer, to provide the answer.

Katie had never actually wanted to become a lawyer. She played the guitar and the piano and sang, and she had acted in plays in high school and college. What she had really wanted to do after graduating was become a performer. She had been thinking of moving to New York and joining the fifteen thousand or so aspiring actors and singers in the city who supported themselves by waiting tables, but Roger and Beverly had convinced her that this was impractical. She had always gotten good grades, they told her, and should apply to law school, medical school, or business school.

Law school seemed the least unappealing, but Katie hated it so much—it was so boring—and became so stressed out that in her first year at George Mason she developed TMJ, temporomandibular joint inflammation. Her jaw locked up and she could hardly talk or eat. It was awful. She persevered, however, and after she graduated, Roger, through his connections, got her a job with a law firm in Atlanta. The firm specialized in processing and litigating fire insurance claims. The work was even more boring than law school and Katie quit after six months.

She had enjoyed clerking for Judge Barrow—engaging with issues of rights brought out the activist in her nature—but she had nothing planned for when the job ended in August. Since her mother's trial, she had been looking for work in Washington, D.C., and living with Alan in his apartment on Dupont Circle. In midwinter, a friend of Alan's who was also a lawyer suggested to Katie that her mother would make a good candidate for an appeal bond. Katie drove down to the Library of Congress and researched the case law.

Despite Beverly's murder conviction, Katie found, she was technically entitled to remain free on appeal if it could be demonstrated that she was neither a flight risk nor a danger to herself or anyone else. At the end of the trial, Lewis had said on the record that Beverly wasn't a threat to anybody and could go home as far as he was concerned. And she'd been released on prior bond, hadn't fled, and had surrendered when Judge Warren ordered it. Katie decided her mom was a prime candidate for an appeal bond.

She and Alan incorporated this research into a brief they wrote and faxed to Murray Janus, asking him to request an appeal bond. Janus duly filed a motion. When Judge Warren summarily denied it, Katie contacted Peter Greenspun, who drafted a more detailed motion asking the court of appeals—Judge Barrow's court—to overturn Judge Warren. The appellate court directed Judge Warren to explain his ruling. When he replied that Beverly Monroe had been convicted of murder, the court found this insufficient and ordered her released on bond pending the outcome of her appeal.

———

Beverly by then had been moved from Cottage 3 to 1 Basement, a long, low room housing B Custody inmates, those classified as moderately dangerous, a category that applied to convicted murderers who showed no signs of violence. Many of the women were semi-literate, and Beverly helped several of them write letters, decipher their paperwork, and calculate fractions so they could learn to budget their canteen money.

The order releasing her came through on a sunny day in May six months after she had surrendered. Her children met her at the administration building and drove her back to Old Gun Road. When they turned into her drive, she saw that the azaleas she had planted along its curve were doing well. The dogwood by the living room window had lost its flowers, but a few white petals still clung to the pear tree. The garden looked a wreck. The kids had maintained the house and mowed the lawn, but saplings had sprung up everywhere—there was a four-foot pine in one corner of the yard—weeds had sprouted in the flower beds, and the strawberries were buried beneath last autumn's leaves.

They sat out on the patio in the back. Katie put on a recording of Bach's orchestral suites. As the sun streamed through the cedars and Bach's stately, elegiac music filled the air, Beverly and her children laughed and cried, hugged each other, sat down in their chairs, then got up to hug each other again. Katie, watching her mother, felt as if they had all endured a harrowing ordeal that was now over. She had to keep reminding herself that it wasn't over yet, that it was far from over.

CHAPTER IX

The Begging Dream

1

On a weekend afternoon early that summer, Dave Riley was browsing in the Civil War memorabilia section of Bob Moates's gun shop in Chesterfield when he ran into one of the jurors from Beverly Monroe's trial. A strange little incident had occurred on the last day of the trial. After the verdict, Riley had been about to leave the courthouse when Sheriff Shirley Reynolds tapped him on the shoulder and said the jurors wanted to talk to him. They were still gathered in the jury room. The foreman told Riley they were all puzzled by one thing. Why, after Riley had already interviewed Beverly once on the morning of March 26, did he go back in and re-interview her after she talked to Wyatt Omohundro? Riley explained that Omohundro had given Beverly a polygraph test and that she had failed it. He had gone in, he said, to confront her with the results. The jurors nodded. It seemed to Riley as if the lights had just been turned on for them.

Riley had been curious about the jury's view of the trial, but he hadn't felt it appropriate to ask any questions then. But now, in Bob Moates's shop, he and the juror fell into a conversation about the evidence. The man said that since he was a gun enthusiast, he had understood the prosecution's forensics case and had explained it to the rest of the jurors. None of them had any doubt that Beverly killed Roger de la Burde, the juror said, but at the same time they thought he was such a despicable person that it was almost justifiable homicide. That was why they had given her what they felt amounted to a manslaughter sentence.

This was pretty much how Riley saw matters. He had liked Beverly. He still did. He had been telling her the truth that day at Drewry's Bluff when he said she deserved a medal for putting up with Roger for twelve years. And he'd been telling the truth when he said he understood why she killed him.

2

Before leaving Goochland, Beverly had decided she wanted Peter Greenspun to represent her on her appeal. Greenspun was happy to take the case. However, he told Beverly that it would be wise to retain the goodwill of Murray Janus, which might be of some use during the appeal, and he had her pay him $5,000 to serve as a consultant as the case moved to the higher court.

In June, Greenspun sat down in his office in Fairfax and read through the trial transcript. As he read, he wondered what the outcome would have been had he represented Beverly. He would have handled the case differently from Murray Janus, he decided. The commonwealth had presented Beverly as a distraught and jealous older woman, displaced in the affections of Roger de la Burde by a younger but equally cosmopolitan woman. In addition, she supposedly had a financial motive to kill because she expected Roger to provide for her by allowing her to live at Windsor for the rest of her life.

Greenspun thought he would have emphasized Beverly's position as a capable and productive mid-level manager at Philip Morris, a figure in the Richmond arts community, the center of her family—which was not often the case with murder defendants—a thrifty, independent woman with a personal financial estate worth some $500,000—more liquid assets than Burde had—who may have enjoyed Roger's company but in no way felt dependent on him and in fact had another man in her life.

A few years before Roger died, Beverly had told Greenspun, Richard Thayer, the man with whom she'd fallen in love when they were both graduate students at the University of Florida, had gotten in touch with her.

While he lived in Texas, they had seen each other periodically, and Beverly actually kept his picture on her desk at Philip Morris. Greenspun thought he might have had Thayer testify. It would have given the jury a more thorough and rounded picture of Beverly Monroe.

Which was not to say that Murray Janus was wrong. You have two different attorneys, you'll get two different approaches.

———

Once she was out on appeal, Beverly decided to act as her own investigator. She talked to Greenspun about contacting the jurors, but he forbade it, so she set off to try to find out everything she could about Zelma Smith. She looked up her name in the office of records in local courthouses. Zelma, she found, had used a variety of aliases: Zelma Mann Smith; Zelma Mann; Zelma Sanderlin. And Zelma had judgments against her for bad checks, in the thousands of dollars, that had never been prosecuted.

After visiting the courthouses in downtown Richmond and in Henrico County, Beverly drove over to the Chesterfield County Courthouse, a low modern building in what resembled a suburban office park. The trip made her nervous. Von Schuch worked there, and she was afraid she might run into him in the hallway. She had also begun to wonder if someone, somehow, was keeping track of her search through the records. Peter Greenspun had said that asking the court clerks for documents could raise a flag, alerting people to the direction of her search, so she had started requesting various files she didn't really want just to hide her tracks.

At the Chesterfield County Courthouse she found a reference to Zelma's sentence-reduction hearing the previous February. While the hearing had been closed, Judge Gill had not sealed the record. Reading the transcript, Beverly learned that Zelma Smith had received a sentence reduction for testifying against her. She also saw references by both Dave Riley and Zelma Smith to Zelma's work as an informant for the FBI and the state police on other cases. Beverly wondered whether Riley and Zelma had a prior relationship. Maybe, she thought, Zelma had worked as an informant for him before. Maybe they knew each other. Maybe, she thought, Zelma and Riley had sat down and together worked out the entire story about Ms. Nelson and the .357 Magnum and the tan raincoat.

Peter Greenspun, to whom Beverly brought this information, found it intriguing, if inconclusive. But even if Riley and Zelma Smith had some prior relationship, which Beverly's research had not established, Greenspun saw no way to incorporate it into Beverly's appeal, which was confined by law to procedural errors made during the trial.

———

By that fall, Greenspun had identified eleven issues that would form the basis of the appeal. Of these, he thought the strongest were the insufficiency of the evidence and the involuntariness of Beverly's statements to Riley. It helped that they were interconnected. Without the questionable statements, the commonwealth had nothing to link Beverly to the death of Roger de la Burde. That meant the statements did not represent some merely formal question of legal or police procedure but went directly to the issue of the defendant's guilt. And that made it much more likely that the panel of three appellate judges assigned the case would engage with it.

Since the commonwealth had successfully argued that Roger de la Burde had in fact been murdered, Greenspun in his brief to the appellate court made a point of acknowledging this possibility. But he offered a different scenario, one he thought was as plausible on its face as the commonwealth's scenario. Krystyna Drewnowska, he speculated, may have gone to the farm after Beverly left on the night of March 4 to present Roger with the official results of the gender of the child she was carrying, provoking a confrontation that ended in Roger's death.

[Krystyna] knew she was disappointing Burde because the baby was a girl. Her testimony was incredible in relating that she told Burde the tests indicated her pregnancy was normal, but that she did not tell, nor did Burde ask, whether the sex identification report was back. This is inconsistent with the fact that Burde told Hazel Bunch that the baby was a boy on March 4, 1992. A reasonable interpretation of this evidence is that, in fact, Krystyna told Burde that the baby was a boy when she initially received the test results and then told him the truth during the evening hours of March 4th, thus causing him to become distraught, angry, or even suicidal. . . . Krystyna's child, and therefore, Krystyna, stood to inherit a full share of Burde's estate valued at close to or over $1 million. Krystyna had a $1 million motive, means (key and Burde's gun) and time (no alibi) to kill de la Burde.

Greenspun often avoided forming opinions about the actual innocence or guilt of the criminal defendants he represented. He didn't need to do that to do his job. A lot of times, it was a good idea *not* to form an opinion. But by then he had spent many hours with Beverly preparing the appeal, and he didn't see how anyone who got to know her could believe she was capable of murder.

Of course that was just an intuition. Beverly Monroe could have been deceiving him. But on top of the insufficiency of evidence establishing guilt, there was also, he felt, real evidence pointing to her innocence: the alibi and the lack of actual motive that underlay the commonwealth's distorted picture of a desperate woman scorned by a caddish lover. None of that would directly concern the appellate judges, of course, but the subliminal notion of justice miscarried might make them more sensitive to the issues raised in the appeal.

3

John McLees, an assistant attorney general for the Commonwealth of Virginia, was in his office at the corner of Ninth and Main Streets when he received Greenspun's petition for appeal. One of twenty-three lawyers who handled post-conviction litigation for the commonwealth, McLees was a balding, broad-shouldered man whose protuberant eyes, small rectangular glasses, and bushy mustache gave him a resemblance to Teddy Roosevelt. Earlier in his career he had worked as a public defender, had, as he liked to put it, defended the unsung heroes of the underclass, but he had gotten tired of helping people get away with hurting other people, so he now worked for the rest of the people—the innocent people. "If you're not a liberal when you're young, you have no heart," he was fond of saying, "and if you're not a conservative when you're old, you have no brain."

Every surface of McLees's office was covered with legal papers. His black metal filing cabinets were stuffed with more documents. McLees had as many as fifty active cases on his hands at any time, involving rape, noncapital murder, burglary, every kind of crime imaginable except capital murder, which another section of the office handled exclusively. These cases tended to drag on for years, but they usually lacked substance, and it did not require strenuous exertion for McLees to knock back the various appeals they involved.

McLees had known from the outset that Beverly Monroe's case—both the direct appeal and, unless she was successful, the habeas petition that would probably follow it—would be different. She was educated, and had the money to hire the state's top lawyers. Greenspun's brief, McLees thought as he read it, was impressive. McLees sent for the trial transcript and the case file. He read everything he could find, including police reports from witnesses who were not called to testify and the depositions in Stuart and Beverly Monroe's divorce. He felt he had procedural arguments he could use to attack a number of Beverly's claims. But he also thought he had the facts on his side. Like many petitioners, she claimed there had been insufficient evidence to convict her. This seemed to McLees almost laughable. Her version of events—that Burde had killed himself in this impossibly awkward manner, that Dave Riley had tricked her into giving incriminating statements, that all the witnesses whose testimony contradicted hers were lying or mistaken—might make for a good novel, he thought, but it hardly impugned the jury's verdict. An old trial attorney's rule held that jurors might believe a defendant's claim that a witness was lying, but if he claimed that two witnesses were lying they grew doubtful, and if he claimed that more than two were lying they usually concluded it was the defendant who was the liar.

McLees was particularly struck by the testimony of Sheldon Gosline. A onetime houseguest of Beverly's, he had no motive to lie, unlike, say, Gavin. McLees was also struck by Beverly's 1990 letter to Roger. You only had to read it to savor the disillusionment, the emotional exhaustion, and the bitterness she felt when, after leaving her husband for the man, after enduring his abuse, rejection, and infidelity for years, she found her position in his life jeopardized by Krystyna Drewnowska. Other people may have had motives to kill Burde, McLees thought, but no one had the abundance of clear, strong motives that Beverly Monroe had.

———

Beverly tried in those months to return to some of the routines of the life she'd led before Roger had died, but her notoriety made that difficult. When she went into the grocery store, people stared at her, with puzzlement and then the shock of recognition. Sometimes they followed her around, just to look at her. After she and a friend attended an art exhibit in August, someone reported it to the *Times-Dispatch,* which ran a gossip item about her visit.

Just because you've been convicted of first-degree murder doesn't mean you can't take in an art show or two, does it?

Well, certainly not if you're Beverly Anne Monroe, the infamous long-time girlfriend of slain Powhatan art collector Roger de la Burde. Monroe, accompanied by an unidentified blonde woman, was spotted at the recent opening of "Sir Thomas Lawrence: Portraits of an Age, 1790–1830" at the Virginia Museum of Fine Arts.

Her celebrity also made it difficult for Beverly to bring in any income. Before Roger died, she had been proud of her financial position. Whenever possible, she had doubled up on her mortgage payments, and her house was almost paid off. Her savings and her equity in her house and the half-dozen real estate properties she'd signed over to Katie came to almost $500,000. But the fees for Murray Janus and the defense experts and investigators had cost some $200,000, and she'd given Peter Greenspun a retainer of $75,000, which was disappearing quickly; like many attorneys, he didn't bill in increments of less than six minutes, so every time he picked up the phone or glanced at a one-paragraph fax she sent him, it cost her.

After her release, she had gone on unemployment. It was embarrassing and demoralizing, sitting there like a deadbeat filling out forms at the agency in order to receive what was little more than a subsistence check, but the money made a difference. She tried looking for a job commensurate with her experience. She thought she had good qualifications—degrees, work history, letters of recommendation—but she never received a single reply to the dozens of letters she sent out about administrative positions advertised in the classifieds.

So she lowered her sights and started going shop to shop, looking for a retail job. People sometimes recognized her from the newspapers and television, and even when they didn't, she made a point of telling them who she was. I'm Beverly Monroe, she would say. You may have heard of me. I was convicted of the murder of Roger de la Burde, but the conviction was unjust and I'm out on bail now appealing it. She felt it was only fair to add that she didn't know how long she'd be able to hold the job, since her bail would be revoked if she lost the appeal.

Most of the people acted sympathetic, though she never heard back from any of them. On one occasion, she went to the Willow Oaks Country Club, where she and Roger had often played tennis with friends, to answer an ad in the paper for a job in the tennis shop. The job paid only $4 an hour, but when she explained who she was, the manager's face went slack with incredulity. She knew he was thinking, Do you know what the members would do to me if they found out I hired a convicted murderer? It was, she supposed, only human to react that way.

One day that winter she stopped in the Book Gallery in the Bellgrade shopping center, where the Safeway she'd visited the night of March 4 was located. She wasn't looking for a job; she had simply always liked the store, which was large and airy and well stocked with the backlist books, like *The Count of Monte Cristo* and *The Stories of John Cheever,* that she and Roger had read together. Sitting in the coffee bar, she fell into conversation with Marshall MacKenzie, the owner. He had read the gossip item about Beverly attending the art exhibit. "So you're the infamous Beverly Monroe," he said with a laugh. He offered her a job on the spot, stocking shelves and handling the cash register. It paid only $6 an hour, but that was more than she would have earned at Willow Oaks, and Beverly took it. Marshall began jokingly to introduce her to customers as the infamous Beverly Monroe.

4

Peter Greenspun had to petition the appellate court to hear Beverly's case, then, once that was accepted, present the appeal itself. Each step was opposed by John McLees, requiring motions and countermotions, briefs in support and briefs in opposition. Six months passed, and then another six months, with little discernible progress on the case. At times, after she had been out on appeal for more than a year, Beverly could almost pretend to herself that the world had forgotten about her. But periodically something would happen to demonstrate that it hadn't.

Corinna filed two suits against Beverly. One claimed that she owed the estate $150,000 for the money Roger had allegedly "loaned" her to buy the lot in Kanawha, which she had sold the year before to pay Murray. The second suit demanded that Beverly pay Corinna $20 million for "financial and pecuniary loss" related to Roger's death and for "damages suffered for the loss of de la Burde's company, counsel, and comfort."

The suits seemed to Beverly gratuitously vindictive, and she wondered how much Corinna truly missed her father, since, as she read in the newspaper that summer, Corinna had decided to hold a series of auctions to liquidate Roger's estate. Everything would go—the books, the furniture,

Roger's Olin Mark III skis, the Steinway baby grand piano, the crocodile masks, the Sam Gilliam paintings. All the objects Roger had collected, everything that amounted to the "legacy" he'd been so consumed with passing on to a male heir, would be dispersed. CURIOUS EXPECTED AT AUCTION had been the headline of the *Times-Dispatch* article, which reported that it would be held—as if it were some sort of carnival, Beverly thought—at the state fairgrounds.

Frank Vegas, the sculptor who had done the imitation Wotruba that Roger had donated to Radford University, called Beverly. He had gone to the auction preview, he said, and had seen some of his own pieces there, works he'd done that Roger hadn't paid him for but had kept at Windsor to show to people. In the list prepared by the auction house, the works were labeled UNKNOWN ARTIST. Frank wondered if there was any way to get them. Beverly said she didn't think so.

Beverly decided to avoid the auction. It would have been too distressing to see Roger's possessions spread out on the fairgrounds. And she was afraid of another sarcastic gossip item in the newspaper: CONVICTED MURDERER BIDS ON VICTIM'S EFFECTS. A friend went, however. She brought back Roger's French tapes. At the sight of the tapes, which she and Roger had spent hours studying, and at the thought that Corinna had gotten rid of all of Roger's belongings in what amounted to a huge yard sale, as if she wanted to dispossess herself of anything that could remind her of her father, Beverly broke down. She couldn't help it.

———

In July, Jeff Johnson, a door-to-door salesman of carpet-cleaning equipment, was working the 2600 block of Old Gun Road. When a slight, brown-haired woman answered the door at a house with gray cedar siding, he began his presentation but then stopped. He recognized her as Beverly Monroe. He asked if she recognized him. When she said she did not, he explained that he was a former neighbor of Roger's. He and his wife, Angela, had lived two miles west of Windsor, on Pleasants Road. He had actually done some work for Roger around the farm.

Belatedly recognizing him, Beverly apologized and invited Johnson into the house. As they sat at the kitchen table drinking iced tea and talking about the circumstances of Beverly's conviction, Johnson told her he had followed the case closely. He had expected to be summoned as a witness, he said. He and his wife were the ones who had called the police to report seeing the black Chevy Blazer pull out of Roger's driveway and speed off on the night of March 4.

The news startled Beverly. She told Johnson the police had said the report about the Blazer had been anonymous. Oh no, Johnson replied. He remembered it clearly. The papers reported Roger's death on a Friday. His wife had called the police the following Monday. Johnson had been in the room with her. She had asked for Captain Poe. Told he was unavailable, she had given the information to someone else. They expected the police to get back in touch with them, but no one ever did. Then, Johnson said, a couple of months later, Greg Neal had come to their house to discuss another matter, a neighbor's child-abuse case. Johnson told Neal about the black Blazer. Neal took the information down, then, Johnson said, told him not to mention it to anyone else, because it might be dangerous—whatever that meant. Again, Johnson said, they expected to hear from someone in the sheriff's office, but they never did.

He and his wife remembered it all pretty clearly, Johnson continued. It had been sometime between nine forty-five and ten o'clock. They knew the time because he had been driving his wife to work at the Westpoint Convalescence Center. As they passed Windsor, the Blazer recklessly pulled out of the driveway, right in front of them and several other cars. The Blazer sat high, on a jacked-up suspension, and had a swinging rear door with a spare tire attached. There was a white-and-silver wheel cover on the spare. The Blazer sped off down Huguenot Trail, traveling so fast that Johnson couldn't keep up with it.

Beverly excitedly called Peter Greenspun and told him about Johnson's story. Greenspun agreed that if the police knew Johnson's identity and failed to disclose it to Murray Janus, this amounted to prosecutorial misconduct. The commonwealth had an obligation to hand over all exculpatory evidence. Unfortunately, he said, he had already submitted the petition laying out the grounds for Beverly's appeal, and Virginia law did not allow him to alter it. Furthermore, a direct appeal was supposed to address not prosecutorial misconduct but errors in rulings by the trial judge.

Beverly was stunned. Evidence had emerged indicating that after she left, someone else may have been at Windsor the night Roger died— someone who may have smoked the Marlboros—and what was more, the commonwealth had known about this evidence but had never provided it to the defense, never allowed E. B. Harmon to try to track down the owner of the Blazer or Murray to question Johnson before the jury, and she could bring none of this to the attention of the appellate judges? Correct, Greenspun said. Unfair as it may seem, those were the rules. He added that she could always include it in a habeas corpus petition if the direct appeal failed.

———

Warren Von Schuch liked to try them and forget them, so he hadn't thought too much about Beverly Monroe since 1992. In November 1994, on Election Day, he was in his office at the Chesterfield County Courthouse minding his own business when his secretary told him he had a call from an irate citizen who had seen Beverly Monroe voting. Von Schuch took the call. He explained that because Beverly Monroe had appealed her verdict, she was still technically a free citizen and therefore entitled to vote like everyone else.

Hanging up, he found it hard to imagine that someone convicted of murder, and in the midst of an appeal, would retain a sufficient sense of civic obligation to take the trouble to vote. But then on reflection, he decided that it was just the sort of thing Beverly Monroe would do.

Later that morning, Von Schuch received a second call about Beverly voting and then a third. The prosecutor was astonished. "No more calls," he told his secretary. "I can't take it anymore." Two years had passed since that bizarre week in the Powhatan County Courthouse, and Beverly Monroe was still haunting him.

5

The Court of Appeals of Virginia agreed to hear five of the eleven claims Greenspun had raised and scheduled oral arguments for December. It was the same court in which Katie had clerked two years earlier. Judge Bernard Barrow, for whom she had worked, recused himself from the case, but Katie had come to know all of the ten judges on the court. She did not attend the arguments, however, and neither did Beverly. Peter Greenspun never liked to have his clients with him in an appellate court. They were at best a distraction from the legal issues. At worst, they risked offending the judges.

The session was held in a windowless courtroom adorned with oil portraits of former judges, in the old Federal Reserve Building on Eighth Street in Richmond. It followed a strict schedule. The three judges—Sam Coleman, Marvin Cole, and Norman Moon—allowed each lawyer ten minutes for argument and five minutes for rebuttal. John McLees, the commonwealth's representative, kept bringing up the forensic evidence and Beverly Monroe's supposed motives. The judges frequently interrupted him, insisting that he discuss the law and defend the issues. They seemed genuinely engaged, in particular by the voluntariness issue, and even allowed Greenspun extra time on rebuttal.

After listening to the lawyers, the judges retired into chambers and voted on the appeal immediately. One of them was then assigned to write the opinion, which could take months or even years. While they were voting, Greenspun called Beverly. It was, he said, one of the most promising oral arguments he had ever given.

———

Three months later, Judge Bernard Barrow was driving back to his Charlottesville office after a run at the university's track. The judge was fifty-seven years old. Six months earlier, he had been married for the second time, to a younger woman. He stopped his new red Porsche at a traffic light. A police car happened to pull up behind him. The officer saw the judge suddenly slump forward against the steering wheel. He leaped out and pulled him onto the sidewalk; the judge had no heartbeat. The officer called for an ambulance, which arrived some fifteen minutes later. The paramedics were able to restart the judge's heart, but when the doctors at the university hospital examined him, they found that in the interval between his attack and the appearance of the paramedics, he had suffered complete brain death.

While the judge remained in intensive care, his family and friends gathered at the hospital. Katie, who by then was working as a staff attorney for the U.S. Civil Rights Commission, drove down from Washington. She ran into Judge Moon in the waiting room. He knew who she was, of course, just as she knew that Judge Moon was a member of the panel that had heard her mother's appeal, and had in fact already voted on whether to affirm or overturn the conviction. Neither acknowledged this, however. Instead, Judge Moon, a thin, professorial man, questioned Katie blandly about her life in Washington. It gave her a strange suffocating feeling to be unable to say anything but to know that he knew whether or not her mother would be going back to prison—and to know he knew she knew he knew—and to try reading his face for a clue as she chatted about her work investigating immigrants' access to government services.

Judge Barrow had written a living will stipulating that he be removed from life support in the event of brain death. His new wife told the doctors she concurred, and they disconnected the machine that had kept his heart beating. The entire appellate court attended the funeral the next day, and Katie saw both Judge Cole and Judge Coleman, the two other members of the three-judge panel. She had known all of them. She had spoken to them almost daily. She had seen them without their robes and had called them by their first names. Judge Jim Benton, who must have known of the panel's decision even though he hadn't participated in it, hugged Katie but made no reference to her mother's case.

A few nights later, she had a dream in which she was on her knees crying and pleading with the judges, who stared down at her in silence. She had the dream again and again, had it so often that she came to think of it as the begging dream. The most disturbing part of it was that the judges never spoke.

———

The appellate panel issued its opinion on May 2. It ruled against Beverly Monroe on all five claims. Judge Coleman, the author, wrote that rule 5A:18 of the rules of practice of the Virginia Supreme Court, known as the contemporaneous objection rule, required a trial attorney to object to issues during trial in order to preserve them for appeal. Since Murray Janus had not objected to the admissibility of Beverly's statements to Dave Riley on the grounds of their involuntariness, the panel refused to consider that claim. "No good cause exists, nor do the ends of justice require that we address the question on appeal," Coleman declared.

The panel used the same objection—that the trial attorney hadn't preserved the issue for appeal—in declining to rule on Greenspun's claim that a comment made during the trial by Judge Warren—that Beverly's statement was "a voluntary statement"—may have improperly influenced the jury. It ruled that Beverly's Sixth Amendment right to counsel was not violated during the meeting at Drewry's Bluff, because no formal prosecutorial proceeding had been initiated. It further ruled that Jack Lewis had not been guilty of prosecutorial misconduct when he informed Zelma Smith she would not be charged with illegal possession of a handgun on the basis of her testimony that she had tried to sell Beverly the .357 Magnum. Finally, it ruled on sufficiency of the evidence. "The Commonwealth proved beyond a reasonable doubt that the circumstances of time, place, motive, means, opportunity, and conduct concurred in linking Beverly Monroe to the crime. . . . We affirm the appellant's convictions."

———

The opinion shocked Beverly and her children, and it infuriated Greenspun. After demonstrating interest in the issues on the case, the judges had ignored them entirely and instead dismissed the appeal on a strict procedural ruling. If they felt they were, as Judge Coleman wrote, "procedurally barred" from reviewing the issues Greenspun had raised, why did they grant the petition to hear the appeal in the first place? The opinion seemed full of spurious reasoning. How could the judges declare that Roger de la Burde had died at 10:35 P.M. on March 4, 1992, and then fail to address the question of Beverly Monroe's alibi? It made no sense. Greenspun asked the panel to reconsider its decision. He was rebuffed. He requested that the entire court review the case en banc. It refused. Frustrated at the appellate level, he petitioned the Supreme Court of Virginia to hear the case.

6

The supreme court scheduled argument on the petition for a morning in November 1995, more than three years after the trial. The day was sunny and mild. Richmond's economy had recovered since the recession of the early nineties, and traffic coming into the city on I-95 was heavier than it used to be. Beverly, always prompt, anticipated the traffic and arrived early with her children. They sat in the leather chairs in the writ courtroom—an imposing chamber, high-ceilinged, with striped off-white wallpaper, and eighteenth-century oil portraits—where the three-judge panel had convened. Peter Greenspun had objected to Beverly attending, but she had insisted. She wanted the judges to see that this case was about a human being.

Katie tried to appear positive for her mother's sake, but she had little hope. The Virginia Supreme Court had made it clear in numerous rulings that it did not view itself as an error-correcting court, overturning the mistakes made by trial judges. That was the appellate court's job. The supreme court existed as a court of last appeal in capital cases, and to rule on technical legal questions. Rarely had it overturned the appellate court in a case requiring it to side against the commonwealth.

Greenspun, who got caught in traffic, arrived late and almost missed the appointed time. He took his seat at the counsels' table and shuffled through his papers. When he stood up to speak, he appeared flustered. The berobed judges, remote and forbidding men in high-backed chairs, their bench on a platform that seemed to tower over the courtroom well, did little to put him at his ease. "What constitution are you talking about, Counselor?" one of them asked when he tried to raise a constitutional point about his client's right to a fair trial. The judges' lack of interest in the case was almost palpable. It came as no surprise to Greenspun when a month later, in what was called a postcard decision, they declined the petition without comment.

———

The Monroes had expected the decision. Although Katie, Shannon, and Gavin were petrified when they realized their mother had to go back to prison, they'd had months to prepare themselves. They knew what she was going to have to go through and they knew she had survived it before. Beverly, although she said nothing to her children, felt worse than she had when she'd first surrendered some three years ago. Back then, her conviction had still seemed like a mistake the appellate courts could correct and she had been able to look forward to release on the appeal bond. Now she knew she could be in for years.

And knowing what prison life was going to be like, far from reassuring her, filled her with dread. She also knew it was going to be worse than it had been. George Allen, who had been elected governor of Virginia in 1993, had made the abolition of parole his primary campaign theme; he called it "truth in sentencing." Ronald Angelone, the new head of the Department of Corrections, was talking about making life in the state prisons a more punishing experience, about putting guards with rifles in prison towers, about building a fence around the women's correctional center at Goochland for the sole purpose of creating an atmosphere of confinement.

After hearing about the supreme court decision from Peter Greenspun, Beverly called Greg Neal, who told her she could spend the weekend with her family if she would show up first thing Monday morning at the sheriff's office. Beverly had decided to sell her house to fund a habeas corpus appeal in the federal courts. That week, she hired a man to sand the floors, but after taking her money, he disappeared—the sort of thing, she thought, that soured you on the human race.

On Saturday, Beverly took a clump of the broomstraw Roger had given her out to Hollywood Cemetery and laid it on his grave. Katie had come down from Washington with her new boyfriend, Andrew Montague, a rangy, quiet young man from Montana she'd met at a Ziggy Marley concert on the Mall. Andy had brought his brother Jason. Shannon and her friend John Mulligan were there, as was Gavin. On Sunday morning Katie suggested they all drive out to the Blue Ridge Mountains. Beverly and her daughters took the Mercury; the men followed in John's Jeep.

They headed straight west, through Charlottesville. The mountains were in front of them. "Midnight Train to Georgia" came on the radio and Shannon turned up the volume. A mood of defiant gaiety, of fatalistic heedlessness—a go-to-hell, fuck-them-all mood—took hold, and they sang along at the top of their voices.

They parked at an overlook on the western slope of the mountains. It was a cold but sunny January afternoon, the sky pearl blue, and they all wore hats and gloves and scarves. They climbed an overgrown logging road up a hillside, where they found a rock outcropping that looked out across the Shenandoah Valley to the Alleghenies.

A wintry haze lay over the distant mountains. Shannon had made some sandwiches and a thermos of coffee. Sitting on the rocks, they shared the food, then became quiet. As the sun sank toward the mountain range, its shadows slid across the valley toward them. They began to feel chilled and decided to head back.

Going down through the woods, Beverly started to jog, and everyone followed. She broke into a run and so did they. Careering through the bare trees, leaping over logs, their arms swinging wildly as the sloping ground gave way before them, they ran faster and faster, the way children run, for the sheer joy of it, feeling with each hurtling step as if they were about to break free of gravity altogether and soar up into the sky, into flight.

Driving home through the darkness, Katie looked at her mother's profile, faintly lit by the glow from the dashboard. They should have left a long time ago, she thought. They should definitely leave now, just turn around, head west, and keep going, south to Mexico or farther, to Peru or Chile or

Australia. Run. Get away. They would at least have the desperate excitement of flight and the satisfaction of defiance, the knowledge that they were not just spinelessly submitting to the dictates of the system.

But she said nothing.

———

They all rose early the following morning. Beverly was tense and distracted. Despite her fears about returning to prison, she was also worried about being late, so worried, in fact, that after breakfast they left for the Powhatan sheriff's office without cleaning the dishes—something Beverly always hated to do.

When they got to the office, Greg Neal had not yet arrived. They waited in the small lobby. Neal eventually showed up, nodded politely on his way in, then after a while came back out to say that no one was free to take Beverly over to the prison until after lunch. He suggested they go out and eat and come back later. Incredible, Katie thought. They considered her mom a murderer, but at the same time they assumed she was completely honorable and trustworthy.

Since no one had an appetite, they stayed in the lobby. Beverly now decided she wanted to talk to Greg Neal privately. Katie said she didn't think it was a good idea, but Beverly insisted, and the police secretary led her back to Neal's desk. Beverly felt a little nervous. She began by saying, "I'm sure, Greg, you know that this is wrong."

Neal didn't seem to know what to say. Beverly told him that one of the commonwealth's claims—that no one but she thought Roger suicidal—was simply false. Neal acknowledged that other people had in fact given statements that Roger seemed depressed. As she prepared for the federal appeal, Beverly continued, she was going to have an investigator take statements. "Will you work with us?" she asked.

"I'll be willing to share my notes and to look at anything you bring me," Neal said. "If there's something I haven't seen, I want to see it."

"Good," Beverly told him. "We'll start from there."

A deputy finally arrived to drive Beverly over to the prison. As they left the courthouse, it started to snow. The snow seemed to Shannon to come out of nowhere. She thought it gave a mystical cast to the trip, swirling above the fields, dusting the corn stubble and the pine boughs. The children followed the fresh tire tracks the patrol car made through the snow, out Maidens Road and over the bridge to Goochland. Their mother occasionally looked back and held her thumbs up. As soon as they reached the prison, the snow, which had seemed to Shannon so cleansing and spiritually refreshing, stopped. Just as she had done three years earlier, Beverly waved a final time then turned and, carrying her cardboard box of possessions, followed the deputy through the door.

CHAPTER X

The Habeas

When Beverly arrived at Goochland's intake center, the guards were friendly but surprised. What are you doing here, Beverly? one of them asked. Beverly explained that her appeal had been denied and she'd called the Powhatan sheriff's office and been told to come on down and turn herself in. We don't have any paperwork on it, the guard said. We can't take you.

At the same time, the prison officials decided not to release her. Instead, they put her back in the cell rented by the Powhatan sheriff's office in which she had first been placed during her earlier incarceration. When Katie found out, she was livid. She called Peter Greenspun, who called Jack Lewis. It turned out that although the Virginia Supreme Court had denied Beverly's appeal, the commonwealth's bureaucracy had yet to act on the decision. Lewis said he would submit the motion to revoke Beverly's bond and have Judge Warren sign it. I'll expedite it, he told Greenspun.

Take your time, Katie thought when she heard this. It was an excruciating irony. Her mom, punctilious to a fault, had surrendered two weeks earlier than she had to, and Greg Neal had not bothered to inform her of this. He himself probably didn't know.

Although Beverly was technically entitled to remain free until the order revoking her bail came through, Katie decided it was not worth the emotional stress, for all of them, of going to the hassle of getting her mother released only for her to have to surrender again a few days later. Still, it was galling to think that because of her mom's cooperative nature, she'd returned to prison earlier than necessary.

———

Katie decided to take a leave of absence from the U.S. Civil Rights Commission to work full-time on her mother's behalf. Peter Greenspun had done a good job filing the state appeal, but he had already cost Beverly more than $90,000, on top of the $200,000 she had spent on her defense. Those expenses had almost depleted Beverly's savings. The habeas corpus petition would be just as expensive. One attorney in Richmond told Katie her mother seemed to have strong habeas claims, but he said it would cost $175,000 to fund the case. He wanted $10,000 just to review the record.

Katie hoped she could find a prominent attorney who would take the case pro bono. She called Gerry Spence, the buckskin-jacketed trial lawyer from Wyoming who was always on TV, and Alan Dershowitz, the Harvard Law professor. Both turned her down. She began writing letters—to law professors, to the heads of legal clinics, to attorneys profiled in *The Washington Post* or the journal of the American Bar Association. Rejection was unanimous.

She talked to Jim McCloskey, the head of Centurion Ministries, in Princeton, New Jersey, which worked on behalf of death row inmates. McCloskey was sympathetic, but he explained that Beverly's circumstances simply were not dire enough to warrant pro bono aid. She had not been convicted of a capital crime; she was not indigent; she still had a house she could sell. And she still had avenues of appeal. The bottom line, McCloskey said, was that Centurion Ministries took cases of last resort. It represented people who had been in prison ten or fifteen years, who faced death or life sentences, who were friendless and penniless, who didn't have assets and a daughter who was a civil rights attorney.

Katie felt she lacked the requisite appellate experience to handle her mother's case. In one of the many referrals she was given, she ended up speaking to Joshua Rosencrantz, a public defender in Manhattan, who warned her against trying to do so. "This law is complex," he told her. "You do not want to attempt to navigate the waters of the habeas alone." But that winter, after her mother had returned to Goochland, she talked to Lawrence Marshall, a law professor at Northwestern University, who had helped free Rolando Cruz, a young man convicted of killing a small girl after police witnesses testified he had given them a dreamlike recollection of being present during the murder.

Marshall said he wished he could help, but he was already swamped with cases, and if he took on new ones, he wouldn't be able to serve the clients he already had. "All of us in this field have our cases," he told Katie. "This is your case. You may feel you don't have the experience, but none of us who do this did when we started. No one will bring the passion and energy to your mother's case that you can. It's you who has to be her savior."

———

That March, Katie attended a conference sponsored by Families Against Mandatory Minimums. The organization was started by Julie Stewart, a former public relations officer for the Cato Institute, whose older brother had been sentenced to five years in prison for growing marijuana. At a cocktail party the night before the conference, Katie met Don Bergerson, a criminal defense attorney from San Francisco, and began describing her mother's case.

"What was the GSR evidence?" Bergerson asked.

Katie had to admit she didn't know what GSR meant. Bergerson explained that GSR referred to gunshot residue. The reason the police had bagged Roger's hands the day his body was discovered, he said, was to protect them until swabs could be taken and sent to the forensics lab. The swabs would reveal whether primer residue, which was invisible to the naked eye, was on Roger's hands. The presence or absence of primer residue on Roger's hands could indicate whether he had shot the gun himself.

Katie brought the trial transcript back to the conference the next day. She and Don Bergerson sat in the cafeteria paging through the testimony of Marcella Fierro, the deputy chief pathologist, and Ann Jones, the firearms expert.

"This is just incredible," Bergerson said. "You've got these forensic witnesses brought on by the prosecution and nobody talking about the GSR. Where's that evidence?"

Suddenly Bergerson stopped on one page. "Look, oh my God," he said excitedly. "Here it is. Look, here it is."

He pointed to the transcript. The passage Bergerson had noticed took place on the second day of the trial, after the testimony of Fierro, Jones, and Charles Pruitt, the commonwealth's fingerprint expert.

MR. VON SCHUCH: I would offer into evidence the lab report of Mr. McClamroch, if it please the Court. It has been filed and authenticated. . . . Do I have the Court's permission to read the contents to the jury?

THE COURT: Yes, sir.

MR. VON SCHUCH: If it please the Court.

"Evidence submitted by Investigator Neal. The date received: 3/9/92 by examiner Donal L. McClamroch, Jr., Division of Forensic Science, in Richmond, Virginia.

Item 5, one sealed gunshot residue kit containing samples from right web, right palm, left web, left palm, and control.

Results: Levels of antimony and barium found on the sample marked right web were indicative of primer residue.

The results of other requested examinations and the disposition of the evidence are being reported separately."

I believe that the residue kit has been offered into evidence already.

THE COURT: Thank you, sir. Are you ready for your next witness?

This was truly strange, Bergerson told Katie. The gunshot residue evidence—a standard test for suicide by handgun—should be at the heart of the forensic case, but the prosecutors had virtually ignored it. Von Schuch had simply read Donal McClamroch's gunshot residue report into the record without bothering to call McClamroch to explain its significance.

Bergerson took the transcript back to his hotel room to study the testimony. The reason the prosecutors hadn't called McClamroch, he told Katie the next day, was that the gunshot residue evidence completely contradicted the commonwealth's forensic case. The report Von Schuch read stated that levels of antimony and barium, the chief chemical elements of primer residue, had been found in the web of Burde's right hand between the thumb and the forefinger. This suggested that he had fired the gun with his right hand, or that at the very least his hand had been near the gun, maybe steadying it.

Fierro and Jones, however, had maintained that Roger had been lying on his right side, with his right hand cupping the right side of his head. If that had been the case, Bergerson said, the web of Roger's right hand would have been buried between his head and the pillow. How could primer residue have gotten onto it? Roger's hand had to be on or near the gun, which strongly suggested that he had in fact shot himself. The prosecution could try to argue that primer residue was a gas that might taint anything within a few inches of the gun when it was discharged. But the fact was that the bulk of the primer residue was discharged from the muzzle and through the back of the gun, around the hammer. The FBI, in the brochure it sent to local police departments, stated, "The elements of antimony and barium, which are found in most primer mixtures for ammunition, have been found to deposit on the back of the hand of a shooter as the firearm is discharged." Bergerson could cite cases of people who had been acquitted on the basis of gunshot residue evidence.

The big question, Bergerson went on, was whether Murray Janus had seen the GSR report. The prosecutors should have turned it over to the defense, along with the autopsy reports and other forensic documents, as part of disclosure. If they hadn't, Janus—who had to have been aware of its existence, since the police always take swabs for GSR tests in cases like this—should have asked for it.

Don Bergerson's theory about the gunshot residue reinforced another forensic detail that had always seemed to Katie to point toward suicide: the absence of blood on Roger's right hand. The gunshot that killed Roger had caused blood to spray out of the wound and across the pillows and the back of the sofa. If, as the prosecution had contended at trial, Roger's right hand had been cupping his head around and beneath the wound, blood should also have sprayed onto his fingers and seeped into his palm. Neal's photographs, however, showed not the slightest evidence of blood on the hand.

During the next few days, Katie searched through Murray Janus's file, which he had given to Beverly after Peter Greenspun took over the appeal. She saw that on several documents Murray had scrawled questions in the margins about the gunshot residue report. "No mention of GSR test?" he had written on the toxicologist's report. "Though Greg Neal has told me he thinks the GSR tests reveal powder on the right hand and nothing on the left hand, we have not seen that report," E. B. Harmon declared in one of his memos, next to which Janus had written, "Did we ever?" Another one of Janus's notes referring to the GSR actually listed Donal McClamroch's name and telephone number.

Katie also reread the trial transcript looking for references to the test.

During Janus's direct examination of his forensics expert Herbert MacDonell, she found the following brief exchange during a discussion of a videotape MacDonell had made of his re-enactment of the shooting.

> Q. In the video in actuality, there appears to be some soot in the right web—of the right web; isn't that correct?
>
> A. Yes.
>
> Q. Was that consistent with Mr. McClamroch's report that you saw last night, where you did the barium testing on the right hand?
>
> A. Yes. There was barium found there which indicates primer.
>
> Q. Was there any soot on the left hand in the experiments you conducted?
>
> A. No. We didn't observe any.

According to his testimony, MacDonell seemed to have read the GSR report only the night before he testified. That would have been the day *after* Von Schuch read it into the record. MacDonell, and therefore Murray himself, apparently had not gotten the GSR report before the trial. Katie felt uncomfortable calling Murray Janus, from whom she and her mother were now completely estranged, to find out what he had actually known about the GSR test. But she called Don Bergerson, who had returned to San Francisco, with her discoveries.

Bergerson said it seemed clear that MacDonell had developed the defense's forensic theory—that Roger had killed himself by gripping the gun frame with his right hand and using his left thumb to pull the trigger—without the benefit of the gunshot residue report. If he'd had the report, MacDonell could have used it to advance a simple, logical, and compelling theory: that Roger had held the gun in his right hand when he fired it, thereby discharging primer residue onto the web of that hand. And this theory could have been supported by a piece of evidence to which Marcella Fierro had attached such importance—the imprint of the gun butt, seen in the photograph of Roger's right palm. If Roger had shot himself with his right hand and died instantaneously, the gun probably would have remained in that hand until Joe Hairfield moved it trying to take Roger's pulse after he had discovered the body.

The charcoal-like stains on Roger's fourth and fifth fingers, which had been the cornerstone of the commonwealth's forensic theory, could have come from old soot on the gun—which Ann Jones had said was one of the dirtiest she had ever seen—or from the fireplace tools or from almost anything. Those stains, unlike the residue on the web, had never been tested. Marcella Fierro's claim that they came from gunpowder was nothing more than speculation, Bergerson pointed out. The GSR test was solid forensic evidence. It was in fact the only solid forensic evidence in the whole case— all the rest being the result of inference—and it trumped Marcella Fierro's guesswork, however educated that may be, any day.

2

Beverly spent two months in Cottage 3 in the same cell in which she'd been held during her first incarceration. Then she was incorporated into the general prison population and transferred to a set of three trailers, classified as B-level custody, that had been placed on the southern edge of the center's property. There were twenty-four women to a trailer, giving them little space to maneuver inside, and they were surrounded by a fence. But the prisoners were also allowed to go outside once or twice a day. That meant Beverly could walk and run in the fresh air. And from the yard she had a view of the wooded river line. Compared to Cottage 3, she felt, it was not a bad place to be.

Early in May, Beverly came across a copy of *Time* magazine that contained an article on a new law signed by President Clinton a week earlier. The legislation, called the Antiterrorism and Effective Death Penalty Act of 1996, was primarily designed to make it easier for federal officials, in the wake of the Oklahoma City bombing, to investigate and prosecute suspected terrorists. But it also provided new limitations on habeas corpus proceedings.

One of those restrictions was a time limit on appeals. Previously, a petition for a writ of habeas corpus could be filed anytime after a conviction. Now, according to the act, petitions had to be filed within a year of the date on which the conviction became final by affirmation in the highest state court. The Virginia Supreme Court had ruled on Beverly's case in January. She was entitled to another ninety days to file a petition for a writ of certiorari, asking for a final review of the case. That deadline had expired in April, which meant Beverly only had until the following April to file her appeal.

———

Later that month, Beverly was awoken one night by a guard and told to get up and pack her things. It was dark. She had to find a box, fit her clothes into it, and figure out how to tape it shut. She and six other women who had been similarly awoken sat up all night waiting for their next orders. They assumed they were being relocated, but they didn't know where. They did know that because the Virginia prison system was so over-crowded, the commonwealth had been shipping inmates to Texas, and they wondered if that distant state was their destination.

Beverly also wondered if Zelma Smith had instigated her transfer. She too was at Goochland, serving out her reduced sentence. Beverly had never run into Zelma, but her counselor, Ms. Fenner, had told her that a note in her file in the prison computer said that Zelma Smith was on her enemies' list. Beverly hadn't even known she had an enemies' list. She had wondered then if that note had somehow been Zelma's doing. Had Zelma complained that Beverly was bent on revenge?

The seven women were given some bread and coffee at sunup, but it was nine o'clock before a mesh-windowed prison van arrived. They were driven to another building, strip-searched, their hands and feet shackled, and led back to the van, which pulled out of the compound. The new type of manacles they wore, linking their hands to a chain around their waists, made it impossible for them to rub their noses or support themselves when the van bounced or turned.

They crossed the James River, and headed south down to Route 288, turning off at the Courthouse Road exit. Just south of the exit was the Poca-hontas Correctional Unit, a low-slung brick building set back behind a parking lot and surrounded by a razor-wire fence. Beverly recognized the place. She and Roger had often driven past it when looking at real estate in the area, where Roger had in fact acquired some land, but she had never given a thought to what it was like inside.

The women were led through the gate and into a holding area. Guards searched them once again, then escorted them into a huge open room. Beverly had an initial blurred impression of people and beds and noise. Women were yelling. The room was hot and electric fans the size of refrigerators sat on the floors throbbing noisily. The walls were painted an incongruous pink.

A woman who introduced herself as Big Frances helped Beverly secure a desirable single bunk. She explained that Pocahontas was known as the Pink Palace. It had been a work camp for male prisoners and was converted into a women's prison because of overcrowding at Goochland. Each of its four dorms held as many as seventy women, who had to share the one open bathroom with two commodes and three sinks. Most of the women could tolerate the noise and the lack of privacy because they were short-termers, with only a few months left on their sentences. This was apparently where Beverly would remain until she was released. She unpacked and got busy learning the routine.

3

Federal Habeas Corpus: Practice and Procedure, a two-volume, two-thousand-page work by James Liebman and Randy Hertz, was the definitive treatment of federal habeas law. It cost $180. To save money, Katie had gone to the Library of Congress and stood at a Xerox machine laboriously photocopying the passages she needed.

The federal law of habeas corpus—"You should have the body," in the literal translation from the Latin—had evolved from English common law requirements that the government reveal the evidence against an accused. Incorporated into the Constitution, it allowed a convict to challenge the lawfulness of his or her imprisonment on the grounds that it represented a violation of constitutional rights to due process.

Liebman recommended that before filing a habeas petition, the appellant conduct a thorough reinvestigation of the entire case. That meant reinterviewing witnesses for any evidence of misconduct by the police or prosecutors. It meant speaking to the jurors for suggestions of jury misconduct. Jim McCloskey at Centurion Ministries had told Katie he often spent five years or more on such an investigation—not only to uncover grounds for possible claims but also because the review standards raised obstacles to presenting new claims once the original petition has been filed. Because of the Antiterrorism and Effective Death Penalty Act, Katie now had eleven months to organize an investigation and write the petition.

An offer for Beverly's house—a depressingly low offer—finally came through in the summer. After Gavin had moved into an apartment, Shannon had tried living there by herself but had lost her nerve—it was too frightening and lonely—and ended up staying with a friend. Still, part of her didn't want to sell the house. It was full of memories, sad memories of Roger and the trial, but also good memories, of her mother finally building a place that was truly her own, of the two of them clearing the rocks and planting the flower beds, of the neighbors helping move the cedar trees. The house, Shannon thought, was a work of art, a gorgeous place to live. By accepting the bid, she and Katie were acknowledging that her mother would never return to it, and that was hard to do.

But they needed the money. Katie accepted the offer. The weekend before the closing, Shannon, Katie, Gavin, and some friends descended on the house to clean it out. Even though Shannon had been living there all those years, it never occurred to her what an absolute pack rat her mother was. There was all this stuff—in the utility room, in the attic crawl space, in the toolshed. There were badminton nets, croquet sets, wooden tennis rackets in their wing-nut presses, pieces of driftwood, the stakes from front-yard election posters, and old wooden toys her mother kept because no one made wooden toys anymore. And there were boxes everywhere, boxes of seashells, boxes of buttons, boxes of fabric scraps, boxes of dolls' eyes. One box Shannon got a particular kick out of was labeled FUTURE HOBBIES.

There was no time to hold a yard sale. They created two piles, one for the Goodwill and one for the dump, and everything went into them except Beverly's artwork and a few personal items—the box of seashells, the dried broomstraw that Roger had given her fifteen years ago and that had sat on the kitchen counter next to a sugar bowl from Pier 1—which they wrapped and put in a self-storage place on Midlothian.

The next day, after the walk-through, the new buyers tried to argue that the Monroes had reneged on the contract by not leaving the fireplace tools behind. The ploy enraged Katie. She and Shannon hadn't wanted to sell, they'd accepted an insulting offer, and now, mere hours before closing, the buyers were gaming them. "Fine," Katie told the real estate agent. "If they want to break the contract over fireplace tools, I don't give a shit."

The buyers backed down and, at the closing that afternoon, Katie handed over her mother's keys.

———

Katie used some of the money to hire Peter De Forest to review the forensic evidence for possible claims to raise in the appeal. De Forest, an expert in trace evidence, was a cautious, skeptical man who worked out of a laboratory in Ardsley, New York. After reading the testimony and examining the forensic reports, it seemed to him that Herbert MacDonell had made so many obvious mistakes that he appeared not to have seriously studied the evidence.

If, as MacDonell had theorized, Roger had gripped the gun frame with his right hand while firing it with his left, there would have been gunpowder deposits from the cylinder blast on the palm of his right hand as well as on his fourth and fifth fingers. However, in the photographs of the death scene, there was no visible residue on Roger's right palm. MacDonell's conclusions were seriously flawed, De Forest decided, but Beverly Monroe's lawyer had accepted them uncritically at the time of the trial.

There were also serious flaws, De Forest thought, in Ann Jones's theory. The commonwealth's firearms expert had made several claims during the trial. One was that the gunpowder pattern on the clay-filled glove she had used in her reconstruction of the shooting matched the pattern of the charcoal-like stains found on Roger's fourth and fifth fingers. But it didn't. The glove fingers showed heavy deposits on their palmar surfaces, the bottom side of the finger parallel to the palm. The death-scene photographs showed that Burde's fingers had no deposits on the palmar surfaces.

It seemed to De Forest that both MacDonell and Jones had come up with—or had been given—hypotheses and then had devised experiments that supported them. Neither had followed the accepted scientific methodology of designing experiments to refute their hypotheses. Strictly speaking, neither MacDonell's nor Jones's reconstruction represented science at all.

Furthermore, neither hypothesis explained the results of the gunshot residue test, which showed primer on the web of the dead man's right hand.

De Forest called Ann Jones to discuss the apparent flaws in her theory. Her reconstruction, he told her, had been unscientific. Jones sounded uncomfortable. She couldn't remember the case, she said. She'd conducted her experiments almost five years ago. The files were in the warehouse and it would take at least a week to have them pulled. De Forest told her he would call her again, but before he was able to talk to her, her supervisor called De Forest. He was sorry, but since the case was still being litigated, Ann Jones was not permitted to discuss it.

For the purposes of the appeal, the forensics seemed a dead end.

———

De Forest had asked Katie to make copies of the autopsy photographs. She had never actually looked at them before, but when she went to pick them up, the receptionist at the photo lab asked her if she wanted to check the quality of the prints. She sat down alone in a chair and pulled them out. It was horrifying to look at these pictures of the naked, dissected body—with gruesome close-ups—of a man she'd known and liked, but she steeled herself to do it. In bed that night, unable to sleep, with the photographic after-images floating in front of her eyes whenever she closed them, she thought, God, what a weird life I have.

———

When Katie contacted the American Suicide Foundation, looking for any studies to support the proposition that someone like Roger de la Burde would commit suicide, she was referred to John Maltsberger, a psychiatrist and professor at Harvard Medical School. Maltsberger, who had spent much of his career studying and writing about suicide, agreed to review the case. Katie sent him portions of the trial transcript, Roger's will and letters, the baby agreement, and the complaint in his Philip Morris lawsuit. That winter, Maltsberger sat down in his Brookline office and read through the material.

What struck Maltsberger most forcefully was that Burde displayed the clinical symptoms of a narcissistic personality disorder. He pulled out his copy of the *Diagnostic and Statistical Manual of Mental Disorders, Fourth Edition* and made a list of the symptoms.

1. has a grandiose sense of self-importance (e.g., exaggerates achievements and talents, expects to be recognized as superior without commensurate achievements).

2. is preoccupied with fantasies of unlimited success, power, brilliance, beauty, or ideal love.

3. believes that he or she is "special" or unique and can only be understood by, or should associate with, other special or high status people (or institutions).

4. requires excessive admiration.

5. has a sense of entitlement, i.e., unreasonable expectations of espe-

cially favorable treatment or automatic compliance with his or her expectations.

    6. is interpersonally exploitative, i.e., takes advantage of others to achieve his or her own ends.

    7. lacks empathy: is unwilling to recognize or identify with the feelings and needs of others.

    8. is often envious of others or believes that others are envious of him or her.

    9. shows arrogant, haughty behaviors or attitudes.

According to the DSM, the presence of five or more of the symptoms indicated a narcissistic personality disorder. Maltsberger thought Burde showed evidence of at least eight, and probably all nine, of the symptoms. The man had an inflated view of his own importance and that of his family; exaggerated his wealth and exaggerated the importance of his art collection; exploited women; and was manipulative and dishonest. Burde also seemed to Maltsberger to have suffered, during the final four weeks of his life, from what the DSM called a "major depressive episode."

Maltsberger, a co-director of the Data Bank of the American Suicide Foundation, was as familiar as anyone in his field with the statistics on suicide. A number of studies had established that a major depressive episode was the cause of 40 to 60 percent of all suicides. "Death Without Warning," a 1993 article in the *Archive of General Psychiatry,* had demonstrated that schizoid and narcissistic personality types were the most common postmortem diagnoses for suicides that followed major depressive episodes. The group most likely to commit suicide in the United States were depressed, aging white males who lived alone and were in poor health. All these statistics, Maltsberger felt, made it likely that Burde had committed suicide, as did the fact that there was a genetic predisposition to depression and suicide, and Burde's mother had tried to commit suicide.

The psychiatrist was not impressed by the testimony of the witnesses who said Burde appeared cheerful and was planning for the future. It was part of Burde's character to dissemble, Maltsberger thought. He could easily imagine Burde pretending to be cheerful if it suited his purpose. Nor was Maltsberger impressed by the fact that Burde did not leave a note. In *Assessment and Prediction of Suicide,* a book Maltsberger had co-edited, one of the chapters presented the results of a study demonstrating that only 12 to

15 percent of the people who commit suicide leave a note. Even writers such as Ernest Hemingway and Hart Crane had killed themselves without leaving a note. Burde may not have left a note because he wanted, for insurance reasons, to obscure the fact that he had committed suicide.

Finally, Maltsberger thought, there was Burde's last phone call, the one to Don Beville, in which he had said everything was resolved and the weight of the world was off his shoulders. The prosecutors had used this as proof that Roger felt upbeat and therefore couldn't have committed suicide. To Maltsberger, it indicated just the opposite. It was a clinical commonplace that when patients made up their minds to commit suicide, their mood often brightened. They saw death not as the terrifying extinction of their lives but as the solution to their problems. Maltsberger had studied cases in which certain people, having made the decision to kill themselves, experienced elation. He had in fact recently completed an article on the subject, "Ecstatic Suicide," that was scheduled for publication in the *Archives of Suicide Research.*

Maltsberger called Katie Monroe. He was not a forensics expert, he said, but from the evidence he'd studied, Roger de la Burde seemed a prototypical candidate for suicide. He would be more than happy to come down to Richmond to testify to that. He was also willing to write a report of his analysis. And to ensure its impartiality, he would refuse any fee.

———

In January, Katie and Andy drove to Salem, Massachusetts, to attend a conference on wrongful convictions. One of the speakers was Richard Leo, then a professor of sociology and law at the University of Colorado, Boulder, and a specialist on police interrogation. Leo gave a talk on false confessions.

A confession was almost invariably considered damning, he said, and tended to dominate any other evidence in a case. Because most suspects who confess are guilty, many police officers and interrogation instructors assume it is impossible for an innocent person to confess to a crime. To ordinary people as well, the idea of someone making a false confession is intuitively illogical. But it happened often enough—while no one knew exactly how often, numerous cases had been documented—to represent a distinct criminological phenomenon.

A false confession, Leo explained, was almost invariably the result of overzealousness, misconduct, or poor training on the part of the police. In some cases, the police became so convinced of one suspect's guilt that they failed to evenhandedly evaluate the evidence. Instead, they devoted themselves to obtaining a confession. Then, once they obtained it, they ceased investigating, and their only goal was to convict the suspect who had made the confession.

Often, the confession itself had been secured by blatant trickery: The police, who are trained to lie, avoided telling the suspect he was under suspicion. Once he'd been lured to the station, the police elicited a confession by, for example, wearing the suspect out, convincing him that evidence (which did not in fact exist) proved his guilt, or appearing to offer a deal. They could also cause him to doubt his own memory by telling him he had failed a polygraph when he hadn't or that he had suffered from a blackout or a repressed memory or a multiple personality disorder. Often, the suspect was close to the victim and in a distraught, vulnerable state of mind. The police, during interrogations that could last for hours, badgered the victim endlessly, refusing to take no for an answer and repeating the incriminating version of the facts. They often offered plausible accounts for how the suspect had committed the offense in a way that minimized or eliminated his culpability. A weak or compliant person who had come to doubt his own memory and who had been given a plausible explanation for his faulty memory and an apparently exculpatory account of the offense could confess to a crime he had not committed.

What Leo was describing seemed to Katie to parallel down to the smallest details her mother's experience. She recalled how Dave Riley had explained to the jury during the trial the way he had repeated his theme over and over and over to Beverly, how the police secretaries described the way Beverly had seemed to go into a trance, how her mother had said Riley had "pounded, pounded, pounded" on her until she felt like she was hypnotized.

Until that night, Katie thought that what had happened to her mother was an isolated, freakish experience. Suddenly, she had a scientific explanation for it, a context, a way of understanding it. Later, she introduced herself to Leo, who agreed to look at her mother's case. And that night she and Andy visited the cemetery in Salem where the women who had been executed during the witch trials were buried. She lit a candle for her mother and left it there among the faded headstones.

———

Back in Boulder, Richard Leo read the testimony from the various witnesses about what had happened at First Division headquarters on March 26, after Beverly failed the polygraph. He then listened to the last fifteen minutes of Dave Riley's interview with Beverly, the portion the investigator had recorded. Beverly's statements reminded Leo of two other cases he had studied. The first involved Peter Reilly, an eighteen-year-old in Canaan, Connecticut, who had confessed to murdering his mother after being told that he had failed a polygraph test. Reilly was convicted but then granted a second trial, and after a new prosecutor found exculpatory evidence in files not turned over to the defense, the judge dismissed the case. The second case involved Tom Sawyer, a recovering alcoholic in Clearwater, Florida, who had confessed to killing his next-door neighbor after the police, who told him he had failed a polygraph test, had convinced him he couldn't remember committing the crime because it had occurred while he was suffering from a dry blackout. Sawyer spent fourteen months in jail before a judge threw out the case.

In the cases of both Reilly and Sawyer, the police interrogators had not threatened or abused the defendants. But they had persuaded them, after exhaustive interrogations, to accept the hypothesis of their own guilt as the only explanation that could account for certain facts. Interrogators in both these cases, Leo had determined, had used the techniques developed by John Reid, which had become popular in the 1970s after court rulings encouraged police, during interrogations, to exchange confrontation for persuasion and skepticism for sympathy.

Riley, it seemed to Leo, had used them as well. And like the investigators in many of the false confessions Leo had studied, Riley seemed to have fixated suspicion on someone close to the victim and then asked the suspect to come to the police station to help solve the crime. Once she was there, he had used his pseudoscientific theory of repressed memories to confuse her further. Following the method espoused by John Reid, he had concocted a scenario he thought she might accept, then used repetition and escalation and encouragement—interrupting, talking over her, telling her she'd feel better once she recovered the repressed memories—to induce her to accept it. Since, as best as Leo could tell, there was no other evidence linking Beverly Monroe to the murder, if indeed murder had been committed, it seemed to Leo a particularly outrageous example of what he called a persuaded confession. Strictly speaking, however, Beverly's statement was not even a confession at all, he thought. It was a nonconfession to a noncrime.

While Riley's behavior at police headquarters on March 26 had been manipulative, the tactics he admitted to—and even seemed proud of—on June 3 at Drewry's Bluff seemed to Leo to involve blatant coercion. Not only did Riley lie about or at least misstate some of the supposed evidence against Beverly—claiming that PBS had not broadcast the documentary she said she had watched with Roger the night of March 4 when in fact it had—but he also threatened her with harsher punishment, a charge of first-degree murder, if she failed to confess, and offered the prospect of leniency, a charge of second-degree murder, if she complied.

Leo called Katie. He said he had studies showing the tactics Riley had used had led to demonstrably false confessions in other cases. Like John Maltsberger, he offered to write up his conclusions and testify if the case wound up in court again, and like Maltsberger, he refused to accept a fee.

———

Leo's analysis of Riley's interrogation tactics seemed to Katie to be borne out by information her mother had unearthed while free on parole. Beverly had conducted a Nexis search at the Richmond Public Library for any prior mention of David Riley in the Virginia press. His name had come up in two 1986 stories about Emerson Stevens, a waterman accused of kidnapping and murdering a twenty-four-year-old woman in the Northern Neck near Chesapeake Bay.

Stevens's first trial resulted in a mistrial. At his second trial, one of the witnesses testified that Dave Riley, who led the investigation, had pressured her to modify her story. "A witness in the abduction and murder retrial of Emerson Eugene Stevens says she tailored her testimony to suit state police special agent David M. Riley during Stevens's first trial in February," the Richmond *News Leader* reported. The *Times-Dispatch* quoted the same witness, Ann Dick, the wife of a retired Maryland state trooper, as testifying that Riley had also bragged of having pressured Stevens during an interview. " 'He said he did everything he possibly could have done [to produce a confession] except taking him and throwing him on the flowers of [the victim's] grave.' "

Katie contacted Ann Dick. The woman said Emerson Stevens's lawyer,

James Parker, had actually filed a formal complaint against Riley with Lieutenant Gordon Rogers of the state police's internal affairs unit. She sent Katie a copy of the letter.

> Dear Lt. Rogers,
>
> As a member of the Virginia State Bar, and as a third generation former police officer, I am compelled to file a formal complaint concerning the investigation and testimony of Special Agent David M. Riley in the trial of Emerson E. Stevens. . . . I am solidly of the opinion that he was convicted as a result of the unlawful and ethically despicable conduct of Agent Riley. . . . Testimony at the trial supported my suspicion that Agent Riley committed perjury, suborned perjury, encouraged witnesses to slant or embellish their testimony, coached and intimidated the witnesses, and badgered, threatened, and intimidated the defendant frequently. It would also appear that Agent Riley made the mistake of focusing his investigation solely on his personal desire to convict the defendant rather than to objectively solve the death of Mary Keyser Harding by the use of accepted methods. . . .

Nothing had come of the complaint, Ann Dick said. Riley, according to the newspaper articles, denied everything, and defense lawyers, Katie knew, often made such complaints primarily to satisfy indignant clients; Parker, she saw, had copied Emerson Stevens on the letter.* But Katie was elated nonetheless. The letter, she felt, could just as easily have been written to describe Riley's behavior toward her mother. It suggested a pattern of prosecutorial misconduct that could clearly form the basis for a habeas claim.

———

Acting on the recommendation in Liebman, as the huge book on habeas procedure was known, Katie hired Roger Goldsberry and Ralph Bennett, two private investigators from Charlottesville, to interview as many of the jurors and witnesses as possible. The team had little luck. Brigitte de la Burde irately refused to discuss the case, insisting it was all behind her now. The memories of Wojtek Drewnowska and Joe Hairfield were vague. Barbara Samuels and Sheldon Gosline and Frank Vegas had disappeared.

---

*Since the letter represented a formal complaint, Edward Carpenter, the commonwealth attorney for Goochland County, was asked to conduct an investigation. He exonerated Riley of any impropriety.

Krystyna Drewnowska failed to return a number of messages left on her answering machine.

Early one evening in February, Bennett did reach the jury foreman, Richard Kistler, at his home. At first Kistler said the jurors had all agreed not to speak to anyone about the case, but Bennett spent a considerable amount of time developing a rapport with the man and finally persuaded him to describe the deliberations.

First of all, the foreman explained, the jury had ruled out the possibility of suicide. Since one of the jurors had tried to re-enact the suicide on a couch in his hotel room and claimed it was impossible, the jury had sent for Burde's couch. Another juror lay down on it and attempted to replicate the experiment. After watching, the jurors decided that while it may not have been technically impossible for Burde to have killed himself in that position, had he decided to commit suicide, he would have certainly chosen a less contorted method. "If you're going to kill yourself," Kistler told Bennett, "you are going to do it the easiest way you can."

The determination that Burde's death could not have been a suicide undercut the basic thrust of Beverly's defense, Kistler pointed out. Her attorney, he said, had from time to time rambled on loosely about other possible murder suspects, including a Philip Morris "hit man," but had produced no evidence to support these propositions.

The jury reasoned that Burde had been on intimate terms with the murderer. "He could fall asleep at the drop of a hat but he would wake up if a needle hit the floor," Kistler said. "So that ruled out somebody sneaking in the house." Beverly Monroe was there that night and she had a motive. "She felt she wasn't in the will anymore and he was probably going to dump her in order to go with this woman he had impregnated," Kistler explained. What had probably set her off, he continued, was overhearing a telephone conversation Burde had with Krystyna. But the jury gave her the minimum sentence, he added, because they felt Burde had "screwed" her over so badly.

Murray was at least right about that, Katie thought when she received Bennett's report.

———

As the deadline for filing the habeas petition approached, Katie kept thinking of the warning that the New York public defender Joshua Rosencrantz had given her not to attempt to navigate the waters of the habeas alone. Since she wasn't a member of the Virginia bar, she needed some sort of assistance. She had hoped Don Bergerson, who had uncovered the GSR evidence, would help her. Bergerson did provide guidance, but he wasn't a member of the Virginia bar, either, so at the end of the year Katie turned to a Richmond lawyer named Don Lee.

Until that fall, Lee had been a staff attorney at the Virginia Capital Representation Resource Center, a nonprofit organization providing legal services for inmates on death row. But he had gotten burned-out. His last eleven clients had all been executed and he had attended each execution. He had become friends with these men, and so had his young children, Jessie and Luke, who would talk to them on the phone when they called collect from prison. Lee had given his clients hope because he had hope, and then the Fourth Circuit of the U.S. Court of Appeals ruled against them and the people to whom he had given hope would be executed. He'd become depressed and had trouble sleeping. His wife, Lisa, told him he had to find less-defeating work. So he had left the Resource Center to form a new firm with two other attorneys.

Katie, who had first met Don the previous spring, when he was still on staff at the Resource Center, liked him immensely. He wore cowboy boots and jeans and an earring, kept his long hair in a ponytail, and could play virtually the entire Bob Dylan repertoire on his guitar. Katie suggested that Don join her as a consultant. She and her brother and sister and their friends could interview witnesses and collect affidavits, she said. She herself would develop the legal issues and rough out the petition, with Don providing focus and direction. Don said he couldn't take the case pro bono, since he needed to support his family, but he agreed to a reduced fee, $100 an hour as opposed to $225, and he told Katie he would bill as he went; she didn't have to give him a huge retainer. "You and the volunteers go put it together," he said. "I'll monitor it, sign it, and take it to court."

4

Tonya Mallory, who'd attended Patrick Henry High School in Ashland with Katie, had a master's degree in forensic science. When she volunteered to help with the habeas, Katie asked her to examine all the scientific evidence Murray Janus had collected prior to the trial. That winter, Tonya called Katie with what she said was a startling discovery. Murray Janus had subpoenaed Krystyna Drewnowska's medical records. Looking through them,

Tonya noticed that on January 24, 1992, Krystyna's doctor, Erika Blanton, had scheduled a "Vac DEC" for February 6, 1992. A line had been drawn through the phrase and *Cancel* was written underneath. Following that, on February 11, 1992, Blanton had written *Schd. f. Vac DEC 3/11*. A line had also been crossed through this notation.

Tonya contacted Dr. Blanton, who confirmed that Vac DEC stood for Vacuum, Dilation, Evacuation, Curettage, the medical term for the four-step procedure that constituted one type of abortion. Krystyna Drewnowska, her medical records seemed to indicate, had scheduled one abortion a month after telling Roger she was pregnant, canceled it, then scheduled a second abortion for the second week in March—*which would have been six days after Roger died*—then canceled that one as well. Instead, on March 11, Blanton's records showed, she received a phone call from the patient, who informed her that the father of the baby had passed away and she "wants paternity testing to verify heirship."

The information seemed to confirm Beverly's story that Roger had regretted his decision to become a father and had been pressuring Krystyna to have an abortion. The issue of these scheduled abortions, Katie recalled, had not come up during the trial. She went through the transcript to find out what, if anything, had been said about the matter. There was one brief exchange, during Murray's cross-examination of Krystyna.

Q. Ma'am, you know Roger told you, had discussions about that if the child was going to be a girl, that you would get an abortion; isn't that correct?

A. That's not correct.

Q. Roger never mentioned the word abortion to you, is that your testimony?

A. Roger never mentioned to me that if it will be known that it is a girl, it's aborted, that there are conditions. He always said whatever child would be born, we would have to wait. And he wants to have a child where he could spend more time, and it will be a child raised the way using our best knowledge and experience, and creating the most beneficial and reasonable condition for the child.

Q. Are you telling us that Roger was happy that you were pregnant finally, and you were going to be expecting as of December 1991?

A. Yes.

Krystyna had not committed perjury, Kate realized, because she had answered Murray's question with the qualification that Roger had not talked to her about undergoing an abortion *if it was a girl*. Had the medical notes been introduced at trial, Katie thought, they would have shown that Roger had twice succeeded in pressuring Krystyna to have an abortion regardless of the gender of the fetus. Given the statements Krystyna had made about how determined she was to have the child whatever its sex, and given the fact that she had canceled the second scheduled abortion after Roger's death—when, faced with the prospect of raising a child on her own, she might have been more inclined to go ahead with it—it was hard to imagine she had arranged the procedures on her own initiative. Evidence pointing to Roger's change of heart, and serious tensions between himself and Krystyna over proceeding with the pregnancy, contradicted the commonwealth's entire scenario, summed up in Jack Lewis's irritating line "It's bye-bye, Beverly; hello, Krystyna and the new baby." It suggested that Roger was confused and probably in a state of panic around the time of his death. And it gave new emphasis to the fact that Krystyna had avoided telling him about the sex of the fetus.

Murray Janus had had Dr. Blanton's notes at the time of the trial. But he hadn't confronted Krystyna with the evidence that she'd apparently twice scheduled an abortion. Katie wondered whether it was possible that Murray, an older Southern gentleman, had looked at Blanton's notes but hadn't known what *Vac DEC* stood for. Maybe he had a reason for not confronting Krystyna. Katie wanted to call him, but given the circumstances, she felt she couldn't.

———

Katie now believed she had two important pieces of evidence—the gunshot residue test and the notes showing the scheduled abortions—that had not been brought to the jury's attention. If the defense had used this evidence, she thought, it could have demolished the prosecution's case.

Don Lee by then had begun to feel some true passion about Beverly's appeal. He'd decided that if Beverly Monroe were guilty, she would never have taken the lie detector test and, as Krystyna Drewnowska did when she finally returned to Virginia and spoke to Dave Riley, would have insisted that her lawyer be present when the police interviewed her. If Beverly were guilty, Don felt, she'd be walking the streets now, a free woman.

She was behind bars not in spite of the fact that she was innocent but *because* she was innocent. *Because* she was trusting. *Because* she'd had nothing to hide.

Don's work at the Resource Center had convinced him that the police and prosecutors frequently ignored correct procedure in the pursuit of suspects they believed to be guilty. He became convinced that this was what had happened in Beverly's case. Dave Riley had used coercive, manipulative tactics on an exhausted, distraught woman. He had broken her down. And when the exculpatory gunshot residue report was issued, Don decided, the commonwealth team had failed to pass it on to the defense counsel and had instead simply read it into the record after presenting their forensics case. That seemed the basis for a claim of prosecutorial misconduct, since the commonwealth had an obligation to divulge exculpatory material.

Don also thought they could make an ineffective-assistance-of-counsel claim against Murray Janus for failing to cross-examine Krystyna Drewnowska about her medical records. But he was uncertain how useful it would be. The judges, he told Katie, probably wouldn't know what *Vac DEC* stood for, either.

Finally, Don wanted to claim ineffective assistance of counsel for Murray's failure to make a motion to suppress Beverly's statements to Dave Riley on the ground that they were involuntary. The courts, however, tended to be skeptical of such claims, since virtually every defendant who was convicted attributed it to ineffective counsel. What was often crucial to such a claim was an acknowledgment by the trial attorney that he had erred. If Murray admitted making a mistake, Don said, they'd have a case the courts could not afford to ignore. So before framing the claim, he would have to speak to Murray himself.

Katie was working in her apartment in Washington the day Lee went to see Janus. Late that afternoon, he called her. "You need to tell me about this phone call," he said.

Don and Murray had discussed the voluntariness issue. Murray had said he thought he *had* argued the involuntariness of the confessions, but if the transcript showed he had not, then he guessed he had not. "He fell on his sword," Don told Katie. But Murray had also mentioned something else to Don, something very troubling. Murray had become convinced that if Beverly hadn't killed Roger, she was covering up for someone who had. And Murray thought that this someone could be Katie herself. There was,

Murray had told Don, incriminating evidence against Katie: a phone call from Beverly to Katie the night of March 4 and Greg Neal's notes of his first interview with Beverly, which said, "Daughter came home at midnight." Katie, Murray had speculated, was enraged at Roger for stringing Beverly along all those years and then deciding to drop her for Krystyna. Katie had the opportunity, since she had no alibi for the evening. Furthermore, Don said, Murray had told him, Katie's the only one with the balls to do it. In short, according to Murray's thinking, Beverly had taken the fall for Katie and Katie was now devoting her life to freeing her mother, out of guilt.

"Don, this is such bullshit!" Katie shouted. She was angry, but she was also hurt. She had been working twelve hours a day on the habeas, and the lawyer she had hired to work with her, her virtual partner, was now voicing suspicions that *she* was a murderer. But Murray seemed to have talked Don into believing it possible. And from the way Murray had laid out his evidence, she had to admit that it did sound suspicious.

Katie told Don it was true she didn't have an alibi for March 4. It was a Wednesday, she didn't know a lot of people in Charlottesville; she had been in her apartment, probably watching *Cheers.* But, she went on, Murray was misremembering things. Her mother had from the beginning explained to E.B. and Murray that when she stopped at home on the way to Windsor the night of March 4, she had called Katie to discuss plans for a Mardi Gras party that weekend. As for the supposedly suspicious line in Neal's report, Murray himself, during the trial, had tried to get Neal to acknowledge that this statement had actually come from Krystyna. Katie pulled out the copy of the report labeled EXCULPATORY INFORMATION that Riley had typed up and given Murray at their meeting the summer before the trial. One statement said, "Krystyna Drewnowska had a key to the victim's home and was at her home, alone, until midnight on 3/4/92." During that meeting, Murray had scrawled next to the statement, "Daughter came home after midnight."

In the end, Katie's account satisfied Don Lee. But she was still a little mad at him for doubting her, even for a moment. And she was more than a little mad at Murray Janus. It was weird. He had always thought Beverly's lack of anger toward Roger and Krystyna was troubling, yet now, because Katie herself wasn't afraid at times to show some anger, he considered that suspicious. Murray, who Katie thought had never understood her mother, seemed to be searching for a rationalization for his defeat at the trial. But in his attitude toward her and her mother, Katie felt, he was just like the prosecutors and the investigators. They had all made certain assumptions about how women behaved, or should behave, and they demonized the women who failed to live up to their preconceived ideas.

———

Sometimes at night, unable to sleep, Katie lay in bed fantasizing about what the trial would have been like if Richard Leo and John Maltsberger had testified, if Murray Janus had confronted Marcella Fierro with the gunshot residue report and Krystyna Drewnowska with the medical records. At times she imagined herself defending her mother, conducting cross-examinations that reduced the commonwealth witnesses to puddles of quivering jelly, introducing surprise witnesses of her own, such as Harriet Newman.

When Beverly Monroe was out on the appeal bond, Harriet Newman, a woman she had known in prison, wrote Beverly a letter describing a conversation she'd had with Zelma Smith after Zelma was transferred to Goochland. In that conversation, Harriet said, Zelma had confessed to inventing the story about Beverly trying to buy the gun from her. Harriet was initially reluctant to become involved in Beverly's appeal, afraid it might hurt her own chances for early release. But Alfred Brown, a private investigator who had worked with Don Lee at the Resource Center, went out to Goochland and, to Katie's surprise, persuaded Harriet to give an affidavit.

I, Harriet Newman, being first duly sworn, do depose and state the following:

I arrived at Virginia Correctional Center for Women in Goochland on February 3, 1993. There, I met another inmate by the name of Beverly Monroe. I recognized her from news coverage I had seen on her trial the previous fall.

I remember in particular a day at VCCW on which I had a conversation with another inmate named Zelma Smith. I knew Zelma because she and I had spent a couple of years together in prison in the 1980's. Zelma and I were waiting to be taken to the medical department in Powhatan, along with several other inmates. While we were waiting, Zelma and I talked about Beverly Monroe's case. I knew that she had testified at Beverly

Monroe's trial, and I asked her why she had testified against Ms. Monroe. Zelma told me that she had done it to get prison time off of some sentences she had pending. She said she had heard about the case and decided to say she was a witness in order to keep from having to return to VCCW. She told me that she would have done anything to keep from returning to VCCW. When I asked her if she had lied in her testimony against Ms. Monroe, she replied, "Yes, you could say that." Zelma told me "they" promised to get her a reduced sentence in exchange for her testimony against Ms. Monroe. She did not tell me who "they" were. She believed that she would not have to return to VCCW if she testified untruthfully against Beverly Monroe. However, she did return, and she was very angry and believed "they" had lied to her.

By the time Harriet Newman's affidavit arrived, the deadline for filing the habeas petition was two weeks away. Katie, who had been working weekdays in Richmond, staying with her father and using the office of a law school classmate, sequestered herself in her Washington apartment to write the final draft.

There was an art to a state habeas petition, Don Lee had explained. All the facts and claims to be raised in a federal habeas had first to be raised with the state in order to be preserved, since in habeas petitions federal judges could entertain only issues on which state judges had ruled. At the same time, Don said, you didn't want the state brief to be so persuasively written that the state judges, traditionally more conservative, agreed to consider it. If that happened and the state judges granted discovery and an evidentiary hearing but then ruled against you, the federal judges to whom you would then appeal the decision were required to adopt the fact-finding that had taken place in state court. Should the state judges, after holding a hearing in which Zelma Smith testified, rule that she was telling the truth, the federal judges would have to defer to that. You wanted your hearing in federal court, Don said, where the judges were more sympathetic to appellants. So the state habeas, he added, shouldn't be *too* good.

Katie thought she would be able to satisfy him on that point. There were so many disparate facts—everything from the mysterious Chevy Blazer and the scheduled Vac DEC to Zelma Smith's sentence reduction and the gunshot residue report—and so many disparate claims—insufficiency of the evidence, prosecutorial misconduct, claims of coerced confessions, ineffective counsel—and so much case law to cite that she began to understand why Murray Janus's closing argument had seemed so rambling.

She also began to get a feel, from the attorney's perspective, for the tension that always exists between lawyer and client over strategy. During weekly visits to Pocahontas, she had discussed all the claims and facts with her mother and they were in agreement on them. Beverly read the drafts of each section of the petition. But her mother also continued to comb her files. Every few days, Katie would receive another long letter with dozens of pages, in her mother's small, precise handwriting, containing thoughts and suggestions on new angles of inquiry to investigate and avenues of legal reasoning to pursue. In those final weeks Katie often felt too swamped even to read them.

Some points Katie considered important didn't make it into the final draft. She had gathered material about the fallibility of polygraphs, about how frequently people fail them and the reasons for it—everything from exhaustion to unconscious foot tapping. Katie often wondered whether the jurors, had they known about Beverly failing the polygraph, would have then understood why Beverly accepted Dave Riley's suggestion that she had blocked out memories of watching Roger shoot himself. No trial attorney would have wanted to risk giving a jury such potentially damaging information, but she thought sitting judges might be more sophisticated. Don Lee disagreed. "Why introduce the polygraph?" he said. "It raises more questions than it answers. Let's just drop it."

Despite such deletions, the final document was 250 pages long. "Man, that's a difficult piece of work to get through," one of Katie's attorney friends said after she showed him the petition. It was true. In fact, the thing was a mess. She wondered if they would have been better off hiring a habeas attorney for $150,000 and spending their time raising the money to pay him, as one lawyer had suggested they do.

But Beverly had already given out huge sums to two lawyers, who had insisted on doing things their way and they had gotten nowhere. For all its sloppy writing and a few unproved assertions—such as the one that Dave Riley and Zelma Smith had collaborated on prior cases—the petition made all the points Beverly Monroe wanted it to make. Katie felt that if nothing else happened, if both the state and then the federal courts rejected it, her mother would at least have the satisfaction of knowing she had gotten her view of what had happened into the public record.

5

The petition was forwarded to John McLees. The attorney general's office usually received such massive documents only in capital murder cases. Despite the size of the petition, McLees didn't think he would have much trouble with it, at least in state court. Many of the claims—that the police failed to preserve exculpatory evidence by not collecting the Marlboro cigarette butts; that the prosecution had engaged in improper argument by alluding to facts not in evidence, such as Beverly spitting at Burde in a restaurant—could be dismissed with the procedural argument that they could have been raised during the trial and on direct appeal but were not.

Nor did McLees think the state court would be impressed by the claim that Murray Janus was guilty of ineffective assistance of counsel. Janus had hired *three* expert witnesses; the petition preposterously argued that he had been ineffective in part because there were additional experts he should have hired but didn't. None of the new claims, McLees thought, presented reliable evidence of actual innocence so compelling as to make it more likely than not that no reasonable juror would have found her guilty. That was the standard, and that was what he would argue in the motion to dismiss.

———

Shannon had left Richmond for New York, where she tried without much success to publicize her mother's case—though she and Katie and Don Lee did appear on the television talk show *Leeza*—and ended up working in a bakery in Brooklyn. Gavin had left the state as well and was living in Atlanta. Both of them just found Richmond too depressing. Katie, needing to work more closely with Don Lee and feeling that one of her mother's children ought to be near her, moved back to the city with Andy, who enrolled in a computer graphics program at Virginia Commonwealth University. Late in the fall, Katie discovered she was pregnant. Andy wanted to get married, and his parents offered to give them a large wedding before the baby was born. But Katie decided to wait and have the ceremony when her mother could be present, even if that meant delaying it for years.

———

Before going to work at the Resource Center, Don Lee had been an associate in the litigation department of a large Richmond law firm, Mays &

Valentine, where he had become friends with Steve Northup, one of the department's senior partners. After Lee left the firm, he and Northup had served as pro bono co-counsel in the appeal of Michael George, a convicted murderer who'd been executed the year before. Lee knew that Northup, who liked to have at least one pro bono case going, had done no pro bono work since George's death. One afternoon, after a game of squash at the Capital Club, he asked Northup if he would be willing to join Beverly Monroe's habeas effort as co-counsel.

Northup read the trial transcript that weekend. It was hard to get the full texture of a trial from the cold transcript, but he was surprised that Beverly had been convicted. Northup had no trouble accepting the thesis that a woman, even an educated and sophisticated woman, could kill a man who'd scorned her for another, younger woman—plenty of documented cases had established that. But the women rarely denied the killing had taken place. Instead, they argued temporary insanity or insisted they were really trying to kill themselves—like Jean Harris, the headmistress of the Madeira School, who shot Dr. Herman Tarnower—or they claimed the shooting was accidental—like Claudine Longet, who'd killed her boyfriend, the professional skier Spider Sabich. Northup found it hard to believe that Beverly Monroe, a responsible working mother without the slightest hint of sociopathic behavior in her background, would kill Roger de la Burde and then pretend to friends, family, and the authorities that he'd committed suicide.

There also seemed to Northup to be a fundamental psychological contradiction in the commonwealth's portrayal of Beverly. It required that you accept the idea that she was at once incredibly guileful and incredibly naïve, that she was sufficiently calculating and coldhearted to kill a man and then lie about it, but also stupid enough to take a polygraph test, lie during the test and flunk it, then resort to another lie, and an incriminating one at that, to explain why she had flunked. Prima facie, this seemed utterly implausible to Northup. It defied common sense. The investigators, he thought, had become so infatuated with their own fanciful version of events that they had lost touch with reality. After meeting Beverly at Pocahontas, and getting a feel for her character, Northup agreed to join Don Lee as pro bono co-counsel.

———

The Virginia Supreme Court rejected the habeas petition without comment in January. With that decision, the time remaining before the expiration of the federal deadline decreed by the Antiterrorism and Effective Death Penalty Act, which had been suspended when the petition was filed in state court, began to run down again. Northup, preoccupied with corporate clients, did not sit down to read the federal habeas petition until two weeks before it was due. He immediately decided the document was much too long. The more concisely a claim could be framed, Northup felt, the stronger it appeared. Northup, a silver-haired man with a lean, weathered face, was a Vietnam veteran and a Harvard Law School graduate, and was capable of both gracious decorum and military bluntness. He called Katie. "This is crap," he told her. "We're going to have to start from scratch."

"You've got to be kidding me," Katie said. She felt he should have voiced his objections months ago.

Northup insisted. If it was going to be filed with Mays & Valentine's name on the front page, it had to meet the firm's standards. He arranged a temporary office for her at Mays & Valentine on the twenty-third floor of the Bank of America building on East Main Street, and for the next two weeks devoted himself to an overhaul of the petition. They started early and worked late. Katie would rewrite sections and then bring them in to Steve, who insisted on more and more cutting. At first she found the process intimidating, but she then began to admire his frankness, because when the writing met his standards, his praise was effusive. "It's brilliant," he would cry, "a work of art!"

When Katie and Northup drove out to Pocahontas to show Beverly the new version, she was frightened by the prospect of dropping claims that could never be raised later. But Northup convinced her that the weak claims only undermined the strong ones. And the final document was still, at 228 pages, the length of a short novel. Northup felt he had made a concession in not insisting on much more radical cuts.

The Sunday before it was due, Katie and her friends stayed up until three A.M. in Don Lee's office, Bob Dylan and Lyle Lovett blaring from the speakers as they proofread the final version, tagged exhibits, and checked case law citations for accuracy. Katie finished printing out the petition just before five o'clock the following afternoon and Don's assistant Gabrielle rushed it across the street to the courthouse.

Two days later, Katie went into premature labor. She had to spend the next two months lying on her side while terbutaline sulfate, which arrested contractions, was administered through a pump attached to her leg. It was her fault, she decided. She had just pushed herself too hard.

6

The case was assigned to Judge Richard Williams in the U.S. District Court for the Eastern District of Virginia. John McLees filed a motion to dismiss. Don Lee filed a reply. Each side asked for extensions.

Months passed.

Katie gave birth to a boy, whom she and Andy named Asher. With the money from the sale of her apartment in Washington, they bought a small house, with white stucco walls, gray trim, and a pillared porch, in a turn-of-the-century neighborhood off Azalea Avenue in north Richmond. She brought Asher with her on Saturdays when she visited Beverly at Pocahontas.

———

By then, Beverly had been in prison for two years. The most difficult adjustment she'd had to make at Pocahontas was to the lack of space and privacy. Each of the seventy or so women in the large dorm considered the two squares of linoleum along the sides of her bed her own private terrain. That was all the personal space the women had. They kept their possessions in a footlocker that fit under the bed; if someone sent Beverly a book, she had to get rid of another book to make room for it. She had no typewriter, no laptop computer, no access to a law library.

The communal living fostered disease. At one point, shortly after arriving, Beverly and some of the other women contracted hepatitis A. But she made a life for herself there. In the back of the building was a fenced-in yard, where she picked small wildflowers as the crackle of gunshots drifted in from a corrections department firing range behind the prison. She taught computer literacy and math courses. And she had friends, like Anita, a Bryn Mawr graduate who'd been convicted of securities fraud and who was a follower of Lyndon LaRouche, and Big Frances, who tucked the sheets around Beverly's shoulders at night.

Shannon took the train down from New York to visit her mother as often as she could. Katie and Asher would come with her. They had to sit across from Beverly in plastic chairs in the rec room. No touching was allowed. With all the other visitors and inmates, the room was so noisy that Shannon found it hard to hear her mother. She'd move her chair closer, and the guards who were walking up and down would tell her to move it back. That was just the rule. In general, the guards were less jerky than the guards at Goochland.

Having a grandchild seemed to have changed her mother, who called Asher her littlest braveheart. The baby, squirming on Katie's lap throughout the visits, gave Shannon's mother something to think about other than her own plight and the disgusting prison food. She became less bitter, less obsessive and aggrieved. She seemed, generally speaking, about as happy as you could expect someone in prison to be.

———

Ever since receiving a kidney transplant at the age of twenty, Don Lee had been taking immunosuppressant drugs, to prevent his body from rejecting the alien organ. The drugs also made him more susceptible to viruses. While he suffered disproportionately from colds and the flu, he did not treat himself as exceptionally fragile. He played squash, baseball, and, despite his small stature, basketball. He drank tequila. In fact, as his wife, Lisa, liked to say, he drank anything you put in front of him. Don Lee believed in the triumph of attitude.

That year, his wrist started swelling and eventually became so tender that anything touching it, even Lisa's hair, caused intense pain. During the winter, specialists at Johns Hopkins Medical Center in Baltimore realized the swelling was caused by a cancerous tumor. They removed it and put Lee on chemotherapy. Although still recuperating, he insisted to Steve Northup that he was well enough to handle the oral arguments Judge Williams had scheduled for March.

———

Judge Williams was a big man, with a full head of white hair, a genial disposition, and a fondness for colloquialisms. His sense of judicial ceremony was strong. On the morning of the hearing, after entering his wood-paneled courtroom, he crossed the sand-colored carpet and, as was his custom, shook hands with all the attorneys before taking his seat on the bench.

The judge had a curious personal connection to the case he was about to hear. Back in the fifties, he had been law partners with Leith Bremner, the legendary defense lawyer who later became Murray Janus's partner and who, back then, had owned Windsor. Judge Williams had fished and hunted on the property any number of times, and he knew it well: the sloping pastures, the white brick house, the tree-lined riverbank. But it was a tangential connection, the kind that regularly occurred in a small city like Richmond, and no one, least of all the judge himself, saw it as anything more than a mildly interesting coincidence.

Judge Williams was a Carter appointee. He was known as one of the relatively liberal federal judges in the Eastern District, someone who responded not just to procedural issues but to the idea of justice. From the outset of the hearing, he demonstrated genuine interest in the issues Lee and Northup were trying to raise. And he seemed pointedly skeptical of Dave Riley's claim to have accidentally forgotten to turn on the tape recorder except during the last fifteen minutes of his post-polygraph interview with Beverly.

"Do experienced state police investigators not know where the on-off button is on a machine?" he asked John McLees in his rich Southern drawl.

"I expect they do," McLees replied. "But everybody makes mistakes."

The judge nodded, then pushed his point. "If there would be a lot of exculpatory evidence in the first part of it, having the tape break or release itself wouldn't be a bad idea, would it?"

But the judge also found it hard to accept the theory, propounded by Herb MacDonell during the trial, that Roger had killed himself by holding the gun upside down with his left hand and pulling the trigger with his thumb. "The contortions of Roger de la Burde—I never heard anyone suggest he is a contortionist," the judge mused. "He had to have been a contortionist in order to commit suicide the way that was done."

Don Lee tried to explain that Beverly Monroe's team had now abandoned that theory because of the evidence in the gunshot residue report, which indicated that Roger's right hand had been holding the gun when it was fired. He said that since the commonwealth had not given the report into evidence until after its own forensics experts had testified, Beverly Monroe was claiming prosecutorial misconduct. Lee added that Beverly was making a separate claim of prosecutorial misconduct on the grounds that Dave Riley and Zelma Smith had a prior relationship. If the judge granted discovery, she could produce the evidence and take the depositions of uncooperative witnesses who would substantiate the claim.

"You found all this out since the trial?" Judge Williams asked.

"Yes, sir. We have."

The judge smiled. "Well, it seems to me that you have some gumshoes that have been so effective that you don't need discovery. You don't want to shoot yourself in the foot by having a gumshoe that is such an efficient person that you don't need discovery."

"We have been unable to talk to Zelma Smith," Don said. "That is one example of the kind of discovery that we do need." Discovery, he added, could help them establish whether Zelma had an agreement to testify in exchange for a sentence reduction.

"Well, the proof of the pudding is what happened," the judge said. "Did she get a time cut?"

"She did."

Judge Williams also seemed intrigued by the new forensic theory suggested by the gunshot residue test and questioned McLees about it. "What's the explanation for the powder residue?"

McLees had attempted—successfully, he thought—to explain away this theory in his brief, but his reasoning now escaped him. "In all honesty, Your Honor," he said, "I can't remember."

A minute later, the judge returned to the subject. "How did it get between the web of the thumb and the forefinger?"

"I don't know," McLees said.

The judge actually gets it, thought Katie, who was sitting in the gallery. After all these years and all these courtrooms, she was finally, she felt, sitting in front of someone who was prepared to listen to her mother's side of the story.

After an hour, Judge Williams adjourned the court. He warned the attorneys that he wouldn't issue an opinion until he had had a chance to study all the briefs. "It is quite a big record that needs to be massaged before an intelligent decision can be made," he said.

———

"In general, the Court is impressed with the substance of many of Monroe's claims," Judge Williams wrote in his opinion, issued a month later. However, he continued, many of them had not been properly preserved for federal habeas corpus review. The claim that the commonwealth had failed to properly disclose the gunshot residue report had not been raised correctly during the trial. The claim that Beverly had received ineffective assistance of counsel because Murray Janus allegedly had not understood and acted on the meaning of *Vac DEC* in Krystyna Drewnowska's medical records was also barred on procedural grounds, since it did not establish "actual innocence."

"The fact that many of Monroe's claims will be dismissed from the action due to procedural default does not bear on the merits of the preserved claims," Judge Williams wrote. "Indeed, the unusual facts and allegations in the remaining claims demonstrate the wisdom of permitting Monroe to develop them further." He granted discovery on the claims that Beverly's statements to Dave Riley were involuntary, that Murray Janus had been ineffective in failing to have them suppressed, that Zelma Smith had a prior relationship with Riley and had been promised a sentence reduction in exchange for testifying, and that the commonwealth should have disclosed to the defense the names of the witnesses who saw the black Chevy Blazer speeding from Windsor the night of Roger's death.

7

That summer, as Don and Katie began writing subpoenas for police records, the lump on Don's wrist returned. After conducting tests, his doctors informed him they would have to amputate his arm. Don was home by August. Much of the time he managed to put a good face on his loss. "I'm going to teach my son to swim even if he can only swim in circles," he joked. But he suffered from intense phantom pain and was devastated, he told Katie, by the fact that he would never again play the guitar.

To complicate matters, when Don returned to his law office, he found that neither of his other partners had been paying attention to the firm's books. It faced a cash-flow crisis that forced them to dissolve it. Don began looking for a steady job at one of Richmond's larger firms, but no one seemed interested in hiring a one-armed litigator recovering from cancer.

Meanwhile, depositions had been scheduled that fall for Dave Riley, Zelma Smith, Greg Neal, Corinna de la Burde, the polygraph operator Wyatt Omohundro, and the two police secretaries who'd witnessed parts of Beverly's statement at police headquarters. Steve Northup was worried that Don, with his health and money problems, might lack the stamina and the interest to conduct them.

"Look," Northup said to Lee when they met to prepare the questions. "You're still struggling. You want to do all these depositions?"

"This is my case," Don told him. He agreed to give Northup the minor witnesses, but said, "I want to do Riley and Zelma, and I'm going to do them."

———

Zelma Smith's deposition was held one early-September morning in a conference room at Mays & Valentine. Don Lee, Steve Northup, John McLees, and Katie Monroe, who had not been allowed in the courtroom during Zelma's trial testimony and was meeting the woman for the first time, were all present.

From the outset, Zelma bristled with hostility, and even refused to state for the record where she was then working.

"Can you tell us why you would rather not say?" Don Lee asked.

"I'm going to be honest when I say this, I feel like I'm being harassed by Ms. Monroe and her attorneys," Zelma said. "I feel that I have had people following me around for Ms. Monroe, and I'm tired of it, and that's why I would rather not say." This pattern of intimidation, she went on, had begun before the trial, when Beverly Monroe's lawyer David Hicks had visited her in jail.

"How did he try to intimidate you?" Don asked.

"Because he came in there, and he was trying to intimidate me," Zelma replied. "You are a lawyer . . . you probably intimidate people too, or try to."

"I've never considered myself to be very intimidating," Don said.

"You know what I'm talking about," Zelma told him. "How you all be doing them tactics."

Steve Northup called for a break. Don, he felt, was allowing Zelma to drag him into pointless confrontations. "Don't take her bait," he told him. "Just move on."

But whatever tactic Don tried, Zelma obdurately clung to her story. Beverly Monroe had paid her to find an untraceable gun. She had never met Dave Riley before. She had never previously served as an informant.

"You never," Don asked, "*snitched* is the word—you never snitched anytime before this in a case?"

"No, sir, not that I recall."

Don Lee brought out the motion Zelma had filed from jail asking for a sentence reduction. In it she described how she had helped the commonwealth—not only in Beverly Monroe's case, but in another case that led to the indictment of a public official. That case, Zelma said, had come up shortly after she talked to Riley about Beverly. He had put her in touch with an agent of the FBI.

"Who is the public official that was indicted based on the information you gave?" Don asked.

"I don't remember his name."

"Do you remember anything about him?"

"Yeah, he was a commissioner."

"And what information about him did you provide?"

"I don't remember."

"Well, it must have been very important information if it led to his indictment."

"I don't remember."

The deposition, Northup felt once it was over, had been a fascinating revelation of the character of Zelma Smith in all her disingenuous complexity, but it hadn't helped establish any facts that would substantiate their claims. The woman had ducked and evaded, bobbed and weaved, with impressive dexterity.

———

The morning after Zelma Smith was deposed, Greg Neal drove into Richmond to give his deposition. Neal didn't get to Richmond much. On his days off in the fall, he was more apt to drive up into the mountains, to hunt on the forested land that he and Jack Lewis owned together. He arrived at the Bank of America building before ten and took the elevator to the twenty-third floor. Steve Northup came out and escorted him to the conference room. He shook hands with Don Lee and Katie Monroe and took a seat next to John McLees at the big table.

The room had floor-to-ceiling windows that faced west. Hawks circled in the air around the skyscraper across the street. At first, they appeared to be in the distance, behind the building, but that turned out to be an optical illusion, for they would swoop toward it, then pass in front of it, landing on a spattered ledge near the building's crown.

After the deposition began, Neal watched as Katie Monroe from time to time scribbled a note on a legal pad and passed it to Northup, who was asking the questions. Neal had originally thought that Katie worked so hard on the appeal simply because Beverly was her mother, but watching her that morning, he realized she was convinced that Beverly was innocent. She seemed to really believe it. So did Northup. If you think Beverly is innocent, Neal wanted to ask, what do you think really happened?

It was not, he thought, a question he'd ever get to pose. That morning, Northup was asking all the questions. The attorney focused on the process that led Neal to determine the cause of Roger de la Burde's death. Neal admitted that he'd originally considered the death a suicide but had changed his mind after Dave Riley, who was convinced from the outset that it was most likely a homicide, discussed the forensic evidence with him. He himself did not conclude that Beverly was guilty until March 26.

"I thought she would pass the polygraph," Neal told Northup.

What Neal didn't have the opportunity to say to Northup was that it wasn't Beverly's failure to pass, in and of itself, that convinced him she was guilty. It was her reaction afterward. Riley, he thought, had definitely put pressure on Beverly to admit she'd been present when Roger shot himself, but even with the pressure, why would she buy his story if she was innocent? It made no sense. If you're innocent, Neal thought, and someone tells you you've failed a polygraph, you wouldn't suddenly switch your story. You'd say, There's something wrong with the machine; go shove it up your ass.

———

Northup liked Greg Neal. He was, the lawyer thought, a straightforward man, salt of the earth. Unlike Zelma Smith, Neal appeared cooperative during his deposition, but he was also cautious, volunteering little, and Northup was feeling disappointed. Then, at the end of the deposition, Northup made a surprising breakthrough. It came during a discussion over whether or not, during the meeting at which the commonwealth team was supposed to have provided Murray Janus and E. B. Harmon with exculpatory evidence, Neal had given them the names of Jeffrey and Angela Johnson, the couple who had reported seeing the black Blazer driving away from Windsor on the night of March 4.

"I can't remember if we gave them the names or not," Neal said. "I can't remember if they asked. I mean, I've known the Johnsons forever. If they would have asked, I would have told them exactly who it was."

Northup found it hard to believe that Janus would not have asked for the names if he knew the police had them. He was even more surprised when Neal explained that one reason he may not have mentioned the Johnsons by name was that he didn't regard them as credible. Northup asked why.

"There's no particular thing that I can think of that they have done to make me feel this way," Neal replied.

In other words, Northup thought, Greg Neal, acting on an unsubstantiated hunch, had apparently withheld potentially exculpatory evidence from the defense. Even if Neal was being completely candid—and Northup had no evidence that he was not—this admission was just the sort of thing that would incite Judge Williams.

———

That afternoon, Northup thought he'd uncovered even more material that would appeal to the judge, who'd seemed skeptical about Riley's failure to turn on the tape recorder during the interview with Beverly. After a break for lunch, Wyatt Omohundro, the polygraph operator, arrived for his deposition.

"Did you show Officer Riley where the switch was for the tape?" Northup asked.

"I don't think I showed him. I think I told him."

Northup asked Omohundro if he was certain.

The polygraph operator said he was. "I remember telling him how to cut the tape off and the switch is under the desk."

"Did he seem to understand what you were telling him?"

"He should. I would think that's pretty clear."

"So you have no explanation as to why he didn't cut it on when he went back in there?"

"No, I do not."

———

Katie was sitting across from Omohundro and John McLees. By the end of the afternoon, she had spent two full days in McLees's company. She had also seen him arguing against Beverly's appeals in court. Don Lee had told Katie he considered McLees a sellout for having gone from representing defendants to prosecuting them. But she was surprised to find she liked the man. When he was not in court, he dressed in jeans. Instead of a briefcase, he carried a soft leather satchel decorated with beads and feathers. He seemed like an aging hippie. During breaks in the depositions, he was friendly and funny. Katie felt tempted to call him up and ask him out to lunch. Off the record, John, she wanted to say to him, how do you really see this case?

———

While McLees was convivial around Katie, he behaved that way toward everyone—it was his nature. He was the sort of man who'd crack a joke with the fellow standing next to him at the urinal. ("Don't fall for Beverly," he told a journalist on just such an occasion, during a break in one of the legal proceedings. "Look at what happened to the last guy who did.") The fact of the matter, however, was that Katie Monroe irritated McLees. He considered her chiefly responsible for Beverly Monroe's habeas appeal, which clearly had engaged Judge Williams and, if it didn't result in an embarrassing reversal for the commonwealth, would at least drag on for years.

The attorney general's office had been involved in rare cases where there truly was a miscarriage of justice. In those cases, it had confessed error and released the defendant. McLees himself had had cases where he thought that if he had been on the jury he might not have voted to convict, but that, nonetheless, reasonable people had done so and it was his duty to represent the commonwealth during the appeal.

McLees had never counted Beverly Monroe's case among them. He had no doubt about her guilt. It was the totality of the evidence rather than any particular piece of it that persuaded him. When appealing their sentences, defendants often argued insufficiency of the evidence by taking each item of evidence and demonstrating that it could be interpreted in a fashion that did not imply guilt. That was what Beverly had done. But how likely was it that an entire array of such evidence, each strand of which could be questioned individually, would end up pointing to an innocent person? Not very likely, in McLees's opinion.

McLees, having read the entire police file, was familiar with the theory that Katie had either killed Roger or had helped her mother cover up a murder. Whenever he pondered the facts of the case, and particularly when he thought about Katie, he came back to the testimony of Sheldon Gosline. Gosline, a graduate student, a smart fellow and as disinterested a witness as you could hope for, had testified that he'd overheard Katie advising her mother not to change her alibi. If you believed Gosline, as McLees did, the implications of what he said, on the stand under oath, were hard to avoid.

———

Steve Northup also thought about Sheldon Gosline. It was entirely possible—Northup assumed it likely—that Beverly and Katie were right: Gosline, a high-strung young man, whom even Jack Lewis had called a flake, had simply garbled his memories of the events surrounding Roger's death. But Northup would have liked to know for sure. He had an assistant try to track Gosline down so he could take his measure, but the University of Chicago had no record of his whereabouts. The man had disappeared. Rumors placed him somewhere in Asia. Northup's assistant finally procured Gosline's purported e-mail address, and Northup sent him a message but never heard back.

Northup figured he was about 97 percent certain that Beverly had not killed Roger. As a lawyer, Northup felt the evidence was insufficient to convict Beverly, but as a human being, he wished he could have proof positive that she was innocent. Absolute certainty, however, was an unobtainable luxury in this case. He would have to live with 3 percent doubt. The prosecution, he thought by way of consolation, had had to accept or try to argue away inexplicabilities far more nagging than Sheldon Gosline's testimony.

———

"What are your views on the accuracy of polygraph examinations?"

"This is a personal opinion."

"I understand."

It was a warm, bright morning in the third week of September 1999. The summerlong drought had caused the trees on the islands in the James River, visible through the tinted windows in the Mays & Valentine conference room, to turn brown early. John McLees and Dave Riley, their backs to the view, sat across from Katie, Steve Northup, and Don Lee at the polished oblong table. Don had his half-empty shirt sleeve pinned up.

"I don't think a polygraph is the end-all and be-all," Riley said. "I've seen people that have failed polygraphs that I knew and proved were innocent." He'd also seen guilty people pass them. "Sociopaths . . . can pass polygraphs all day long. They love to take polygraphs, because the truth doesn't mean anything to them."

"I had a client once," Don Lee said, "who refused to take a polygraph because he had taken three already and twice he was lying and he passed and once he was telling the truth and he failed."

Lee was in a good mood. He enjoyed jousting with Riley, whom he knew, having once represented a member of the Poison Clan, a Jamaican drug gang that had committed a murder in Virginia Beach that Riley had investigated. But Lee was also finding this by far the most productive deposition he and Northup had taken. They had scheduled Riley's deposition last in the hope that they would uncover something incriminating from the other witnesses that they could then use to confront Riley. That hadn't really happened. But as it turned out, Riley was astonishingly forthcoming. His attitude was that he had done nothing wrong and therefore had nothing to hide. So he described in detail the origins of his suspicions about Beverly and his feelings toward her.

"She was a very intelligent woman, very articulate woman," he said. "Attractive, educated, cultured. I liked her. I still like her."

"And was she cooperative?"

"Very, very cooperative."

Lee and Northup, expecting this deposition to be extensive, had arranged to conduct it on two separate days. On this, the first day, they continued until five o'clock in the evening. Riley spoke tirelessly for hours, about how he had proceeded with the investigation, how he had talked Beverly into coming to First Division headquarters to take the polygraph, and how, afterward, he had gotten her to agree that she could have been present when Roger shot himself.

"I lied to her," Riley said. "I know you people are shocked, but we lie to people, suspects, every day. I do it every day that I talk to suspects. It's part of my job."

"I'm shocked," Don Lee said, and quailed in mock horror.

"I know you are," Riley told him. "But anyway, I lied to her."

———

The second day of Riley's deposition was to take place the following week. As the date approached, Don Lee came down with pneumonia. He had a racking cough and a throat so sore he could hardly talk, but he insisted on proceeding. That morning, before the deposition began, Katie took the elevator down to the building lobby and bought him some throat lozenges.

Don was still so weak from his amputation that when he had attended the depositions Steve Northup conducted, he had been nodding off and propping his head up with his arm. If it had been anybody else, Katie thought, she would have been elbowing him, saying, Man, we need both of you here. But Don wasn't getting any sleep. He was drugged and exhausted and in pain and depressed. She could very easily imagine him pulling out, saying, Katie, I understand you and your mom got problems, but I got my own fucking problems here. You guys are barely paying me. I'm sick as a dog. I got no job. My wife and I can't make ends meet. I lost my fricking arm.

But Don hadn't done that. Even with pneumonia, he'd shown up to finish Riley's deposition. Katie worshipped the guy.

———

Riley was just as loquacious and relaxed as he had been the preceding week. He leaned back in his chair and put his feet up on the polished conference table. He talked about how he had explained to Corinna that her father had been murdered and then had convinced her to cooperate in gathering evidence against Beverly. The other members of the Burde family, he said, were leery of the police. He finally realized that this had to do with Roger's claims of aristocratic lineage and his art collection. "Roger's claim to French aristocracy was total fraud," Riley explained. "The story about his father being a turn-of-the-century Indiana Jones type and acquiring an African art collection was total bunk."

He had learned, he continued, that Roger had acquired much of the African art while in Nigeria during the 1960s, in violation of an antiquities law forbidding the export of such works. "I had to get into this in order to get the family to cooperate," Riley said. "And I finally cracked it. Everything in this case was a mystery wrapped up into an enigma disguised as a riddle."

Katie, listening, thought: Had to get into it in order to get the family to cooperate? Did that mean the family's apprehensions about the legitimacy of the art collection was simply a barrier Riley had to overcome? Or did it mean that the family had cooperated with the police out of fear that the collection's taint would be exposed? She wanted Don to pursue this lead, but, maybe because of the pneumonia—he was stopping frequently when overcome with bouts of coughing—he let the opportunity pass and proceeded instead to the notes he had subpoenaed from Riley.

Certain pages contained lists of questions and talking points Riley had written down prior to his first interview with Beverly. Don read aloud one that referred to a possible evidence ploy. "Tell her we found a print in the crevice of the gun that definitely was not Burde's to see how she reacts."

"I didn't do that, I don't believe," Riley said. "That was something I was thinking about to throw a ruse up to her to see how she would react to it."

"So at this point in time then you were trying to think of ways you could trip up, if we will, Beverly Monroe?"

"Test her reactions, yes."

Don studied the page. "Were you considering using a ruse like that in the first interview with Beverly Monroe?"

"Yeah," Riley replied. "It was just something that popped into my mind. I just wrote it down. I write myself notes all the time like this."

At that point, Don asked, Beverly Monroe was considered the prime suspect?

"She was certainly leading the pack, yeah. She was way at the top by a long length."

"And that justified not investigating the others at this point in time?"

"It justified investigating her first very thoroughly."

Riley fiercely disputed the story Beverly had told on the witness stand, that after she had signed the statement that day at Drewry's Bluff, Riley had asked her to stay, and on the walk through the woods out to the old battlements, had pressured her to plead to a lesser charge.

"This wasn't Dave Riley dragging her around by the handcuffs in the park, you know, beating her with a club," he said. "I was just replying to what she had to say. I was trying to make appropriate responses to her anguish. I truly felt sorry for her at that point. I did."

Riley was a personable guy, Northup thought as he sat listening to the detective, the kind of guy you'd like to go drink a beer with. He had some hubris, it seemed clear, but he was also articulate and engaging. He came across as a zealous, good cop, bright and sharp, experienced, but a cop who played his hunches. In this case he had been confronted with a woman, Beverly Monroe, who hadn't acted the way Riley's hunch told him people in her situation would act. Everything that had happened subsequently had followed from that misguided hunch. Northup felt that if he could demonstrate this to Judge Williams, he could prevail in court. Beverly was convinced Riley was corrupt and vicious, but Northup disagreed. He kept telling Beverly, "We don't have to prove Riley's evil to win this case."

———

After lunch, Don brought up the topic of Zelma Smith. "When in the course of an investigation you get information from a jailhouse snitch, do you generally have any concerns about the credibility of the story that the person is telling you?"

"Absolutely."

"And why is that?"

Riley sighed at the obviousness of this question. "Because they're in jail," he explained. "They probably got a criminal background. They're prone to lie. And I went into it with the belief that she was probably lying."

Don asked Riley what made him change his mind.

"Just everything about the way Zelma described Beverly," Riley continued. "I came to believe that this person had truly been in the presence of Beverly Monroe. Now, whether this stuff about the gun was true or not, I couldn't say."

———

The week after taking Riley's deposition, Katie and Don met Steve for a strategy session. Discovery, they all felt, had produced a gold mine. They had found no irrefutable evidence that the commonwealth knew Beverly was innocent but prosecuted her anyway. But what they had unearthed, Don said, was more than enough material to substantiate the voluntariness claim.

He mapped out the main points on a legal pad. While Greg Neal and others first treated Roger's death as a suicide, Riley made a rush to judgment that it was a homicide, persuaded Neal to accept the theory, and quickly targeted Beverly Monroe as the chief suspect. Instead of conducting a proper investigation, Don went on, he disregarded evidence that contradicted his theory, ignored other potential suspects such as Krystyna or Wojtek Drewnowska, and began making plans to ensnare Beverly Monroe, a trusting, grief-stricken woman who had no experience with the police. On March 26, using psychologically coercive techniques he had freely described in his deposition, Riley conducted an interrogation of this distraught woman, most of which he suspiciously failed to record, convincing her she had been present when Roger de la Burde shot himself. On June 3, at Drewry's Bluff, Riley had used that statement and other fabricated evidence to coerce Beverly to sign a written statement. During the trial, these statements represented the key evidence against Beverly, but her lawyer, Murray Janus, failed to move to suppress them on the grounds that they had been given involuntarily.

It was a good claim, Northup felt. He didn't know if Judge Williams would buy it, but on the law and on the facts, it was valid. He had been a trial lawyer for twenty-five years by then. He knew when he had a good claim and when he had nothing but specious legal argumentation.

Don agreed. What they needed to do now, he said, was file a motion asking for an evidentiary hearing. If they could get an expert like the criminologist Richard Leo in front of Judge Williams, he said, Leo could show how the police had repeatedly used similar techniques to induce demonstrably false confessions.

Northup also wanted to depose a final witness, Deborah Pollock, one of the two secretaries who had observed Riley's interrogation of Beverly. What he hoped to establish was that despite Riley's disclaimers to the contrary, the detective had not in fact forgotten to turn on the tape recorder but had intentionally neglected to do so, ensuring that no physical record would exist to show just how coercive the interrogation would be. Instead, he had arranged for the two secretaries to watch parts of it, confident that they could later produce a coordinated and sanitized version of what had transpired.

Deborah Pollock, who no longer worked for the state police, knew little and remembered less. She had been asked to watch the interview, she said, because a male officer was talking to a female suspect. If the female later charged the officer with improper conduct, she could testify that nothing inappropriate had happened.

"Had you on prior occasions observed questioning of witnesses from the observation room?" Northup asked.

"No, I don't recollect."

"That was the first time you had ever done this?"

"Yes."

"Did you ever, after your observation of the questioning of Mrs. Monroe, did you ever observe witnesses being questioned?"

"No, I did not."

"So this was the only time in your two years there that you observed witnesses being questioned? Is that correct?"

"Yes, that I remember."

Pollock's recollection seemed to Northup to contradict the common-wealth's assertion that it was routine for witnesses uninvolved in investiga-tions to watch the questioning of suspects. Judge Williams, he thought, would find it most interesting.

———

In November, Don Lee began having intense headaches and temporary loss of vision. X rays revealed that he had three tumors in his brain. It was non-Hodgkin's lymphoma, a form of cancer unrelated to the disease that had taken his arm. While in the hospital in December, Don suffered cardiac ar-rest. Katie felt sure he was going to die.

But Don didn't die. Lisa brought him home, and they began traveling to New York, where Memorial Sloan-Kettering Cancer Center offered a spe-cial treatment for patients with both cancer and immune disorders.

In February, Judge Williams's clerk called Steve Northup. Pointing out that Northup and Lee had finished discovery more than four months ago, she asked what they planned to do now. Northup said that they intended to file a motion asking for an evidentiary hearing but that the lead counsel had become seriously ill. The clerk told Northup to take his time.

Katie and Northup realized Don was in no position to return to work anytime soon. Although it meant a substantial increase in his duties, Northup decided to take on Don's role in the case and drove out to see him at his house outside Ashland. Beverly had agreed that he should become lead counsel. "If you can get back on your feet and get involved again, I know you will," he added. Don nodded.

Northup kept the visit brief. Don was in a wheelchair by then. He had a blood tumor in one leg. The chemotherapy had caused his face to swell, and his pain medication made him drowsy. Don had been a true believer in Beverly's case, Northup thought, but he was dealing with more stark and fundamental matters now. It made no sense to try to have a conversation about habeas strategy.

———

In March, Katie saw an article in *The Washington Post* about Mitchell Moore, a policeman for twelve years with the Atlanta police department, who had flunked a lie detector test about drug use when applying for a job with the Secret Service. Moore and six other job applicants had filed a suit challenging the polygraph tests administered to job applicants by the FBI and the Secret Service. The policeman's attorney was quoted in the article comparing polygraphs to "voodoo science" and complaining that innocent lives had been ruined. That says it all, Katie thought.

———

The following month, Don Lee broke his collarbone while putting on his shirt. X rays showed that the cancer had metastasized. His doctors told him he had only two weeks to live, but those two weeks passed and so did another two and Don was still alive. One Saturday night in mid-May, he and Lisa went to a movie. On their way home, they were involved in a minor car accident. No one seemed hurt, but the next day Don became ill and had to be taken to the hospital, where the doctors discovered that because he was so fragile, he had suffered massive internal bleeding. He died that night.

"Don fought death all his life," Lisa said in her eulogy at the funeral two days later. "He was going to fight the cancer to the end, so death cheated and took him in a car accident." Katie had not been Don's closest friend, just a client, but she was devastated. Don didn't want to die. It wasn't fear so much; he just felt that at thirty-nine, he was too young to go. He had two children he needed to raise, clients to defend, causes to advocate.

Andy tried to console Katie by saying that Don's spirit was still alive in the habeas petition and that in that sense, he was still with them fighting the fight. But Katie couldn't be consoled. To her, Don's death was an utter, irredeemable loss.

———

On July 4, Katie returned with Andy and Asher from a trip to Billings to see Andy's family. Going through the mail, she found a letter from Steve Northup in a cream-colored Mays & Valentine envelope. The envelope contained a copy of a letter Judge Williams had sent to Northup. Since it was appropriate to do so, the judge had written, he was referring this case to magistrate judge David G. Lowe. That was all it said.

God, what does this mean? Katie thought. She had gone to see Northup just before her vacation. While they'd both been distracted by Don's illness and death, now that he had passed away, they were planning to draft the motion for an evidentiary hearing. But Judge Williams was dropping the case, as if he'd lost interest in it. Katie had fastened so many of her hopes on Don Lee and Judge Williams. She felt she had finally found in Don a champion for her mother and in the judge a court willing to entertain Beverly's claims. Now both of them were gone, and with them all the momentum her mother's case had acquired in the last eighteen months.

CHAPTER XI

Findings of Fact

1

Judge Williams had not explained the reasoning behind his decision to relinquish Beverly Monroe's habeas appeal to magistrate judge Lowe. Katie at first feared that he was simply disposing of a case that seemed to have gone stale, and Don Lee's illness and death notwithstanding, she blamed herself and Steve Northup for failing to move back in the fall, when they clearly had Judge Williams's interest. But then Northup talked to Beverly Powell, a former law partner of Don Lee's who had also been a clerk for Judge Williams. Beverly Powell said she thought the judge's decision may have been a way of prompting some action in a case he did not want to see die.

Magistrate judge Lowe, while a man with a more conservative reputation than Judge Williams's, made it clear both that he intended to move the case forward and that he was, at the very least, open to the proposition that Beverly's statements to Dave Riley may have been improperly given. "I listened to that last half-hour of tape, of that March 26 interview," he said to John McLees and Steve Northup during oral arguments prior to the evidentiary hearing he granted, "and I've got to tell you, it's frightening."

The question Judge Lowe had to decide was whether Murray Janus had been ineffective in failing to move to suppress the statements during the trial on the grounds of involuntariness. Like Don Lee before him, Steve Northup knew Beverly's case would be strengthened immeasurably if Janus admitted making a mistake. Prior to the evidentiary hearing, he had a meeting with Janus, to feel him out about the degree to which he would be willing to cooperate. Janus, while circumspect, was also polite and outwardly agreeable. His recollection was fuzzy, he said, but he promised to review his files to find out what exactly he had done prior to Beverly's trial to research and prepare for a possible voluntariness claim.

Two weeks later, returning from an out-of-town trip, Northup found a voice-mail message from Janus, who said he'd reviewed his files and didn't see any need to meet again. The reason he hadn't made a voluntariness claim was twofold, Janus told Northup over the telephone. First of all, Beverly had denied making the specific statements attributed to her by Riley and had accused the police secretaries who witnessed her interview with Riley of exaggerating what she'd actually said; an attorney couldn't argue that statements his client disputed making were given involuntarily. Second, Janus continued, he'd tried unsuccessfully to make a voluntariness claim in a previous case, involving a man named Rogers, who'd confessed to murdering his girlfriend. Since it hadn't worked with Rogers, Janus explained, he had decided it wouldn't work with Beverly Monroe.

This dual rationale struck Northup as extraordinary, since that was precisely the reasoning John McLees had used in the oral arguments before Judge Lowe earlier in the month to dispute the need for an evidentiary hearing. When Northup asked, Janus admitted that McLees had recently been to see him. Northup now struck Janus's name off his list of witnesses. A few days later, McLees sent him the commonwealth's witness list. Murray Janus was on it. Beverly Monroe's former attorney would now be testifying against her at the upcoming hearing. There was a bitter irony to this development, but it did not surprise Northup. Janus, had he had the heart, might have acknowledged what seemed to Northup indisputable errors in his handling of the trial. But in Northup's experience, ego trumped heart every time.

2

Judge Lowe's courtroom was next to Judge Williams's in the federal courthouse, a converted Art Deco post office building on Main Street, across from the state capitol. Although a magistrate judge ranked below a judge proper in the court hierarchy and often handled routine matters such as traffic violations on federal property, Judge Lowe's courtroom was nonetheless handsomely appointed. The stained-oak paneling created an atmosphere of formal gravity, as did the magistrate's raised bench, the docket clerk's rail-topped desk, the elevated witness stand with the worn leather Bible resting on its box front, and the view through the large windows of the capitol's white columns.

One morning in early December 2000, as a watery winter light filtered through the wooden venetian blinds that hung in the windows, the courtroom's pews gradually filled with spectators. They sat quietly or talked among themselves in low voices. The weather had been unseasonably cold the night before, but the courtroom was warm, and most of the spectators had folded their overcoats and slipped them beneath the pews. Beverly's ex-husband, Stuart, who regularly visited his former wife in prison and now regretted his failure to attend her entire trial eight years earlier, was among them.

Many of the visitors wore yellow ribbons pinned to their lapels. They had been Katie's idea. Yellow was Beverly's favorite color. Katie had decided this show of support for her mother was worth the risk of offending Judge Lowe, who might perceive the ribbons as an attempt to sway him emotionally on what were supposed to be purely issues of law.

Katie, Shannon, and Gavin sat in the first pew. Shortly before nine o'clock, a marshal led Beverly into the courtroom. A jolt of horrified disbelief stirred her supporters when they saw the bright flash of nickel plating at her waist; Beverly's hands were manacled behind her back, linked to a chain belt. As the marshal removed the handcuffs, Beverly waited patiently, wearing a smile of embarrassed resignation. No one spoke. The marshal, a dark-browed, heavyset man in a brown blazer, motioned for her to follow him across the blue-gray carpeting to the counsels' table, where Northup and his co-counsel, Fred Gerson, awaited her.

In the years since her trial, Beverly Monroe's wavy chestnut hair had become laced with gray. But, a number of the spectators noted, she looked surprisingly healthy. Her porcelain skin and vivid hazel eyes were clear. As she passed her children, Shannon stretched a hand across the rail to touch her mother. The marshal abruptly knocked it away.

"That's not allowed!" he warned. He pointed a finger at Shannon. "Don't do that again."

Judge Lowe had set aside two days for the hearing. Eight years after the trial, many of the central participants—Dave Riley, Beverly, Corinna de la Burde, Murray Janus, even Warren Von Schuch—would come together again to explain for the magistrate's benefit the circumstances of Riley's investigation, Beverly's confessions, and the tactics used in her defense. The magistrate, a former federal prosecutor, was a witty man who wore a neatly trimmed white beard. He had prepared thoroughly for the case, reading the voluminous transcript, the lengthy depositions, and the numerous motions and briefs. When he anticipated the thrust of a witness's testimony, he gazed out the window with a bored look. At times he made mordant and even caustic asides. "You know, I'm not the dumbest man in the world," he said to Northup's junior counsel Fred Gerson when he thought Gerson was belaboring an obvious point. But the judge also listened intently to the central witnesses, stroking his elegant beard. He seemed genuinely receptive to the argument made by Beverly's attorneys. At one point, after a discussion of Riley's tactics, he nodded and said, "Trooper Riley is a very overbearing personality."

For much of those two days, Dave Riley had been sitting in a witness room down the hall from Judge Lowe's courtroom waiting to testify. The room was small and airless, with grim fluorescent lighting. Witnesses called to appear in other proceedings had taken every seat. The wait was tedious, but Riley was used to testifying and he was used to the unpredictably long waits that preceded the summons to the witness stand. Still, Riley felt exasperated. He remained proud of the work he had done on the case. He had always considered himself a diligent investigator, thorough but not overzealous—except perhaps for a few years in the early eighties, when he had first been promoted from patrolman to special agent and had been guilty, he would admit, of a little hot-dogging. Now, as a result of the exertions of Beverly Monroe and her daughter Katie, he was being described in court papers, and even in newspapers and on television, as a rogue cop who had harassed, intimidated, and tricked a vulnerable woman.

Late in the morning of the second day, Riley left the crowded witness room and paced up and down in the narrow hallway outside Judge Lowe's courtroom. Now in his mid-fifties, he had fought to control his weight for years and then given up and accepted it. Since Beverly Monroe's trial eight years earlier, he had put on at least twenty pounds. His reddish-blond hair and mustache had turned white. His children had grown up and moved out of the house. He found it hard to believe that the case, after so much time, was still unresolved.

Riley thought of the execution taking place tomorrow night—he believed it was tomorrow night; Virginia was executing so many people these days it was hard to keep the dates straight—of a murderer he'd helped convict. The murder was committed in 1995. The guy had gone through all his appeals, state and federal court, and now he was getting his needle. Beverly Monroe, by contrast, had received only a twenty-two-year sentence, the mandatory minimum for first-degree murder with a handgun, and eight years later she was still fighting it. The attorney general's office, Riley figured, had put more time into her appeals than it had a lot of capital murder cases.

A short while later, just before he was scheduled to testify, Riley inexplicably developed a nosebleed. Pressing a finger to his nostrils, he hurried down to the men's room to stanch it. On his return, he ran into Steve Northup, who was waiting outside the courtroom while Judge Lowe briefly took up another matter. "You gave me a nosebleed," Riley joked. "The thought of this cross-examination gave me a nosebleed."

Northup laughed. Ever since meeting Riley at his deposition a year earlier, he had found him to be surprisingly likable. Beverly too had liked Riley at first, Northup made a point of reminding himself. Everybody liked Riley. And that, Northup additionally reminded himself, was what had made Riley so dangerous.

———

Corinna de la Burde also sat in the witness room waiting to testify. Katie had seen her on the first day of the hearing, when all the witnesses gathered in the courtroom, and had run into her in the coffee shop next to the courthouse, but they had said nothing to each other. It was the first time Katie had seen Corinna since the trial. Corinna seemed to have aged, but then, she thought, they'd all aged. Katie herself now had a few strands of gray in her hair.

Katie had thought for years that if she could sit down with Corinna, show her the forensic evidence indicating suicide, and explain how Dave Riley had tricked Beverly into making her self-incriminating statements, she could persuade Corinna that her mother was in fact innocent. When Katie had mentioned this to Northup, he had written the word NAÏVE in large letters on the blackboard in the conference room, and then he had underlined it. Even so, Katie had written Corinna a letter a couple of years earlier, suggesting they get together, look over the evidence, and try, as she had put it, to bridge the gap. Corinna had never answered, and Katie had decided that in the end it might prove overwhelmingly difficult for Corinna to face the possibility that her father had actually committed suicide, that she had been misled by the police, and that she had helped convict a woman who had once meant a great deal to her.

Gavin, like Katie, had said nothing to Corinna when he saw her. It still galled him that once the police had revealed to her their suspicions of Beverly, Corinna had not come to him or his mother to discuss them. He hadn't imagined she was capable of duplicity, and he had been stunned during the trial to learn that when she had taken him out to dinner, for his birthday, the month after Roger died, she was already clandestinely cooperating with the police in their investigation of his mother. She'd never given him the slightest hint that she had become convinced that Beverly had murdered her father.

Gavin had seen Corinna once since the trial, at a restaurant down by the river, where he had been working as a waiter. One night, running a plate of food over to another waiter's table—he could still remember the order: pasta with chicken and broccoli—he had found Corinna and her boyfriend sitting there. He had tried to remain calm and friendly. "How you all doing tonight?" he asked as he placed the plate on the table. Corinna, recovering from the shock of seeing him, had forced a smile and asked him how he was doing. How do you think I'm doing? he wanted to say, but instead he merely replied, "Fine, Corinna," and turned away. The chance encounter shook him so badly that he had rushed back into the kitchen and leaned against the wall, hyperventilating.

That had been six years ago. Gavin had not seen Corinna since. On the second day of the hearing, when Corinna was scheduled to testify, he staked out the first seat in the front pew. He wanted to be able to look her in the eyes the moment she entered the courtroom and to have an unimpeded view of her as she testified. He had no intention of trying to intimidate her. He wanted simply to make eye contact with her, to try to learn what she really thought and felt, and to convey to her his own feelings.

When the marshal opened the double doors and Corinna walked into the courtroom, she kept her eyes down. She was so apprehensive about testifying that she had been unable to sleep the night before. As she began to speak, she felt a quaver in her voice and worried that it was audible. Three times during her testimony, she glanced over at Gavin but then looked away without holding his eyes. Gavin seemed to be trying to frighten her, but as she went on, her voice grew stronger. Dave Riley, she told Judge Lowe, had informed her what to expect from the meeting at the Marriott with Beverly in which she explained to Corinna how she might have been present when Roger killed himself. Such a statement, Corinna remembered Riley telling her, would be tantamount to a confession of murder. "I hoped like hell she wasn't going to say it," Corinna said to the judge, "but she did."

Afterward, returning to the witness room, Corinna felt uncertain about how successful her testimony had been. But the sight of Beverly at the counsels' table, and of her children arrayed behind her, had reignited the anger she felt toward the entire family for the death of her father and, now, for forcing her back into court to relive the experience. It had been eight years since her father had been murdered—she made a point of always using the word *murdered,* because that's what it was. A jury had said so. Her family had been unable to heal, to move on, because the Monroes kept dragging out the appeal. Corinna and her mother and sister needed some closure on this, and they weren't getting any.

———

McLees also called Warren Von Schuch. It's like a reunion, Katie Monroe thought as the prosecutor crossed the courtroom. Everyone was there except Krystyna Drewnowska, who, Katie had learned, had married one of the attorneys she'd retained to represent her during the trial.

Von Schuch, wearing a camel-hair blazer, passed in front of Beverly on his way to the witness stand. He avoided looking at her. He hadn't followed her case and had been surprised to learn she was still locked up. People he'd convicted for gunning down their victims execution-style had served less time than Beverly Monroe. Von Schuch figured her case was too high-profile for the parole board to want to touch. And it surely hadn't helped matters that instead of showing remorse, she'd spent all these years fighting the verdict.

After Von Schuch took the oath, Judge Lowe asked him how he had expected Murray Janus would explain Beverly Monroe's confession to the jury.

"The defense was going to be that her will was overborne by Detective Riley," Von Schuch said.

"Does it surprise you that Mr. Janus never made that objection?"

Von Schuch startled both teams of lawyers, and complicated the issue, when he said he was under the impression that, indirectly at least, Murray Janus had put forth this argument. "That's what I thought he was doing," Von Schuch explained. "I don't recall right offhand what his closing argument was, but that was part of his case: Look, these statements were not true, and so forth and so on. She was pressured to make them."

McLees stood up. "Did you argue and try to convince the jury to the contrary, that they should believe that her statement—"

"—Yes."

"—was a ploy to explain her failure on the polygraph?"

"We did not get to the polygraph test in the case in chief."

"Okay, I beg your pardon," McLees said. "Did you argue that her statement was something that they should regard as incriminating rather than something that was just a misconception that Riley planted?"

"We argued that her statement was incriminating."

"I have no further questions," McLees said.

The judge nodded at Von Schuch. "Thank you, sir."

———

For most of the two-day hearing, Murray Janus, wearing a black suit and white shirt, sat in a conference room across from Judge Lowe's courtroom reading the *Times-Dispatch*. He had expected to be dragged into the case one way or another. It went with the turf. Virtually every habeas petition that was filed alleged ineffective assistance of counsel. Even Mafia bosses elbow-deep in the blood of victims blamed their lawyers if they were found guilty. When you'd been convicted, there was no one else to blame but the lawyer.

Still, it irritated Janus, particularly because he felt he'd put on a good defense. When he'd heard about the specific complaints against him in Beverly's habeas petition, he'd searched his memory, but years had passed, he'd tried dozens of cases since then, and he had no recollection of a number of the issues she had raised, such as the existence of the GSR report or the details in Krystyna Drewnowska's medical records. But whatever those documents may or may not have contained, he couldn't imagine that they would have affected the outcome of the trial.

There was, Janus believed, no would've, could've, or should've in this case. He'd had an appealing client who'd taken the stand and told her story. He had an alibi supported by multiple witnesses. His client had had enough money—and this rarely occurred—to hire *three* expert witnesses. Janus felt he'd done everything he could. Beverly had received a fair trial. In the end, the jury simply hadn't bought her story. And that had pretty much been out of Janus's hands.

After all these years, Janus still could not believe that Beverly had given those statements to Dave Riley. They were tantamount to a confession. Why she did it was truly a mystery, second only to the mystery of how Roger de la Burde had died.

John McLees called Janus late in the morning on the second day of the evidentiary hearing. When McLees began asking him about his qualifications, Judge Lowe breezily dismissed the exercise as pointless. "I've known Mr. Janus for years and years," he said. "We graduated from the same law school class. He opposed me when I was a U.S. attorney. We don't need to go into all that."

Katie, sitting in the first pew behind the counsels' tables, wondered if this familiarity would prove crucial. How likely was it that Judge Lowe would find that Murray Janus—a man he had known for so long, and a man, moreover, who had just been ranked the top criminal defense lawyer in the state in a listing of the "legal elite" by *Virginia Business* magazine—had provided incompetent counsel?

Katie's anxiety was heightened by a sense of helplessness. Sitting three feet behind Beverly—who was next to Steve Northup—but allowed neither to touch her mother nor to confer with Northup about the testimony being given, she could only watch as the climax of their years of work unfolded. She had taken several sheets of yellow legal paper and ripped them into quarters and all morning she had been passing notes over the rail to Northup and Fred Gerson. A marshal, finally noticing this breach of etiquette, told Northup that Katie would have to stop or she would be ejected from the courtroom. Northup held up his hand. "We can handle it," he said to Katie.

On the stand, Janus reiterated the rationale he had given Steve Northup for not making a voluntariness claim on Beverly Monroe's behalf: She had denied making certain statements to Dave Riley; he had failed with a voluntariness claim in the Rogers case. He also added a third reason, that arguments about Beverly's March 26 statements to Riley might somehow prompt a reference to the failed polygraph test. "I was scared to death, frankly, Mr. McLees, that the polygraph evidence was going to come in," Janus said. "This was just a tactical decision that I made."

"Are there any notes or memos in your file that record that tactical decision and the reasons that you made it?" Northup asked.

"No, sir," Janus said. "Not that I am aware of."

Northup pointed out that while Beverly may have quibbled about the specifics of what she'd said to Riley on March 26, she never denied signing the written statement on June 3 at Drewry's Bluff.

"And it certainly would have significantly aided the defense of her case if you had been able to suppress that written statement prior to trial, wouldn't it?"

"Yes, sir," Janus said. "I would acknowledge that."

"You can't dispute that?"

"No, I would acknowledge that."

———

That same day, during Riley's cross-examination, Northup asked the investigator if he had decided Beverly Monroe was a suspect even before meeting her.

"Yes," Riley said. "She was a suspect if in fact it was a murder." He added that before making a final determination on the nature of the death, he had been waiting for the forensics report.

"I understand that, Mr. Riley," Northup said.

"Mr. Northup," Judge Lowe suddenly interjected. "With that question in your mind, I'm convinced it was murder."

This comment startled Northup. "Pardon me?" he asked.

"I'm convinced it was murder," the judge said again.

When Katie, still sitting in the first pew, heard those words, she became transfixed with dread. No forensic evidence had been presented during the hearing. Procedural restrictions had prevented the various judges who had reviewed the case, in all the phases of its appeal, from considering on its merits the expert opinion and circumstantial evidence Katie had put together indicating that Roger had committed suicide. But Judge Lowe seemed to have dismissed what he had seen of it and now, in open court, he had announced that he considered Roger's death a homicide.

If Lowe thought it might have been a suicide, he would have to be more inclined to consider Beverly innocent. If he considered it a murder, however, her mother would have to be regarded, as Katie had always admitted, as a primary suspect. Judge Lowe was supposed to rule strictly on the issue of the voluntariness of Beverly's statements to Riley and on Janus's alleged negligence in failing to move to suppress them, but in making his determination, he had the right to consider the totality of the evidence submitted during the trial. He would, Katie thought, find it paradoxical to rule that Beverly Monroe had been coerced into confessing to a murder if he believed that in all probability she had committed it.

——

At the end of the second day, Judge Lowe gave the two teams of lawyers sixty days to prepare written briefs on the evidence collected during the hearing. He would then hear oral arguments, he said, and after that make his ruling. When the judge left the court, the marshal stepped forward and replaced the manacles on Beverly's wrists.

Katie, standing behind her mother on the far side of the rail separating the courtroom well from the spectators' gallery, said, "Chin up, Mauska."

Beverly smiled.

"Give her a hug for us, Steve," Shannon told Beverly's attorney.

Northup enveloped his client in a powerful embrace. For Katie, Shannon, and Gavin, watching only two feet away, that was as good as it was going to get.

3

Four months later, Judge Lowe held the final round of oral arguments. Since no evidence was to be presented, Beverly was not allowed to attend. This time Katie sat next to Steve Northup at the counsels' table.

Dave Riley, Northup told the judge when it was his turn to speak, had effectively hypnotized Beverly Monroe on March 26, and when she was in this state of heightened suggestibility, he had induced her to believe she'd been present when Roger killed himself. She remained in a state of posthypnotic suggestion for weeks, visiting her therapist, discussing these supposed memories with Corinna de la Burde, and talking to Riley in recorded conversations about her struggle to recover them. While these statements were highly incriminating, Murray Janus had failed to move to suppress them, and that failure had resulted in Beverly Monroe's conviction. It was, Northup said, an egregious case of ineffective assistance of counsel that could not be excused by Janus's recent claim, unsupported by any documentation, that he had been guided by tactical considerations.

"Defense counsel," Northup told the judge, "can't come in and just by a benediction utter the magic words I made a tactical decision, and then keep this court from doing its own independent analysis as to whether that decision was objectively reasonable, given what was facing defense counsel at the time."

Katie was so elated by Northup's presentation that the next day she sent out an enthusiastic e-mail to the supporters on her mailing list. "I believe that if ever there were a situation where a judge's decision might be affected by an attorney's oral argument, this would be it, because our lead attorney, Steve Northup, did a fantastic job. He really wiped the floor with the government's attorney! Please continue to keep us in your thoughts and prayers. We are in the very final stretch."

Countless times Katie had imagined Steve calling her and telling her to come to his office, and then, when she arrived, throwing a habeas writ down on his desk and telling her that her mom was free. Don't even go there, she'd say to herself when she found the fantasy overtaking her thoughts. But after the oral arguments, despite strenuous efforts to control herself, her mind could not resist returning to it again and again.

———

Katie and Steve did not expect Judge Lowe to issue his report for several weeks. But just sixteen days later, Katie woke up from an afternoon nap—some friends of Andy's had come over the night before and they'd stayed up until four A.M. talking and drinking wine, something she hadn't done since college—to find a message from Northup on her answering machine. "Bad news," he said. The judge's "Report and Recommendation" had just been delivered to his office. It was sixty-three pages long, well written, tightly argued, comprehensive in its treatment of the issues, and it sided with the commonwealth on every single item of contention.

Listening to Steve's message, Katie suddenly felt nauseous. She sat down on the living room couch. Asher was still at preschool and the room was quiet except for the murmuring air conditioner in the front window. Her mother's baby grand piano, with some of Asher's plastic toys on its scratched mahogany lid, stood next to the fireplace. The silent emptiness of the house seemed unbearable. She thought she should go down to Mays & Valentine, but then she decided she was too upset to talk to Steve. She was afraid that if she saw him, she'd start crying and wouldn't be able to stop. She called Andy at work and told him the news, then took a long walk through the neighborhood.

Virginia's late-spring humidity thickened the air. The tall Norway maples, profusely green from the heavy rains the month before, afforded the rows of tidy brick houses a cooling shade. The streets were silent. You rarely saw people outside in this neighborhood. Katie had never intended to live in Richmond. Both Shannon and Gavin had gone far, far away. It was the only way they felt they could get on with their own lives. Katie, the most ambitious and restless of Beverly's children, was the one who had ended up remaining behind.

Later, after she was sure Steve would have left the office, she drove down and picked up a copy of the report, which his secretary had left at the reception desk. In her car, she took it out of the envelope and started to read it, but at the first page she was overcome with a feeling of bitterness and despair so strong she couldn't continue. When she returned to the little stucco house with the gray trim, there was a message from Steve on the answering machine. "Call. Feeling really low about this." She tried his home number but couldn't get through. Which was just as well, she thought. She didn't really want to talk to anyone. All she wanted to do was to crawl into bed and lose herself, if possible, in sleep.

———

The next day, feeling less numb, Katie read the report. The forensics, Judge Lowe declared in his section titled "Findings of Fact," proved that Roger de la Burde's death was a homicide.

> Before discussing Petitioner's claims, it is important to understand, as the jury did, one incontestible fact: Roger de la Burde did not shoot himself. Despite Petitioner's protestations to the contrary, the forensic evidence rather conclusively establishes the shot that killed Burde was fired through the fourth and fifth fingers of his right hand as he was holding his head with that hand, probably while asleep.

The judge then noted that Beverly Monroe made three separate statements—to Riley on March 26, to Corinna on April 1, and in writing to Riley on June 3—any one of which would be sufficient to establish that she killed Burde. Furthermore, he wrote:

> Considering all of the circumstances surrounding her statement, the conclusion is inevitable—her admission that she was present when Burde "committed suicide" was made in furtherance of her goal of convincing Riley to end his investigation and declare that Burde's death was a suicide, not a homicide. It was a statement which was freely and voluntarily made. Monroe was a highly intelligent woman; she had a college degree, worked in a patent research department, had been through a divorce, had raised three children, was free to leave whenever she chose, and had been advised of her right to an attorney. What prompted her statement was not Riley's overbearing manner, it was not the surroundings, and it was not a collapse of her will. It was her conscious choice to offer Riley an explanation for the damaging results of the polygraph examination rather than risk a further investigation into the nature of Burde's death.

Finally, Judge Lowe concluded, since Beverly Monroe's statements were given voluntarily and since Murray Janus, as he had testified at the evidentiary hearing, was "white-knuckles scared" that a motion to suppress them would lead to the disclosure of the polygraph results, he had made a reasonable tactical decision not to make such a motion. The judge ended by saying,

> Accordingly, it is RECOMMENDED that the petition for a writ of habeas corpus be DENIED and that this action be DISMISSED.

Katie and Steve had always known that the appeal, like all habeas petitions, had only an outside chance of succeeding. In their most realistic moments, they had predicted that the magistrate might buy some of their claims—perhaps that Beverly's statements had been coerced—but then rule that Murray Janus's failure to suppress them did not reach the standard required for a finding of ineffective assistance of counsel.

But reading Judge Lowe's report, Katie felt as if she were back in the Powhatan County Courthouse listening to the jury's verdict. All the work they had done in the past eight years—the evidence they'd uncovered, the legal reasoning they'd developed—seemed to have been a complete waste. The judge had rejected it in its entirety. Katie couldn't understand his thinking. While he had said in open court back in the fall that he found the taped section of Riley's interview with Beverly "frightening," he now wrote that Beverly's hesitant, uncertain tone at the time was due to the fact that she had become "suspicious and reluctant to re-hash her statements . . ." Lowe, she thought, sounded more like a prosecutor arguing for a conviction than an impartial adjudicator balancing the evidence.

Northup agreed. Over the next few days, as he reread the magistrate's report and absorbed its arguments, he began to feel less depressed and more indignant. The tone of the report, the contemptuous dismissal of every single one of Beverly's witnesses as uncredible, seemed nakedly arrogant. Lowe clearly had a preconceived notion of Beverly Monroe's guilt, Northup decided, based on conclusions he had reached by reading the trial transcript and looking at the trial exhibits before the evidentiary hearing had even begun. He had decided that he understood the forensics better than anyone else and that Beverly Monroe was guilty. His evaluation of all the testimony during the hearing had obviously been colored by that assumption. In other words, Lowe revealed clear bias.

But the magistrate may have made a critical mistake, Northup realized. By basing his findings of fact on the conclusion that the forensics proved Roger de la Burde had been murdered—when the forensics had not been the subject of any testimony during the hearing and indeed were not a part of any of the habeas claims Judge Williams had permitted them to pursue—Lowe may have allowed them to raise, for the first time during the appeal, the question of how Roger had actually died.

"He's reopened the door to the forensics," Northup told Katie during a meeting the following Monday. While Katie had always wanted to contest the commonwealth's forensics case—especially after she had discovered the gunshot residue report—she had been unable to fashion a legal claim that the courts were willing to consider. The fact of the matter was that both the prosecution and the defense had offered the jury forensic theories and the jury had favored the prosecution's. No issue of due process was at stake. But now Lowe may have given them the opportunity to challenge the prosecution's forensics.

After the meeting, Steve took Katie to lunch at a Chinese restuarant on

Shockoe Slip. When the meal was over, Katie pulled the fortune from her cookie. It read: "Your greatest dream will come true." It was ridiculously corny, of course, probably printed in China by someone who couldn't even read English, but you take your omens where you find them. She slipped it into her purse.

———

A short time earlier, a coroner in California who had learned of Beverly's case had suggested to Katie that she get in touch with Martin Fackler, the president of the International Wound Ballistics Association. Katie now sent Fackler—a retired naval surgeon, a graduate of Yale University Medical School, and the author of more than two hundred articles on wound ballistics—a package containing the forensics reports and testimony, along with the photographs from the autopsy and death scene.

The package reached Fackler at his office near Gainesville, Florida. Fackler, it turned out, was aware of the case. He knew Ann Jones, the commonwealth's firearms expert, and several years earlier, at a meeting of the Association of Firearm and Toolmark Examiners, she had discussed it with him in great detail, dwelling on what she considered to be the unscientific methodology of the defense's forensics expert, Herb MacDonell. Fackler, who knew MacDonell and thought highly of him, felt that Jones was being a little harsh, but she was, he remembered, in quite a tizzy about it.

As Fackler sifted through the material Katie sent him, he became aware of what he considered a striking anomaly in the prosecution's theory. The charcoal-like stains on the fourth and fifth fingers of Burde's right hand had always been the cornerstone of the commonwealth's theory. What they supposedly revealed was that the murderer had slipped the gun barrel between those fingers as Burde's hand cupped his forehead and then fired the fatal shot. The problem with this, as Fackler saw it, was that when a shot is fired, gunshot soot explodes outward from the gun barrel, in the form of an expanding cone.

This meant that the gunpowder marks on Burde's fingers had to be slightly smaller in length than the mark on the forehead. If, as the prosecution would have it, Burde's fingers were closer to the gun barrel than the forehead, they would have been exposed to a more narrow spread of soot. But the autopsy photographs included pictures in which a ruler had been placed next to Burde's fingers, proving the mark on his fourth finger to be two and a half inches long. The photographs of the wound, however, showed a gunpowder stain only about an inch long; the autopsy report descibed it as 15/16 of an inch in length. The laws of physics don't allow that, Fackler thought. If Burde had been murdered as the prosecution described, the mark on his forehead would have to be slightly larger than the mark on his finger, not half the size.

It seemed indisuptable to Fackler that Roger de la Burde had not been murdered as the prosecution had contended.

He then tried to figure out how he *had* died. Fackler had a Smith & Wesson similar to Burde's. He took it out and examined it. The gunshot residue report indicated that the right hand had been near the gun when the shot went off. Perhaps, he thought, Burde had held the gun upside down, pulled the trigger with his left thumb, and used his right hand to steady the barrel. If that had been the case, the soot stains on the fingers must have come from gunpowder that sprayed out of the gap between the cylinder and the barrel.

Fackler cut out a circle of white paper. He then worked the circle of paper into the gap between the barrel and the cylinder. When he was finished, the paper surrounded the barrel like an Elizabethan lace ruff. It represented the direction in which the soot would have sprayed. Fackler found that if he held the gun upside down with his left hand and gripped the barrel between his thumb and the tips of the index and middle fingers of his right hand, his fourth finger lined up right next to the paper. That was how Burde's ring finger had become so stained, he concluded. Fackler's fifth finger, slightly curved, rested atop the gun's cylinder, on the far side of the paper, which accounted for a pronounced soot smudge near Burde's fifth fingernail. It was, Fackler discovered, a natural, comfortable, and quite solid way of gripping the gun. And it also explained the presence of the primer residue on the web.

Herb MacDonell was right in saying Burde had held the gun in his left hand, Fackler decided, but wrong in arguing he had wrapped his right hand around the cylinder.

———

"It just doesn't work," Fackler said of the prosecution's forensics theory. He was talking on the speakerphone to Katie and Steve, who were sitting in the Mays & Valentine conference room. As Fackler explained his analysis, Katie began practically trembling with excitement. For the last eight years, while never doubting her mother's innocence, she had never really known what happened to Roger on the night of March 4, 1992. Now she felt she had finally found the answer. Northup, too, was excited. He had always been somewhat skeptical of the forensics in the case, since they seemed to involve more creative speculation than actual science. In fact, he'd begun to suspect that the entire field of forensics might be little more than voodoo. But Fackler's explanation seemed so clear and simple and self-evident as to appear indisputable. "It's all a question of physics," Fackler said. "And it's all pretty straightforward."

———

Fackler refused Katie's offer of a fee. In cases where a genuine injustice had obviously occurred, he said, he wanted to be able to take the witness stand and tell the jurors he had not been paid for the conclusions he had reached.

When Katie sat down to write the objections to Judge Lowe's report, she made Fackler's analysis its centerpiece. As she began working, she and Steve discussed the tone of the memorandum. If they were too harshly critical of Judge Lowe, if they appeared disrespectful of his reasoning, would they risk offending Judge Williams? But in the end Northup decided, as he put it, to take the gloves off. Unless Lowe's report was attacked as forcefully as possible, Williams might simply accept it.

The magistrate's conclusions, Katie wrote, were "contrary to the actual physical evidence" and in a few instances actually went "beyond what is contained in the trial record." His "incorporation of his erroneous forensic conclusions into his consideration of Monroe's claims prejudiced him against her and prevented him from conducting the correct factual and legal analyses. . . . First, he improperly premised his consideration of Monroe's voluntariness claim on his preconceived opinion that Burde was murdered. Second, he arbitrarily ignored pertinent evidence and made erroneous factual findings and thereby failed to consider and weigh the requisite circumstances surrounding Monroe's statements."

The memorandum, which Katie wrote in six weeks—putting Asher in day care for ten hours at a stretch in order to complete it—was ninety-two pages long and accompanied by 233 pages of exhibits. Northup thought it was the best thing she'd written, but Katie wondered if it would make a difference. The ultimate irony in the case, she thought, was that Lowe, by making his presumptuous assertions about the forensics, had given her the opportunity to solve, to her satisfaction anyway, the mystery of how Roger died. If Fackler had appeared nine years earlier, she thought, her mother would never have been convicted. Now it could be too late.

Northup also realized there was only a remote chance that Judge Williams would consider Fackler's forensics. Federal judges were technically supposed to conduct de novo reviews of a magistrate's recommendations, which did not come cloaked with the presumption of correctness, but the fact was they usually deferred to them. Fackler's explanation of the forensics did not even constitute new evidence. He was simply one more in a line of experts, and Judge Williams might feel that regardless of the merits of Fackler's conclusions, they had no bearing on the claims before him. There was also pressure on federal judges—from the families of victims, from Congress, from the appellate courts, and from the sheer backlog of cases—for legal finality, to prevent cases from sputtering on interminably. McLees would no doubt argue that by asking Judge Williams to consider Fackler's analysis at this late date, Katie and Steve were engaged in nothing more than a desperate last-ditch effort to keep alive a case Judge Lowe had emphatically and definitively put to an end. At this point, Northup thought, he and Katie were throwing Hail Mary passes.

Northup had a copy of the objections hand-delivered to John McLees on June 15. After that, there was nothing to do but wait.

4

On a Saturday morning in mid-July, four weeks after filing the objections, Katie drove out to Pocahontas with Asher. It was a beautiful, mild day, the sun bright in an iris-blue sky. She parked in the lot in front of the prison, and then reparked when a guard sitting in a black SUV told her all the cars had to face in one direction. It was another stupidly arbitrary prison rule. There was no point in even asking the reason for it—you just submit. She and Asher walked up to a white prison guardhouse, where they were searched by a guard wearing disposable gloves. Then Katie took Asher by the hand and led him out into the prison yard, down a path enclosed by a high chicken-wire fence topped with coils of razor wire.

Asher, who was three, paid no attention to the wire. Katie had been taking him to see Beverly since he was an infant and he accepted it unthinkingly. She hadn't yet explained to him that Pocahontas was a prison and that his grandmother was incarcerated there. The time for that conversation— and the concomitant explanation of Roger's death and Beverly's trial and conviction—would come soon enough. For the present, Asher simply took for granted that this was where his grandmother lived.

A short flight of steps led down to a door. Beyond it was a large, low-ceilinged room cooled by a massive floor fan. Two guards at a folding table watched as inmates and their visitors sat talking on molded plastic chairs. Many of the visitors were children, and the guards had set out coloring books and board games for them. One prisoner was playing cards with her family. Another prisoner was helping her two boys pick up the mah-jongg tiles they'd spilled. Katie bought herself a Diet Coke and some crackers for Asher from the vending machines and had him pick out a couple of books for his grandmother to read to him.

Beverly appeared a few minutes later. She had come down with a virus earlier in the week and had an eye infection and was feeling peaked, but she made a fuss over Asher, who enthusiastically hugged his grandmother. Beverly was now sixty-four, the oldest woman in Pocahontas. Prison life was wearing her down. Morning count was at five forty-five. Every day, she taught four ninety-minute classes of computer literacy, for which she was paid 45 cents an hour; and she spent her evenings keeping up with her correspondence, often using a flashlight, because the guards sometimes simply turned off the lights in the dorm without warning. Since her friend Anita had been let out, she was not close to anyone in Pocahontas; she tried to safeguard what little privacy the prison afforded. But she was friendly with the other inmates, who came to her for maternal advice and help with paperwork and personal problems and who seemed to think she had the answer to whatever question might occur to them: How long would it take for a letter to reach St. Louis? What was the name of the creeping vine that covered the baseball diamond's backstop? Where was Guadeloupe?

Katie told Beverly that McLees's response to the objections had arrived the day before. As Katie and Steve expected, McLees asked Judge Williams to strike the new forensic evidence on the grounds that it was irrelevant to the claims that formed the basis of the appeal. McLees also argued that Fackler had misinterpreted the evidence and reached erroneous conclusions. When Katie and Steve had called Fackler to discuss McLees's response, Fackler had said the arguments were laughable. He wanted to fly to

Richmond immediately to present his findings to Judge Williams. Steve had told him that unfortunately, there was a strong chance he'd never get the opportunity. Fackler was outraged. He felt he had solved the mystery, and he couldn't believe that procedural technicalities would prevent Judge Williams from considering evidence that might establish a convicted person's innocence.

Beverly said she found Fackler's analysis interesting. She was less excited than Katie, she added, since it proved what she had known all along—that Roger had killed himself. It didn't matter to her, she said, how Roger had actually held the gun. She didn't want to think about it. "Who needs to know?" she asked. Thinking about the specifics of how he had killed himself forced her to visualize it, which was painful, but it didn't solve the real mystery of why he had killed himself. Nothing ever would. And so, as with her father's death, she was better off simply not thinking about it.

Katie explained to her mother that Steve had no idea how or when Judge Williams would rule. They did know that in the unlikely event Williams ruled in their favor, McLees would certainly appeal to the Fourth Circuit of the U.S. Court of Appeals, which was the most conservative appellate court in the federal system. It would, it seemed safe to say, almost assuredly side with the commonwealth, as it did on almost every criminal conviction it was asked to consider. That meant Katie and Steve would then have to appeal to the U.S. Supreme Court. The legal battle would continue for a few years, but since the Supreme Court rarely took cases in which there was not at least one dissenting opinion in any of the appellate decisions, the prospect for redress there seemed extremely remote.

"I want my *life* back," Beverly said angrily. But the emotion soon subsided. She and Katie had been forced to accept that in all likelihood she would be in prison for some time to come. Parole did not appear imminent. The Virginia legislature had abolished parole in 1994, but since Beverly had been convicted prior to that date, she was technically eligible for early release. But the parole board, which still existed only to consider cases like Beverly's, had granted virtually no paroles for violent crimes since the law had passed. Its members never met as a body, never saw or spoke to the prisoners applying for parole, and voted by e-mail. Once a year petitioners were allowed to meet with one, and only one, of the five board members and argue an inmate's case.

At one such meeting, Steve and Katie told board member Charles James that Beverly fit all the requirements for parole. She had served the requisite one sixth of her sentence, her behavior while in prison was exemplary, and since she had never before been charged, much less convicted, of any previous crime, there was little chance she would be a repeat offender. Their research showed she had already served more time than the average inmate with her sentence and record. James had said it was not yet time for Beverly Monroe to be set free. "How will you know when it *is* time?" Katie asked. "We'll know," James said.

Katie watched as Asher climbed into his grandmother's lap and she began reading him a book. At times Katie felt battle-weary. So many people had come and gone on the case over the years and she was still here, still in Richmond, still fighting for this one seemingly lost cause. If she had stayed at the Civil Rights Commission, she would, like her law school classmates, be earning a decent salary by now instead of scraping by on Andy's paycheck as a sales clerk in a computer store and the $7 an hour she paid herself, irregularly, from the remnants of her mother's savings. They could be saving money instead of living month to month, budgeting every dollar, waiting for a tax refund before they could afford to visit Andy's parents in Montana.

People sometimes asked her whether she ever got sick of working on her mother's case. They wondered if she should finally just declare defeat and get on with her life. But if she wasn't doing this work on behalf of her mother, no one else would. As hopeless as it sometimes seemed, she wasn't prepared to give up. And anyway, she thought, in what sense was she supposed to get on with her life? She couldn't see herself joining a corporate law firm and litigating aspects of the telecommunications act, as Steve did. The work she was doing was the only work that made sense, and if she wasn't doing it for her mother, she'd be doing it for someone else. In fact, she was already spending part of each week advising people who had heard about her and who called her concerning friends or family members who they said were wrongfully convicted.

Katie decided Roger would have been proud of her for making the choice she had made. That she was not earning a lot of money would, of course, have disappointed him, but he had always hated the police and the power of the state, and she felt he would have respected her for trying to take on the system. For years Katie had missed Roger—and so had her mother, who would become disconsolate on the anniversary of his death—

but neither of them missed him any longer. March had come and gone this year and her mother had not once mentioned Roger.

Katie herself rarely thought of Roger anymore. She thought instead of blood spatter, of the diameter of the bullet wound, of the gunpowder-stained fingers. When she examined the death-scene photographs, she concentrated on the forensically relevant details and avoided looking at Roger's face. The man himself had disappeared behind the forensic evidence his death had generated.

It was Roger, she thought, who was in a sense responsible for everything that had happened to Beverly since he killed himself, as Katie now felt certain had occurred. He would, of course, have had no way of anticipating that Beverly would be convicted of murdering him. But Katie had no idea what he had thought would happen as a result of his death. Had he considered it at all? She'd accepted the idea that she would never know. The truth was, it no longer mattered.

Asher was getting tired. They had been at the prison for more than two hours and his nap time was approaching. Katie told her mother they had to go. Beverly hugged her daughter and her grandson. Katie hoisted Asher onto her hip.

"Good-bye, Mouse," she said, and added to Asher, "Say good-bye."

"Good-bye, Mouse," Asher said.

Beverly watched from the molded plastic chair as Katie, holding Asher in one arm, opened the door out into the prison yard. She paused, framed in the brilliant sunshine, then waved a final time.

After she was gone, Beverly sat for a moment looking at the door. Katie would be back next weekend, or the weekend after that. She never let more than two weeks go by without visiting. They'd decide what their next step would be once Judge Williams's opinion arrived. It did you no good to think about anything beyond the next step.

5

Judge Williams had set Monday, September 17, as the date for oral arguments on the motion to dismiss Magistrate Lowe's recommendations. When that court date arrived, it followed by just six days the attacks on the Pentagon and the World Trade Center that had left thousands dead. The grief and horror sweeping through the country made Beverly's particular plight seem puny, even to Katie, but it also compounded the feeling she had that she was living in a world where everything had gone terribly wrong.

At first Katie and Steve Northup thought Judge Williams would postpone the hearing. But he didn't. Life went on. The few people gathered at the courthouse that morning, however, all felt jittery and sad and lost. Judge Williams entered the high-ceilinged courtroom and took his seat directly, without stepping down to shake the hands of the attorneys as he usually did. Katie wondered if this was because she was sitting next to Steve at the counsel's table. Maybe the judge thought it would be improper to shake hands with the petitioner's daughter.

From the outset, it seemed to Katie from Judge Williams's demeanor that he had lost his earlier interest in the case. He looked tired and distracted, didn't display his usual flashes of humor, and the routine questions he asked were devoted to procedural matters. He didn't seem to grasp Northup's request to allow the forensic specialist Martin Fackler and other witnesses to appear before him. He wanted to know if Northup was asking him to send the case back to Magistrate Lowe to hear additional testimony. When Northup explained that they wanted Williams to hear the witnesses himself, the judge sighed in exasperation.

At lunch afterward, in a cavernous and eerily empty Italian restaurant, Katie and Steve decided that the judge had already made up his mind about how he would rule. It was almost inconceivable that he would reject Lowe's recommendations. Williams's bearing and lack of interest in the substantive issues before him clearly indicated he had just been going through the motions in the courtroom. "His opinion's probably already two thirds written," Katie said. She felt totally depressed.

———

Since Judge Williams had issued previous opinions promptly and since he didn't seem prepared to do much pondering, Steve and Katie expected his ruling to come in a matter of weeks. But October passed, and then November and December, with no word from the court. Katie kept herself busy around the house. She and Andy installed a new roof and renovated the upstairs bathroom. They decided to repaint the stucco exterior's fading gray, and Katie tested different colors, painting swathes of each on the side of the house before deciding on yellow. But she didn't get the painting done. Asher, who was in day care, was coming down with an earache almost once a month.

The weirdly mild winter made it seem as if time had somehow stopped, and so did the continuing silence from Judge Williams. More months passed without a ruling. Was the judge writing a detailed opinion in support of Lowe that would crush their chances for an appeal? Had he forgotten about the matter? Were all their briefs lost in a sea of paperwork? The months of uncertainty were making Katie twitchy, but there was nothing she could do. Steve refused even to call the judge's clerk to try to find out when they might expect a ruling.

By spring, Katie was both dreading and longing for the decision. She found it increasingly difficult to stand the tension, but until the moment the ruling arrived, she could at least hold out hope. So she developed avoidance rituals: If the phone rang in her office, off the living room, she wouldn't answer it or even look at the Caller I.D. panel, afraid it might say MAYS & VALENTINE. Instead, she would wait to see if the house phone then rang. If it did, that meant one of the few people with both numbers was urgently trying to reach her. When she went out in the afternoon—the most likely time for Steve to call—she wouldn't even check her messages when she got back. She was too scared. She would wait until Andy came home and ask him to look.

One morning in late March, Katie got up around eight, after Andy and Asher had already left the house. It was a clear, warm day, the daffodils and forsythia in bloom, and she planned to go for a run and take a shower, but she sat down in her pajamas to check her e-mail and didn't get up until two. She was just stepping out of the shower when the office phone rang. It stopped, and then the house phone rang. She was afraid to answer it, but this time she couldn't help checking the Caller I.D. It said MAYS & VALENTINE. She waited for Steve to leave a message. She knew that if the judge had ruled against them, Steve would say something like "Bad news. We got the opinion today, and unfortunately it was what we expected." Instead, he said, "Katie, it's Steve. Call immediately."

Trembling, standing in the bedroom with the towel wrapped around her, she dialed the number.

"Are you sitting down?" Northup asked.

"Should I be?"

Northup said he had received the judge's order. He read her the penultimate sentence. " 'Petitioner's amended petition for a writ of habeas corpus is *granted,* petitioner's convictions are *vacated,* and a writ of habeas corpus is issued to the respondent.' "

In other words, Beverly was to be released. Katie fell to the floor. She was sobbing, her body jerking with convulsions. All Steve could hear, listening on the phone in his office, was a lot of undifferentiated screaming.

Hanging up, Katie threw on some clothes. She was shaking so badly, it took everything she had to keep from wrecking her car on the way downtown. She hadn't felt such incredible emotional turbulence since the day Roger died. The emotions were different, but the intensity was the same. She was in shock, but these occasional jolts of joy were coming through. She started honking the horn and shouting through the open window whatever came into her head: Don Lee's name, her mother's name, Steve's name. Other drivers stared at this crazy woman honking and yelling.

When Katie stepped off the elevator at the twenty-third floor of Mays & Valentine, the receptionist rushed over to hug her. In the hall on the way to Steve's office, lawyers kept coming out of their offices to shake her hand. Secretaries were crying. The whole floor was alive with people congratulating her. Katie started crying when she saw Steve, and so did he. The emotion was contagious. Then Steve put in a call to the prison and told Major Hill, one of the senior officials, that he had an urgent message for Beverly Monroe. "I hope you're calling to tell her she's going home," Major Hill said.

Steve said that he was, but he asked Major Hill not to reveal the news. When Beverly came on the line, he switched on the speakerphone. "I have a sixty-seven-page opinion and a two-page order," he said. As Steve began reading the order, Katie heard her mother burst into tears.

———

In his opinion, Judge Williams agreed with Magistrate Lowe that Beverly's statements to Riley were voluntary, writing that "the tactics engaged in by Riley were deceitful, manipulative, and inappropriate. However, the Court cannot find that his tactics were, in this case, unlawful or unconstitutional." Williams also ruled that Murray Janus made a legitimate tactical decision in not challenging the voluntariness of Beverly's statements, and that even if Janus had done so, the trial judge would have admitted them.

Judge Williams, however, rejected the magistrate's conclusion that the forensics established that Roger de la Burde had been murdered. Investigators had failed to gather critical evidence at the death scene, he wrote, and "the forensic evidence presented by the prosecution at trial was unclear and contradictory." Williams pointed out that the prosecution had ignored the matter of the gunshot residue report showing the primer residue on the web of Roger's right hand. He noted that the prosecution's own forensics experts had acknowledged it was entirely possible Roger had killed himself. "[T]he Court has grave concerns with regard to the forensic evidence presented by the Commonwealth and sustains petitioner's objections to findings of fact with regard to forensic evidence."

But Judge Williams's main concern was with the fact that the prosecution had withheld from the defense the names of the witnesses who saw the black Chevy Blazer speeding away from Windsor the night Roger died. He also ruled that the evidence indicated Zelma Smith had, at least implicitly, been promised a reduced sentence in exchange for testifying against Beverly. Had the jury been aware of these facts, he declared, the verdict may well have been different. "The prosecution's case against Monroe was not overwhelming," he wrote.

But unlike Magistrate Lowe, Judge Williams was extremely guarded in his views about what had actually taken place, declaring that "consideration of the material, exculpatory evidence—particularly with regard to Zelma Smith, whose testimony was critical to support the Commonwealth's theories as to motive and malice—demonstrates that the evidence, when viewed in its entirety, may not support the Commonwealth's version of events beyond a reasonable doubt."

———

Late that afternoon, Steve Northup called John McLees at the attorney general's office. He said he wanted to discuss expediting Beverly's release. McLees said he didn't think the attorney general was going to agree to let her out. The order's pretty clear, Northup replied. McLees said the judge's opinion was preposterous. It accused the commonwealth's prosecutors and law enforcement officers of misconduct, and the attorney general's office could not allow that charge to stand unchallenged. He was going to appeal Judge Williams's decision to the Fourth Circuit, McLees said, and he was going to ask the court to stay the order for Beverly's release.

Northup thought that given the fact that Beverly was sixty-three and had already served seven years in prison, the attorney general's office might simply agree to drop the matter and allow the poor woman to go home. But he knew he couldn't count on any gesture of compassion from the commonwealth.

Katie and Shannon, who'd moved back from Brooklyn, stayed up that night drinking wine and calling friends with the news. Katie went to bed exhausted but was wide awake by five in the morning. First light was beginning to fill the windows with a faint gray. She went downstairs and made herself a cup of coffee and sat in the silent living room as the shadows slowly faded. Steve had told her about the conversation with McLees. It hadn't dimmed her elation. They'd known all along that if they prevailed with Judge Williams, the commonwealth would appeal and that in recent years the Fourth Circuit had overturned virtually every habeas writ—and there weren't many—issued by the lower courts. What mattered was that after ten years—and it was ten years ago this month that Roger had died—a federal court had acknowledged that her mother's conviction was wrong. It was a true victory. But her mother was still in prison, and Katie had a lot to do.

6

The following Tuesday, the attorney general's office asked Judge Williams to issue a stay preventing Beverly's release from prison during the appeal. As a matter of routine, the judge complied. The next day, Steve Northup filed a motion asking the judge to reverse himself and allow her to go free. Williams scheduled a hearing on the matter for Thursday afternoon.

Katie and Shannon attended, though Shannon hated going back to that courthouse. Just being in the building made her skin clammy and put knots in her stomach.

During the hearing, Judge Williams was in fine form, magisterially framing procedural complexities and bantering with the attorneys. When Stephen McCullough, a young assistant attorney general, explained that he was representing the commonwealth because John McLees was on vacation, the judge smiled and said, "He's psychic."

Steve Northup argued that Beverly posed no danger to society and was not at risk of flight, because she had strong ties to Richmond. Her two daughters, her son-in-law, and her grandson, who had never seen her in any setting except prison, all lived there. Furthermore, twice before—prior to the trial and during her appeal—she had been out on bail and had voluntarily surrendered.

McCullough insisted that the public had an interest in seeing that a person convicted of first-degree murder remain in confinement. Beverly, he said, was a much greater risk of flight now than before, because she knew she had little chance of succeeding on appeal and had the means and intelligence to figure out how to flee the country to a foreign refuge. McCullough pointed out to Judge Williams one reason he felt sure the judge's habeas writ would be overturned by the Fourth Circuit: because the judge had not deferred to Magistrate Lowe's recommendation.

"I am required to conduct a de novo review," Williams replied. "If I have to defer to a magistrate's recommendation, you can be sure I won't be referring many more cases to him, and you can broadcast that loud and clear."

The hearing lasted less than half an hour. At its conclusion, the judge said, "I will rule on this matter expeditiously."

Northup had hoped the judge might actually rule from the bench, but since Williams had a set of written motions before him and since the case would be scrutinized by the Fourth Circuit, he apparently believed he needed to explain his decision in a written opinion. Thinking it possible that the judge would issue the opinion before the end of the day, Northup went back to his office to wait, but five o'clock came and went and the courthouse closed with no word.

———

Beverly heard about the hearing by watching the local news. She hadn't talked to Katie since Tuesday. It was so hard to get through and Katie, of course, couldn't call her. That night, she tried to call on the prison's pay phone a couple of times, but the line was always busy. Lights-out came at nine, but she was able to watch the eleven o'clock news, which repeated the story about the hearing, on someone's miniature portable TV.

Beverly had never slept particularly well at Pocahontas—it was too noisy and crowded—but in the week since Judge Williams had issued the writ, she'd hardly slept at all. As she lay awake on her bunk, "Midnight Train to Georgia" started playing on her neighbor's radio. It reminded her of that trip they'd all taken out to the Blue Ridge Mountains the day before she turned herself in after losing the appeal. When the song had come on the car radio, Shannon had turned it up full blast and they had all sung along at the top of their voices. It was one of Beverly's best memories, and now the music brought it flooding back. Unable to sleep and having given up trying, she passed the hours reliving that trip.

The next day she got up at five as usual, for morning count. There was some construction going on in the dorm—they had repainted the walls a pale yellow and were now redoing the floors—and she couldn't take a shower. She dressed in blue jeans and a blue work shirt and had a cup of coffee for breakfast. She knew from the TV news that the judge's order might come today. She didn't want to jinx anything, however, so she kept to her usual routine, teaching her classes and helping one of her students, who was getting out the following week, with her résumé. It needed a lot of work.

That afternoon, a writer dropped by to see her. They were sitting in a small room off the prison entrance. If the ruling was going to come, it was going to come soon. Beverly was trying to distract herself by reminiscing about the handsome old houses in Marion, her North Carolina birthplace, when Major Marilyn Hill appeared in the doorway. "Beverly, there's a call," Hill said.

The two went into Major Hill's office next door. The wait for this call had been as hard for Hill as it had been for Beverly. Major Hill liked Beverly a lot—she was like a mother to the other women, and she never acted out and had that devoted family and cute grandson—and she'd felt all day like she was at an execution hoping for the call from the governor commuting the sentence. Usually it didn't come. Beverly stood by the desk as Hill listened to the person talking at the other end of the line. Then Major Hill hung up and said, "Beverly, your release has come through. Go pack your things."

Beverly stepped back out into the hallway, holding her hands to her face and shaking her head in disbelief, and waited for the electric buzzing noise that opened the barred door into the dorm. Suddenly feeling faint, she leaned against the wall and wiped her forehead. She started to slide down the wall but then caught herself and straightened up. The lock buzzed and the door swung open.

Beverly climbed the short flight of stairs to her dorm, a huge open room crammed with bunks, where women were lounging around playing cards, doing one another's hair, and listening to music. The possibility of Beverly's release had been the talk of the prison for a week. Everyone had seen or heard about all the TV news coverage and they were all rooting for her, since Beverly was popular and any inmate's good fortune made the rest of them feel more hopeful about their own situation.

As soon as they saw Beverly come up the stairs and into the dorm, some of the women held their thumbs up as a way of asking her if she'd gotten the good word. Beverly held her thumbs up in reply, and the women in the dorm started cheering. As Beverly made her way down the long rows of bunks to her own, women came up and hugged her or pounded her on the back or just tried to touch her arm, as if some of her luck might rub off on them. The cheering grew louder and louder, spreading through the other dorms and the rec rooms—everyone in Pocahontas knew what it meant—until it swept the entire prison.

———

As soon as Steve Northup got the judge's order, he tried to call Katie and Shannon, who were working at Shannon's new apartment, but the line was busy; it turned out they were talking to a local television reporter who'd just heard the news. Northup set out in his car for the prison with several copies of the order.

"The Commonwealth of Virginia is DIRECTED to RELEASE THE PETITIONER FORTHWITH," Judge Williams had written. In the accompanying opinion, he had abandoned the tone of judicial restraint he had used when issuing the writ and had excoriated the commonwealth in scorching language.

> Nothing can be more egregious in a criminal case than denying a defendant the raw material needed to secure a fair trial. This is so whether the prosecuting authority deliberately or inadvertently fails to disclose information necessary for the defendant to have a fair trial. This case is a monument to prosecutorial indiscretions and mishandling.

It was extraordinary, Northup thought. Judge Williams had reviewed exactly the same material as Magistrate Lowe—the transcripts, the exhibits, the motions on appeal, the depositions—and had come to a diametrically opposite conclusion. What did that say about the system? It said judges were human beings who brought their own liabilities and preconceptions to their cases. It also said the courts were a crapshoot.

When Northup reached the prison, some of the inmates, watching through the barred windows, recognized him from the television news. "There's the lawyer!" one shouted. Steve waved. Major Hill met him at the door. "If I ever get in trouble with the law, I want to hire you," she said, and led him inside. Northup was flattered by the compliment, but he wondered if he deserved it. Of the four pro bono cases he'd taken on over the years—two of them death-penalty appeals—this was the only one in which he'd enjoyed even partial success. And it wasn't over yet.

———

A few minutes later, the Channel 12 news van pulled up outside the prison. The previous week, Judge Williams's ruling had been a front-page story in the *Times-Dispatch,* and Beverly's actual release would be even bigger news. By the time Katie and Shannon got there, two additional news vans had arrived, satellite dishes raised, miked-up reporters milling around outside the wire fence. More prisoners now were watching all the commotion through the barred windows. They recognized the two women and started shouting. Katie and Shannon waved. Andy drove up with Asher in their white Suzuki station wagon. Asher clung sleepily to his dad's neck while Andy, holding him in one arm, walked over to the prison gate with Katie. Andy couldn't believe that after all these years and all these failed appeals, Beverly was suddenly going to be set free, just like that, on a Friday afternoon. He simply couldn't believe it.

"This is too bizarre," he told Katie.

"Not as bizarre as the day she was convicted," Katie said.

———

Inside, in Major Hill's office, Beverly and Steve and Hill and Warden Tammy Estep were waiting for the official fax from the Department of Corrections ordering Beverly's release. Beverly and Major Hill were making plans to stay in touch. The warden was taking care of the final paperwork. She gave Beverly a check for $371, drawn on a DOC checking account. It was the balance of her prison bank account.

Beverly felt giddy with jubilation and relief. All the inmates had wanted to help her pack and there had been a second wave of cheering when she left the dorm. She also felt vindicated, but beneath the vindication was an undercurrent of anger. Steve had brought her a copy of Judge Williams's ruling. She'd hardly been able to focus enough to read it, but he'd pointed out the key phrase: "monument to prosecutorial indiscretions and mishandling." It confirmed what she'd been trying to tell people all these years as she watched their politely skeptical expressions: that she'd been set up or framed or taken advantage of; that the trial had been a travesty of justice; that the commonwealth of Virginia had violated its own laws in going after her, one of its own citizens, the way it had. As a result, she'd lost ten years of her life, not to mention her house and savings and job, and not to mention what this had done to Katie and Shannon and Gavin.

But at the moment, in Major Hill's office, none of that was at the front of her mind. She was too excited anticipating the moment she would walk through those prison doors. People had already been asking her what she would do first when she got out. The women in Pocahontas talked about it all the time: They were going to go to the mall or get a steak or take a long, hot bath—material things. All Beverly wanted to do was hug her children and grandson and visit her mother, who was eighty-five and very frail.

Beverly had no money except for a small Philip Morris retirement account, which she couldn't even access yet without incurring a penalty. She and Katie had talked many times about how, when she got out, she would move in with Katie and sleep on the futon in the small upstairs office, and that's what she was going to do. They had also talked about starting a foundation to expose wrongful convictions. But that was way off in the future. If the commonwealth appealed Judge Williams's ruling, they would have to fight that first. That was in the future, too. For the time being, she'd be happy playing with Asher, working in Katie's garden, and walking in the woods.

The inmates, excited by the television crews and Beverly's release, continued to shout and carry on and wave from the windows, and a little tension cropped up between Major Hill and Warden Estep about how to handle it. Hill thought they should be allowed to blow off steam and celebrate Beverly's departure, while Estep wanted to quiet everyone down and restore order. The warden's view prevailed. Major Hill got on the prison intercom and asked for quiet. "Don't do it for me, do it for Beverly," she told the prisoners. "If you all don't stop the noise, she can't leave."

———

Everything had happened so quickly that Katie and Shannon had only had time to call Gavin, who was still living in Atlanta, and a few friends. They now began to arrive. Among them was Tonya Mallory, who'd deciphered Krystyna Drewnowska's medical records, and a couple of Beverly's old Philip Morris colleagues. They all gathered in a small group in the parking lot.

The prison doors opened and a guard wheeled out a dolly with three cardboard boxes marked BEVERLY MONROE. At the sight of them, Katie broke down sobbing. Andy tried to store the boxes in the back of their little station wagon, but with Asher's folded stroller taking up so much space, there wasn't room, and Tonya put them in her SUV.

For a while everyone waited in silence. It was a bright day but cold and windy. The late-afternoon sun glittered on the razor wire that scrolled along the fence tops. The three flags on poles in front of the prison rippled and snapped. And then Beverly, still wearing her jeans and work shirt, accompanied by Steve Northup and Major Hill and Warden Estep, walked out the front door. When she saw the small crowd, she stopped and raised her hands as her daughters rushed toward her.

—

That December, a three-member panel of the Fourth Circuit of the U.S. Court of Appeals held oral arguments on Beverly's case. In March, a year after she was released from prison, it issued an opinion unanimously upholding Judge Williams' decision to overturn her conviction and set her free.

Author's Note

I first learned of Beverly Monroe's case from an article about her appeal that appeared in *The New York Times*. I was intrigued and tried to learn more, but I soon discovered that aside from the stray article in the *Times*—which was prompted by a letter that one of Beverly's nephews had written the reporter—virtually nothing had been published about the case outside the Richmond newspapers. Even there, the coverage was primarily devoted to the 1992 trial.

I contacted Katie Monroe and she sent me the habeas petition. As I read it, curiosity gave way to perplexed fascination. Like everyone ever involved in the case, I wondered how it was possible for an intelligent, educated, independent woman to confess to being in the room when her lover killed himself if in fact she was nowhere near the house. People can and do vividly remember events that never took place, just as they can and do block from their minds memories of actual events. If Beverly Monroe was not guilty, her case involved both syndromes: She had been persuaded to produce a false memory because she'd been convinced she had a repressed memory.

My interest in the mystery of Beverly Monroe's confession soon broadened into an interest in all the mysteries in the case. Did Roger de la Burde kill himself? If so, why? If not, who killed him—if it wasn't Beverly—and why? Was there another visitor at Windsor the night he died? Who smoked the Marlboros? Who drove the Blazer? The case, I began to realize, was in a way about mystery itself, and about how we, both as individuals and collectively, through our social and judicial institutions, deal with mystery. But it was also about police procedure in the post-Miranda years, about the mechanics of prosecution and defense in today's court-rooms, habeas law, the questionable nature of forensic science, male pre-sumptions and female accommodation, and finally the clash of sensibility and class that occurs when an affluent woman goes on trial in a rural area where she is a stranger.

I read the more than fifteen thousand pages of legal documents, tran-scripts, exhibits, and depositions, and spent the better part of two years trav-eling to Richmond to attend legal proceedings and conduct interviews. During that time, I interviewed Beverly Monroe for more than sixty hours at the Pocahontas Correctional Unit, often for several hours at a time and for several days in a row. I interviewed Katie Monroe just as intensively. I also interviewed Shannon Monroe for several days over a period of months in Brooklyn and spent one long evening talking to Gavin Monroe.

In addition, I interviewed virtually all of the lawyers and investigators in the case. Many of these interviews—such as the ones with Dave Riley, Jack Lewis, Warren Von Schuch, and Murray Janus—involved multiple sessions and telephone calls to follow up on points and to check facts. Sources made available to me the entire police file on the case, including material that was not introduced in trial. I was also able to read legal correspondence and memorandums, investigators' reports, witness statements, and raw tran-scripts of interviews with potential witnesses. While some of this material could not, for the sake of privacy, be incorporated directly into the book, it helped shape my understanding of people and events.

I had no contract with Beverly Monroe or her children, and made it clear to them from the beginning that the book was to be independent; they would have no control over what I ultimately wrote. In the end, my ap-proach to the case was determined by the irreducible mystery surrounding many of the key facts. While the evidence against Beverly Monroe was cir-cumstantial, there was also no definitive proof that she had not killed Roger de la Burde, and as a reporter I had to limit myself to what could be estab-lished. I thought the only fair and journalistically honest way to structure the narrative was to develop the points of view of the various participants in the events as they unfolded.

The thoughts, feelings, and actions attributed to people in the book were either described to me by the participants themselves in interviews with me or taken from trial transcripts, depositions, or, in a few instances, the re-ports of investigators. At no time have I attributed thoughts or feelings to individuals that did not come from the individuals themselves.

More than 95 percent of the dialogue, I would estimate, is literal, either based on scenes I witnessed or taken directly from transcripts of recorded conversations or of depositions or of the trial. Almost all of the remaining dialogue was recounted, either to me or in sworn testimony, by the individual who had spoken the words. I edited the dialogue for brevity but did not add to, transpose, or in any way reorder or compress the language that appears in quotes. Only a few short passages of dialogue—for example, Warren Von Schuch's comment to Katie Monroe at the end of the trial that he was only doing his job, and Murray Janus's comment to Peter Greenspun in Acapulco that he missed the voluntariness issue—came from those to whom the comments were made. Neither Von Schuch nor Janus denied making the statements, but neither could remember making them, while the listeners remembered them vividly and contemporaneously told others, who confirmed the accounts.

In describing the thoughts and feelings of the participants, I tried to remain as faithful as possible to the actual language they used. But since the process involved a degree of summary and interpretation, I showed parts of the manuscript to a number of the people I interviewed, on both sides of the case. I made it clear that I in no way required or sought their approval of my editorial decisions and the characterization of events and people but merely wanted them to verify factual accuracy.

The names of four people appearing briefly in the narrative have been changed: Richard Thayer, Hazel Bunch, and Chuck and Barb Collins. In the few instances during the trial and in court papers when attorneys used Mrs. Bunch's actual name, I substituted the pseudonym.

The trial was videotaped, and while a complete tape no longer exists, I was able to view portions of it.

The physical descriptions of places in the book came from my visits to those locations—Windsor, Beverly's jail cell in Goochland, the courtrooms, the morgue, the Virginia Museum, Drewry's Bluff, the interrogation room at First Division headquarters, Hollywood Cemetery, to list a few. The descriptions of the weather were verified with the National Climatic Data Center. The proper names in the book are those that were in use at the time of the action. Some of the characters have subsequently married, and other changes have taken place: Mays & Valentine is now Troutman Sanders Mays & Valentine; Bremner, Baber & Janus is now Bremner, Janus, Cook & Marcus.

Finally, sometime after I started work on this book, my daughter Jessica, who was living with her mother in the same small Brooklyn neighborhood where Shannon Monroe lived, coincidentally applied for a job and was hired at the bakery where Shannon worked. It occurred to me that some people might try to construe this as a possible conflict of interest. While I had no intention of abandoning the book, I didn't think it was fair to ask my daughter to give up her job, either. I can assure the reader that my daughter's work in no way influenced the editorial decisions in this book. But I did once get a free espresso.

Acknowledgments

This book would not have been possible without the willingness of Beverly Monroe to share the story of her entire life, which required her to discuss the memories of her father's suicide, the complications of her marriage and divorce, her life with Roger de la Burde, his death, her arrest and trial and life in prison. Most of those subjects were painful, and I am grateful to her for her candor. Nor would the book have been possible without the cooperation of Katie Monroe, who spent countless hours discussing the case with me, over coffee at her house or on the telephone, and of Shannon and Gavin, who, after the family made the initial difficult decision to talk to me, freely discussed their family history and shared their journals and letters.

The following people, almost all of whom had never discussed the case with a journalist before, also granted me extensive interviews: Peter Greenspun, E. B. Harmon, Murray Janus, Lisa Davis Lee, Jack Lewis, John McLees, Greg Neal, Steve Northup, Dave Riley, and Warren Von Schuch.

I also interviewed Don Bergerson, Alan Block, Peter De Forest, Mary Dodson, Ruth Doumlele, Martin Fackler, Suzanne Hall, Arthur Hodges, Nancy Hugo, William Jefferson, Richard Leo, LaTonya Mallory, Lawrence Marshall, Andy Montague, Peggy Palmore, Shirley Reynolds, and Julie Stewart.

I talked to Corinna de la Burde about the case during the evidentiary hearing, and she described to me then her feelings about testifying, her conviction about Beverly Monroe's guilt, and the effect on her family of the ongoing litigation. Later she decided against granting an in-depth interview.

Krystyna Drewnowska's new husband, the attorney Tom Coates, did not respond to repeated requests by letter and telephone to interview his wife.

I am grateful to Stuart Monroe and Marcella Fierro for confirming facts; to Rob Cizek, news director of WTVR, for giving me access to the station's videotapes of Beverly Monroe's trial; to Larry Traylor of the Department of Corrections, Warden Tammy Estep of the Pocahontas Correctional Unit, Dick Sanfilippo of the Virginia Correctional Center for Women, Robert Holloway of the Office of the Chief Medical Examiner, and David Botkins of the Virginia attorney general's office, for their help in arranging interviews and access to sites off-limits to the public.

Arthur Hodges's articles in the Richmond *Times-Dispatch* were a useful source of information. Richard Couture's *Powhatan: a Bi-centennial History* provided background, as did Blair Niles's *The James: Iron Gate to the Sea* and Richard Kluger's *Ashes to Ashes: America's Hundred-Year Cigarette War, the Public Health, and the Unabashed Triumph of Philip Morris.*

I want to thank my agent, Jennifer Rudolph Walsh, especially for her support during the dark months of 1999, and Courtney Hodell and my editor, Jon Karp, for their enthusiasm. I also want to thank my father, the author Jay Taylor, for reading preliminary versions of the manuscript.

Most of all I want to thank Jeannette Walls, who read numerous drafts and passages and was unwavering in her encouragement and faith.